AN
ECONOMY
OF
VIOLENCE
IN
EARLY MODERN
FRANCE

AN ECONOMY OF VIOLENCE IN EARLY MODERN FRANCE

*Crime and Justice
in the
Haute Auvergne,
1587–1664*

Malcolm Greenshields

The Pennsylvania State University Press
University Park, Pennsylvania

Library of Congress Cataloging-in-Publication Data

Greenshields, Malcolm R.
　An economy of violence in early modern France : Crime and justice in the Haute
Auvergne, 1587–1664 / Malcolm R. Greenshields.
　　p.　cm.
　Includes bibliographical references and index.
　ISBN 0-271-01009-6 (alk. paper)
　　1. Violent crimes—France—Auvergne—History—16th century.
　2. Violent crimes—France—Auvergne—History—17th century.
　3. Violence—France—Auvergne—History—16th century.　4. Violence
—France—Auvergne—History—17th century.　I. Title.
HV6969.A9G74　1994
364.1'5'094459—dc20　　　　　　　　　　　　　　　　　　93-10328
　　　　　　　　　　　　　　　　　　　　　　　　　　　　　　CIP

Published by The Pennsylvania State University Press,
University Park, PA 16802-1003

It is the policy of The Pennsylvania State University Press to use acid-free paper for
the first printing of all clothbound books. Publications on uncoated stock satisfy the
minimum requirements of American National Standard for Information Sciences—
Permanence of Paper for Printed Library Materials, ANSI Z39.48–1984.

For Bonny

Contents

Preface

In the fall of 1979, near the hamlet of Combelles, a few miles above Arpajon-sur-Cère, I met a peasant. He preferred, of course, to call himself an "agriculturalist" and "stockman," but his family had been in the region for centuries and he began to refer more frequently to "paysans" as the conversation progressed. The activities of the farmyard seemed more typical of peasant polyculture than of contemporary Western agriculture or stock-raising. Every morning, some of his five daughters led the geese out of their shed attached to the end of the house and every evening called and drove them back to safety. A division of the same shed housed two pigs. Near-feral chickens scratched at the ground and attempted to rush into the house whenever the front door opened. A wretched promiscuity of rabbits, one with an eye missing, huddled and fought in two tiny cages.

Hunting season was just beginning and the hunters were all around. Little knots of armed men in extravagant bush dress punctuated the roadside, and the occasional carload of them roared hopefully into the yard to ask for directions. To the mercifully distant report of rifles (although I never saw any game), I explained to my new acquaintance that I was interested in the history of crime. He immediately grew quite serious, picked up a twig and drew a map of the department of Cantal in the dust. He would show me, he said, why there was now no crime problem in the Cantal. On his map he traced the major roads leaving the region. All the gendarmerie needed to do was block these routes and their quarry was at bay. These mountains, the ideal "repair of brigands" in the seventeenth century, were now an empty trap. But later, in the archival documents, the glamor of brigandage gave way to face-to-face encounters between ordinary rural inhabitants in the fields and hamlets of the Haute Auvergne, occasions of which scholars, historians such as Robert Muchembled of France, and anthropologists like Julian Pitt-Rivers of Britain and the redoubtable Canadian Erving Goffman, have made much.

My own first face-to-face encounter with an Auvergnat had given me much, and there were to be many more such encounters, helpful and amicable, with persons to whom I must express my thanks: Mlle. Léonce Bouyssou, director of the Archives Départementales du Cantal, her generous assistants, Mlle. Mercoeur and M. Pougnet; Dr. Pierre Couderc and his family; the bookseller and scholar M. Muzac; M. Christian Marchi; and above all, the De Solans and Estèves: Guy and Odile, Pierre and Agnès, André and Catherine. Many generous colleagues have helped and encouraged me, among them, James Thomson, James Tagg, Raymond Huel, Charlene Sawatsky and Brent Shaw. My wife Bonny, along with Mary, John, David, Stephen, and my most trusted friend and colleague, Michael Hayden, deserve a thanks that words cannot express.

Introduction

It seems that whenever human beings gather, some of them hurt others. They inflict pain to subordinate, to retaliate, to avenge, to defend, to acquire, and to protect their acquisitions. They wound and kill to please others and themselves, to please human beings and gods. In the following chapters, we shall examine violence between human beings in itself and in the particular context of the Haute Auvergne between 1587 and 1664.

In the broadest sense, this book is about one stage in the development of violence, a short but significant step in the long slow evolution from private to public justice, or more properly, in the seizure and centralization by the state of the power of vengeance. The chronological limits of the study are dictated by the most coherent set of documents for the region, the reports (*procès verbaux*) of the mounted police (*maréchaussée*) between 1587 and 1664 and by the establishment of a royal investigation of crime in 1665, the *Grands Jours d'Auvergne*. The documentary base for this study was therefore produced during a period when French royal justice was attempting to become a more intrusive part of ordinary life, when the crown or the state claimed as its exclusive property the official violence that medieval ideals had limited to regulation by the nobility as well as the monarch. This transition necessitated, or so it was thought, demonstrations of officially sanctioned violence by royal justice against a violent society.

Although official justice seldom managed to penetrate very deeply into the life of the community, its occasional intrusions have generated documents that allow us glimpses of a self-contained rural society, informed by what I have called the economy of violence. An endless round of provocations and retaliations, of affronts and private, violent justice, this "economy" could be a matter of individual quarrels or of massive, collective uprisings. Moreover, at any stage in its unfolding, the official forces of order could become a part of it, an additional provocation, or a violent, judicial riposte.[1]

Upon closer examination of the incidents that comprise this phenomenon we can also gain some insight into the nature of interpersonal violence during the period. Physical violence was a widely accepted solution to conflict as well as the most direct personal affront in much of early modern society and therefore, at the level of individual confrontations, violent behavior was common. It often involved a defense, an assertion or a violation of what I have termed "psychic property," which could be defined as all that a person possesses, mentally or physically, that can be violated: honor, dignity, space, possessions, and the physical person. The dimensions of psychic property varied with the characteristics of both persons in a confrontation, as well as with the particular situations in which they perceived themselves to be. The examples of violent behavior that are to be observed in everyday confrontations and interpersonal negotiations during the early modern period may sometimes strike a histrionic note to the twentieth-century reader, but this is a true rather than a false note, which confirms the theatrical quality of public behavior and social interaction, in which feelings, values, and inner struggles were readily externalized and for which the audience was always important. This theatricality emphasizes the great importance of the psychic property at issue.

A constant of these situations of violence is that they took place in the Haute Auvergne or Upper Auvergne, the mountainous area of south-central France that is now, roughly speaking, the department of Cantal. Relatively isolated, it supported a livestock and dairying industry in addition to the subsistence agriculture that characterized most regions of France. Its people therefore shared in both the "immobile" tradition of the French peasantry and the more mobile and independent pastoral pursuits that moved from the winter valleys to the summer mountains and back each year in search of pasture and fodder for animals. Remote from the increasingly dominant centers of French culture, the Haute Auvergne also had a reputation for "backwardness," an archaism of

---

1. Interestingly, after the completion of this manuscript, I discovered in a recent edition of Niccolò Machiavelli, *The Prince*, trans. R. Adams (London, 1977), an essay by Sheldon S. Wolin that uses the phrase "the economy of violence" (185–93).

customs and behavior that, some recent scholars have argued, included a propensity for interpersonal violence.

Although the Haute Auvergne has not benefited directly from a regional monograph, some recent studies have touched upon this region. Arlette Lebigre's work *Les Grands Jours d'Auvergne* (Paris, 1976), while it includes some cases from the Haute Auvergne, is a general study of a much broader area and does not make many geographical distinctions. In her study, the preponderance of violence is clear. Iain Cameron's study *Crime and Repression in the Auvergne and the Guyenne, 1720–1790* (Cambridge, 1981) includes, along with its examination of France's national police force, a discussion of crime during the period. Cameron concluded that theories about the eighteenth-century decline of violence "must be subject to severe regional qualifications" (198). The area that seems to have persisted in a pattern of extravagant brutality was the Auvergne, particularly the Haute-Auvergne. The catalogue of violent incidents Cameron offers, taken from administrative correspondence of the eighteenth century, is immediately familiar to anyone who has read seventeenth-century justice documents (193–98). A significant difference from the earlier period is the impression that in contrast to the rambunctious nobility we shall study in the first part of the seventeenth century, "by the eighteenth century there is scarcely a trace of noble violence to be found" (197).

There are problems in comparing the data in Iain Cameron's work with those from the same area for the seventeenth century.[2] Nevertheless, his findings, when compared to those of this study, lead to an important hypothesis about change in the society of the Haute Auvergne, whose elites seemed to have been tamed. Cameron's impressions support those of Abel Poitrineau, who found in the evidence for his study *La Vie rurale en Basse-Auvergne au XVIIIe siècle (1726–1789)*, 2 vols. (Paris, 1965), "the persistence of an archaic type of criminality, characterized by the importance, always preponderant, of acts of physical violence" (1:619). It is with these impressions of a later period that we can begin to examine crimes of violence in the Haute Auvergne.

The Sources and Their Limitations

In this study I shall use a variety of sources, including memoirs, jurists' commentaries, statutes, intendants' reports, administrative correspon-

2. Unfortunately, the only available documentation for the Auvergnat sections in his book

dence, local criminal court records, and other archival records. Recent historians of criminality and justice who have used these kinds of sources have shown a heightened awareness of the limitations and possibilities of each type of document. The memoirs of contemporaries, for example, along with the correspondence and reports of various officials on the scene, are in various degrees impressionistic and selective, but they can be valuable in revealing elite or official attitudes and preoccupations.[3] Similarly, institutional dictionaries,[4] royal edicts, and early manuals of judicial procedure[5] are highly informative but, in many ways, practically limited. The above types of sources are all necessary to any study of crime and justice; but for the student of criminality there also remains a more arduous course: the study of the immense series of archives left by the various courts and authorities of the Ancien Régime.[6]

---

consisted mainly of administrative correspondence and of the impressions of eighteenth-century visitors to the province. By contrast, Cameron found much more impressive documentation for the Périgord in the records of prevotal courts.

    3. For the Haute Auvergne: Espirit Fléchier, *Mémoires sur les Grands Jours d'Auvergne en 1665*, ed. A. Cheruel (Paris, 1856) and reports of the intendants Jean de Mesgrigny, *Relation de l'état de la province d'Auvergne en 1637* (Clermont-Ferrand, 1842), and Antoine Lefèvre d'Ormesson, *Mémoire sur l'état de la généralité de Riom en 1697*. There are many copies of the latter in existence, that in Aurillac being B. M. Aurillac MS. 6. Abel Poitrineau has consulted all of the copies and published an annotated version (Clermont-Ferrand, n.d.) to which I shall refer in this work. Two collections of administrative correspondence are particularly useful for the Haute Auvergne: Georges B. Depping, ed., *Correspondance administrative sous Louis XIV*, 3 vols. (Paris, 1851), and Roland Mousnier, ed., *Lettres et mémoires adressées au chancelier Séguier*, 2 vols. (Paris, 1964).

    4. Examples of this genre: Marcel Marion, *Dictionnaire des institutions de la France aux XVIIe et XVIIIe siècles* (Paris, 1968), and most recently Roland Mousnier, *The Institutions of France under the Absolute Monarchy, 1598–1789*, trans. Arthur Goldhammer and Brian Pearce, 2 vols. (Chicago, 1979–84). See also H. F. Rivière, *Histoire des institutions de l'Auvergne*, 2 vols. (Paris, 1874).

    5. André Isambert et al., *Recueil général des anciennes lois françaises depuis l'an 420 jusqu'à la révolution de 1789*, 29 vols. (Paris, 1823–33), is a useful compendium of royal edicts and statutes; volumes 12–17 have been used for this study. On criminal procedure, Adhémar Esmein, *Histoire de la procédure criminelle en France* (Paris, 1882) remains a standard work. John Langbein, *Prosecuting Crime in the Renaissance* (Cambridge, Mass., 1974) is a comparative study making extensive reference to Esmein. Of sources of the period, Pierre Liset, *Practique judiciaire pour l'instruction et décision des causes criminelles et civiles* (Paris, 1603), and Jean Imbert, *La practique judiciaire tant civile que criminelle* (Cologny, 1615) are examples of manuals in use during the period of this study. A helpful work that used procedural manuals extensively is the published thesis of André Laingui, *La responsabilité pénale dans l'ancient droit, XVIe–XVIIIe siècle* (Paris, 1970).

    6. Recently, scholars have turned their attention to judicial archives with a variety of methods and results. Articles containing suggestions for research have encouraged a systematic examination of the documents and a critical regard for the idiosyncrasies of local jurisprudence. Two early examples include one brief but highly influential essay by François Billacois, "Pour un

Of great importance for the present study are the criminal justice documents in Series B of the archives of the department of Cantal (Archives départementales du Cantal), which include records from the *présidial* of Aurillac, the royal *bailliage* courts, and some seigneurial courts. The problem of record survival,[7] however, is acute. No court offers a good series of registers or a substantial collection of consecutive dossiers for the period before 1665. While there is an abundance of cases, they are in dossiers and minutes scattered over two dozen different courts, and many are not properly classified. Pieces of evidence from the same case often turn up in various different cartons. The kinds of quantitative studies pursued by other students of criminality are therefore not possible with these documents.

In addition to these limitations, researchers have posed troubling questions about the representativeness even of "good" series of court records. The reluctance or inability of a large part of the population to pursue justice in the courts, based on social and economic factors and upon the very structure of the system itself, must therefore be considered in any assessment of the source material in judicial archives. A problem often lamented by students of crime, that of the "dark figure" of unreported or unrecorded crime, therefore seems even darker in light of the nature of court records.[8] But another source, unique, I believe, to

---

enquête sur la criminalité dans la France d'Ancien Régime," *Annales E.S.C.* 22, no. 2 (March–April 1967): 340–49, and Yves-Marie Bercé, "Aspects de la criminalité au XVIIe siècle," *Revue Historique* 239, no. 1 (1968): 33–42. Billacois included a suggested form for a "fiche d'affaire criminelle" that would enable students to conduct a systematic, collective study in French justice archives.

7. If the researcher is working with a continuous series of bound registers, there is some hope of estimating the rate of survival of associated loose pieces of evidence. But when the evidence consists mainly of bundles of unbound and often disorganized bits and pieces from trials, investigations, and sentences, there is no way one can confidently assess how representative the material is.

8. One of the major questions that troubles both criminologists and historians of crime is that of the "dark figure" of unreported crime: How are statistics of reported crime representative of actual deviance? Studies of local royal (*bailliage*) courts in Normandy first revealed that the clientele of the local royal courts did not reflect the full range of social groups. In an article on the *bailliage* of Mamers, Alain Margot found that trials often involved a local elite whose members had the means, the confidence, and the litigious mentality to use official justice: well-to-do peasants, merchants, lawyers, nobles, and legal practitioners. The lower orders would make a complaint only when a certain threshold of tolerance had been reached; that is, when blood began to flow or when a series of thefts had made the problem excessive or insoluble within the family or the local community. Only then was the day-laborer, the marginal weaver, or the poor peasant willing to enter the forbidding world of law, literacy, and punishment. A. Margot, "La Criminalité dans le bailliage de Mamers 1695–1750," *Annales de Normandie* (1972): 185–224. The expression "dark figure" referring to unreported crime (or perhaps at times to

the Haute Auvergne, offers at least a partial solution. One suggestion by students of more recent periods has been the use of police records, which often report offenses whether they reached the courts or not. Although the Haute Auvergne did not enjoy the presence of large regular police forces, there was one regular police-like force that patrolled the province in our period. The mounted police (*maréchaussée*) under the command of the *vice-bailli prévôt des maréchaux*, whom we shall usually call the *vice-bailli* or *prévôt*, has left traces of its activity in a series of reports (*procès verbaux*) that cover the period 1587–1664. This is an invaluable source, and unusual for the period in which it was written. While the *maréchaussée* has usually been discussed in connection with prevotal cases (*cas prévôtaux*)[9]—most often those involving "marginality"—and generally for a later period, these records indicate a wider interest and a looser attitude toward jurisdiction; it is hoped that these documents will complement the series of criminal records and other archival materials.[10]

Aside from the questions of numbers and coherence, the limitations of both types of documents are many. In the royal and seigneurial court records, most dossiers offer no resolution to the cases they contain. But usually there are complaints by the offended parties and the depositions of witnesses; frequently there are also records of interrogation, surgeons'

---

that undiscovered by researchers) is used by many if not most students of criminality and criminology. For examples, see Alfred Soman, "Deviance and Criminal Justice in Western Europe, 1300–1800: An Essay in Structure," *Criminal Justice History* 1 (1980): 8–11, Howard Zehr, *Crime and the Development of Modern Society* (Totowa, N.J., 1976), 15, 17; Hermann Mannheim, *Comparative Criminology* (Boston, 1965), 109–13, 375–76.

9. Royal justice further distinguished social groups by providing the most summary forms of justice in "prevotal" cases to "marginal" deviants such as vagrants and military deserters. Both unintentionally and by design then, there seems to have existed under the Ancien Régime what could crudely be called "class" law. *Cas prévôtaux* were distinguished by both the nature of the offense and the *qualité* of the offender. Any offense committed by soldiers, mendicants, or vagabonds was included, as were offenses such as robbery, sedition, armed assault, and counterfeiting. The *maréchaussée* do not seem to have been very precise about these distinctions in the seventeenth century.

10. A.D. Cantal, *Fonds de Comblat*. Any challenges to the competence of the *vice-bailli* usually came *after* the investigation of an offense had begun, so that the incident in question was recorded in the reports along with the subsequent challenge. Admittedly, this inclusion does not eliminate the tendency of the *maréchaussée* to do the specific task for which it was formed; this tendency will be discussed more thoroughly as we examine and assess the police reports. A partial transcription of the *procés verbaux* exists as *Documents inédits sur la justice et la police prévôtes* (Riom, 1906), edited by Marcellin Boudet. For reasons of accuracy and completeness I have used only the original manuscripts for this study; a fuller discussion of Boudet's version appears in Chapter 2, note 2.

reports, and other useful or interesting information. In reassembling these cases, one must also contend with the idiosyncrasies of court clerks, who translated, organized, and probably summarized the statements of witnesses and accused, in script that is often difficult to read. The result is that scholars have had to exercise not only persistence but also considerable ingenuity to extract the secrets from justice archives.

In the cases recorded by the *maréchaussée*, there are also sometimes solutions without problems: trials and executions for which the original offenses have not been explained elsewhere in the *procès verbaux*. There is as well a great variation in the detail of explanations, from the most cryptic summaries to many pages of narrative. More often than not, however, there are simply statements of the facts of each case, scattered under the various dates at which incidents, pursuits, captures, trials, and executions occurred, sometimes several years apart. Moreover, the great variety of tasks performed by the *maréchaussée* sometimes meant that police attention was drawn away from "ordinary" crime, and the legal competence of the police meant that they may have concentrated their attention on certain social groups such as soldiers and vagrants.

The available documents are thus not sources from which sophisticated statistical correlations should be made. But there is much to be learned from them nonetheless. The readers of justice documents are struck by one central fact: that they are reading about behavior, the behavior of many individuals three centuries ago. In the more detailed interrogations and investigations, individuals explain their behavior and that of others; in doing so, they give us their own reactions and attitudes to the event in question, to others in their community and to the representatives of official justice in the milieu of official institutions. Whether or not one solves the mystery surrounding an accusation, the persons involved reveal, even in their perjuries, precious clues to their own identity and attitudes. We can observe the reactions and the attitudes of the officers of the justice system toward the accused, the victims, and the witnesses who are from various social strata, with various degrees of wealth, of literacy, and of self-confidence. In the treatment and sentencing of offenders we can see the reactions of an elite, both to different types of individuals and to the offenses they have committed. The reports of the *maréchaussée*, on the other hand, provide a broader survey, imperfect though it is, of crime between 1587 and 1664.

Methods and Questions

Several different approaches will be used to exploit the documents, which are essentially of two types: police reports and court records. The former can be used to do some limited quantification, to assist a discussion of various aspects of crime and repression in general terms; where the documents permit, reference can be made to specific cases in more detail. Police reports will thus help to give us an idea of the proportions of crime reported to the *maréchaussée,* and overcome some of the limitations of the court records. Court records, on the other hand, can be used in ways that police reports cannot. From a careful reading of all the pieces in each case I shall reconstitute detailed incidents that typify or illustrate aspects of other cases from both types of sources. With these sources and others to supplement them we can learn something of behavior, of justice, and of life in the Haute Auvergne.

The questions one can reasonably ask of the documents assembled for this study are numerous, and many have been raised in the discussion of other studies of criminality. What sort of place was the Haute Auvergne? What of its inhabitants and their "police" forces? How and why were crimes committed? When and why were they considered crimes? We can also attempt to discover the identity of criminals and the patterns of criminality. Did violence predominate? The outlines of behavior within and interaction among various social groups are also of interest. Do they look more like the "vertical solidarities" proposed by Mousnier in his *Fureurs paysannes* (Paris, 1967), the class conflict described by Porchnev in *Les soulèvements populaires en France de 1623 à 1648* (Paris, 1963), or is some other pattern evident? And what of the nobility of the Haute Auvergne? Was its reputation for violent liberties deserved? Were noble offenses punished or was "class justice" common? In keeping with the question of "modernization," one might also ask how official justice was proceeding with its expropriation of private vengeance. Further to the question of vengeance: Was unofficial violence sometimes considered a form of justice? We must also examine the official procedures and penalties faced by those accused of crimes.

Yet further, we might ask: Do the offenses to be examined mark the bounds of behavior that was acceptable, not only to judicial officials, but also to members of the rural community? Supposing that they do, we have, then, in the documents of criminal justice, an outline of the shape of certain mentalities from a specific time and place. But we are able not only to observe the border points marked by extreme behavior. It should be possible to find some features of what was "normal" as well as what was unacceptable. The archives have given us human specimens, normally silent beneath the literate expressions of the day, forced into the light of judicial examination; a dim, artificial light perhaps, but one that can illuminate for us some aspects of a society now extinct.

To examine violence is not to explain it fully. Such explanations can only be attempted after a lifetime of study. This book is a beginning in relatively uncharted territory; it proposes ideas about the nature, causes, functions, and repression of violent criminality in the Haute Auvergne in the period 1587–1664. In the process, both the role of violence in that society and certain aspects of the mentality of Haute Auvergne emerge.

Crime in Early Modern France

While we concentrate on the Haute Auvergne, however, this study must also be seen in a wider context. The systematic study of crime and repression in early modern France and Europe is still in its adolescence if not infancy, but the field has a few inchoate traditions of which it is well to take note. At this point there are still more problems than conclusions in many areas, but these problems themselves have been valuable in revealing the dimensions of the task and some directions for future research. No work such as the present study can proceed without at least a cursory look at some of the findings in the recent historiography of early modern crime and justice.[11]

11. A number of recent essays deal with bibliography and method. I am particularly indebted to A. Soman of the C.N.R.S., Paris, for two unpublished essays in which he describes many of the problems of sources, method, and historiography discussed here: "Deviance and Criminal Justice in Western Europe 1300–1800: In Search of a Method," which is an early draft of "Deviance and Criminal Justice in Western Europe, 1300–1800: An Essay in Structure," (subsequent references will be to the published works) and "Some Reflections on Torture and Other Punishments as Administered by the Parlement of Paris in the 16th and 17th centuries," now published as "Criminal Jurisprudence in Ancien-Régime France: The Parlement of Paris in the Sixteenth and Seventeenth Centuries," in *Crime and Criminal Justice in Europe and Canada* ed. Louis A. Knafla (Waterloo, Ontario, 1981), 43–76. An important contribution to the discussion of sources is Louis-Bernard Mer, "La procédure criminel au XVIII siècle: l'enseigne-ment des archives bretonnes," *Revue historique* 274 (1985): 9–42. An earlier bibliography of French studies appears in André Abbiateci et al., *Crimes et Criminalité en France sous l'Ancien Régime 17e–18e siècles* (Paris, 1971), 263–68. Also useful are Steven G. Reinhardt, "Crime and Royal Justice in Ancien Régime France: Modes of Analysis," *Journal of Interdisciplinary History* 13, no. 3 (1983): 437–60, and the essays in *La Faute, la répression et le pardon.* Actes du 107e Congrès national des sociétés savantes, section de philologie et de l'histoire jusqu'a 1610, vol. 1

While the term is used fairly freely, the meaning of crime is not always clear. As J. A. Sharpe has noted recently, "crime in any reasonably developed society is a very unsubtle analytical category" ("History of Crime," 188). The definition of crime is therefore the first of several problems that need to be addressed, if only briefly. It is a problem that troubles both criminologists and historians of crime. Herman Mannheim, a criminologist, "searching for a workable definition of crime, . . . had no doubt that any purely formal definition was inadequate."[12] G. R. Elton has admonished historians of early modern crime to avoid anachronistic classifications of offenses, and a spirited debate has arisen over such essential questions as the distinction between crime and sin and the appropriateness of various classifications used by historians of crime.[13]

One simple definition of crime explains it as any act that transgresses the criminal law. Such a definition should not be dismissed out of hand merely because of its simplicity; it provides a guideline sensitive to changes of law in any society with a developed system of criminal justice, and it does not offend the basic distinction between law and communal morality. This distinction, however, is an important one: between *mala per se*, actions that offend morals, and *mala prohibita*,[14] actions that offend

---

(Paris, 1984). For a European survey, see the introduction by V. A. C. Gatrell, Bruce Lenman, and Geoffrey Parker to *Crime and the Law: The Social History of Crime in Western Europe Since 1500* (London, 1981), 1–10 and the first essay by B. Lenman and G. Parker, "The State, the Community, and the Criminal Law," ibid., 11–48. English works on crime and justice are assembled in an extensive essay by L. A. Knafla, "Crime and Criminal Justice: A Critical Bibliography," in *Crime in England, 1550–1800*, ed. J. S. Cockburn (Princeton, 1977), 270–98 and in J. A. Sharpe, "The History of Crime in Late Medieval and Early Modern England: A Review of the Field," *Social History* 7 (1982): 187–203.

12. *Comparative Criminology* (Boston, 1965), 64.

13. "Crime and the Historian," in Cockburn, ed., *Crime in England, 1550–1800*, 1–14. Elton comments on "a mildly anachronistic confusion" among the contributors to the volume as to the definition of crime. He objects for example to J. A. Sharpe's description of cases of adultery and blasphemy as crime in the latter's essay "Crime and Delinquency in an Essex Parish, 1600–1640," ibid., 90–109. Elton worries about the accuracy of studies in which "offenders of this kind" are "lumped together with vagabonds and thieves." He recommends a legal rather than a social definition of crime. Sharpe has replied that "Elton's discussion" itself is the more anachronistic because it "takes too modern a view of crime" ("History of Crime," 188–89), although Sharpe advocates at the same time an "institutional" definition of crime that seems not too distant from that of Elton. See also J. A. Sharpe, *Crime in England, 1550–1750* (London, 1984) in which Sharpe continues the debate, arguing that early modern folk did not distinguish clearly between crime and sin: "disorder and ungodliness were not readily separable entities" (4–5). See also T. Curtis, "Explaining Crime in Early Modern England," *Criminal Justice History* 1 (1980): 117–37.

14. Mannheim, *Comparative Criminology*, 26, 30.

official law but not necessarily any "higher" laws. There were clearly cases in which the law as it were "created" crime. The Haute Auvergne, for example, was divided into areas of unequal taxation on salt. Faced with this inequity, many Auvergnats thought smuggling a reasonable response. Salt was necessary to the pursuit of livestock-raising and cheese-making; to many Auvergnats therefore, smuggling was not "true" crime. The law had, in effect, "criminalized" the inhabitants of a region.[15] One could make a similar observation about other official measures, such as edicts prohibiting dueling or forbidding the carrying of weapons, in both cases attempts to suppress customs that may have threatened order but were not necessarily thought evil.[16]

Crime, it would seem, also had a pre- or extralegislative meaning. Offenses against the law were not always offenses against the community; and some offenses against the community or its morality were not regarded as demanding the sanction of official justice. This study, while relying mainly on the documents of criminal justice authorities, will deal with both sorts of offenses. As we shall see in the chapters to follow, just as there were both official and private offenses, so were there official and private forces of justice, repression, or vengeance.

Fundamental questions about the nature and functions of crime are interesting but similarly inconclusive, for they depend to some extent on the definitions that precede them. Nevertheless, such questions can stimulate fresh analytical perspectives and free us from merely legal considerations. Were deviants the instruments of evil, or expressions of the natural reversion to the originally sinful character of human beings? Were criminals making a calculated, rational choice? Was crime patho-logical and dysfunctional, a social sickness, or was it a healthy and boundary-making activity that fostered social unity in a common recogni-tion of behavioral limits? Was it a primitive form of political expression,

---

15. For a description of the salt tax in Haute Auvergne, see M. Deribier du Chatelet, *Dictionnaire statistique ou histoire du département du Cantal*, 5 vols. (Aurillac, 1852–57), 2:101–8; Henri Vitrolles, "La Gabelle en Haute-Auvergne," *Revue de la Haute Auvergne* (1970–71): 325–38. On smuggling, see Charles Felgères, "Contrebandiers et faux-sauniers en Haute-Auvergne aux XVIIe et XVIIIe siècles," *Revue de la Haute Auvergne* (1927–28): 187–209 and 251–72. For the eighteenth century, Olwen Hufton, *The Poor of Eighteenth-Century France* (Oxford, 1974), 284–305, gives an overview with specific mention of the Haute Auvergne (297) and Iain Cameron, *Crime and Repression*, makes several references throughout. Interestingly, the relative respectability of smuggling persists. I spoke to several citizens of Aurillac who claimed "criminal" ancestry on the clear understanding that their forebears were smugglers, daring but harmless.

16. See the extensive references to these two offenses in Chapter 3.

a sort of safety valve for the energies of discontent, or relatedly, a necessary expression by the powerless of the "power to be"? Were social disorganization, anomie, or the imitation of deviant behavior responsible for offenses? Did the categorization or labeling of the weak by the powerful promote, and even create, criminality?[17] To these questions one can only reply that one single theory cannot comprehend the variety of violent criminal activities found in the documents. That there was a popular as well as an official meaning to the terms "crime" and "justice" has also been argued usefully by those concerned with the study of "social" crimes such as poaching, wrecking, smuggling, and rioting. The view of law as a sort of ideology or a tool of ideology is similarly useful but not comprehensive.[18] It is important, however, that students not treat any of these theories dismissively, for their most important feature to the sincere researcher is that they are not mutually exclusive.

This study shall in the main be concerned with crimes of violence. Crimes in this context are actions that could be prosecuted by the criminal courts. Violence here is the exercise of physical force against human beings. Any discussion or enumeration of violent crimes will follow as closely as is practical the classifications used by those who composed the documents. The nature, the causes, and the functions of violent criminality shall be treated as they arise in the archival material of the Haute Auvergne.

While much fine work is under way, it is clear that the questions above, and others, still need examination for the period and place under study here. Judging from the archival research of many, the problems of record survival and of the "dark figure" of unknowable offenses are more

17. There are many discussions of various views of crime. For a recent survey of the variety of approaches to deviance and its repression, see Stephen J. Pfohl, *Images of Deviance and Social Control, A Sociological History* (New York, 1985). H. Mannheim's *Comparative Criminology* is devoted to such a discussion. H. Zehr, *Crime and the Development of Modern Society* contains a summary. Durkheim believed that deviant behavior could reinforce the strength of social groups because they would become more unified in self-defense against it. See, for example, Émile Durkheim, *The Rules of Sociological Method*, trans. Sarah A. Solway and John H. Mueller, ed. George E. G. Catlin (New York, 1964).

18. For examples of this view, see essays in Douglas Hay, Peter Linebaugh, John G. Rule, E. P. Thompson and Cal Winslow, eds., *Albion's Fatal Tree: Crime and Society in Eighteenth-Century England* (New York, 1975), and particularly D. Hay, "Property, Authority and the Criminal Law," ibid., 17–63. Hay sees the law as a flexible, awe-inspiring instrument that could be manipulated by the propertied classes for their own protection. For an analysis of this view and others in related works, see Terry L. Chapman, "Crime in Eighteenth-Century England: E. P. Thompson and the Conflict Theory of Crime," *Criminal Justice History* 1 (1980): 139–55.

acute for the sixteenth and seventeenth centuries than for the eighteenth. Added to the problem of fragmentary evidence are the not inconsiderable paleographic difficulties presented by some manuscripts of the sixteenth and early seventeenth centuries. Much recent research in France has therefore been concentrated on the late seventeenth and the eighteenth centuries, rather than on the period under study here.[19]

The existing historical studies of crime and justice show a wide variety of approaches. In some cases historians have concentrated on a single crime or type of crime. Studies of infanticide, homicide, smuggling, poaching, witchcraft, and other offenses have all contributed to the growing body of scholarly works on crime in several parts of Western Europe.[20] Others use a single source to study a wide range of offenses or behavior.[21] Yet others have used a range of sources to produce integrated studies of crime and justice.[22]

The geographic range of studies varies considerably as well. The value

19. Soman, "Deviance." Soman laments the lack of sixteenth- and seventeenth-century French studies "a situation which is easily explained by the continuity, accessibility and, above all, the legibility of the extant sources" ("Criminal Jurisprudence," 43).

20. There is a multitude of single-crime studies. See for example A. Abbiateci, "Les incendaires devant le Parlement de Paris . . ." in Abbiateci et al., Crimes et criminalité, 130–32; François Billacois, "Le Parlement de Paris et les duels au XVIIe siècle," ibid., 330–48, and The Duel: Its Rise and Fall in Early Modern France, edited and translated by Trista Selous (New Haven, Conn., 1990); Carl I. Hammer, "Patterns of Homicide in a Medieval University Town: Fourteenth-Century Oxford," Past and Present 78 (February 1978): 3–23; Keith Wrightson, "Infanticide in European History," Criminal Justice History 3 (1982): 1–20; C. Winslow, "Sussex Smugglers," in Albion's Fatal Tree, 119–66; D. Hay, "Poaching and the Game Laws on Channock Chase," in Albion's Fatal Tree, 189–254. Witchcraft has received much attention although not always in the context of criminal justice history. For a dated but still useful survey of the enormous bibliography on that subject, see Albert G. Hess, "Hunting Witches: A Survey of Some Recent Literature," Criminal Justice History 3 (1982): 47–79. For France see Robert Mandrou, Magistrats et Sorciers en France au XVIIe siècle: Une Analyse de psychologie historique (Paris, 1968); A. Soman, "The Parliament of Paris and the Great Witch Hunt," Sixteenth-Century Journal, 9, no. 2 (1978): 31–35 and "Les procès de sorcellerie au Parlement de Paris (1565–1640)," Annales E.S.C. 32, no. 4 (May–June 1977): 790–814.

21. Probably the best-known work of this sort is E. Le Roy Ladurie's Montaillou, village occitan de 1294 à 1324 (Paris, 1975), translated by B. Bray as Montaillou: The Promised Land of Error (New York, 1979), which uses a single inquisition register to draw a portrait of life in a medieval Pyrenean village. (One could also regard it in a sense as the study of a single crime: heresy.)

22. More in the tradition of the recent historiography of crime are André Zysberg's work based on the archives of late seventeenth- and eighteenth-century galleys and the various studies of local court records. See A. Zysberg, "Galères et galériens en France à la fin du XVIIe siècle; Une Image du pouvoir royal à l'age classique," Criminal Justice History 1 (1980): 51–115, and "La Société des galériens au milieu du 18e siècle, Annales E.S.C. 30, no. 1 (January–February 1975): 43–65. The complete work has been published as Les Galériens: Vies et destins de 60,000 forçats sur les galères de France (Paris, 1987).

of village and regional studies has generally been acknowledged, as has the value of overarching "world" history. But the question that troubles some historians of crime is the extent to which one can credibly move from local particulars to great generalizations. This is the sort of question, however, that can only be satisfactorily answered when studies that move to generalizations from local evidence are vindicated, corrected, or contradicted by much further research. European research into the history of crime is not yet at the exhaustive stage where this process of comparison can produce conclusive results. This does not mean of course that hypotheses cannot be tested and trends suggested from limited studies. Indeed, the experimental air surrounding the pioneers of research into crime history has allowed hypotheses to flourish.

The most persistent early hypothesis tested by historians of crime is based on a dichotomy between crimes against property and crimes against persons. In its simplest form, the theory holds that the development of modern societies is accompanied by a modernization of crime. Criminality in archaic or feudal societies such as seventeenth-century France is characterized more by violence against persons than by property crimes like theft. "Bourgeois capitalist societies" (eighteenth-century France) by contrast experience more theft than violence.[23] The retreat of violence with the rise of capitalism and theft had a pleasing symmetry that worked well with both Marxist historiography and modernization theory.[24] This theft-violence (vol-violence) thesis was not, however, without its detractors, and as the number of crime studies increased, inconveniently "archaic" societies were found in the Massif Central and other parts of

23. This theory was first tested in France by a group of students under Pierre Chaunu. Initial samples from the records of a Norman royal court confirmed the hypothesis in 1962, and over the following ten years it became the prevailing wisdom. See, for example, B. Boutelet, "Etude par sondage de la criminalité du bailliage de Pont de l'Arche (XVIIe–XVIIIe siècles)," Annales de Normandie (1962): 235–62. The other studies in this series include P. Crépillon, "Un Gibier des prévôts: Mendiants et vagabonds entre la Vire et la Dives (1720–1789), Annales de Normandie (1967): 223–52; Jean-Claude Gégot, "Étude par sondage de la criminalité dans le bailliage de Falaise (XVIIe–XVIIIe siècles): Criminalité diffuse ou société criminelle?" Annales de Normandie (1966): 103–64; Marie-Madeleine Champin, "La criminalité dans le bailliage d'Alençon de 1715 à 1745," Annales de Normandie (1972): 47–84; A. Margot, "La criminalité dans le bailliage de Mamers 1695–1750." Annales de Normandie (1972): 185–224.

24. Reinhardt, "Crime and Royal Justice," 437–38. For further summary of this hypothesis and research into it, see Georges Duby and Armand Wallon, eds., Histoire de la France rurale (Paris, 1975), 2:550–51. Pierre Deyon, Le Temps des prisons (Paris, 1975), "Le recul de la violence et le sauvegarde de la propriété," 78–79, also summarizes research from various parts of France.

eighteenth-century France.[25] Moreover, the problems of the "dark figure" and questions concerning the relation of court records to actual deviance have gradually robbed this theory of much of its centrality to historians of crime.[26] All that having been said, the theft-violence theory still preoccupies historians of crime, at least indirectly, and it must be given credit for providing them with a basis for debate and a spur to further research into the place of crime in the economy of early modern life.[27]

Violence, the other dominant aspect of criminality, has always fascinated historians, who have traditionally studied war, revolt, revolution, assassination, and other "politically" motivated forms of violence. To those interested in seventeenth-century France, the peasant revolts of the early and mid-seventeenth centuries have held a particular fascination. Much of the debate on peasant revolts concerns the interaction of various groups within the social hierarchy of the seventeenth century, and the social alignments it reveals. Given the infinite gradations of status within early modern society and the multiplicity of factors at work, these are not simple matters; but there is a fundamental disagreement among scholars about the nature of seventeenth-century society. On one hand, historians such as Roland Mousnier and and Y.-M. Bercé perceive a "vertical" society of orders in which the traditional inhabitants of rural France, the nobility of the sword (noblesse d'épée) and the peasantry, resisted the taxes and the urban royal officers (often noblesse de robe or nobility of the robe) of an intrusive and centralizing monarchy.[28] On the

25. For example, see O. Hufton, *The Poor of Eighteenth-Century France*, 360–61; T. J. A. Le Goff and Douglas M. G. Sutherland, "The Revolution and the Rural Community in Eighteenth-Century Brittany," *Past and Present* 62 (February 1974): 96–119; Julius Ruff, *Crime, Justice and Public Order in Old Régime France: The Sénéchaussées of Libourne and Bazas* (London, 1984); I. Cameron, *Crime and Repression*, 191–93.

26. Research in sixteenth- and seventeenth-century English records has recently shown a trend of decreasing property crime; J. A. Sharpe, *Crime in Seventeenth-Century England* and *Crime in England, 1550–1750*.

27. Muchembled, for example, takes care to establish that he is describing "a violent society," and the comparisons made more explicitly by earlier historians seem to be taken for granted in his work. See, for example, Muchembled, *L'Invention de l'homme moderne: Sensibilités, moeurs et comportements collectifs sous l'Ancien Régime* (Paris, 1988), and *La Violence au Village: Sociabilité et comportements populaires en Artois du XVe au XVIIe siècles* (Turnhout, 1989). Gregory Hanlon makes the standard comparison clearly at the beginning of his "Les Rituels de l'aggression en Aquitaine au XVIIe siècle," *Annales E.S.C.* 40, no. 2 (March–April 1985): 244–68.

28. R. Mousnier, *Fureurs Paysans: Les paysans dans les révolts du XVIIe siècle* (Paris, 1967). This work was translated by B. Pearce as *Peasant Revolts in Seventeenth-Century France, Russia, and China* (London, 1971). Y.-M. Bercé, *Histoire des Croquants—Études des soulèvements populaires au XVIIe siècle dans le sud-ouest de la France*, 2 vols. (Geneva, 1974), and *Révoltes et*

other hand is a school of thought represented by Boris Porchnev, who argues in *Les soulèvements populaires* that a class front of the urban and the rural poor confronted the powerful allied interests of bourgeois, nobility, and monarch. Thus, as seen by both schools of thought, violence defines and illuminates social structures, relations, and attitudes.

The functions of collective violence have also received attention, particularly from Y.-M. Bercé.[29] First, according to Bercé, revolt provided a festive interruption of the daily routine and a release from the normal order of life.[30] Second, it was a rite of purification in which the xenophobic tendencies of communities were satisfied by attacks on outsiders, or on those who were socially or culturally isolated, whether they were tax collectors, Jews, passing soldiers, or other strangers. Such attacks were attempts by the community "to recover its original purity" (137). But finally and most important, this sort of violence constituted a popular administration of justice: "It could be considered a folk penal custom, in which the putting to death of those responsible for public misfortune constituted the final level of punishment" (135).

Violence can thus sometimes be considered a response to perceived threats or to transgressions of communal boundaries, social, fiscal, cultural, moral, or geographic. If we continue with the theme of common boundaries, but return to considerations of crime "proper," or at least of the interpretation of criminal justice records, the work of Yves Castan (*Honnêtété et relations sociales*) stands as a monument to his ingenuity and imagination. From a variety of sources, including pieces of evidence from criminal cases, Castan has achieved a remarkable reconstruction of the intricate system of social relationships and the mental patterns of eighteenth-century Languedoc. He uses crime as an indicator of limits, perceptions, and priorities, showing the boundaries of convention and the desperate protection accorded the honor and self-esteem of individuals, men and women, and the family. In his sensitivity to words as well as deeds, the author reveals the cultural boundaries and the complex relationships between the Occitan-speaking commonality and the francophone elites of Languedoc. In eighteenth-century Languedoc the greatest number of offenses that saw the judicial light of day were concerned with

révolutions dans l'Europe moderne (Paris, 1980). Fuller discussion and documentation of these theses will be presented in Chapter 4.

29. Bercé, *Révoltes et révolutions*, 132–34. See also Natalie Z. Davis, "The Rites of Violence," in her *Society and Culture in Early Modern France* (Stanford, 1975), 152–87.

30. *Révoltes et révolutions*, 134–35. Translations, unless otherwise cited, are my own.

violations of *honnêtété* (honesty or decency), a sort of "common decency" or code of behavior. Men wished above all to be seen as truthful and honest, while women were often judged by their sexual morality and physical attributes. Most people spoke the local idiom of Occitan, and to speak French when not a member of the social elite was to put on airs or to insult one's fellows. Toward the end of the period, the array of attitudes and comportments Castan has delineated seem to have been changing as the social importance of wealth increased and the niceties of an older code were more frequently ignored. Castan actually attempted to quantify attitudes and expectations as well as simply to categorize offenses. No one can ignore the way in which Castan has used the documents of criminal justice to transcend the narrow examination of criminality, jurisprudence, and judicial institutions.

Castan's example was one of the most innovative and complete when it appeared; what is more, it added historical precision to the already existing social scientific literature on subjects such as honor and encouraged other scholars to make more imaginative and adventurous use of their sources. The result has been a range of studies of human behavior that are at once broader in the common characteristics of mentalities that they bring to light, and more microscopic in the depth with which they examine changes in attitudes and comportments, including the uses of violence and the claims of honor.[31]

In summary, the current state of research into the history of crime and

---

31. Some examples of historical work on the problems of violence, honor, and changing sensibilities include Muchembled, *L'Invention de l'homme moderne* and *La Violence au Village*; Hanlon, "Les Rituels de l'aggression"; Elisabeth Claverie and Pierre Lamaison, *L'Impossible Mariage: Violence et parenté en Gévaudan* (Paris, 1982); Steven G. Reinhardt, *Justice in the Sarladais, 1770–1790* (Baton Rouge, La., 1991); N. Z. Davis, *Society and Culture in Early Modern France*; James R. Farr, *Hands of Honor: Artisans and their World in Dijon, 1550–1650* (Ithaca, N.Y., 1988); and Billacois, *The Duel.* On the use of judicial violence, see Pieter Spierenburg, *The Spectacle of Suffering* (Cambridge, 1984). The most useful social scientific work on interpersonal confrontations is by Erving Goffman, particularly his *Relations in Public: Microstudies of the Public Order* (New York, 1971). The anthropological work on honor, social status, and interpersonal relations is invaluable. See, for example, J. G. Peristiany, ed., *Honour and Shame: the Values of Mediterranean Society* (Chicago, 1966), and the seminal essays by Julian Pitt-Rivers: "Honor and Social Status," in ibid., 19–77; especially 21–22; Pitt-Rivers, *The Fate of Shechem, or the Politics of Sex; Essays in the Anthropology of the Mediterranean* (Cambridge, 1977), *The People of the Sierra* (Chicago, 1961), and "Social Class in a French Village," *Anthropological Quarterly* 33 (1960): 1–13. John Davis, *People of the Mediterranean* (London, 1977), provides some qualification and criticism of Pitt-Rivers's work. David D. Gilmore's *Honor and Shame and the Unity of the Mediterranean* (Washington, D.C., 1987) and *Manhood in the Making: Cultural Concepts of Masculinity* (New Haven, 1990) are also valuable. Most students have been guided as well by the influential works of Norbert Elias on court society and the "civilizing process."

justice gives evidence of several different tendencies followed by historians using quantitative and other methods. The desire of the first researchers to draw significant and far-reaching conclusions, testing hypotheses such as the theft-violence theory, persists. This tendency has been tempered, however, by the discovery of contrary evidence and by the caution of scholars who are not sure what fraction of deviance, or of justice, court documents represent.[32] Some scholars therefore still search for a profile of crime through court records, while others propose that researchers try to discover how the institutions of justice worked and where they fit in the long-term process of change from private vengeance to the acceptance of royal justice. While not ignoring the latter objective, Castan and subsequent researchers also have shown that much can be learned about societies, behavior, and attitudes, as well as crime and justice, from a careful scrutiny of justice records. Others are gradually discovering how violence informed and expressed the vitality of society and culture in early modern France. Along with other studies of popular culture, inquiries into violence and conflict have begun to trace changes in sensibilities that reflect more faithfully the unity of life than did the compartmentalization of these changes into various discrete movements such as the Catholic Reformation, or the development of absolute monarchy. It seems now that whether one examines changes in religious sensibilities, the development of royal institutions, or the evolution of attitudes and methods with regard to criminality and its repression, there is usually a sense that the period of this study was one of increasing internalization of private sentiment, individualization of sin, official repression of theatrical displays of spirit, centralization of repressive means, and literate homogenization of beliefs, mores, and cultural prac-tices. To discuss on a broad national or European basis the effect of imposing an urban sensibility on country folk, or the pacification of elites as part of an overall civilization process, or a new religiosity when we still have an unsure grasp on the old, may be premature. But such discussions are part of a stimulating evolution toward a new understanding of our ancestors and ourselves.

We have moved our discussion from the definition of crime to the

---

See for example N. Elias, *The Civilizing Process*, vol. 1, *The History of Manners*, and *The Civilizing Process*, vol. 2, *Power and Civility*, both translated by E. Jephcott (New York, 1982).

32. It seems highly probable that much justice was done outside the courts; hence the advocacy of linking court records with some infrajudicial documents such as notarized compro-mise agreements (*accommodements*). See, for example, Reinhardt, *Justice in the Sarladais*.

question of what other phenomena the documents of crime and particularly of violence can define for us. Aside from the early preoccupations of criminal justice historians, the scholars of seventeenth-century collective violence have demonstrated how early modern violence could represent a form of "justice" and how it can also delineate social roles, alignments, and attitudes.

Whatever the sources or the modes of analysis, most researchers are ready to admit that while statistics may be improved, the dark figure of total deviance will elude students of early modern crime just as it frustrates those who quantify the crime of today. Nonetheless, the need for further studies of every sort on a local, national, and European scale, using every sort of method, is evident. It is time as well to explore ways in which documents can be interpreted qualitatively, methods of capturing and analyzing some of "what it was like" from the fragments of early modern society that remain to us. After all, court documents often give us the very words of people who wrote no memoirs. Their "crimes" were often their only extensively recorded actions.[33] With this basic reality in the forefront, the following study continues some of the traditions and examines some of the questions posed by others who have studied crime, early modern Europe, and early modern France in particular. It is a study of local documents, employing some limited quantification, in an area that has not yet been extensively studied for the period in question. It is hoped that it will add to the knowledge of a time, a place, and a people.

---

33. In another context, R. Darnton has persuasively issued the call for such methods and interpretations, and has demonstrated their potential for at least showing just how foreign to us early modern sensibilities could be. See Darnton, *The Great Cat Massacre and Other Episodes in French Cultural History* (New York, 1984).

1 The Haute Auvergne, 1587–1665

L'Auvergne est montagne.
—Annette Lauras-Pourrat, *Guide de l'Auvergne mystérieuse*[1]

The mountains of early modern times have been described as "zones of fear," the habitat of wild and solitary folk who disdained the more peaceful agrarian regularity of the plains.[2] The culture of herding peoples, it has been said, evades the closely regulated rhythms of agricultural societies and allows a greater individual freedom, a culture sympathetic to the outlawry that results when this easy liberty clashes with the forces of a stricter order.[3] In the following chapters I shall examine, through police and criminal justice records, the sometimes violent behavior of a mountain people in seventeenth-century France, a people whose economy and society were heavily influenced by the rhythms of transhumant stock raising and dairying.

But to give fuller meaning to such an examination, we must pay attention to what two of the most perceptive scholars of similar phenom-

1. (Paris, 1976), 14. Literally, "The Auvergne is mountains."
2. John R. Hale, *Renaissance Europe, 1480–1520* (London, 1971), 41.
3. E. J. Hobsbawm, *Bandits* (London, 1969), chapter 2, esp. 25, 28. Hobsbawm refers to the role of herdsmen and shepherds throughout this book as well as in his *Primitive Rebels* (London, 1959). Hobsbawm also makes frequent reference to mountains as a gathering place for brigands.

ena have called "the insertion of criminal acts into the norms of local life."[4] The contours of life in the Haute Auvergne followed those of the mountains and valleys, whose power to affect human endeavor is still evident to the motorist who takes the high country roads into the Cantal or attempts to follow the twisting, narrow route from, say, Aurillac to Viellevie, as it grips the rocky hillsides. Basic to the "norms of local life," then, are the structures, physical, economic and social, the relations human beings developed with the land they inhabited and with each other. Before going further into matters of crime and justice, therefore, we must look at these bases in the Haute Auvergne.

The Land

The boundaries of the Haute Auvergne were those of the present-day department of Cantal, with the exception of a few parishes on the northeastern border taken from Basse Auvergne to make up the department. On the northeastern border lay Basse Auvergne, to the west the River Dordogne, to the south Quercy and Rouergue and on the southeastern border, Gévaudan.[5]

If it is generally true that Auvergne is "montagne," it is particularly so of the Haute Auvergne, which is essentially a massif within the Massif Central. Its dramatic relief affected many facets of Auvergnat life: its isolation, climate, economy and society, down to the oft-lamented character of the inhabitants. At the center of the region stand the volcanic peaks of the Monts du Cantal, and from them flow the rivers that dissect the country into valleys flanked by lesser peaks. The altitude of the land falls away on the outer fringes of the basaltic massif only to rise again on the borders of the province. Aside from the river valleys, the altitude seldom dips below 600 meters and most of it is above 1,000

4. E. Claverie and P. Lamaison, *L'Impossible Mariage: Violence et parenté en Gévaudan* (Paris, 1982), 10.

5. The best reference work on the Haute Auvergne remains M. Deribier du Chatelet, *Dictionnaire statistique ou histoire du département du Cantal*, 5 vols. (Aurillac, 1853). The author has assembled a mass of factual detail, dealing alphabetically with place names and subjects. These include historical essays on subjects as diverse as the borders of the Haute Auvergne, cheese-making, salt, and justice. Abel Poitrineau, *La vie rurale en Basse-Auvergne au XVIIIe siècle (1726–1789)*, 2 vols. (Paris, 1965), also devotes considerable passages to the Haute Auvergne; for geography; see 38–39. The most comprehensive recent work on the region is G. Manry, ed., *Histoire de l'Auvergne* (Paris, 1974), which includes a geographic section, 12–23.

Haute Auvergne

Fig. 1. The Haute Auvergne and some of the surrounding French provinces

meters. Thus there were natural barriers within the province as well as obstacles to communication with the outside.[6]

To the traveler, much of the landscape appears to have been strewn with stones and boulders, and the architecture that remains to us from early modern times is characterized by the use of stone: stone fences rather than wood; stone houses and barns often with basaltic corner

6. A. Fel and S. Derrau, *Le Massif Central* (Paris, 1970); A. Fel, *Les Hautes Terres du Massif Central* (Paris: 1962) and P. Arbos, *L'Auvergne* (Paris, 1932), provide geographic descriptions of the region.

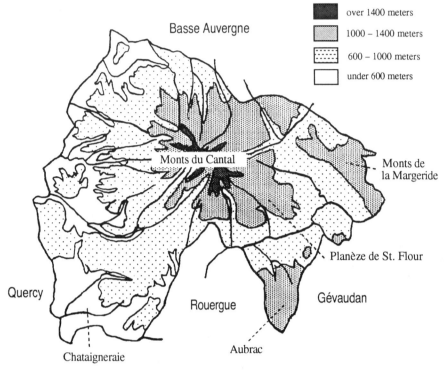

over 1400 meters

1000 – 1400 meters

600 – 1000 meters

under 600 meters

Fig. 2.   Mountains of the Haute Auvergne

stones and window ledges; stone drains, water pipes and even stone shingles or roof tiles, each with a hole drilled through the center for a wooden roofing peg. It is not surprising that often the first weapons that came to hand in every sort of dispute from a petty quarrel to a large insurrection, were stones.

While the Massif Central has been referred to as the center of France and the Haute Auvergne as the "heart of the massif," it is too far south to be a geographic center and is really a hydrographic center. Close to the Mediterranean, it has been regarded by Parisians as part of the "South," and indeed such a description could be partly justified by some aspects of language and culture. But to those from less extreme climates to the south it was "la montagne," cold, wet, remote, impoverished, and inhospitable.[7] Both descriptions to some extent apply. Certainly the climate is rude. The winters are cold and damp, with snow in the

7. Derrau and Fel, Massif Central, 5.

mountain passes for several months of the year. Elsewhere the winter days alternate between severe frost and chill rains. If there was indeed a "Little Ice Age," the late sixteenth- and early seventeenth-century inhabitants may have suffered winters even less kind than those of recent times.[8] The registers of grievances (cahiers de doléances) to the Estates General of 1614 complained of freezing crops in late spring and early autumn frosts as well.[9]

The growing season is short and often interrupted by frost. Even when the number of frost-free days was adequate for grains, however, growth and especially maturity were often inhibited by heavy rains. In the Monts du Cantal today, the average annual precipitation is over 2,000 millimeters and much of the province receives between 1,500 and 2,000 millimeters. Only in the east, particularly in the valley of the river Alagnon and on the surrounding plateaus, is there significant diminution of the rains.

While France is surely among the most naturally endowed of agricultural countries, the Haute Auvergne was a poor relation of other French provinces. In addition to the severe climate and the unfavorably rough terrain, its soils tended to be leached, stony, and often heavily acidic or lacking in minerals. The frequent patches of clay soils had a great propensity to retain moisture, which caused further problems in a damp climate. To those who wished to cultivate crops, the land presented a series of obstacles. After deforestation came a succession of onerous tasks: stones had to be removed (a job often reserved for children), drains dug, fertilizer applied, and frequent tillage operations completed. Even when all of this work had been done, the violent caprices of the weather, the intrinsic poverty of the soil, or the low germination rate of frost-damaged seed might make all labor futile.[10]

8. E. Le Roy Ladurie, Times of Feast, Times of Famine (New York, 1971) discusses the observed absence of sunspots and increased glaciation, which together with reports of bad weather and poor harvests, probably from the 1590s until the 1660s, suggest there may have been a period of subnormal temperatures or Little Ice Age. See also G. Parker, Europe in Crisis, 1958–1648 (New York: 1979), 17–28.

9. See for example "Le Cahier de la noblesse de Haute Auvergne aux États Généraux de 1614," ed. Pierre-François Fournier, Revue de la Haute Auvergne (1947–49): 117–21. Similar complaints are found in many of the cahiers of 1614, such as those from Basse-Auvergne, A.D. Puy-de-Dome 5c Aa 3rr. The most accessible printed examples are in the cahiers edited by Yves Durand, Cahiers de doléances des paroisses du bailliage de Troyes pour les États Généraux de 1614 (Paris: 1966).

10. My thanks to the Chambre d'Agriculture in Aurillac for physical, soil, and rainfall maps of the Cantal. The geographic sections of P. Arbos, L'Auvergne, and Derrau-Boniol and Fel, Massif Central, are also useful guides. The principles of soil moisture-retention and the problems

The Agrarian Setting

In light of the above characteristics it is not surprising that the Haute Auvergne has long been described as an area of mediocre production. Despite this mediocrity, however, the obvious obstacles to communication necessitated the local production of grains in areas ill-suited to that purpose. Although rivers abounded, they were usually barriers, for few were navigable. Difficult terrain made transportation hazardous and expensive and the mountain roads were often troubled by inclement weather. Such a multitude of obstacles created excellent sites for the toll bridges and barriers scattered throughout the province, sources of friction as well as a further inhibition to the flow of goods, most of which were carried on pack animals or in two-wheeled carts.[11] As with many other parts of France therefore, the Haute Auvergne contained pockets of precarious agriculture on which the local populace was dependent for subsistence.

The environment in which crops and livestock were raised was as varied as the topography of the Haute Auvergne. To use the terms of Roger Dion, it was an area of agrarian "opportunism" where various structures could be observed in different conditions,[12] in contrast to the

---

of agronomy briefly mentioned can be gained from any introductory works on those subjects. A good example is Roy L. Donahue, John C. Shickluna, Lynn S. Robertston, *Soils: An Introduction to Soils and Plant Growth* (Englewood Cliffs, N.J., 1971). See also Abel Poitrineau, *La Vie rurale en Basse Auvergne*, 2 vols. (Paris, 1965), 1:270–71.

11. Abel Poitrineau, *La Vie rurale*, 1:263, 448; 2:113.

12. The discussion of field shapes and systems of cropping is wide-ranging; rather than arriving at any single conclusion, it teaches that there are no easy explanations for the multiplicity of structures in France. Two most influential contributions to this debate have been Marc Bloch, *Les caractères originaux de l'histoire rurale française* (1931) and Roger Dion, *Essai sur la formation du paysage rural français* (Tours, 1934). Dion contrasted the collectivism of strict triennial rotations and communal *vaine pâture* in northern open field areas with the archetypal individualism of southern polyculture in the Midi, where peasants could erect barriers around cropland (*ager*) and graze their animals on the abundant wastes (*saltus*). The area between north and south was not subject to one classifiable and consistent system; it contained a variety of conditions and customs that gave rise to many different systems. While both Bloch and Dion saw the various arrangements of arable, waste, and meadows as a means of ensuring grain production for subsistence and feed for necessary animals, Bloch divided France into areas of *champs ouverts et allongés*, *champs ouverts et irréguliers*, and *enclos*. He saw in the collectivist open-field systems of the north an achievement of medieval equilibrium that required communal enforcement of triennial cropping patterns and grazing the fallow. Enclosure often occurred on former open-field areas because some element such as the availability of pasture or the introduction of a new forage crop changed the balance among the elements of production. But although his theory of developing field systems is somewhat evolutionary, he stresses that

open-field collectivism of northern plains and the "individualism" of the Midi. There were areas such as parts of the Margeride where agrarian collectivism enforced a regular agricultural calendar supervised by an organized village community, and some fields quite elongated in shape could be found on plateaus. But much of the province was characterized by small, irregularly shaped fields that peasants had the liberty to enclose. Enclosures were usually either hedges or low walls of dry stone, many of which dated from ancient times. Between fields were paths seldom more than six feet wide.[13]

The nucleus of such holdings was not a village proper, but a hamlet, like those Marc Bloch described in his discussion of the areas of enclosure in France, and bearing some similarity to those of nearby Gévaudan.[14] Léonce Bouyssou, studying a large area around Aurillac, traced the development of these hamlets from the *mas* (house or farm) of late medieval times, a term that signified both the handful of buildings and the adjacent holdings, and even lent its name to the mountain pastures. Thus it was different from the *mas* or *meix* of Provence or Bourgogne, which referred only to the house and agricultural buildings. The hamlet

---

peculiarities of local conditions could produce innumerable variations. The literature on the subject is vast and includes parts of some of the classics in French historical research such as F. Braudel, *The Mediterranean and the Mediterranean World in the Age of Philip II* (London, 1972), Le Roy Ladurie, *Les Paysans de Languedoc* (Paris, 1962), as well as other works by Bloch and Dion. For the Haute Auvergne, Léonce Bouyssou, "Etudes," provides evidence of field shapes, sizes, and enclosures. Also of use are André Fel, *Les Haute Terres*, and Abel Poitrineau, *Basse Auvergne*, For a bibliographic introduction to the discussion of agrarian structure, see Hugh Prince, "Regional contrasts in Agrarian Structures," in *Themes in the Historical Geography of France*, ed. Hugh D. Clout (London, 1977), 128–84. Eighteenth-century village and field plans showing various degrees of enclosure along with some irregular open fields are in A.D. Cantal 1B–16B. It is interesting that in some cases meadows were directly adjacent to houses while arable was further away, for example, the village of Las Cols (on the Planèze de St. Flour) 1787 A.D. Cantal 7B 633.

13. Bouyssou, "Etude," 130–32. The enclosures of the Haute Auvergne originated in various ways. Some barriers were the result of clearing land, a process that left trees and hedges of great age and mixed varieties. Much of the land was also stony and therefore stones were removed and piled at the edges of fields. Bouyssou also cites cases from the fifteenth century that show peasants enclosing land because of persistent incursions by their neighbors and the neighbors' livestock. Enclosure required the permission of the *seigneur* although "this must have been only a formality" (131). See also André Fel, "Petite Culture" in Clout, *Themes*, 215–45.

14. Bloch, *Caractères*, 57–65. Bloch refers to "a handful of houses" (*Caractères*, 61); Fel, "Petite Culture," 230, notes the weakness of communal organization in the Haute Auvergne. See also Poitrineau, *Basse Auvergne*, 1:595; Claverie and Lamaison, *L'Impossible Marriage*, for descriptions of the hamlet and the "ousta."

had originally represented a family community made strong by the "Roman" power of the patriarch to keep the patrimony intact when passing on his legacy.[15]

We can imagine our setting as a series of quite separate hamlets, the houses and outbuildings with enclosed gardens nearby; arable and hay meadows distinct from each other and usually enclosed. Further afield were extensive pastures, waste, and woodland. In other cases it was possible to see an isolated house and buildings, separated from their neighbors, perhaps containing more than one branch or generation of a family. With time, the tenure of the fields might change hands and thus the contiguous parcels of land would no longer be exploited by the same person or family. Rights of passage could then grow more important in the daily trips between the field and buildings.

Within this setting, the peasants of the sixteenth and seventeenth century practiced a most rudimentary agriculture, from what is known of techniques and production. The usual rotation was biennial, using both spring- and fall-seeded grain varieties, a practice that left half the arable fallow every year. The existence of common pastures (*couderes*), and of waste reduced the necessity of grazing the fallow. Although this may have been practised, there was no enforcement of the communal grazing rights on fallow land (*vaine pâture*) common to the collectivist villages of northern open-field areas. Great care was lavished on gardens, which were fertilized as heavily as possible. Manure was always in demand and many payments in kind included pots of it. Fowl were often kept close by and whenever nearby forest or waste permitted, pigs were raised by individual families for the table; grain was still the important crop, however, and also a principal medium of exchange.[16]

The visible structures of the countryside allowed for a measure of individuality in agricultural operations; but for many, especially in hard times, it was a freedom of dubious value, for the results of arable farming in Haute Auvergne were generally dismal. Rye was a major crop, followed by oats. Wheat, the preferred cereal grain, often fared badly in the short, damp, growing season. Even in the mid-eighteenth century, seed:yield ratios on poor land were 3:1 or worse; on better land a farmer could

15. Bouyssou, "Etude," 123–24.

16. Ibid., 151–52, 228–32; Poitrineau, *Basse Auvergne*, 104, 270, 324; James Goldsmith, "Agricultural Specialization and Stagnation in Early Modern Auvergne," *Agricultural History* (1975): 219; M. Leymairie, "La propriété et l'exploitation foncières aux XVIIe siècle dans la Planèze de St. Flour," *Revue de la Haute Auvergne* (1965): 483.

expect 4:1. By comparison, in areas like the Paris Basin, more suited to arable farming, yields could rise to 8:1 or better; dryland farmers today regularly expect yields of at least 20:1 or 30:1. In the Chataigneraie of the south, chestnuts were an important source of food, fodder, and oil. Because of an abundance of flowering plants in pastures, meadows, and orchards, there was also considerable honey production, although the dampness and the dearth of sunlight in many areas resulted in mediocre yields. Gardens produced most of the common kitchen vegetables of the period as well as some hemp. The potato, which was to enhance the productivity of the land, was not cultivated extensively until the late eighteenth century. The most notable absence among the crops of the period was that of grapes; even in the fifteenth century when wine was made in many unsuitable parts of France, vines were restricted to the southernmost parts of the province bordering Rouergue and Quercy, and wine was always among the notable imports.[17]

Crop failures occurred frequently during the sixteenth and seventeenth centuries; with them came famine and sometimes plague. In the last two decades of the sixteenth century, in 1614, 1628–32, 1642, and 1693, crops failed all over the province. Plague was epidemic for several years after 1587, and it struck with particular force during the period 1627–30. Between the years of misery was mediocrity. While there were some large domains where grain was grown on a commercial scale, the subsistence economy of Haute Auvergne could not bear much pressure and mountain communities lost their weakest members through death, disease, or flight whenever the ceiling of production produced by a stagnant technology failed to meet their needs. The uncertainty of peasant subsistence was epitomized in the dramatic variations, local, seasonal, and annual, of grain prices.[18]

17. Bouyssou, "Etude," 232, 276; see also the essays by Jean Jacquart and E. Le Roy Ladurie in Histoire de la France rurale, ed. G. Duby (Paris, 1975), 2. Le Roy Ladurie discusses eighteenth-century production in Auvergne in a summary of the work of Abel Poitrineau; Jacquart, 237–39, discusses yields for the sixteenth and seventeenth centuries. Also Albert Rigaudière, La Haute Auvergne face à l'agriculture nouvelle au XVIIIe siècle (Paris, 1965), and André Fel, Les Hautes Terres du Massif Central (Paris, 1962).

18. Jean Jacquart in Duby and Wallon, Histoire, 2:246–47; James Goldsmith, "Agricultural Specialization," 220, refers to the Haute Auvergne as having a Malthusian economy. The fullest elaboration of the problems of stagnant production, shortage, and disease is in E. Le Roy Ladurie, Les Paysans de Languedoc (Paris, 1965). The problem of subsistence and its demographic illustration have occupied many historians of the Early Modern period, for example, Alain Croix, Nantes et le Pays Nantais (Paris, 1974). Series of grain prices for our period are in manuscript in Mercuriale d'Aurillac, A.D. Cantal, F259; Michel Leymairie has contributed to a series of grain prices for Haute Auvergne used by James Goldsmith in "The Rural Nobles of

The Mountain Pastures

Economic hope lay beyond the agricultural hamlets of the basins and valleys, in the mountain pastures. In addition to the subsistence grain-growing economy, the Haute Auvergne supported an extensive pastoral economy, more suited to the environment and hence more successful. The mountains were well-watered natural pastures and they formed the basis of the transhumant stock-raising and dairying activities which distinguished the region as an exporter of cheese, butter, and livestock to centers in Quercy, Rouergue, and Languedoc. The most important and productive pastoral areas were in the western part of the province, the regions of Aurillac, Mauriac, and Salers.

The pastoral economy in our period has been analyzed most thoroughly

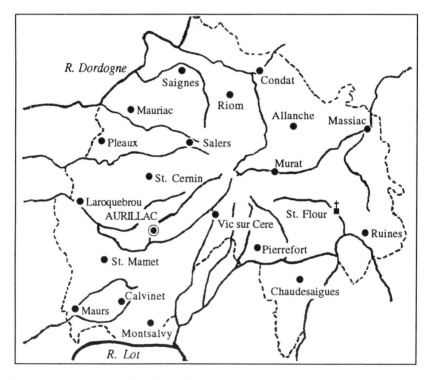

Fig. 3.   Major towns of the Haute Auvergne

by Léonce Bouyssou, James Goldsmith, André Fel, and Abel Poitrineau. The area of summer pasture was known as *la montagne* (the mountain, also *montanha, montana, montanea*, etc.) a term that came to refer to function rather than topography, although in most cases it could be applied to both. The animals, mostly cattle, sometimes sheep or horses, were wintered in the lower valleys and basins of Haute Auvergne and elsewhere and brought up to the *montagnes* on or near "La St. Urbain" (Saint Urban's Day, 25 May), returning to winter quarters at the end of September or in early October.[19]

Mountains were generally divided into "heads" of pasturage (*têtes d'herbage* or *herbatgia*), which varied in size according to the quality of pasture. The most common definition of a *tête d'herbage* was that it could support one cow with sucking calf, six sheep, or one mare with foal; pigs and goats were not usually included. While in most areas the cattle were used for dairying, there were some specialized "fattening" mountains (*montagnes à graisse*) thought to ensure rapid weight gain in animals.[20]

Herdsmen and shepherds were usually called *vachers* and *bergers* in the documents, but they could also be referred to as *messages* (*mesatgi*). They were hired by communities, partners, or individuals and spent the summer in mountain huts (*burons, mazucs*) that served as lodgings, cheese factories, and warehouses. In nearby forest or waste areas, the herdsman often kept pigs. The life of a Cantalian dairy herdsman, although relatively free from communal or seignurial scrutiny, was nonetheless quite labor intensive and demanded considerable skill. It was probably not so free and easy as the existence of the Pyrenean shepherd Pierre Maury in Le Roy Ladurie's *Montaillou*.

In autumn, herdsmen brought large round chunks of cheese (*fourmes*) down from the mountain, using cattle as draft animals. Dairy products as well as some livestock were sold at the market fairs.[21] Despite the abundant summer pastures, the need for arable in the more temperate lowlands limited the amount of land devoted to winter fodder. Local law prohibited the summering of more cattle than one could keep in winter,

19. The detailed account of the pastoral system in Haute Auvergne is Léonce Bouyssou, *Les Montagnes Cantaliennes du XIIIe au XVIIIe siècle* (Aurillac, 1974), which forms the basis for remarks on *Montagnes* in Duby and Wallon, *Histoire*, for example, 118.

20. L. Bouyssou, *Montagnes*; "Etude," 227.

21. Goldsmith, "Agricultural Specialization"; Bouyssou, *Montagnes*, 21–26; E. Le Roy Ladurie, *Montaillou, Village occitan de 1294 à 1324* (Paris, 1975), also published in English as *Montaillou: The Promised Land of Error*, trans. Barbara Bray (New York, 1979). See also Duby and Wallon, eds., *Histoire de la France rurale*, 2:118–19.

and although such laws were almost impossible to enforce, the reality of shortages encouraged a variety of practices, including the importation of animals wintered outside the province. Hay meadows and winter fodder were therefore a source of conflict in the Haute Auvergne and in other areas of transhumance such as the Alps or the Pyrenees.[22]

While the pastoral economy was important to the Haute Auvergne and more suited to the land than arable farming, it would be a mistake to ascribe to it any great technical progress. In addition to the imbalance between summer pasture and winter fodder, the animals used were not particularly productive. The cattle of the Haute Auvergne were usually the native Salers. Even today, improved animals of the same breed dominate much of the pasture land in the Cantal, and if the present small red cattle are an improved race, the early modern beasts must have been deficient indeed. While they are generally hardy, Salers cattle do not produce much meat or milk, although the rather wild diminutive females can be good mothers. Cheese production, even on the best pastures, was not remarkable. Despite changes in terms of tenure, there was no significant intensification of livestock or dairy production in our period.[23] In any event, as we shall see, peasants were not the primary beneficiaries of the lush mountain pastures, for during the Ancien Régime their well-being was tied to the subsistence grain-growing economy of the lowlands.

Thus the peasants and other ordinary folk in the Haute Auvergne were locked in a technically stagnant and unproductive economy. But technique alone could not solve their problems; the lack of productivity was only one component of a complex that conspired against their economic and social welfare, a trap in which geographic isolation, a severe monetary shortage, a lack of outside capital, and an overextension of credit reinforced a rather archaic and sometimes predatory seigneurial regime.

Seigneurs and Tenants

A seigneury in much of the Haute Auvergne was a series of rights and privileges that could pertain to various parts of the original *mas*, ancestor

22. Fel, "Petite Culture," 231; Bouyssou, "Etude," 275–77; Chabrol, "Coutumes locales du haut pays d'Auvergne," in *Coutumes*, 4:1211. Such conflicts were also common in the nearby Gévaudan, for example, and constituted a source of violence: E. Claverie and P. Lamaison, *L'Impossible Mariage*, chap. 2 and 12.

23. James Goldsmith, "Agricultural Specialization," 231, gives a yield of 2 quintaux or 162.25 lbs. of cheese per cow on the best pastures.

of the hamlet. The seigneur's or lord's only economic function, as far as his tenants were concerned, was to collect fixed payments of various kinds. While there were lands free of seigneurial obligation (*allodia* or *alleux*), they were probably not so common in the Haute Auvergne as in the Basse Auvergne, where Abel Poitrineau found them to equal 30% of the land in the eighteenth century.[24]

The seigneurial tenant, called *page, emphitéote, tenancier, manant* or, if well-off, *laboureur* (husbandman or plowman), received his tenure from the seigneur for an unlimited time and could bequeath his rights to his heirs. In return he owed the seigneur various obligations and payments at rates that in theory, were fixed for all time. The peasant was not usually identified as the inhabitant of a seigneury but rather of a particular hamlet and parish, and might owe payments to different lords.[25] The obligations varied from place to place both in their form and amount. Generally they consisted of regular annual payments and of other payments on occasions that occurred irregularly with more or less frequency.

The annual rent (*cens*) was the primary recognition of the status of the seigneur. It was paid partly in cash and partly in kind on gardens, fields, houses, meadows, and sometimes on common pastures as well. The rent paid on gardens, for example, was usually paid in cash while that on other lands was paid in produce. In the Haute Auvergne, payments in kind were primarily in cereals although they also included such things as hay, cheese, fowl, beeswax, eggs, livestock, or vegetables at different times of year. Fowl, for example, were delivered to the seigneur at Christmas and wax was presented in March.[26]

Although there was considerable variation, from a bushel of grain per acre of land to a pittance, the amounts of fixed rent were traditionally small. During the seventeenth century, however, the provincial nobility (*gentilshommes*) were accused of increasing or manipulating it to their profit: allowing or forcing arrears to build up and then demanding a ruinous amount of grain when it was scarce and expensive; selecting the best of whatever produce was required and using especially large measures. In other cases they would accept a payment in kind rather than in cash

24. On *alleux*, Abel Poitrineau, *Basse Auvergne*, 1:341–43; E. Le Roy Ladurie, in Duby and Wallon, *Histoire*, 423; P. Goubert, *Ancien Régime*, 95–96.

25. The seigneurial system is described in Bouyssou, "Etude," chapter 2, "Le régime seigneurial," 133–51, and A. Poitrineau, *Basse Auvergne*, 1:141–249, 341–51. *Manant, tenancier, emphitéote,* and *page* are some of the terms that can be taken to mean lease holder or tenant.

26. Bouyssou, "Etude," 141–43.

after a seigneurial officer had set the price of the produce below the prevailing market price of the locality.[27]

Obligations even more open to abuse were the annual services of labor and cartage (corvées) demanded of tenants. While these were not thought to have been part of most seigneuries in the fifteenth century, they seem to have been widespread and often abused by the seventeenth, along with many illegal "corveés sans titre" (unwarranted services). Auvergnat tenants were required to assist the seigneur in haymaking, harvest, and other agricultural labor on the domains he exploited directly. More costly to some peasants were the duties called bovades (bohadas), which required the use of oxen on the seigneur's domain. Where the number of oxen was not specified, the seigneur might try to improve on custom by demanding several teams for the specified period, or by forcing the plowman to fulfill all of the bovades at one critical time of year and neglect his own work. Vinades obliged the tenant to travel to vineyards and bring back wine for the seigneur, often a demanding trip that was supposed to be taken in winter.[28]

In addition to these regular services and dues there were others less regular and usually less frequent. The acapte was paid upon a change in tenant or seigneur. New tenants also paid an entry fine (droit d'entrée) when beginning their tenure, essentially the price of their possession of the land. Lods et ventes, which could be quite heavy, were demanded of those who bought land subject to the fixed annual rent of the cens.[29] Other troublesome payments were the dues for the use of seigneurial ovens or mills (banalités) and the tolls (péages) on bridges and roads. Substantial fees (percières) were charged on land newly cleared, often for temporary cropping.

---

27. Abuses of the system are most fully documented in the journal of the greffier Dongois in the Grands Jours d'Auvergne 1665–1666, A.N. U749; for a printed version of the documents, see Les Grands-Jours de Clermont, Registres tenus par le Greffier Dongois (1665–1666), printed as Les Grands Jours d'Auvergne, edited by Ulysse Jouvet (Riom, 1903), cited hereafter by date as Dongois, Registres. See especially the arrêts of 9 January 1666 and 15 October 1665, as well as the letters to the intendant Colbert from Auvergnats and intendants of Auvergne, 1661–1665, in Depping, Correspondance Administrative, vols. 1–3. These letters will be described more fully in Chapter 6. See also Arlette Lebigre, Les Grands Jours d'Auvergne (Paris, 1978), chap. 4.

28. Bouyssou, "Etude," 143. The interesting thing about these seigneurial dues is that they seem to have changed very little over three centuries if one compares the studies by Bouyssou for the fifteenth century, with the complaints and arrêts of the Grands Jours in 1665–66 and Poitrineau's work on seigneurial revenues in La Vie rurale en Basse Auvergne, esp. 1:341–51, and if one compares the Haute Auvergne with other parts of France. For a general statement, see Goubert, Ancien Régime, 78–152 and appendix.

29. Bouyssou, "Etude," 143–45. Poitrineau, La Vie rurale en Basse Auvergne, 1:341–42, 347–49.

The charges that allowed for the most invention on the part of seigneurs were originally called *les tailles aux quatre cas*. But the number of "cases" in which such payment could be demanded were sometimes multiplied by seigneurs with a whimsical sort of avarice, and they were still being levied at the height of the seventeenth century. These included substantial payments for common happenings such as the marriage of the lord's sons, daughters, and even granddaughters, or the entry of his offspring into religious orders. Occurrences less likely in the seventeenth century were payments for the lord's assumption of noble status (*nouvelle chevalerie*); ransom for a seigneur held captive by the enemy or payments on his departure for a crusade to the Holy Land. Presumably, as Léonce Bouyssou suggests, these charges had been instituted to compensate the bourgeois who found himself newly beset with the military rigors of nobility.[30]

The above are only a few examples of the various dues that could be levied. Not all of these rights were in the hands of each and every seigneur, but two features of the system are fairly clear. The first is the persistence of payments in kind that had often been commuted into cash elsewhere in France; these were still in force in the eighteenth century. The second feature is the ultimate profitability, for some seigneurs at least, of the system as a whole, not merely in the product it claimed directly, but in its cumulative effects on a peasantry beset with crop failures, high taxes, and increasing indebtedness in our period. This profitability was reflected in the general gains in property made by the nobility and by the bourgeoisie of the period. The expansion of elite property holding in turn changed the type of tenure so that relatively short-term contracts of lease and the exploitation of domains through sharecroppers (*métayers*) or lease holders became more common.[31]

Credit and the Expansion of Domains

During the period 1500–1675, many of the great domains of the Haute Auvergne were built by a combination of seigneurial dues, grain specula-

30. Bouyssou, "Etude," 146–47; Poitrineau, *La Vie rurale en Basse Auvergne*, 1:348. *Arrêt* of 9 January, 1666 in Dongois, *Registres*, indicates that many versions of these *tailles* along with numerous "corvées sans titre" were still in existence.

31. James Goldsmith, "Agricultural Specialization," illustrates this profitability, and the expansion of noble and bourgeois holdings is a major theme in Bouyssou, *Montagnes*. For *métayage*, Bouyssou, "Etudes," 149–50; *Montagnes* gives a detailed discussion of various rental arrangements.

tion, and the manipulation of credit. With this expansion came two other phenomena: an increase in the use of sharecropping leases and the growth of the area devoted to hay meadows in the lowlands at the expense of the arable.

The work of James Goldsmith and Léonce Bouyssou on the mountain pastures of Haute Auvergne has been particularly valuable in documenting changes in land tenure and in analyzing the process by which lands changed hands. An important factor in the underdevelopment of the region was the system of credit. The Haute Auvergne, like much of rural France, was a region where, in the words of the intendant Mesgrigny, "money is extremely scarce." But the particular isolation of the province aggravated the problem. There were no large cities with substantial populations of bureaucrats and wealthy bourgeois who could provide capital.[32] Because of this shortage, those with money or marketable goods tended to become creditors easily, and money was used as little as possible in the ordinary business of rural life. The whole province, as Mesgrigny complained in 1637, suffered from an overextension of credit with "brutal terms" befitting the rather brutal society. Loans were secured by notarized I.O.U.s backed by the threat of legal action and prison. Often, the loan was backed by a mortgage on land (explicit rates of interest were illegal).[33]

32. *Relation de l'état de la province d'Auvergne en 1637*, 186. Lefèvre d'Ormesson also remarked on the lack of large cities, *Mémoire sur l'état de la généralité de Riom en 1697*, ed. Abel Poitrineau (Clermont-Ferrand, n.d.), 52–54.

33. Mesgrigny explained the problem of credit "there are some great chicaneries through the injunctions of arrest, which is the particular style of the province, where no money at all is lent by interest agreements [*constitution de rente*] but [is secured] only by personal bond and the bodies [of the debtors], even when it concerns the most eminent, the term of the bond having elapsed, the creditor issues an injunction to the debtor to surrender to the royal prisons of the jurisdiction"; *Relation de l'état de la province d'Auvergne en 1637*, 157–58. Mesgrigny further complained that the bourgeois of the province were guilty of these practices against both *gentilshommes* and "communes" (187–88). The *conseillers* from Paris to the Grands Jours d'Auvergne encountered the problem immediately upon arriving in the Auvergne, "On Friday morning 25th, they were convoked by the President to inspect the prisons of Riom, which they did, and . . . they set at liberty many wretches who had been prisoners for a long time for very small debts"; Dongois, *Registres*: 26 September 1665. Abel Poitrineau, *La Vie rurale en Basse Auvergne*, 1:495–506, noted that the monetary shortage was still severe in the eighteenth century and that the system of credit was still primitive: "This is credit in its rawest form" (501). The authority for the Haute Auvergne is James Goldsmith, who used inventories after death for the early seventeenth century and notarial archives for the end of the century to demonstrate the frequent use of notarized I.O.U.s: *Nobles* and "Agricultural Specialization," 217–19 and note. On the general question of monetary shortage, see the foundational essay by Jean Meuvret, "Circulation monétaire et utilization économique de la monnaie dans la France du XVIe et du XVIIe siècles," *Etudes d'Histoire Moderne et Contemporaine* 1 (1947): 15–28.

In a capital-poor province, seigneurs in need of revenue for expansion turned first to seigneurial dues paid in grain and cheese. At times of scarcity when prices were high, those who had excess grain to sell could make large profits from the seasonal and annual fluctuations in grain prices. The income from seigneurial dues, which amounted to about one-third of noble incomes, thus became one means of capitalizing the expansion of domains.

The difficult conditions of the sixteenth and seventeenth centuries, the crop failures, scarcity, and high prices combined with the system of credit in the Haute Auvergne to undermine the peasants captive to the seigneurial system. Arrears in the payment of dues accumulated into significant debt when crops were poor and prices high. Debts were backed by land and therefore foreclosure became a means of further expanding domains. James Goldsmith found, for example, that between 1570 and 1675 one family near Salers acquired 44% (79,920 livres) of its new domain holdings through debt cancellation. In the village of Albepierre, where no domains had existed in 1535, they took up 30% of the land by 1681.[34] In the central mountains of the Haute Auvergne by 1688, the elites controlled 60% of the *montagnes* (33% noble, 29% bourgeois, 5% ecclesiastical) according to Léonce Bouyssou; by the late eighteenth century the proportion of "upper-class" holdings had risen to 75%, with nobles directly holding 45% of *montagnes*. By contrast, the arable at lower altitudes often remained in the control of peasants in the seventeenth century, although even there the elites controlled a large proportion of woods and meadows.[35]

The increase in domains on mountain pasture also brought about a change in types of tenure. Most *montagnes* were leased to tenants who held short-term contracts (four to eight years) supplying grain, butter, cheese, and various work obligations (*corvées*) to seigneurs. As a result, two-thirds of noble income in the Haute Auvergne came from domains.

34. Ibid., 222–27.
35. Bouyssou, *Montagnes*, 56–58. Proportions of lowland holdings varied a great deal and may have been considerable. Michel Leymairie in his survey of the Planèze de St. Flour in 1688 showed that cereal production dominated the Planèze and that 75% of arable was in peasant hands. The nobility and bourgeoisie held a large part of meadows (35%) woods (64%) and montagnes (57%) but only 23% of grain-growing land. By contrast, A Poitrineau's study of Vic sur Cère in 1769 showed that nobles and "privilégiés" alone held 34.8% of *montagnes*. Bourgeois held under 7% in each category; peasants held 51.8% of arable and only 13% of montagnes. "Propriété et société en Haute Auvergne à la fin du règne de Louis XV: Le cas de Vic," *Cahiers d'Histoire* (1961): 425–55.

For their part, tenants were seldom able to meet the required payments and often performed increased work obligations in lieu of rent.

The growth of commercial specialization in dairying also increased the need for winter fodder, putting further emphasis on hay meadows and leading to a reduction in the amounts of land reserved for grain.[36] Thus the agricultural structures of the Haute Auvergne were changing during the period of this study as domains became a potent economic force; the victim of change was usually the peasant. The poor arable, seldom sufficient, was cruelly inadequate in hard times; crop failure during the period exaggerated this inadequacy. The staggering growth of royal taxes, particularly the *taille*, after 1628 and the years of plague in the periods 1587–90 and 1628–30 were added disasters.[37]

In the predominantly rural economy there was little local industry to which the threatened peasants could turn. Aurillac, the largest commercial center, had a leather industry and there were a few other pursuits, most of them closely related to the land or to domestic needs: shoemaking, weaving, wood cutting, milling, tinkering, and peddling of various sorts. There was a tendency among economically marginal peasants to gain their subsistence by these means. But the mountains simply could not feed their inhabitants. The Haute Auvergne in this period had "an isolated, weakly capitalized and largely underdeveloped economy."[38]

The Mountain People

The inadequacies of the local economy informed another fundamental feature of life in the Haute Auvergne: the tradition of escape. Probably the most persistent export of the Haute Auvergne was people. Emigration was a natural course for the impoverished Auvergnat and it became a

36. Goldsmith, "Agricultural Specialization" and Bouyssou, *Montagnes*.

37. For the plagues, the best single source remains the *Chevauchées* of the *vice-baillis* for the years in question. For the *taille*, Lefèvre d'Ormesson, in his *Mémoire sur l'état de la généralité de Riom en 1697*, wrote: "the généralité of Riom is one of those which pays the most taille to the king" (169). Actually it ranked fifth in France (*Mémoire*, 169n.). The amount grew from less than 800,000 livres in 1628 to over 4,000,000 in 1640. The three *élections* of Haute Auvergne paid slightly over 30% of these amounts, spread among a population that was probably somewhere between 160,000 and 170,000. See also Poitrineau's essay in G. Manry, ed., *Histoire de l'Auvergne*, 287–314.

38. Goldsmith, "Agricultural Specialization," 217.

demographic constant from the Middle Ages to the present day. Emigration was remarked upon by every commentator of the Early Modern period and it is doubly important to any student of the Haute Auvergne as it links two of the most important characteristics of life in the region: first, the poverty discussed above; and second, the southern orientation of the Haute Auvergne, increasingly challenged during the period under study by the influence of Paris. While there was a specialized pastoral economy that increased its hold during this period, the direction of trade and emigration to Quercy, Rouergue, Toulouse, and Spain had been established much earlier, and a map of fifteenth-century trade routes would show little change.[39] Although the region was within the jurisdiction of the Parlement of Paris by the sixteenth century, the destination of the justice documents belies the Mediterranean orientation of many aspects of Auvergnat life. Both temporary and permanent emigrants went south to find work or trade in an easier climate, to escape the law or perhaps, as Robert Mandrou has suggested of early modern travelers, simply to escape.[40] They traded cheese or livestock, worked in vineyards, worked as sawyers, peddlers, and porters or pursued whatever trade they had previously practised. In Spain, which still seems to have held its golden allure, unskilled Auvergnats often did the jobs Spaniards refused to take, such as carrying water and other menial tasks.[41]

Linguistically, the Haute Auvergne was a part of the south and its

39. Bouyssou, "Vie rurale," (1945–46): 84–85.

40. R. Mandrou, *Introduction à la France Moderne, 1500–1640* (Paris, 1961), 187–300.

41. The phenomenon of Early Modern emigration received considerable attention, both during the Early Modern period and in recent times. In 1637 Mesgrigny suggested that the rude climate and the need for money to pay the *taille* were strong motives behind emigration; *Relation de l'état de la province d'Auvergne en 1637* (Clermont-Ferrand, 1842), 182. Later, Lefèvre d'Ormesson estimated the seasonal emigrant population at 6,000 men; *Mémoire sur l'état de la généralité de Riom en 1697,* 174. Jean Bodin wrote that the great part of work in Spain was done by French laborers, winemakers, carpenters, shoemakers, etc., particularly from Auvergne, "L'Emigration de la Haute Auvergne," quoted in M. Trillat, "L'Emigration de la Haute Auvergne en Espagne du XVIIe au XXe siècle" *Revue de la Haute Auvergne* (1954–55): 257–94. Trillat used the records of Spanish hospitals, passports, and examples of the circulation of money to study emigration. He discovered, for example, that from 1617 to 1619 about 100 emigrants died in the Hôpital St. Louis des Français in Madrid. In 1626 it was estimated that there were 200,000 Frenchmen in Spain. Other authors have dealt with the Auvergnat emigrants in various parts of France and in Spain; R. Le Blant, "L'Evolution social d'Auvergnats parisiens au XVIIe siècle," *Actes de 88e Congrès des traités savantes* (Clermont-Ferrand, 1963), 696–707. P. F. Fournier, "Emigrants auvergnats en Espagne au XVe siècle," *Revue d'Auvergne* (1924–27): 240–241. L. Bourrachet, "Les immigrants saisonniers auvergnats en Haut Agenais," *Revue de la Haute Auvergne* (1960): 173–80. P. Arbos, "L'Emigration temporaire en Auvergne," *Revue d'Auvergne* (1931): 41–45.

common people spoke an Occitan patois. Accounts in Aurillac were written in French only after 1464, and those in St. Flour were still in Occitan in 1467. Direct control by the crown in 1531 hastened the spread of official French and the first printing presses, introduced slightly earlier, gave literate Auvergnats access to more of written French. French thus became the language of the elites while the local patois remained the tongue of the majority.[42] In justice documents, witnesses' testimony (with the exception of some insults) was recorded in French and those who wished to succeed in officialdom gravitated toward Paris.[43] Pierre Liset, a native of Salers for example, became *premier président* of the Parlement of Paris, in 1529.[44] At a much humbler level, Paul Lacarrière, the third *vice-bailli*, *prévôt des maréchaux*, the chief of the region's mounted police, was the first of his family to study in Paris.[45]

In local law and custom, the southern influence of written law dominated the most populous parts of the Haute Auvergne. The customs of inheritance and the distribution of power within the family were similar to those in much of the Midi. As we have seen earlier, the father had the freedom to name heirs. A son could renounce his inheritance and the father's power, although this was unusual. When they married, women and their possessions were legally under the sway of their husbands; even after marriage, sons usually remained under the father's control. If a family had both sons and daughters, the latter were usually dowered and excluded from the inheritance. The tight-knit family communities of the Haute Auvergne placed an emphasis on the security and integrity of their patrimony against outsiders.[46]

In religion, the region differed from its southern neighbors in its almost total rejection of Protestantism. Although the city of Aurillac had been designated in the Edict of January, 1562, as a place where Protestant worship was permitted, during thirty years of religious war, most of the Protestants were killed or driven away. Aurillac, along with the rest of the Haute Auvergne, suffered severely during the wars. The city was

---

42. Manry, *Histoire d'Auvergne*, 250–51, 279–80, and chap. 8.

43. A.D. Cantal series B dossiers criminals, particularly the *informations*.

44. Abbé Chaumeil, *Biographie des personnes rémarquables de la Haute Auvergne* (St. Flour, 1867), 179–81.

45. Procès Verbaux du Vice-Bailly, 7 March 1636, A.D. Cantal, Fonds Comblat (hereafter cited as *Chevauchées*).

46. Bouyssou, *Vie rurale*, part 3, chap. 1, 47–58. For the seventeenth century, Michel Saby, "L'Âme paysanne et la vie rurale en Haute Auvergne au XVIIe siècle," *Almanach de Brioude* (1975): 157–78.

taken and sacked by Protestants from the Rouergue in 1569 and in 1572, when the news of Saint-Barthélemy reached the Auvergne, Aurillac, alone of all the cities in the upper and lower province, joined in the frenzy and eighty remaining Calvinists or alleged Calvinists were killed. During each phase of the religious wars the Haute Auvergne was the scene of bloody strife. By 1589 at the death of Henry III, Aurillac, Maurs, and Salers were staunchly royalist, some other centers were in the hands of the Protestants, and all of the major towns in the *prévôté* of St. Flour were held by the Catholic League. St. Flour itself became the rallying point of Catholic fanaticism, and not until 1594–95 was the province finally free of major sectarian struggles. In subsequent years, the traditions of violence established in a generation of war remained strong among the nobility of the mountains. The Haute Auvergne at the beginning of this period was therefore impoverished and insecure, preyed upon by a nobility accustomed to military liberties and to the traditional subservience of its peasantry.[47]

The people of the Haute Auvergne in the late sixteenth and early seventeenth centuries were born into a series of interesting contradictions. In contrast to the evidence of "individualistic" agrarian structures, the relative freedom of the herding life and of the occasional independent peasant holding (*alleu*) along Mediterranean lines, was the strict and archaic seigneurial regime. A subsistence grain-growing economy lay in uneasy balance with the vigorous and growing commercial exploitation of the mountain pastures. The region was isolated and communication difficult, yet it witnessed massive migrations, seasonal, temporary, and permanent. The southern habit of written law was sometimes mixed with the customary traditions of the north; the invading culture of official French and the legal jurisdiction of the Parlement of Paris met with popular Occitan. One could add as well that the *gabelle* divided the province along the rivers Alagnon and Jordanne between the tax-free salt to the north and the *gabelle* of Languedoc to the south.

Out of this mountain crucible came the Auvergnats, whose behavior we are to examine. As to their appearance, Abel Poitrineau has suggested that *montagnards* were probably taller and healthier than the poor peasants of the Limagne in Basse Auvergne. Lowland peasants ate great

---

47. Manry, *Histoire de l'Auvergne*, chap. 9, deals with the fate of the Auvergne during the religious wars, as do H. Hauser, *Notes et documents sur la Réforme en Auvergne* (Paris, 1909) and A. Imberdis, *Histoire des guerres religieuses en Auvergne pendant les XVIe et XVIIIe siècles* (Riom, 1846).

quantities of bread (400 kg. per annum) and are thought to have been scarcely five feet tall on the average.[48] But the inhabitants of the mountains had access to more dairy products and the use of wasteland where pigs and goats could forage. The diet of the majority, however, was probably still quite farinaceous, although cheese is frequently mentioned as a part of meals. The poorer peasants at Vic-sur-Cère in the eighteenth century ate rye bread from large round loaves that were sometimes kept for three or four months before consumption. While pork was the most widespread source of meat, the traditional feast of boiled salt pork and garden vegetables was an occasional luxury. At Vic, salted goat's meat replaced pork. The inhabitants of our hamlets in good times at least, were relatively sturdy specimens.[49]

The impression of contemporaries was of a rough people, rustic, coarse, taciturn, parsimonious, quick-tempered, and sometimes brutal. Espirit Fléchier's contemporary account of the Grands Jours d'Auvergne in 1665 is full of disdainful reference to the wonderful roughness of the Auvergnats, to their primitive, violent behavior, and even to the ugliness of the local women.[50] A most extensive catalogue of Auvergnat characteristics in the Early Modern period came from Louis Estadieu, an eighteenth-century tax official who toured the Haute Auvergne in 1753 and again in 1779, remarking on the idiosyncrasies of places and their inhabitants.[51] The people of St. Flour, for example were, "very uncivilized, coarse, rude . . . great drunkards." Those of Allanche were "boorish, nasty, insular . . . " In the high mountain villages of the Salers region (which he said was known as "the end of the world") Estadieu decided that the closed, suspicious character of the inhabitants was due to "the harshness of the climate." When they saw a man "from a milder climate," they acted as if they had seen a ghost, and the author met great resistance when trying to secure a declaration of their possessions for tax purposes. The most remarkable feature of the society he observed was the traditional southward emigration, which in some villages took away two-thirds

48. Poitrineau, La Vie rurale en Basse Auvergne, 1:101–6.

49. Ibid. and Poitrineau, "Société et propriété": Bouyssou, "Etude," 274–75.

50. Espirit Fléchier, Mémoires sur les Grands Jours d'Auvergne en 1665, ed. A. Cheruel (Paris, 1856).

51. The journals of Estadieu were assembled and published by Gabriel Esquer as "La Haute Auvergne à la fin de l'Ancien Régime, Notes de géographie économique." Revue de la Haute Auvergne (1905): 381–97; (1906): 90–108, 150–68, 256–78, 395–428; (1907): 125-58, 278–313, 384–432; (1908): 237–76; (1910): 209–35; (1911): 84–94.

of the adult males. He concluded that this drain of manpower was due to the impoverished economy of the region.

These are interesting firsthand impressions, albeit a century after the period that concerns us, and we have similar observations in the reports of the Intendants Mesgrigny and Lefèvre d'Ormesson as well as in the commentaries on the Grands Jours. It is not unusual, however, for elite "strangers," especially those whose official functions require them to intrude, to encounter the hostility of the locals. After all, as Robert Muchembled has put it so succinctly in his discussion of late medieval and Early Modern xenophobia, "L'étranger inquiète" (The outsider disturbs).[52] Nor is it surprising for such men nervously to describe a habitual reticence and unfamiliar customs with ethnic and social condescension, framed in terms of local "character." These outsiders, often urban, were of a different, perhaps even, as it has been argued recently, a "modernizing" order. Although we must make use of their observations, we must be careful not to adopt their perspective, which in the hands of students becomes yet another example of what has been called "the enormous condescension of posterity."[53]

52. R. Muchembled, L'Invention de l'homme moderne: Sensibilités, moeurs et comportements collectifs sous l'Ancien Régime (Paris, 1988), 19.
53. E. P. Thompson, The Making of the English Working Class (Toronto, 1968), 11.

2 The Forces of Order

"In the upper region, there are few rich houses in the cities," wrote the Intendant Mesgrigny in 1637. Indeed, to an outsider, the cities of the Haute Auvergne would have seemed little more than insignificant piles of domesticated stone in the wild, immense shadows of the volcanic massifs. Life was overwhelmingly rural. But behind the city walls dwelt the agents of royal justice—the forces of order.[1] We have noted briefly the conditions of life in Haute Auvergne for the majority, the rude climate and the harsh necessity of an isolated life. Release from these painful circumstances was achieved in drink, and in rough festive dancing, or in flight to the fortunate south. As we shall see in Chapter 3, release also came in sudden, purgative explosions of violence. But what were the institutional forces that restrained, deterred, or punished offenses?

The formally established forces of "order" were after all the authors of our criminal justice documents. Into this elite world of law and French literacy the antagonists went to continue a process that had begun, like a thousand other quarrels, in the countryside. But now the official cast of the proceedings, the necessity of formally identifying oneself as to name, age, status (*qualité*) and residence, the solemn oath and the demand for a sort of precision uncommon in the everyday world, changed enemies into accuser, accused, and perhaps criminal.

The *Maréchaussée* and the *Vice-Baillis*

While there existed an impressive array of titles for officers and of ordinances defining procedure and jurisdiction, the early modern forces

---

1. *Relation de l'état de la province d'Auvergne en 1637* (Clermont-Ferrand, 1842), 186.

that functioned as official police in the present-day sense of that term were rather puny when compared to the machinery of surveillance and control in our contemporary states. The most coherent "police" force in the Haute Auvergne, was the *maréchaussée* or mounted police led by the *vice-bailli, prévôt des maréchaux*. Literally the title *vice-bailli* could be taken as "vice bailiff," but "sheriff" may be more meaningful than "bailiff" to many English speakers, and it more accurately represents the functions of the office. *Prévôt des maréchaux* would literally be "provost of marshals," although given the obscurity of the latter to modern readers, *prévôt* will probably serve us just as well. In the reports of the *vice-baillis* for 37 of the 77 years between 1587 and 1664, we have a catalogue of patrols, crimes, pursuits, captures, trials, and punishments that comprehends most sorts of offenses and their repression.[2]

Although the office of *vice-bailli* was a creation of the late sixteenth century, its roots were medieval and the district under the control of the officers conformed to ancient boundaries. The Bailliage des Montagnes d'Auvergne was created in the thirteenth century and later subdivided into districts called *prévôtés*, under the direction of *prévôts*. The three southern *prévôtés* of Aurillac, Mauriac, and St. Flour, which followed the same borders as the districts of the archpriests of those areas, became known as the Bailliage des Montagnes and also as the Haute Auvergne. The *prévôté* of Aurillac was later subdivided to form a fourth *prévôté* of Maurs.

The first *prévôts*, administrative ancestors of the Early Modern *vice-baillis* of Haute Auvergne, enjoyed a wide range of powers that gave them

2. *Procès verbaux* in the Fonds de Comblat, A.D. Cantal, exist for the years 1587–95, 1606–17, 1627–31, 1636, 1646, 1647–50, 1652, 1654, 1655, 1659, 1660, and 1664. M. Boudet, ed., *Documents inédits sur la justice et la police prévôtales* (Riom, 1906) is a partial transcription of some *procès verbaux*. Anyone who uses Boudet to follow the *chevauchées* of the *maréchaussée*, however, will find that he was selective, paraphrasing here, omitting there, and generally concentrating on the bizarre and illustrious at the expense of the workaday incidents that made up the life of the *maréchaussée*. For some reason he omitted the entire year 1606, and of 1611, for example, a year in which there were five murders, as well as numerous executions, robberies, and feuds, he writes, "The record for 1611 . . . mentions not one noteworthy event" (74). While his transcription is a good introduction to the *procès verbaux*, after wrestling with some of the confused dates, inconsistencies, and omissions, I decided to ignore it, and all incidents referred to here under the designation *Chevauchées* are taken from the existing original thirty-seven years of *procès verbaux* in manuscript. Of much greater value to the student of the seventeenth century is his narrative *La justice et la police prévôtales* published in the series L'Auvergne, Historique, Littéraire et Artistique (Riom, 1902), especially the first essay "L'institution prévôtale en Haute Auvergne," which discusses the formation of the *maréchaussée* and its jurisdiction, and the second "The functions of the vice-bailli des montagnes."

control over public order and justice as well as the responsibility of receiver or collector (*receveur*) of royal revenues in each *prévôté*. This unity of the coercive powers of force and the farm of royal finance led, as one might expect, to the corruption of justice for economic ends and the office fell into disrepute. In 1516 therefore, all prevotal powers in the Auvergne, except for the investigation of criminal cases, were suppressed.[3]

But problems of public order in the years following grew serious, especially after military defeat at Pavia in 1525 released bands of soldiers and left garrisons of troops who preyed on the local populace.[4] In 1526, therefore, a permanent "police" force was introduced to the Auvergne. A captain and six *archers* or constables formed the core of this troop, which was to contain and punish the offenses of soldiers, brigands, and vagabonds on the highways and in public places. The captain was authorized to recruit when necessary more men from the towns and seigneuries. Gradually the number of *archers* grew, but the terrain they patrolled was simply too vast and too difficult to enable a quick response to sudden alarms of trouble.[5] The Monts du Cantal, which separated Haute from Basse Auvergne, made this force ineffective in the upper province. Although the problem of policing the Haute Auvergne was recognized early in the century, it was only after the outbreak of the Wars of Religion that the situation was thought to be critical. Well-armed men and disorder were everywhere in the Haute Auvergne. By 1572, Protestant bands from Rouergue were ravaging the countryside near St. Flour, and in Aurillac Catholic noblemen murdered "heretics" and pillaged their houses. At the fringes of military confusion there was crime, vagabondage, and general insecurity.

In January 1573, the *général de finances*, a royal bureaucrat at Riom, described the problems of disorder. There had been an increase in the

---

3. The document of suppression is printed in Chabrol, *Coutumes générales et locales de la province d'Auvergne*, 4 vols (Riom, 1786), 1:cxxlii. See Boudet, "Institution prévôtale" x–xi. *Prévôts* apparently predate the creation of the Bailliage des Montagnes, and Chabrol held in his *Coutumes générales* (1:lxxi) that they were suppressed about 1257; Emile Delalo, writing in the *Dictionnaire statistique . . . du Cantal* on the borders of the Cantal (2:511–12) thought that they had been suppressed a century later, while Boudet, "L'institution prévôtale," xi–x, gave evidence of a continuous line of *prévôts* at St. Flour in the fourteenth and fifteenth centuries.

4. Pavia was the signal defeat of France under Francis I by the imperial forces of Charles V on 24 February 1525. For a survey of the power politics involved, see Gerald Q. Bowler et al., *Europe in the Sixteenth Century* (London, 1989), 229–35.

5. Boudet, "Institution prévôtale," x–xiii.

numbers of "vagabonds" and "scoundrels" who operated freely in the Auvergne, especially since the late troubles, committing "many robberies, plunder, depradations, violence and oppression."[6] The *prévôt général*, head of the *maréchaussée* in Auvergne, resided in Basse Auvergne, twenty difficult mountain leagues[7] from Aurillac, so that before he could be notified of their crimes "the criminals have the leisure to carry out their wicked designs and retreat far away with complete impunity." Even if the high country had not been so inaccessible, the *prévôt général* had his hands full in the Basse Auvergne alone. The people of the Haute Auvergne were therefore, "deeply troubled and disgraced," for "even so, the ordinary justice of the high country of Auvergne has no strength at all with which to carry out its decrees and judgments."

When seen beside the dramatic list of miseries it was meant to cure, the remedy prescribed in 1573 seems rather pitiful. A "vis bailly," lieutenant of the *prévôt général*, along with ten *archers* and all the powers attributed by statute to other prévôts des maréchaux, was to ensure the repose and well-being of the inhabitants of the Haute Auvergne. The new officer was to be chosen from among three candidates nominated by the provincial estates, and known to be a man of "judgment, integrity, and sufficiency." The last-mentioned quality may have been a financial sufficiency, for the offices in the force were venal, and after the introduction of the *paulette* in 1604, they could also be hereditary, or, in the ironic description of the day, "immortel."[8] Of the ten *archers*, the *vice-*

---

6. "Extrait du libre du Roy de la court du bailiage du hault Auvergne estably pour le roy a Aurillac" (10 January 1573), Fonds Goyon-Grimaldi, A.D. Cantal, series E. The extract and the letters of provision for the first *vice-bailli* are printed in Boudet, *Documents inédits*, appendix 4, 161–71.

7. Jean-Baptiste Franiatte, in his *Tableau des poids et mésures en usage dans la ci-devant Haute Auvergne* (Riom, 1802) attempted to introduce Auvergnats to the conversion from traditional to Revolutionary units of measurement. He estimated one French league (*lieue*) to equal 4.44 kilometers (2.8 miles) and one league of the Haute Auvergne (lieue du Cantal), 5.9 kilometers (3.7 miles). The Intendant Lefèvre d'Ormesson considered a mountain league to be twice as long as the ordinary French league and his modern editor Abel Poitrineau almost agreed, calculating it at 8.3 kilometers (5.2 miles). See *Mémoire sur l'état de la généralité de Riom en 1697*, 37 and 37n.

8. The problem of venality of offices was of serious concern to many in the late sixteenth and the seventeenth century. The authority on the subject is Roland Mousnier, *La Vénalité des offices sous Henri IV et Louis XIII* (Paris, 1971). The practice was especially galling to members of the nobility who saw it as the means by which filthy lucre replaced noble birth and noble qualities as the way to power and financial advantage. A fertile source of such complaints is the collection of *cahiers* to the Estates General of 1614 in which nobles both decried the growth of venality and demanded that the number of noble officeholders be increased. For examples, see

bailli could choose nine and the tenth was appointed by the crown to be a recorder (*greffier*).[9] Later the number of *archers* increased, and for most of the period 1587–1664 the *vice-bailli* usually had fifteen of them, although the numbers gradually increased and by the beginning of the eighteenth century, there were twenty-four. These men were to police a rugged area of almost 6000 square kilometers and a population that probably varied between 150,000 and 200,000. The initial annual salaries of *archers* were 180 livres and that of the *vice-bailli* 400 livres. Some of the funds for the force were taken from the contribution of 1400 livres that the Haute Auvergne had formerly given to the *prévôt général* of Auvergne and the rest were to be raised by the collector of *tailles*.[10] *Prévôts des maréchaux* and their men were prohibited by law from demanding any other expenses, salaries, or *épices* (fees) from the citizenry, a prohibition that was not observed.[11]

The record begins in December 1586 with the reign of *vice-bailli* Jean Lacarrière (1586–1602), and it is from the accounts of Lacarrière and his descendants, Jacques (1602–36) and Paul (1636–64), along with the evidence of the appropriate statutes, that we can define the functions of the *vice-baillis* and assess the value of the documents they left behind.[12] The term *vice-bailli* and its variants (*vibailli, visbailly,* etc.) were not new, for *vice-baillis* and *vice-sénéchaux* had existed as early as the thirteenth

---

Nobles of Berry, B.N. MSfr. 3328, 42, 45–46; Beauvaisis, B.N. Clair 742 Art. 11; Provence B.N. MSfr. n.a. 5174, fol. 94; Burgundy A.D. Cote d'or 3473, fol. 6; Lyonnais B.N. MSfr. 4782, Art. 136, Art. 68; Chaumont en Bassigny, B.N. MSfr. n.a. 2808. J. M. Hayden, *France and the Estates General of 1614* (Cambridge, 1974) provides a thorough study of the *cahiers,* and M. R. Greenshields, "The Relations of Sentiment between the Peasants and the Rural Nobility in the Cahiers to the Estates General of 1614" (M.A. thesis, University of Saskatchewan, 1978), a closer look at the noble and peasant *cahiers.*

9. "Extrait du libre du Roy de la court du bailiage du hault Auvergne."

10. Ibid. The numbers of *archers* appearing at the semi-annual musters varied. See also Iain Cameron, *Crime and Repression in the Auvergne and the Guyenne, 1720–1790* (Cambridge, 1981), 2, 19, appendix 1, and Boudet, *Documents inédits,* 11.

11. The *dossiers* of trials in which the *vice-baillis* were involved show evidences of *épices* and the *Chevauchées* also contain instances in which *archers* kept the horse or arms they confiscated. The older tradition of the *prévôts* persisted here. By an ordinance of July 1539 *prévôts* had been allowed to keep half of fines they levied for "délits de chasse"; A. Isambert et al., *Recueil général des anciennes lois françaises depuis l'an 420 jusqu'à la révolution de 1789* (Paris, 1822–33), 12:570.

12. Jean Lacarrière was *vice-bailli* from 1587 to 1602, his son Jacques from June 1602 to 1636 and Paul, son of Jacques, took control of the family office on his return from Paris, 7 March 1636 until the end of the period under study here. The *vice-bailliage* remained in the Lacarrière family until the office was suppressed. Boudet dated the suppression 1730 (*Documents inédits,* 151) but the date of the edict suppressing the office is 9 March 1720; I. Cameron, *Crime and Repression,* 4n.

century; Doucet mentions them in areas as diverse as Normandy, Dau-phiné, and Provence.[13] But the officially designated functions and compe-tence of the *vice-bailli* were not really cloaked in the mystery of the ages. The edict creating the office simply stated that the new *vice-bailli* of Haute Auvergne was to have the same powers as other *prévôts des maréchaux*.[14] For our period these powers had been defined piecemeal in a series of edicts and statutes from the edict of 25 January 1536 until the most comprehensive statement of competence and procedure in the Ordinance of 1670. The latter was, for the most part, a summing-up of previous developments and established practices, a codification rather than an innovation.[15] In his role as a guardian of the peace and agent of the crown, the *vice-bailli* appeared in many guises, as a chief of police, a military policemen, a soldier, a judge of last resort, an examining magistrate and even on occasion as a diplomat. This classification of his tasks disguises the basic unity of his work, which simply involved responding to trouble and preventing potential troubles. For much of our period, especially in the early years, the *vice-baillis* showed little concern about the niceties of jurisdiction.

As mounted policeman and chief of the provincial *maréchaussée*, the *vice-bailli* was to tour the province regularly with his *archers*, checking with local authorities for reports of trouble, pursuing and capturing suspects, and judging the appropriate cases. His police function was not limited to any particular offense, for he was specifically authorized to capture all offenders and then hand them over to the appropriate judges.[16] In practice, therefore, the *vice-baillis* responded to all sorts of alarms and made very little distinction among them. The records often imitate the

13. R. Doucet, *Les institutions de la France au XVIe siècle*, 2 vols. (Paris, 1948), 1:117, 119, 257, 26, 252. The ordinances concerning *prévôts des maréchaux* in the sixteenth and seventeenth centuries usually made mention of *vice-baillis* and *vice-sénéchaux*. For example, see the Ordinance of February 1566, Isambert, *Recueil général des anciennes lois*, 14:200; Ordinance of May 1570, ibid., 425; Ordinance of 1660, Isambert, *Recueil*, 16:391.

14. "Extrait du libre du Roy de la court du bailiage du hault Auvergne estably pour le roy a Aurillac."

15. "Attributions et jurisdictions," edict of 25 January 1536, Isambert, *Recueil*, 12:531. Other ordinances and edicts in the Isambert collection that deal with the powers and precedences of the *prévôts des maréchaux* are generally repetitive up to and including the Ordinance of 1670. They include the ordinances of 3 February 1549, ibid., 13:144; January 1560, ibid., 14:81–82; February 1566, ibid., 200 articles, 41–47; edict of January 1572, ibid., 251; May 1570, 14:425–27; January 1629, 16:276; August 1647, 17:63; December 1660, ibid., 391; August 1670, 18:374–79 (Titres 1 and 2).

16. Ordinance of February 1566, Art. 41, Isambert, *Recueil*, 14:200.

language of statutes and procedural manuals, saying that the *vice-bailli* received a report and pursued the matter "instantly," "immediately afterwards," or "without stopping in town."[17] The emphasis was always toward rural crime, and the temptation to stay in the cities and towns was frowned upon. An ordinance of 1549 specified that *prévôts des maréchaux* were to "devote themselves" continually to *chevauchées* (mounted patrols) of the rural areas without staying in any city longer than two days. A patrol of the entire district was to be made every three months and reports were also to be composed quarterly by the recorder (*greffier*).[18] These admonitions were restated repeatedly, for example in 1560, 1566, 1570, and 1660. The ordinance of May 1570 encouraged the *prévôt* or *vice-bailli* to mount his horse as soon as he was told about an incident.[19]

The places over which the *vice-baillis* kept especially close watch were highways, public places, and markets. Fairs, an attraction for vagabonds, pickpockets, and highwaymen, were of particular interest and in the thirty-seven years for which there are reports, the *archers* of the *vice-bailli* patrolled more than 700 market fairs. The *vice-baillis* of the Haute Auvergne seem to have exercised exemplary discipline in the matter of patrols. In a normal tour they visited most of the major towns and cities of the province: Mauriac, St. Flour, Salers, Laroquebrou, Murat, Maurs, Marcolès, Vic, Pierrefort, Chaudesaigues, and many smaller places as well. The route taken varied with each patrol in order to surprise malefactors in the act. While *prévots des maréchaux* were required by the ordinance of 1549 to live in their own district,[20] the *vice-baillis* were not allowed any jurisdiction in their town of residence. In times of serious danger the *vice-baillis* seem to have ignored this restriction and at the beginning of his tenure, Jean Lacarrière asserted his authority to keep public order and assure the quarantine of infected persons in the plague of 1587 that swept Aurillac.[21]

17. For example, *Chevauchées*, 1588, 19 May.
18. Ord. 3 February 1549, Art. 9; Isambert, *Recueil*, 13:144.
19. Ord. May 1570, Art. 185; Isambert, *Recueil*, 14:425–27.
20. Ord, 1549, Art. 9, 12; Isambert, *Recueil*, 13.
21. Boudet, *Documents inédits*, 7. Boudet gives no reference for this particular regulation, and I have found none in the ordinances for the period. But it is true that aside from the fairs and major civil or military emergencies, the *Chevauchées* contain no crime from the city of Aurillac proper. For details of the plague of 1587, see *Chevauchées*: 1587, 25 June; 28 June; 3 July; 6 July–25 August. On 1 October the *vice-bailli* was able to resume his travels, but the disease was still in the area (20 November). On 11 December, Lacarrière was warned away from the gates of Mauriac by the news that all of the innkeepers were dead and their houses infected.

While the patrols themselves often resulted in captures and arrests, the formal dealings with local authorities, no matter how turbulent the times, were usually fruitless. When the *vice-bailli* met with the consuls or other local officials of a town during his tour, he would always ask them if there were any problems with which he could lend a hand (*mainforte*). The reply was almost always no. Consuls, other royal officials, seigneurs, and local authorities of all sorts jealously guarded their jurisdictions against incursions by this freewheeling police force.[22]

Although a force based in Aurillac was better able to respond to trouble than the original troop of the *prévôt général* of Auvergne had been, conditions in the high country made pursuit and capture difficult. Unless a suspect was captured during the commission of a crime the response to information was still clumsy; inevitably a great deal of time elapsed between the initial incident, the report of an informant, and the arrival of the *maréchaussée* at the scene of the crime. Usually the suspects had fled the area if not the country; after an unsuccessful pursuit, the *maréchaussée* spent their time questioning witnesses and beginning proceedings against the absent accused. Although this problem was never really solved, during the seventeenth century in relatively peaceful times, the *vice-baillis* kept some of their men stationed in the major towns such as Maurs, Salers, and Mauriac. A lieutenant and usually about a half-dozen *archers* were stationed in St. Flour and called to Aurillac only during large-scale disturbances or for the semi-annual muster, always well attended because it was also payday.[23]

The *vice-baillis'* role as military policemen brought them into contact with a problem of order that plagued much of the early modern period. Both on the regular patrols and in response to specific requests, the *maréchaussée* maintained a careful surveillance over armies on the march, garrisons, and the disbanded soldiers whose experience with the legalized plunder of war often led them to continue as bandits or troublemakers. When need be, the *vice-baillis* themselves served as military officers. *Maréchaussée* activities related to armies tend to dominate the records during the times of national crisis, particularly during the period

22. For example, see murder cases, *Chevauchées:* 1648, 18 August; 1649, 5–6 July; 1595, 30 November.

23. Ord. 1549, Art. 10. The reports were to be sent to the *Connétabli,* "Supreme organ of the maréchaussée," in Paris: Mousnier, *Institutions,* 1:141–42. Theoretically, these reports were to be compiled daily and sent to Paris every three months. The records of the Lacarrières were signed only at the end of each year.

1589–95, when the Catholic League held sway in St. Flour. During this period the *vice-bailli* Jean Lacarrière was involved in a steady round of surveillance, investigation, and skirmish. In June 1593, for example, he was busy with investigations into the depredations of soldiers lodged in the parish of Anglars[24] and the following August he traveled the "length and breadth" of his country to prevent violations of the truce of that month.[25] Throughout the previous two years the *vice-bailli* had been more soldier than policeman, battling the forces of the League at La Chappelle,[26] Mur des Barrès,[27] in the Rouergue,[28] and at Pierrefort.[29]

These time-consuming military efforts often interfered with ordinary police work in the early years and their presence in the records of the *maréchaussé* renders quantification of criminality all but impossible. While the successful pursuit of suspects was difficult in ordinary times, the confusion of allegiances and the scattered knots of partisan soldiery throughout the Haute Auvergne often made it impossible.[30] In October 1589 the *vice-bailli* and his *archers* approached the city of St. Flour in hot pursuit of a horse thief named Pierre Mercyr. His quarry slipped into the city, but the *vice-bailli* was refused entry because the city "during the present troubles had declared itself for a party against His Majesty." Jean Lacarrière sent two *archers* into the city and they managed to capture Mercyr; but the consuls and other inhabitants supported the horse thief against the police, who were forced to withdraw empty-handed.[31] During the seventeenth century, the *vice-baillis* were seldom called to serve as military commanders, but they were active as military policemen right up to the last years of our period, as when during the Fronde, the *vice-bailli* Paul Lacarrière supported the inhabitants of several parishes against unauthorized bodies of soldiers attempting to lodge in the area and live off the fat of the land.[32]

24. *Chevauchées:* 1593, 25 June.
25. Ibid., August.
26. *Chevauchées:* 1591, 6 November.
27. *Chevauchées:* 1592, 17 May.
28. Ibid., 8–10 June.
29. Ibid., 20 June.
30. For a general discussion of the problems of *gens de guerre,* see L. Welter, "Détresse de l'Auvergne du fait des 'gens de guerre' dans la premier moitié du XVIIe siècle," *Bulletin historique et scientifique de l'Auvergne* (1959):166–76.
31. *Chevauchées:* 1589, 9 October.
32. *Chevauchées:* 1652, 15 October, 26 October, 21 November. Actually the royal armies caused more grief in the Haute Auvergne than did the Frondeurs, who left the Upper Province virtually untouched.

The men of the *maréchaussée* were also used to support other arms of royal government. They provided escorts for both foreign dignitaries and important Frenchmen. Among their most unpopular tasks was the support they provided to the collectors of taxes, particularly the royal *taille*, either escorting the tax convoy (*voiture des tailles*) or enforcing the seizure and auction of property for arrears in taxes, or suppressing the "rebellions" against the tax collectors by families and by larger groups. This most distasteful and dangerous of tasks was also continued throughout the period from the beginning of disturbances in the *prévôté* of Mauriac in 1588, to the difficulties of the 1630s through the 1650s.[33] In 1637, the Intendant Mesgrigny complained that many of the civil functions of the *vice-bailliage* should be removed and given to minor royal functionaries (*sergents royaux*) because such preoccupations sapped the strength of the *maréchaussée* needed for criminal matters.[34] Thus the *vice-baillis* and their *archers* were used for a diverse array of purposes as a military and police force. We even find the *vice-bailli* performing as a diplomat when he undertook successful negotiations with the Leaguers under the Sieur d'Apchier at St. Flour in 1594.[35]

Perhaps the most interesting function of the *vice-bailli* was that of magistrate. This power made him an effective policeman, but it was a power that was exercised with increasing care after the initial unfettered days of the religious wars. The cases in which he had most complete control were those called prevotal cases (*cas prévôtaux*). These are quite clearly set out in the Ordinance of 1670, but they had already, for the most part, been defined in a series of previous ordinances. Boudet's description of *cas prévôtaux* is most apt, dividing them into two types: cases deemed prevotal (1) because of the nature of the offense or (2) because of the status (*qualité*) of the persons involved.[36] Broadly speaking, the first sorts of offense involved threats to the public order and affronts to the crown. Many forms of theft were prevotal, including highway robbery, robberies involving the breaking and entering of inhabited dwellings, robberies with violence, armed robberies, and those committed at fairs. One could also include here the crime of sacrilege with breaking

---

33. For example, *Chevauchées*, 1588, 3 November; 1590, February; 1636, 16 October; 1649, 14 July, 16 October.

34. *Relation de l'état de la province d'Auvergne en 1637*, 193–94.

35. *Chevauchées*, 1594, 12 February, 22 April, 6 May. Jean Lacarrière in this case was instrumental in bringing about an agreement between the king's governor de Messilhac and d'Apchier which ended five years of League dominance and depredation around St. Flour.

36. Boudet, *Documents inédits*, 5.

and entering, which often involved the theft of religious treasures or relics. Public violence, premeditated assault, sedition, riot, and popular revolt were within prevotal competence; to prevent these offenses the *vice-bailli* or *prévôt* was also commissioned to suppress illegal public gatherings, the unauthorized levy of armed men and the carrying of illegal weapons. Finally these cases included counterfeiting which, although it was only detected in a few instances, was prominent among official fears in an age that saw a chronic shortage of coin and in an area that experienced a steady influx of foreign coinage.[37]

Cases deemed prevotal because of the status of the persons involved included two major groups: soldiers and the homeless or vagrant. Desertion or complicity in desertion were prevotal cases along with all violence and other "outrages" committed by soldiers, whether they were garrisoned, camping, or on the march. The *vice-bailli* was also a judge of last resort in instances of mendicancy by the able-bodied, and in all cases of crimes and misdemeanors committed by vagabonds or homeless persons no matter where they occurred.[38]

In matters of criminal procedure the *vice-bailli* generally followed the accepted practices of other judges. The major difference was that his competence over contentious cases was to be decided in the nearest *présidial* court by an assembly of at least seven judges.[39] During the tenure of the first Lacarrière, the matter of competence seldom arose, but under Jacques and Paul Lacarrière, challenges to the judicial competence of the *vice-bailli* became quite common. We even find Paul Lacarrière refusing to pursue a suspect because the case was outside his competence, a practice that would have been unthinkable forty years before. The trouble came not only from litigious prisoners but also from other judges, especially those in the *présidial* at Aurillac and in the *bailliage* of Salers.[40] This jurisdictional jealousy must have been widespread in France, for in August 1647, a royal edict protested the impediments placed in the way of *prévôts des maréchaux* by the officers of royal courts, who frequently

---

37. The assessment of the value of money in Ancien Régime France required considerable skill, for coinage had no face value and foreign coinage was used throughout France. Exchange rates and devaluation were established by ordinance. Hence perhaps the great fear of counterfeiters; see P. Goubert, *Ancien Régime*, 62–64: "The day-to-day handling of coinage in old France took the kind of expertise that probably not two men in a hundred possessed" (64).

38. Ord. 1670 Title I, Art. 12.

39. Ord. February 1566, Art. 42.

40. For example, *Chevauchées*: 1648, 18 August.

wrangled over the question of competence. *Vice-baillis* and *prévôts* were therefore encouraged as much as possible to render justice "on the spot."[41]

Over prevotal cases the *vice-bailli* served as judge without appeal and had at his disposal the entire range of penalties and methods available, including torture and death. His judicial competence went well beyond prevotal cases, however, because he was also an examining magistrate in many nonprevotal affairs, usually those that involved malefactors caught "in the act" (*en flagrant délit*) or "public outcry" (*clameur publique*). In these instances the *vice-bailli* usually sent the cases before a competent judge after he had completed the investigation and interrogation of the accused.

The legally sanctioned powers of the *vice-bailli* were therefore considerable. In prevotal cases he participated in the proceedings from the initial report of an incident and the capture of a suspect up to the pronouncement of sentence, in other cases he played a major part in the complexion of the proceedings.

But the power of the *maréchaussée* cannot finally be defined by statutes. For if everyone decided to disobey the law no police force is numerous or powerful enough to enforce it. The true power of the *vice-baillis* therefore waxed and waned depending on the incident at issue, and the persons involved. The religious wars, tax revolts, and noble feuds often revealed the *vice-bailli* and his men for what they were, a small band of royal agents hoping that the name of the king and the terrors of summary justice would make up for the poverty of arms. The condemnations of the defaulting accused (*contumace*), and the long list of scandalous crimes revealed by the Grands Jours d'Auvergne of 1665–66 revealed the limitations of the *vice-baillis* of our period, who could only act successfully when sure of the weakness of their foes or of the approval of some significant part of the society in which they operated.

The Courts and Officers

The solitary position of the *maréchaussée* as a national police force is reflected in the wide range of its activities. But there were other bodies and institutions, official and unofficial, that concerned themselves with

41. Ord. August 1647.

"police" work. The royal courts, including the *présidial* of Aurillac, the court of appeals at Vic-sur-Cere and the *bailliage* and ordinary royal courts elsewhere all had bailiffs, ushers, and officers (*huissiers*, *sergents*) to carry out their business, delivering summonses, reading decrees, and taking prisoners. Indeed, the Intendant Mesgrigny devoted a section of his *Rélation* to royal notaries and sergents, decrying the excessive number of these functionaries in "all" the cities, towns, and villages of Auvergne. According to his account, many of these officials had no legitimate title to their offices, but simply declared themselves hereditary officeholders and began to collect fees for the enforcement of court decrees.[42] The *présidial* at Aurillac, for example, had five *huissiers* and no fewer than twenty sergents.[43]

In the towns, the consuls kept watch over the morals and behavior of the citizenry, attempting to keep order, to exclude undesirables, and to ensure that the inhabitants were well provisioned and protected. They had a *commissaire de police*, watchmen, and guards about whom we can only find complaints that they were not able to fulfill their task.[44] *Police* in the sixteenth and seventeenth centuries referred not only to crime prevention but also the overseeing of rubbish disposal and other general maintenance functions. The consuls of Aurillac seem to have had a hand in everything. In 1594 they resolved to send a letter to the king protesting that while the nobility owned half of the property in Haute Auvergne, the weight of royal taxation fell on the poor "laboureurs."[45] They considered, in 1649, an appeal from the *vice-bailli* for help in arresting some horsemen of the notorious Sieur de Canillac. A more successful project in 1632 was the closing of a filthy street behind the College des Jésuites where "the children of the school go to relieve their bowels."[46] The consuls also expressed their concern over garden raiding,[47] the deplorable state of the local hospital,[48] adulterous women and immoral nuns,[49] and about the clamorous goings on in the taverns at night.[50]

---

42. *Relation de l'état de la province d'Auvergne en 1637*, 193–94.
43. Jean Malmezat, *Le Bailliage des Montagnes d'Auvergne et le Présidial d'Aurillac* (Paris, 1941), 132.
44. For example, 15 March 1624, Archives Communales d'Aurillac, BB[14].
45. 1594, A.C. Aurillac, AA[21].
46. 18 January 1632, A.C. Aurillac, BB[10].
47. 20 November 1566, A.C. Aurillac BB[10].
48. 18 February A.C. Aurillac BB[14].
49. 13 March 1669, A.C. Aurillac BB[29].
50. 18 June 1642, A.C. Aurillac BB[15].

Although the *vice-bailli* was on hand to protect their city against the ravages of passing troops, it was on the initiative of the consuls that the citizens gave the Duc de Candale a "present" of 14,000 *livres* for taking his troops around the Haute Auvergne rather than through it in 1654.[51] The consuls periodically brought cases before the *présidial* of Aurillac. The strains between town and country are evident in some of these, as when the consuls protested the tolls (*péages*) levied by the Marquis de Conros or when the commissioner of *police*, Aigueparses, was humiliated by the Sieur d'Anjou, who insulted him and threatened him with a beating.[52]

Perhaps one could also place nobles and their henchmen among the forces of order. Although this role was a tradition that expressed itself through the seigneurial courts, there is little evidence that the provincial nobility often acted as a police force, except when defending their own interests. The rare occasions when this sort of activity comes to light are usually cases involving transgressions tried in the seigneurial courts, when a suspect was apprehended by the henchmen or tenants of a seigneur; often these were cases that involved the direct self-interest of the nobles concerned. We shall discuss the nobility and some of the actions of their courts more fully later, but suffice it to say for the present that when one encounters the nobility in criminal justice documents, they are as often cast in the role of disrupters as of pacifiers.

The most effective and numerous police force was unofficial, its investigations and pursuits spontaneous. For it was upon the great mass of people in the Haute Auvergne that order ultimately depended. Most of the detective work was done and information given by ordinary folk in the place where an incident occurred and then reported to the agents of official justice, although the actual seizure of suspects was usually the work of official police forces. The surveillance that really prevented crime was the ceaseless watch of neighbors in the towns and villages, the jealous guard over one's property and people, and the natural interest in any departure from the daily routine. Neighbors, however, were not likely to worry about all the transgressions against official laws and statutes. They did not concern themselves with someone else's refusal to pay taxes or evasion of the salt tax, only with offenses that were threatening to the community or some of its individual members: theft,

51. 23 January 1654, A.C. Aurillac BB¹⁵.

52. 6 November 1662, A.C. Aurillac BB¹⁶. This interminable case is also found in the records of the Présidial, A.D. Cantal, IB, 928.

for example, or excessive violence. Without this surveillance, however, the official forces of order would have been totally ineffective, for there was no sure network of communication or systematic surveillance other than the courts and the patrols of the *maréchaussée*. When members of the community went a step further from this police function and began to mete out their own "justice," they became part of the problem in the eyes of official police forces.

The courts themselves were usually one of the last stages in the economy of violence[53] and they are also the source of our most detailed evidence. Aurillac was the center of judicial activity in the Haute Auvergne and at its center was the *bailliage* and *présidial* court. The *présidial* had been erected in 1551,[54] one among sixty such courts in France, forty-three of which were in the jurisdiction of the Parlement of Paris.[55] According to edict, the *présidial* courts were created to relieve the parlements of the many relatively unimportant cases that clogged them, and thus to reduce the length of proceedings.[56] But the crown had other reasons for the creation of a new royal court. Jean Malmezat saw it as a further extension of royal power into the provinces. It was also an excellent opportunity to sell royal offices. Even at the beginning of its existence the court appears to have been somewhat bloated, with almost eighty offices ranging from *présidents* of the court to *huissiers*, and the numbers were to grow like the disease of venality itself. The growth of judgeships is an example: In 1551 there were seven *conseillers* at Aurillac; by 1651 the court had thirteen.[57]

The importance of the *présidial* and the desirability of its offices are matters for debate. Lefèvre d'Ormesson wrote in his memoir that the

---

53. The reader must keep in mind the fact that the initiation of official proceedings could and often did become yet another affront between enemies that would lead to further rounds of private vengeance. Thus popular and official justice were intimately related, each becoming a weapon in the pursuit of the other, and the pursuit of honor. Most recent scholars have remarked on this relationship. Especially thorough on the relationship between popular and official justice are Steven Reinhardt, *Justice in the Sarladais, 1770–1790* (Baton Rouge, La., 1991), and E. Claverie and P. Lamaison, *L'Impossible Mariage: Violence et parenté en Gévaudan* (Paris, 1982), both of whom show litigation as a provocative step in the contest between antagonists. The phenomenon may have been more marked in the later periods these authors discuss, because, as Reinhardt argues, by the late eighteenth century, royal justice was beginning to lose its impressive force.

54. "Edit de Création," Présidial d'Aurillac, A.D. Cantal IBI. The general edict is also found in Isambert, *Recueil,* 13:248.

55. Marion, *Institutions,* 450.

56. "Edit de Création."

57. Malmezat, *Le Bailliage des Montagnes,* 131.

offices were highly prized. The position of lieutenant-general at Aurillac, although cheaper than at Riom or Clermont, was still worth 50,000 livres and that of judge 10,000–12,000 livres.[58] While the officers of the *présidial* had an undeniable prestige for most of our period, by the late seventeenth century, according to Jean Malmezat, the offices of the court were not really valuable in either dignity or revenue. The price of *présidial* offices did not follow rising prices generally and there were not enough cases to keep all of the officers busy. The office of *présidial* judge actually began to decline in value toward the end of the seventeenth century, and was even advertised as an easy and idle occupation.[59] Although the court claimed to be the highest in the Haute Auvergne and it certainly dominated the judicial life of the province, the structure was not strictly pyramidal and the jealous disputes among courts never stopped. Officers of the *présidial* decided on the competence of the *vice-bailli* and also deliberated on some of the prevotal cases he presented to them. But while the *vice-bailli* could act as a judge of last resort, appeal against *présidial* sentences of death or of condemnation to life in the galleys could be made to the Parlement of Paris. The attempts of the *présidial* to absorb many of the functions of other courts were resisted, especially by the *bailliage* of St. Flour and the court of appeals at Vic. But the *présidial*, because of its location in Aurillac, the major trading center on the best highways in the Haute Auvergne and also the residence of the *vice-bailli*, managed to dominate the recalcitrant *bailliage* courts at Murat, Salers, Calvinet, Vic, and St. Flour. St. Flour and Vic did retain their power to appeal to Paris in all except *présidial* cases, even though Mesgrigny had recommended in 1637 that Vic be joined to Aurillac to stop the expensive bickering between judicial officers. The *bailliage* of Calvinet also retained its independence.[60] Criminal cases in the segneurial courts of high justice (*hautes justices seigneuriales*) were usually appealed to Vic, Aurillac, or the local *bailliage* courts.

The separate and warring jurisdictions could easily mislead one into thinking them mutually exclusive, but there was a certain social cohesion in the small world of the bureaucrats and judges, the *officiers* of Haute Auvergne. A good example is the relationship between the *présidial* court and the *consulat* of Aurillac. Not only were most of the royal bureaucrats related to the consuls, but during the seventeenth century, at least half

58. Lefèvre d'Ormesson, *Mémoire sur l'état de la généralité de Riom en 1697*, 164.

59. Malmezat, *Le Bailliage des Montagnes*, 222–26.

60. Ibid., 126–27.

of the consuls were quite often royal officers themselves; by the end of the century, all three consuls held royal office.[61] The officials of Aurillac and the Haute Auvergne spoke and wrote French, married into each others' families, sent their sons to study in Paris or Toulouse, tried to buy seigneuries or marry higher into the nobility and kept their hold on their offices. The Teilhard family was reputed to be the richest among the nobility of the robe in the Haute Auvergne, controlling positions on the *bailliage* court at St. Flour, the appeals court at Vic, the salt-tax court at Murat and several appointments in the farm of royal revenues.[62] In Aurillac, the Senezergues held the office of royal prosecutor or crown attorney (*procureur du roy*) for three generations,[63] the Broquins and the Delorts kept the office of *lieutenant général* until it was taken over by the Verdières and Lacarrières in the mid-eighteenth century.[64] *Lieutenants criminel* came from the de Cebie family and *lieutenants particulier* from the Du Laurens, who also provided other judges as well as the *vice-bailli* who preceded the Lacarrières. The royal and seigneurial justices were also related. In Salers, for example, we find André de La Ronade acting as both a royal and seigneurial judge.[65]

The humbler positions in the justice bureaucracy were also venal and often inherited, including *archer* and *greffier* or recorder. But probably the best example, which demonstrated the tight-knit quality of the society of officials and its potential for social mobility, was the family of the *vice-baillis* who held the office until its suppression. Descended from a bourgeois of Aurillac, the three *vice-baillis* continued in office for all of the period under study here. Second *vice-bailli* Jacques Lacarrière married the daughter of a receiver or tax collector (*receveur*) and *greffier*. Their son Paul inherited the office in 1636 and married the daughter of Pagès, Sieur de Vixouse, and also an official. Paul's claim to nobility failed to withstand the examination of noble titles in 1666. But his son Antoine-Raymond married well, and, after the family office was suppressed, became the *grand prévôt* of Montauban. The social apogee of the Lacarrières was reached in 1789, when a descendant of the sixteenth-century

61. Ibid., 133–35.

62. *Registre des Sentences*, A.D. Cantal 9B 2. See also Mesgrigny, *Relation de l'état de la province d'Auvergne en 1637*.

63. Dossier 167, 33, Fonds Delmas, A.D. Cantal. T. B. Boutillet, *Nobiliaire d'Auvergne*, 10 vols. (Clermont-Ferrand, 1846–53), is also a good source by which to follow the fortunes of various families.

64. Dossier 167, 38, Fonds Delmas.

65. Ibid., and Bailliage de Salers, A.D. Cantal 14B.

bourgeois of Aurillac was chosen as a representative of the nobility to the Estates General.[66]

An ordinary Auvergnat who entered this cosy world of justice officials faced some daunting mysteries. Often illiterates who spoke only Occitan, the plaintiff, the accused, or the witnesses confronted a group of officials who asked endless questions, challenged their truthfulness and translated their words with a mysterious set of symbols into a foreign language. Words repeated in gossip or spoken in heat of the moment, things done without thought, now took on a rather frightening solemnity. Precision was required of people who told time by the sun, remembered only the festive saints' days as dates and counted vaguely in scores and dozens. One could be insulted as to one's integrity and do nothing in reprisal. An incident that had been no more than one of a thousand such occurrences became a criminal act. Village enemies became plaintiff and accused, nosy villagers became witnesses and their words, often no more than gossip to begin with, attained great importance, even the weight of condemnation.

To some extent we face the same sort of situation as Yves Castan, that of an illiterate rural Occitan population passing through the hands of a bilingual and literate elite. Because of the instant translation, the editorial hand of the clerks, and the lack of detail that marks the documents of the early seventeenth century, our pieces of dossiers often lack the sort of spontaneity one would like, but they can still provide one of the few opportunities we have to witness the speeches of the illiterate.[67]

The above are some basic features of the Haute Auvergne and its world of official justice in the late sixteenth and the seventeenth century. On the one hand was an agrarian, pastoral people, independent in some respects but often closely tied to seigneurs. On the other hand were the meager forces of repression: a small mounted police force, a quasi-urban judiciary, its officers, and their subordinates. The potential energy of rural society, although dispersed in small communities, seems to have been out of all proportion to the capacities of its police; the physical and economic environment of the rural inhabitants during our period probably aggravated the effect of this disproportion.

---

66. Boutillet, *Nobiliaire*, 2:40; Chabrol, *Coutumes*, 4:834; in Boudet, *Documents inédits*, appendix 1, 149–54.

67. For a concise statement of Castan's research problems, see his "Mentalités rurales et urbaines a la fin de l'Ancien Régime" in André Abbiateci et al., *Crimes et criminalité en France sous l'Ancien Régime 17e–18e siècles* (Paris, 1971), 109–86.

3 Crime: The Varieties of Violence

The character of these people is as rude as the climate.
—Louis Estadieu, after a tour of the Haute Auvergne in 1779.

At about eight o'clock on the morning of 16 July 1659, Pierre Cassans of the parish of Ladinhac near the southern border of the Haute Auvergne took his scythe to cut hay in a nearby meadow. On his way to work, he stopped to climb a cherry tree near the Quier house and ate a few cherries. Françoise Quier spied him, and the sight of Cassans climbing out of the tree seems to have put her into a rage. She ran out of the house, shouting to her sister "Come quickly out of the house . . . the devil is loose!"[1] She then screamed at Cassans, who by now was retreating down the path to his field, "Thief! Rascal! Robber! You'll pay for this! I'll throw you out of . . . La Goudalie!"[2] The promised retribution was exceeded by Anthoinette Quier, who came to her sister's aid with seven or eight large stones[3] and began to pelt their enemy. Cassans dropped his scythe to the ground and covered his head, falling under a hail of blows. The Quier sisters vented their fury on the prostrate man, all the while shouting together, "Kill him! Kill him!" In a "doleful and piteous voice," Cassans cried for help: "Justice, ay ay ay, hurry!"[4] Those were his last

---

1. The case, which continued from 17 July until 26 September 1659, is found in the records of the Présidial of Aurillac A.D. Cantal IB 927. An *inventaire* lists 20 documents marked "A" to "T" of which 18 were found. All the relevant pieces hereafter belong to A.D. Cantal IB 927. The account of the attack begins with the deposition of Catherine Aymerial, ibid.
2. Deposition of Jeanne Martin, ibid.
3. Deposition of Catherine Aymerial.
4. Deposition of Jeanne Martin.

words. When his assailants had left, his wife rushed to his side, pleading with the neighbors to help. Cassans's body was carried to his house where a neighbor, Jeanne Martin, applied a poultice of egg white to his wounds. When a local judge arrived the next morning he discovered the grieving widow and another woman keeping watch over the shrouded body of Pierre Cassans.[5] The surgeon who examined the body found that the left side of the victim's head had been crushed and that he had several contusions on his head and neck, each about the size of the palm of a hand, made "with partly sharp and partly blunt instruments, such as stones, crowbars, clubs or other such things." Like many others in a similar situation, the Quier sisters fled the country, giving up home and property for their moment of triumph.[6] They had suffered mistreatment, had savagely brought Pierre Cassans to their own "justice" for the crimes they had shouted in accusation, and then had to evade the agents of official justice.

Were Françoise and Anthoinette homicidally upset over a handful of cherries? Or is this one of those cases where, in a village setting, a long-held grievance or resentment erupted suddenly, releasing the tensions of enmity in a ferocious outburst that, to our minds, seems disproportionate to the provocation? Pierre Cassans, a peasant from the village of La Goudalie, had had some sort of working contact with the two rather fierce unmarried sisters of the village; the pieces of testimony, abundant though they are, never make the relationship clear. Françoise Quier only allowed that Cassans had "mistreated" her.[7]

This account of the death of Pierre Cassans is a reconstruction from court documents, one of several we shall employ; it is drawn mainly from the depositions of witnesses, including the dead man's widow. The purpose of this chapter is to familiarize the reader with violent crime in

---

5. *Plaincte et denonciation par Jehanne Guarde veufe de Pierre Cassans*, marked "A" 17 July 1659. Evidently the widow had been thinking of her perilous future through the night. When asked if she wished to start proceedings for reparations from the Quier sisters, she asked if her declaration to the judge might be used as a complaint (*plainte*) "In consideration of her poverty and wretchedness and the fact that she is burdened with the three children her husband has left her."

6. *Sentence* marked "S," 26 September 1659. Both women were sentenced contumaciously by the Présidial of Aurillac to be hanged. Their property was sequestrated, 20 livres was to pay for prayers for the soul of Pierre Cassans and 200 livres went as compensation to the widow, who had to pay the expenses of the procedure. An *épice* of 23 livres was paid to the councillors of the *présidial*. Any remaining income from the estate went to the seigneur of the place, the Baron de Lagarde.

7. Deposition of Gerard Baduel, *Information* marked "C" 17 July 1659.

the Haute Auvergne during the period under discussion. In doing so, it will also attempt to impart some idea of the reality of violence, to begin an examination of patterns of behavior and to discuss the factors that may have moved Auvergnats to violent displays. What was important to them? What were they attacking or defending? How and when did they fight, and why?

But the reconstruction of old passions is an uncertain business, and it presents us with a vexing question that lies at the heart of many historians' debates, whether they are discussing the meaning and use of language, the nature and uses of historical documents, the limits of conjecture from evidence or the intrusion of anachronistic sensibilities into historical interpretation: Just how far can we go? This problem has been the source of some fascinating controversies, not least among them the debate surrounding the sixteenth-century account of the trial of Arnauld du Tilh for usurping the conjugal place and property of Martin Guerre. Critics of Natalie Davis have raised questions about her recent interpretation of the case, thereby contributing to a never-ending problem of historians. When is an historian with a particularly powerful imagination too much beguiled by the protagonists in her documents, and when, in turn, are her readers too susceptible to the same beguilement at the skillful touch of the historian? Criminal justice documents have clearly shown an enduring propensity to provoke renewed passions and accusations of unfaithfulness; unfaithfulness to the evidence, to the readers and, finally, to Martin Guerre and his contemporaries.[8]

While historians may argue passionately about respecting the "sovereignty of the sources," and the "tribunal of the documents,"[9] it is clear that one cannot hope to discover the truth or falsehood in each case reassembled from fragmented records more than three hundred years old. The usefulness of statements made under interrogation lies in their

8. The debate began with Natalie Davis, *The Return of Martin Guerre* (Cambridge, Mass., 1983), an adventurous interpretation of the *Arrest Memorable* (1561) by the judge Jean de Coras, and of other documents pertaining to the case. The most telling exchanges concerning Davis's work are in Robert Finlay, "The Refashioning of Martin Guerre," *American Historical Review* 93, no. 3 (June 1988): 553–71. Finlay essentially claims that what Davis saw as informed imagination was, in fact, invention, and warns sternly that, "speculation, whether founded on intuition or on concepts drawn from anthropology and literary criticism, is supposed to give way before the sovereignty of the sources, the tribunal of the documents" (571). In "On the Lame," *American Historical Review* 93, no. 3 (June 1988): 572–603, Davis replies with a defense of imaginative and reasonable conjecture from evidence that will admit of more than one possibility, arguing that indeed the sources are particularly sovereign in her work.

9. Finlay, "Refashioning," 571.

plausibility, which in turn allows the discovery of other truths about the speakers.[10] This art of the plausible must take account, not only of the specific and explicit case in question, but also of the inadvertent revelation, the clue to attitudes, and to the fabric of ordinary life. What is more, it is important to remember that these messages can sometimes exist as much (or more) in perjuries as they do in accurate testimony. The specific character of various court documents will be more fully explained later, when our Auvergnats come to have their day in court. If occasionally the reconstructions include a repetition or a digression from the point of inquiry, we must try to strike a balance between analytic order and the untidy realities of human lives.

We shall begin with a brief look at what can be known of the overall nature of crime in the period under study, and then proceed through an examination of offenses and their significance, concentrating on violence or offenses against persons. From the *Chevauchées* or *procès verbaux* of the *vice-baillis,* we can get an overview of offenses; from the more detailed records of the criminal courts, we can return to the murders with which we began and a discussion of what violent behavior was like.

Crime in the *Chevauchées*

Numbers have a certain authoritative elegance, marshaled in columns, providing summaries and comparisons at a glance. But even though they be used in good faith, figures taken from sources such as the *Chevauchées* can mislead as much as they inform. The *vice-baillis* sometimes wrote that a suspect was accused of "many" or "several" (*plusieurs*) murders or thefts. One *rébellion* could involve five thousand peasants or a single family. At other times, beside a vaguely stated case, there are detailed descriptions of crimes, points of procedure, and sentences. A great number of cases fall between these extremes of precision and vagueness. Each figure

10. For the emphasis on plausibility, I am indebted especially to Alfred Soman of the C.N.R.S. who mentioned in a conversation in Paris in 1980 that while court records can never be trusted to tell the truth in any absolute way, they do give us plausible accounts of various happenings. It is interesting that E. Claverie and P. Lamaison found that the depositions and complaints in their Gévaudan cases were remarkable for their *lack* of verisimilitude, their improbability; such an assessment nonetheless indicates that those authors did gain from their sources a sense of what *was* plausible. See their *L'Impossible Mariage: Violence et parenté en Gévaudan* (Paris, 1982).

therefore conceals a series of decisions on the acceptability of the evidence.

One must also take account of the diverse activities of the *maréchaussée* alluded to in the previous chapter. During the years 1587–95 the *vice-bailli* Jean Lacarrière was preoccupied with plague, religious civil war, and military duties. During the regency of Marie de Médicis, 1610–17, prohibitions against assembling armies, weapons, and military threats were a cause for concern. The period from 1628 to 1650 saw various times of widespread popular unrest. In frantic times when military or political troubles beset the country, the reports speak of widespread "excesses" or "riot" (*excès, rébellions,* or *outrages*), after which there are pages of detail describing a few of the most serious incidents. Through it all, however, the *archers* of the *maréchaussée* patrolled the market fairs and highways, and the individual offenses they reported are still much more numerous than large-scale disturbances and rumors of war. Thus one can get an idea of what happened and of the overall proportions of specific crimes. But to attach authoritative figures and "rates" to offenses or to calculate correlation coefficients between, say, theft and the price of grain, would attribute to the sources a sophistication they do not possess.

In defense of the records of the *maréchaussée,* it must be said that they are police reports, often describing specific offenses that could not be prosecuted successfully; that they often give information about the identity of the accused, the approximate date and nature of the offense, and the outcome of police action. Furthermore they represent a reasonably coherent source, consistent in outlook, reporting crime in a whole region for particular periods for which such sources are lacking.

Given the above precautions, we can start the examination of offenses. The following table provides an estimate of the offenses and accusations reported for thirty-seven years between 1587 and 1664.

Offenses in Police Reports, 1587–1664

Some of these figures require serious qualification, which will be given in the discussion of the various types of offenses; nonetheless, one can observe a few outstanding features. The first is the preponderance of violent offenses and offenses against persons. Homicide, assault, rebellion, abduction, rape, and dueling constitute about half of all offenses (51%). Theft, arson, counterfeit money, and forgery, the clearest of-

Offenses	Number of offenses	%
Homicide	184	20.1
Assault	215	23.5
Rebellion	31	3.4
Abduction	17	1.9
Duelling	9	1.0
Rape	7	.8
Illegal Weapons	7	.8
Arson	6	.7
Theft	246	26.9
Vagrancy	81	8.9
Counterfeit Money	7	.8
Sacrilege	3	.3
Forgery	1	.1
Prison Escapes	4	.4
Illicit Assembly	42	4.6
Illicit levies of troops	11	1.2
Illegal lodging of troops	28	3.1
Desertion	15	1.6
Total offenses reported	914	100.1

(Additional arrests, sentences, trials, and decrees in which the offense is unclear: 119.)

fenses against property, make up less than one-third (29%). The proportion of offenses against persons to those against property is roughly 64% to 36%. Even considering the preoccupation of the *vice-baillis* with highway robbers, sneak thieves, and fairs, the most common criminal offenses threatened persons rather than property.

Some historians of criminality have argued that crimes against persons dominated the seventeenth century while those against property became more important in the eighteenth. Our estimates do not approach the spectacular 83% of violence in the Norman *bailliage* of Falaise during the seventeenth century; nor do they equal the 70% discovered in the records of the Grands Jours d'Auvergne of 1665. But then in the first case, the *maréchaussée*, unlike the authorities in Falaise and local authorities elsewhere, did not usually pursue those guilty of threats, insults, and local *charivari*; nor did the *bailliage* courts deal so often as the *maréchaussée* with the crimes of vagrants, cutpurses, and highway robbers.[11] It has also

11. This thesis and its sources are given in outline in the Introduction. For the *bailliage* of Falaise, see J. Gégot, "Etude par sondage de la criminalité du bailliage de Falaise," *Annales de Normandie* (1966): 103–64. The *sondage* is of 88 cases from the seventeenth and eighteenth centuries. Gégot found by contrast that violence accounted for only 47% of the cases for the

been argued that violent offenses in the Auvergne were often traditionally settled out of court, while theft was the reason par excellence for prosecution, although recent research has revealed such conclusions to have been premature.[12] Taking the above factors into consideration, the first half of the standard thesis on early modern crime seems to remain intact. But an important distinction has been added, especially when the work of Iain Cameron on eighteenth-century Auvergne is recalled: to a greater extent than in some other areas in France that have been studied, violence was a constant in the life of the Haute Auvergne throughout the Ancien Régime.

In dealing with violence, it is best to come straight to the point, to discuss homicide and assault. The first remarkable feature of these two offenses in the *Chevauchées* is the large number of homicides relative to the number of assaults: 184 to 215. Assault, it seems, was more a local preoccupation and did not often, in the opinion of villagers, warrant the intervention of the regional mounted police.

Another point to be made about assault and homicide concerns the problem of terminology. Homicide is easy to identify because murderers leave corpses. The victim has been *tué, assassiné*; he is *mort*. Assault in the *Chevauchées* is another matter, of sometimes vaguely depicted excesses, violence, attacks, blows (*excès, violences, attaques, coups*). While the *vice-baillis* used the words "excesses or outrages on his/her person" (*excès or excédé en sa personne*) in 36 of 215 cases, other circumstances indicate as well that these were violent attacks. It is difficult therefore to determine the gravity of these incidents, although their inclusion in the reports might be in part a measure of their severity; mild assaults were probably trivial matters, unrecorded by the *vice-baillis*. Thus the overall statistics conceal some uncertainties about the nature of offenses they describe. Let us therefore pause for a closer look at rural homicide and assault and the forms they took in the fields and hamlets of the Haute Auvergne.

---

eighteenth century. In 115 cases from the seventeenth century in the archives du Cantal the proportion of violence was 81.7%, but the records did not permit a systematic *sondage* like that of Gégot. For a general summary of this thesis, see E. Le Roy Ladurie's section in Duby et al, *Histoire de La France rurale*, 547–53. Figures for the Grands Jours from A. Lebigre, *Les Grands Jours d'Auvergne*, 139. More recently, Gregory Hanlon found that 65% of cases in the neighboring cities of Agen and Clairac concerned physical violence. "Les Rituels de l'aggression en Aquitaine au XVIIe siècle," *Annales E.S.C.* 40, no. 2 (March–April 1985): 244–68, figures on 245–46.

12. Iain Cameron, *Crime and Repression*, 179.

The Fields of Combat

Perhaps it is most appropriate to begin our discussion with an examination of the duel, one of the least measurable but conceptually most suggestive forms of violence. It is particularly useful because it combined in a structured way some of the features of many violent confrontations. It was a ritual of violent justice, containing elements of judgment and proof, vengeance and reconciliation. It was the formal defense of oneself in a face-to-face society, and it also demonstrated solidarities, alliances, fraternity, and a sort of equality. Conceptually at least the duel also had an integrative and restorative function, although it took on the character of a modish, anachronistic disruption. The restoration of lost honor, salvation from civil death, even at the cost of physical injury or death, is a feature of the mentality of our period that was repeatedly attempted in less contrived ways. The affront, the challenge, the provocation and the riposte, the degrees of premeditation, were measured and employed by both criminal justice authorities and by ordinary Auvergnats. Moreover, the history of the duel, its general acceptance, followed by its criminalization and the gradual withdrawal of elites from its formal exercise, parallels in some ways the expropriation by public authority of the private right to vengeance. And, for that matter, the vestigial survival of the duel parallels the survival of the ideal, still current in popular culture from Rostand's Cyrano de Bergerac to Clint Eastwood's western heros, that honor is above the commands of the state, or the king.

The formal duel of early modern times, according to one of its most notable students, was a peculiarly French passion, although it was originally borrowed from the Italians.[13] The late sixteenth and early seventeenth centuries, of primary importance to us here, were its heyday. During our period, dueling was regarded variously as a "national mania," a serious source of disorder, a disgraceful "affront to God" and a heroic activity befitting men of honor.[14] It was an atavistic quest for truth, justice, and honor, and a murderous innovation that signified rebellion against God's anointed on the French throne. While related to the judicial duel and the single combat by champions that flourished during the Hundred Years' War, by the late sixteenth century, duels were "extrajudicial," rituals of private vengeance or justice. In 1602 they were

13. F. Billacois, *The Duel: Its Rise and Fall in Early Modern France*, ed. and trans. by Trista Selous (New Haven, Conn., 1990).
14. Ibid., chapter 1.

made illegal, but if statutes are any indication, the rage continued: between 1602 and 1646 alone dueling was the subject of at least thirteen royal edicts, ordinances, and declarations, as well as of the canons and decrees of the Council of Trent. The illegality of the duel may even have been a spur to nobles who wished to assert their traditional "liberties," before the growing power of the state.[15]

The ritual itself was still intact in the early sixteenth century, when the offended party would "call out" the author of an affront by presenting him with an oral challenge or a written *cartel de défi* (card or note of challenge). The duelists would then ask the king for a field on which to fight, and the duel would take place in a closed space, often in town, during the daylight hours, with the combatants mounted and armored. The procedure was acceptable enough that at one point even the Emperor Charles V and Francis I of France proposed to duel, although the challenge was merely symbolic. But it could not coexist legally for long with a monarchy attempting to expand its judicial competence. As it began to lose official sanction, and to receive religious condemnation, the duel also gradually lost much of its formality. By the late sixteenth to early seventeenth century, a simple challenge sufficed, and the closed field was no longer the rule; duellists had begun to fight anywhere, day or night, often moving to the country, the better to evade the authorities. They fought on foot with rapiers and without armor, honor without livery, honor represented only by the bodies and the swords of the combatants, while the seconds increasingly joined the fray, making the duel into a "small collective battle."[16]

Despite the popular romantic importance of the duel, however, dueling does not occupy a prominent place in our documents. All of the duels for which there is a record appear in the *Chevauchées* and the details are not usually so extensive as for some other cases of violence. Perhaps this lack of information is due to the character of the duel itself as "private justice," which did not demand a recourse to official justice. The *vice-bailli* usually learned about a duel after it had taken place and someone had been killed or wounded. But in the case where a challenge had been

---

15. See Isambert et al, *Recueil général des anciennes lois françaises*, April 1602, 15:266. June 1609, ibid., 35; July 1611, ibid., 16:21; 25 June 1624, ibid., 156; February 1626, ibid., 175; May 1634, ibid., 408; 1 October 1614, ibid., 82. For other examples, see ibid., 29:120.

16. Billacois, *The Duel*, 65.

offered, either rumor or a reluctant duelist sometimes informed the *vice-bailli* and he rode out to warn the parties involved.[17]

The encounters involved ranged from the formal presentation of a challenge by the challenger's second(s) and a precise place and time for the meeting, to much more haphazard affairs in which one man called the other into combat and the fight began forthwith. One suspects the validity of the term "duel" used in reference to some encounters such as that in which two nobles and their henchmen killed the Sieur de Barriac at St. Paul des Landes in July 1627.[18] Interestingly, it has been asserted that the more vaguely termed *rencontres* (chance encounters) should be classified as duels.[19] But the nobles of Haute Auvergne made a clear distinction between the two in their grievance to the crown of 1614: "If it please the King, moderate the rigor of the edict concerning "rencontres" while maintaining that concerning duels so that those who get involved by mere chance and without any premeditation not be deprived of the grace of their prince and sovereign lord."[20]

On rather scant evidence, there appear to have been no particular seasonal variations, but the period of most duels detected in the record follows that suggested by other scholarship, which has placed the climax of early modern dueling at the time of the Fronde. Seven of the nine duels mentioned in the *Chevauchées* occurred before 1629 and the last was mentioned in 1652. The duelists in our records were mostly, although not exclusively, nobles.[21] In most cases the combatants were neighbors or lived in the same area; in one case a challenge was exchanged between members of the same family.[22] The last two are suggestive of changes in attitude by both the potential duelists and the authorities. When the Baron de Miramont sent a written challenge to his father, the Marquis de Montclar, in August 1647, the latter simply turned the card over to the justice authorities; aside from the intriguing family connection, the

---

17. *Chevauchées* 1614: 6 November; 1627: 20 November.

18. *Chevauchées* 1627: July.

19. *Chevauchées* 1652: 17 December.

20. Printed in *Revue de la Haute Auvergne* (1947–49): 112–21.

21. The duels in *Chevauchées* 1607: 5 February; 1627: 20 November, were between non-nobles. Out of eighteen duelists in all, fourteen were noble, or styled themselves as such. One study of duels in the records of the Parlement of Paris suggests that dueling by the late seventeenth century had ceased to be a noble pastime and had become instead a phenomenon associated with soldiers. See F. Billacois, "Le Parlement de Paris et les duels au XVIIe siècle," in Abbiateci et al., *Crimes et criminalité*, 33–48.

22. *Chevauchées* 1647: 13 August.

situation interestingly combines the anachronism of the *cartel de défi*, which is thought largely to have gone out of use after about 1615, with the altogether modern appeal to royal justice. But then perhaps there was an archaic streak among Auvergnats; although it has been stated that the last official judicial duel occurred in 1547, there was one at least semiofficial one that took place in the Haute Auvergne in 1591, to which the governor and lieutenant-general de Missilhac sentenced one Captain Rouerguas.[23] The final contest reported may also be instructive. The unfortunate loser of a duel was found at Espinat near Aurillac in December 1652; in this case not only was a warrant of arrest issued against the duelists, it was also stipulated that the corpse of the loser had to face trial.[24] The final vengeance was to belong to the prince.

Duels certainly existed in the Haute Auvergne but the documents suggest that an Auvergnat was much more likely to die or to be wounded in an ambush or a chance encounter than in a "proper," premeditated duel. Moreover, the struggle for honor was continuing apace in fields that were in many ways more firmly "closed" than those of the early judicial duel, as we can see by returning while the body is still warm for a postmortem of the murder of Pierre Cassans, the unfortunate cherry thief stoned to death by two women. If we look at the time, the place, the events, and the participants, the Quier sisters' action and other similar incidents can help us reconstruct an environment where many of the sensibilities affected histrionically by duelists take on an almost concrete solidity in the lives of ordinary people.

The incident occurred in summer, the Haute Auvergne's cruelest months, accounting for a disproportionate number of reported violent incidents.[25] This was the hottest time of year when the days were long and the work, haymaking and grain harvesting, the hardest. There was a pressing need to gather forage for the long winter when the cattle would return from the high summer pastures. It was a time of expectation; for many, the only time of relative plenty. It was also a period of conflict when everywhere hands were extended to grasp the fruits of the land.

23. *Chevauchées* 1591: 16, 17, 22, 18 September.
24. Billacois, *The Duel*, 11–13.
25. Roughly 25% of violent incidents in the *Chevauchées* took place in July and August and half in the months between May and September. The overall percentages are as follows for a total of 407 reported which could be dated:

Jan.	Feb.	Mar.	Apr.	May	Jun.	Jul.	Aug.	Sept.	Oct.	Nov.	Dec.
8%	8%	8%	7%	8%	9%	14%	11%	8%	7%	6%	6%

July and August were the months during which tithes and other dues were collected, a process that sometimes involved a struggle, either because the collectors used excessive force in seizing the tithes, or because they were violently hindered from doing so.[26] There was probably a higher level of population during these months as well; because the seasonal migration of labor that characterized the area was a winter phenomenon and the migrants, usually young men, returned home in spring and summer. As Abel Poitrineau's regional study has shown, these migrations were especially strong in mountain communities where winter was a long "dead" season of unemployment or underemployment, and those with strength or skill to sell could find better markets elsewhere. The mountain populations in summer saw an increase in the number of young, vigorous males.[27]

In the documents surrounding the murder of Pierre Cassans, and in other cases we shall examine, one begins to get a glimpse of the village or hamlet as a community in which the inhabitants lived and worked in close proximity, and in which such intense hatreds could develop. It was well-nigh impossible to avoid coming face to face with almost everyone in the parish, and one was often in the eyes of another. When the explosion occurred it quickly became a community affair, a public spectacle watched by the neighbors who afterwards helped the wounded and consoled the bereaved. But it was not merely the village of La Goudalie that saw the affair. Jean Boussart, for example, was in the "village" of Gontefaux from where he saw and heard much of the goings-on in La Goudalie,[28] less than half a mile away, and Catherine Aymerial in the nearby village of Cassans heard "a disturbance coming from the direction of La Goudalie."[29] Despite the rural, individualistic, agrarian

---

26. In August 1628, for example, two *archers* of the *maréchaussée* were sent to help the collectors of the Canon of Conques who had been continually harassed by two local seigneurs (*Chevauchées* 1628: 19 August). The reverse situation occurred in St. Simon in 1659 when a *fermier* of tithes was accused of mistreating the local inhabitants and wresting tithes from them by force of arms. Some other examples are found in *Chevauchées* 1609: 4 August; 1611: 3 August; 1617: August; 1664: 10 August.

27. In addition to the more specific studies of the Haute Auvergne cited in Chapter 1, note 41, A. Poitrineau, *La Vie rurale en Basse Auvergne*, 1:560–72, provides a good discussion of mountain emigrations, as does E. Le Roy Ladurie, *Les Paysans de Languedoc* (Paris, 1966), 1:93–111; F. Braudel's description of the general characteristics of mountain populations is also valuable (*The Mediterranean* 1:24–53), as are the remarks in J. K. J. Thomson, *Clermont-de-Lodève 1633–1789* (Cambridge, 1982), 23, 49–52.

28. Deposition, 17 July 1659.

29. Deposition, 17 July 1659.

character and the mountainous terrain of the Haute Auvergne, and the isolation of the villages, individuals were not isolated from the larger community. We have discussed the small, irregularly shaped enclosures that characterized the land around mountain villages of the Massif Central; village plans for the Haute Auvergne confirm generalizations with detail. Usually a cluster of houses surrounded a central road or path. Nearest the houses were gardens and hay meadows; usually there was also a nearby *couderc* or common pasture. The hay meadows were often separate from the rest of a tenant's land; in many cases, it would have been necessary to pass through the field of a neighbor or to take a circuitous route to reach one's meadow from one's house.[30] Men worked together or in separate fields that were close together and also close to the village. Hay was cut and grain harvested at roughly the same stages during the dry days of summer. Meadows and other fields were therefore quite busy and well peopled, not necessarily with large haymaking crews but with individuals or family groups working within separate enclosures. Court documents and our knowledge of the physical layout of the communities both suggest the close proximity of life and work in the populous valleys of the province that form the location for numerous acts of violence. The fields were more public than one might think.[31] Borders were important and all too easy to violate.

To complicate things further, physical and mental boundaries were closely allied, combined into what I have called elsewhere "psychic property," a sense of oneself that included both inner and outer territory, both honor and space, subject to violation.[32] The duel required an acknowledgment that one's opponent was worthy of the honor of combat. In this intimate world of the countryside, where one's peers were all

30. For general information on the different types of fields see Marc Bloch, *French Rural History*, trans. Janet Sondheimer (Berkeley and Los Angeles, 1966), 24, 28, 35, 58–59; A. Poitrineau, *Basse Auvergne* 1:141–53, 186–265, and numerous passages in Duby and Wallon, *Histoire rurale de la France*, vol. 2. Examples of village and field plans can be found in A.D. Cantal 16B and 15B 397.

31. Most violent incidents occurred in the areas of greatest population around major cities such as Aurillac, Murat, St. Flour, Salers, and Mauriac. Aurillac, the seat of the *présidial* court and the headquarters of the *maréchaussée* as well as the major town of the province, was the center of a basin and the scene of many such incidents. This is probably due partly to the accessibility of the *maréchaussée* in the area who were not always summoned for incidents further away.

32. M. Greenshields, "Women, Violence and Criminal Justice records in Early Modern Haute Auvergne (1587–1664)," *Canadian Journal of History / Annales Canadiennes d'Histoire* 22 (August 1987): 175–94.

around, the elements of the duel, as it were, were ever present. It was in fact that world where the obsession with individual and collective self-regard and the regard of others could be almost constant: "honor and shame are the constant preoccupation of individuals in small scale, exclusive societies when face-to-face personal, as opposed to anonymous, relations are of paramount importance and where the social personality of the actor is as significant as his office."[33] It is important to note too that honor, especially given the instability of a relatively egalitarian village setting, required a degree of aggressiveness: it could not always be assumed but must be asserted and defended. It was not only a matter of a person's individual self-worth or "claim" to a certain regard; it also needed the agreement of others to accord the degree of honor claimed by an individual.[34] The ultimate means of convincing others who questioned the rightness of a claim to honor, or who committed an affront, was violence; just as honor was often connected to the physical person and, by extension, to property, so was the defense of honor often a matter of physical attack. In the case of Pierre Cassans and the cherry tree we may have an example of the extension of honor to property, for it was commonly a matter of dishonor not to be able to defend one's possessions (défendre son bien), especially when publicly confronted with a theft or violation. It has been noted too that this was an issue to which widows were particularly sensitive, because they were at such a disadvantage and had to go to court in order to protect what they could not guard by force, a rule that could be extended to other unattached women, and to which the Quier sisters showed themselves to be spectacular exceptions.[35]

"At the center of social organization," Erving Goffman has written, "is the concept of claims, and around this center, properly, the student must consider the vicissitudes of maintaining them."[36] Moreover, Goffman has analyzed not only territorial claims and "personal space," but also the myriad of negotiations and rituals that all human beings daily undertake to reassure, challenge, pacify, support, and defend each other and themselves. In the context of early modern life and violence,

33. J. G. Peristiany in his Honor and Shame: The Values of Mediterranean Society (Chicago, 1966), 11.

34. Julian Pitt-Rivers, "Honor and Social Status," in Peristany, ed., Honor and Shame, 19–77, 21–22.

35. See Hanlon, "Les Rituels de l'agression," 259–61. As he puts it "widows forgave nothing," because of their weakness. (260).

36. E. Goffman, Relations in Public: Microstudies of the Public Order (New York, 1971), 28. See especially chapter 2, "The Territories of the Self," 28–61.

Goffman's remarks on territorial claims and their violation are quite useful especially when combined with those on the duel and those of Julian Pitt-Rivers on Mediterranean ideas of honor and shame. On the most obvious level in the fields of the Haute Auvergne, we are examining a collection of "fixed" territories to which the claimants had an established right and whose violation, as we have already seen, could be the occasion of retaliatory violence. One can also observe violations by actions or words, of personal space, of the body and of the space or territory that each person claims for temporary use in the normal movements and activities of the day. Intensifying these possibilities yet further was that of a slight to honor, which in any event was not easily separable from spatial territory. If, in Goffman's words, the modern person "goes about constrained to sustain a viable image of himself,"[37] how much more strenuous must this have been to an Early Modern one obsessed with the assertion and maintenance of an honor that had often to be vindicated at the expense of a competitor? If the look or stare of another can be pregnant in the relative anonymity of many of our contemporary societies, how much more significant must it have been in the intimacy of the mountain hamlets?

Add to these subtle elements the important variable of a particular situation cast within the particular culture and period under examination here. Take, for example, the seemingly ordinary matter of hay. While pressure on hay land was common to many parts of France, it was particularly acute in the Haute Auvergne for several reasons. The dominant tradition of transhumant herding and dairying ensured a constant flow of grazing animals to the uplands. But the imbalance between the large tracts of mountain pasture and the restricted acreage for growing winter forage meant that the latter was always at a premium; for fuller exploitation of the summer pastures, animals were brought from other provinces. The disproportion between mountain pastures and hay meadows was further emphasized by the winter herd restrictions in customary law.[38] The need for arable land aggravated the effect of these restrictions. Hence hay was precious, too valuable to be trampled by the neighbors. These pressures on lowland meadows and fields at least partly explain the acute sensitivity to trespass in meadows and the general sensibility to violations or seizures of property, which may have provoked violent

37. Ibid., 185.
38. Chabrol, *Coutumes* 4:602. Bouyssou, *Montagnes*, 20.

incidents such as the following confrontation between Jean Giraldon and Jacques La Guiole.

On a Thursday afternoon near the end of July, Jean Giraldon was taking an oxcart of hay from his field to his home. The shortest way was through a field belonging to Jacques La Guiole. Giraldon began to lead his oxen through the field, ignoring the protest of La Guiole, who was working nearby and did not want his own hay to suffer damage. Giraldon made his way through the field without incident. But after he had completed his passage, he paused to savor his victory and make his challenge absolutely clear, shouting to La Guiole "that he despised him."[39] This was too much for La Guiole, insult on top of trespass, and he rushed at the invader with his hay rake. Giraldon waited by his cart and then promptly broke his *aiguillon* (a long wooden lance, sometimes with an iron tip, used for driving oxen) on his opponent's neck.[40] With a cry of "Justice," La Guiole fell to the ground where he received a few cuts from the knife of Giraldon. The latter, having subdued his opponent, replaced his knife in his belt and continued on his way.[41]

Again we see the offense, the riposte, and the violent exchange. It is as if the trespasser wanted to clarify the challenge with a further humiliation, to leave no doubt as to the meaning of his violation of territory, his own self-enhancement and the negation of another's. The words of disdain simply clarified the violation as one of honor. This time the riposte, the administration of informal justice, was unsuccessful but the incident was a similar explosion, spontaneous, violent and public. The incident above is not unlike others that involved property, rights of passage, the possession of hay or nearby pasture. The consciousness of limits, borders, and possession was keen. For example, the entire Badeul family including women, children, and servants became embroiled in a violent conflict near Brezons on 27 July 1665 over passage through a hay meadow.[42] The disputed right to a cut of hay also led to violence on 27 July 1632, again near Brezons.[43] On 28 July 1640, the right to the second growth on a common meadow near Salers was a source of conflict.[44]

---

39. Deposition of Guillaume Tourquet, August 1648, Juridiction de Brezons A.D. Cantal 16B 280.

40. Deposition of Antoine Succet, 1 August 1648, ibid.

41. Deposition of Pierre Costin, 1 August 1648, ibid. Again the incident was observed by several witnesses working in nearby fields.

42. 27 July, 1665 Jurid. de Brezons, A.D. Cantal 16B 280.

43. 27 July, 1632 Bailliage de Salers, A.D. Cantal 14B 307.

44. 28 July, 1640 Bailliage de Salers, A.D. Cantal 14B 307.

Another July dispute of 1641 in the high mountains involved a cartload of hay and rights of passage.[45]

While the summer in the fields and villages of the Haute Auvergne saw many such violent incidents, the days of festivals and fairs throughout the year were also times when a festive release combined with alcohol to overcome the communal constraints on behavior. Rude festivities could then become violent, even lethal, as when a boy in the parish of Crandelles near Aurillac was killed by some young men who had disguised themselves and conducted a dance through the parish (danse masquerade) from the neighboring parish of Ytrac in 1646.[46] Drunkenness, the excitement of the festive crowd, the rapid resort to violence and the sensitivity about points of honor appear repeatedly in the documents for the Haute Auvergne. The affinity between Auvergnats and alcohol was a characteristic that more generally separated mountain folk from lowlanders in other areas like the plain of Languedoc; even within the Auvergne itself Abel Poitrineau noted a similar difference between the peasants of the agricultural Limagne and the more pastoral people of the mountains. Emigrants from the Auvergne were reputed to be heavy, choleric drinkers who were always ready to fight for their honor.[47] Alcohol decreased the sense of propriety that prevented unintentional violations of others' property and honor, and often led to self-aggrandizement and an assertion of claims that extended far beyond those of sobriety. Wine could blur the borders of psychic property, and increase the possibilities of confrontation and conflict.

45. 15 July, 1641 Bailliage de Salers, A.D. Cantal 14B 307.

46. *Chevauchées* 1646: 5 February, 8 February, 12 April. The occasion was probably the Purification of the Blessed Virgin Mary, held on 2 February. Not counting Sundays, the inhabitants of the diocese of St. Flour, which encompassed the Haute Auvergne, were to observe 45 feast days in the mid-seventeenth century. *Calendrier des Festes de l'Evesche de St. Flour* (1640?) A.C. Cantal 346F 33 ter. Another similar murder took place in the village of St. Curiot on a feast day in October. At least half a dozen village men were implicated. *Chevauchées* 1654: 15 October.

47. A. Poitrineau thought that some of the irritability of Auvergnats was due to undernourishment as well as drink; see his *La Vie rurale en Basse Auvergne*, 1:619–620. This theory was proposed more generally by R. Mandrou in his *Introduction à la France moderne*, 324. Olwen Hufton found that "No other city immigrant was reckoned so quick to anger, so ready to pick a fight and enforce his rights" than the Auvergnat of whom it was written 'The Auvergnats . . . are the roughest folk and the greatest drinkers' "; see her *The Poor of Eighteenth-Century France* (Oxford, 1974), 101 and note. See also I. Cameron, *Crime and Repression*, 12. Interestingly, the cheap wine of Paris was, in one case, called "auvergne" probably after the "auvernat," the name given to the grape used to produce it. See T. Brennan, *Public Drinking and Popular Culture in Eighteenth-Century Paris* (Princeton, 1988), 95–97.

Sunday was a sort of weekly festival attracting a large public gathering where antagonisms sometimes surfaced. Seating arrangements and precedence in church could themselves incite quarrels between men such as the Sieur de Bac and the Sieur de Bardeties who had a continuing feud over which of them was to precede the other into church. In 1615 a fracas broke out inside the parish church of Jabrun near Chaudesaigues. The parishioners at least fought outside the church at St. Martin Cantales in 1629. The combatants in one quarrel of 1647 were even so considerate as to wait until mass had ended.[48]

The crowded alcoholic atmosphere of a festive day played an important part in the assault of young Jean Tourdes. In the evening of Tuesday, 1 September 1654, Hugues Navarre overtook Jean Tourdes near a bridge about two kilometers from Aurillac and struck him with a large club.[49] Under blows from Navarre, Tourdes screamed repeatedly for mercy and forgiveness, "Please, forgive me. Leave me be!"[50] But Navarre was unforgiving, inexorable. He forced his victim to the ground, hitting him about the head and shoulders into silence and then continued to spend his rage on the unconscious form at his feet. Finally Jean Tourdes was left bleeding from the wounds on his swollen head and battered shoulders.[51] Navarre rode away and Tourdes did not move until his father François came and carried him to the nearby village of La Ponetie.

48. Chevauchées: 1592. One Sunday, the vice-bailli even rode to their parish to attend mass and prevent any violence between them. For the other cases, Chevauchées 1615: 15 January; 1629: 30 May; 1647: 3 January.

49. This case is scattered in several different places, the main body of documents being in Présidial d'Aurillac A.D. Cantal IB 925. The plainte is found in A.D. Cantal IB 1058 and there is also an account in Chevauchées 1654: 18 October.

50. Deposition of Pierre Philip, shepherd, Arpajon. Information A.D. Cantal IB 925. The date given on the depositions in this Information is 4 October 1654, but the preamble also states that the witnesses are responding to the monitoire, which was not posted in the church at Arpajon until 18 October. It seems most likely that the monitoire was published earlier than the date indicated. Seven other witnesses repeat in full or in part the words of Tourdes, but all indicate that they heard the story from Pierre Philip. Two later witnesses, Durand Courbaisse, deposition of 27 February 1655 and Jean Goluy, 5 March 1655, do not mention the words of Tourdes.

51. Philip Berger, ibid., and Plainte of Tourdes 11 September 1654, A.D. Cantal IB 1058. While the plainte claimed that Navarre had used his sword during the beating, the report of the surgeon, 4 November 1654 A.D. Cantal IB 925, makes no mention of weapons. The report, made over a month after the incident, gives some idea of the severity of the beating, describing Tourdes: ". . . whom we discovered in his house, lying on his sick-bed, racked by continuous fever which greatly impaired and gave considerable pain to his head; and having examined and palpated his body, we discovered three tumors on his head, that is to say, two contusions, one on the left parietal bone and the other on the top of the head, and the third, on the right parietal bone, with an open laceration and cavity, plus two bruised areas on the shoulders."

On 11 September, François Tourdes notified the *vice-bailli* Paul Lacarrière and made a complaint on behalf of his son who, he said, had only
regained the ability to speak after ten days in bed. Lacarrière immediately
went to see the victim who gave under oath a statement similar to the
one already given by the father. Returning from a fair at Marmanhac, the
story went, Hugues Navarre had supped with Tourdes and others in a
tavern in Aurillac. The table-talk had become heated and Navarre "with
swearing and blasphemy" had insulted Tourdes and threatened to kill
him. After Tourdes had left the tavern and begun his homeward journey,
Navarre followed him and attempted to carry out his bloody promise,
using both a large stick and his sword.[52]

Why was Hugues Navarre, a twenty-eight-year-old *notaire* from the
village of Boussac, angry with Jean Tourdes? Unfortunately we know
little about Tourdes except that he was from Le Crouzet, a mile away
from the home of Navarre and that the two parties knew each other. No
status is given for him and the only references to his age are "boy" and
"young man." The choice of punishment and submission over combat
may also indicate Tourdes's social inferiority. His father was able to write
his own name in a fairly confident hand and was willing to pay the fees
necessary to move the case along.[53] He was probably at least a well-to-do
peasant. In any event, Tourdes and Navarre supped together in the
cabaret of Jean Montel.

After a general summons for information (*monitoire*) had been published and witnesses had been questioned, Navarre submitted to interrogation.[54] Part of his story seems plausible and whether true or not, it
certainly reveals some of his sensibilities. According to Navarre, he had
been looking for a fellow notary on his return from the fair at Marmanhac, and was told that his man was at the inn with the consuls of
Arpajon. Jean Tourdes was sitting nearby and had been drinking heavily,
as was often the custom on the day of the fair. Surrounded by men of
local importance, young Tourdes in his cups began to shout insults, not
directly at Navarre, but at notaries in general, saying "that all notaries
were forgers and that they were worthless"—strong words, given the

52. "Plaincte pour Jean Tourdes," 11 September 1654. A.D. Cantal IB 1058.
53. The only fee for which there is a record in this case was a "quatre ecus" noted at the
bottom of an order sending "parties et cause" before the *lieutenant criminel* of the *baillage* and
siège présidial of Aurillac. 24 October 1654 A.C. Cantal IB 925.
54. "Monitoire" (4 October?) and "Extraits des registres du visbailliage," (27 October 1654)
A.D. Cantal IB 925.

situation. Navarre said he was not pricked by these insults; but by his own admission he immediately defended his own honor, replying to Tourdes "that he was a man of honor, as were the other notaries," and he compared Tourdes's drunken words to those of Pierre Falict, presumably a well-known local drunkard, "sergent of Arpajon who has wasted his substance in the inns getting drunk every day." Still insisting that he had not felt any great ill will toward Tourdes, Navarre said to the contrary that Tourdes was so wounded by this last verbal thrust that he stumbled from the room, so drunk that he had to be helped down the steps by the innkeeper. According to Navarre, that was the end of the affair. He denied having beaten Tourdes and insisted that he had carried no weapon with him on that day.[55]

With the interrogation (*interrogatoire*) of Navarre the case becomes much clearer and one begins to understand the importance of the *milieu*. The time was the evening, in a common phrase in such cases, "after having eaten supper." Hugues Navarre was surrounded by his peers— another notary and some of the petty eminence of the parish of Arpajon—men by whom he was known and among whom his reputation was important. There he was loudly insulted by Tourdes, a boy perhaps flushed with the courage of drink and the compulsion for bravado in a public place. His honor and his worth were attacked; a notary or solicitor, village notable, certifier of contracts was called a forger and told he was worthless. The fuse was irrevocably lit in this highly charged milieu and the explosion occurred shortly after, on a well-traveled road in the early evening.[56] Hughes Navarre could not forget nor would he forgive the breach of decency and the insult to honor, and he did not trouble to find a secluded spot in which to mete out justice to Tourdes. The latter knew instantly the reason for the attack and his last words that evening were a plea for forgiveness. Tourdes had first violated the territory of Navarre and his company and then committed the almost irrevocable affront of an insult in the presence of notable witnesses. If this was so, the logic of honor demanded a thrashing.[57] A semiprivate thrashing was not so

55. "Interrogatoire," A.D. Cantal IB 925.
56. André Laingui, *La Responsabilité pénale*, quotes various jurists' commentaries to show that in considering the excuse of provocation in criminal offenses the proportion between provocation and riposte, the time elapsed between them, the public environment of the insult and the status (*qualité*) of the persons involved could mitigate judgment in theory in the courts of the Ancien Régime (295–303).
57. The case of Tourdes v. Navarre continued at least until 5 March 1655, after which the record stops. On that day a witness on his way to testify for Tourdes was attacked by two men "who said to each other 'that's our man' " and beat him with a stick. The victim managed to

prestigious or fulfilling a compensation for an affront as one administered before witnesses, but at least it fulfilled the didactic purpose of beating an offender and followed the strict letter of the laws of vengeance. To give Tourdes a humiliation of greater or equal value to that Navarre had received in front of friends and colleagues would probably have required witnesses of the same level and number.[58]

The village inn or tavern, perhaps somewhat humbler than the Aurillac version, was sometimes the locale of violent quarrels. Even the request for payment of a bill could be a provocation to one inclined to violence and sensitive on the matter of honesty or poverty. When innkeeper Anne Guion asked Bernard de Conquans to settle his account, he flew into a rage, calling her a *putain* (whore) and *carrogne* (hag, jade, impudent slut), and said that he owed her nothing and that if she didn't leave him alone, he would kill her. At the point of violence several men forced Conquans to leave the house. Outside he continued to shout oaths and insults and then returned to the house with his sword drawn. Again the drinkers forced him outside to protect the innkeeper, who was pregnant. There he found the serving-girl Anne Delbos and began to beat her with his sword. The unfortunate Delbos raised her arm to protect her face and under repeated sword blows her arm was mutilated and she was left a cripple.[59]

Gambling was perfectly suited to the provocation of insults to honor, because it frequently combined the problems of challenges to honesty, money, and steady face-to-face contact. When alcohol was combined with gambling and a lethal weapon was close to hand, a trifling quarrel could develop into a very grave incident indeed, even among friends, as happened in the case of François Sales, the unfortunate innkeeper of La Peyrousse, a case that also affords us a closer look at the village cabaret or wineshop, an arena of sociability and conflict.[60]

July 22 was an important feast day in the religious calendar of the Haute Auvergne.[61] After darkness had descended on the day's activities,

fight his way free of his assailants and was shot at with a pistol as he ran away; deposition of Jean Goluy, 5 March 1655. A.D. Cantal IB 925.

58. Hanlon, "Les Rituels de l'agression," 254–55.

59. "Plaincte pour Anne Giron contre Bernard Conquans," Juridiction de La Besserette, A.D. Cantal 16B 212. To this story I must add the cautionary note that it is taken from a *plainte* and the tendency of the plaintiff to paint a grim picture of innocence violated might have ignored a more substantial provocation of the accused.

60. Juridiction de Conros, A.D. Cantal 16B 432.

61. It was the feast day of Saint Mary Magdalen; *Calendrier des Festes*, A.D. Cantal 346 F33ter.

six adults and two children remained in the village inn at La Peyrousse, and the door had been bolted for the night. The inn was a humble house, for master, mistress, and guests stayed in the same room. In one corner of the large fireplace slept the innkeeper, François Sales.[62] His business associate, a village tailor named Jean Delboin, had fallen asleep on a large chest under the window; Jeanne Delrieu, wife of Sales, had taken her two children to bed with her. Yzabeau del Mas, a fourteen-year-old serving-girl, slept on a bench drawn up beside the bed of her mistress.[63] At a table before the fireplace two men played cards, their prize a bottle of wine. Gervais Pradel, with his back to the fire, and Ramond Laborie, who faced him, were both acquainted with the sleepers in the room, although neither was native to La Peyrousse.

After a late meal of bread, cheese, and wine, both men had intended to go home and the innkeeper had even lent his sword to Laborie so that he would not have to travel unarmed at night. But Pradel had wanted to play cards and so they sat, playing and drinking in the light of a small lamp while the others fell asleep. Laborie had leant the innkeeper's sword against a bed behind him.[64]

At midnight the mistress of the house awoke to the sound of angry shouts. By the time she had roused herself, the two gamblers had come to blows, struggling in front of the fireplace. She cried out to her husband to awake and stop the fight. Sales rose and stepped between Pradel and Laborie, remonstrating with them while the struggle continued. What happened next is not clear. Someone, most likely Laborie, dealt the innkeeper a strong sword blow. Sales fell to the floor, bleeding profusely from the left thigh and crying out that he was dead. His wife ran to him and took him in her arms. The fight stopped suddenly and the three men in the room carried Sales to a bed. An attempt was made to stanch the flow of blood with a cloth bandage ("un estoppard de linge") but the sword had slashed an artery and he continued to lose large quantities of

---

62. The fireplace was probably a type that still exists in the Cantal, and elsewhere on the Massif Central. The opening below a high mantel might be eight or ten feet across and four feet deep. On either side of the grate in the middle, benches were placed so that one was actually sitting in the fireplace. In evening, it was often the center of activity, and one of the few places other than beds, or the table, where one could sit. Often a *cantou* or salt box served as a seat. For some clear illustrations of vernacular domestic architecture, see Claverie and Lamaison, *L'Impossible Mariage*, chapter 3. I have also heard such a fireplace itself called a *cantou*, but do not know whether this usage was general.

63. Deposition of Jean Delboin in *Information*, 25 July 1626. A.D. Cantal 16B 432.

64. Deposition of Jeanne Delrieu, *Information*, 23 July 1626.

blood. The serving-girl had also been wounded, in the hand, as she ran past the fighting men to fetch help.[65] When the neighbors (two peasants and a widow) reached the scene, the wounded man was lying on his bed and the remorseful Laborie and Pradel were standing nearby, sober, bewildered, and at a loss. Laborie at first offered his apologies to Sales and said he had not intended to hurt him. Pradel then said that Sales had saved his life by taking the blow intended for him. Clearly, the full import of the situation began to dawn as the victim lay dying before them. Laborie quickly said that it was not he but Pradel who had struck the blow in question and that he himself was innocent. As they argued between themselves, Jean Delboin told them gravely "that they had done something for which they would be very sorry."[66] Laborie then pathetically contended that the wound was merely a scratch. None of the others in the dim light of the room had actually seen either man strike the fatal blow. As they realized the danger of their position, Pradel and Laborie politely took their leave of the victim, stepped out of the house, and fled. A surgeon was called and tried unsuccessfully to stop the bleeding, saying that Sales would soon die. Gerauld Destanne, the local seigneurial judge, was notified of the wounding, and perhaps thinking it a matter of small importance, sent his secretary to investigate. When informed that Sales was dying, however, he immediately rode to la Peyrousse and began the careful investigation, which is all that remains to us of this case.[67]

Such reconstructions are also interesting because they give us some of the texture of seventeenth-century life in Haute Auvergne. The shabbiness of the dimly lit inn ("cabaret et lotgis"), which was nothing more than a small village house, the sleeping arrangements of the family and their servant, and the meager evening meal including the cheese so essential to the Auvergnat diet are the sorts of details that are often repeated in the documents of the courts. Other aspects of the case have much in common with other spontaneous explosions of violence. The accused, the victim, and the witnesses were all acquainted as the documents often say "by sight and frequent contact." The time was a late evening meal in midsummer on a feast day. Cards and wine were involved in the provocation of an insignificant brawl that became serious and finally became a crime investigated by official justice. At the moment of

65. Deposition of Izabeau Delmas, ibid.
66. Deposition of Jean Delboin, 25 July 1626.
67. *Information*, 23 July 1626.

crisis, the servant ran to seek the support of the neighbors and when the seriousness of the incident became apparent, members of the community sought out the agents of official justice.

In addition to the explosions of violence there were cases in which a more calculated vengeance or violence was at work. Again we can often see the process of provocation, the threat to honor, dignity, or property followed by violent retaliation or informal justice, after which the agencies of official justice were brought into play. In general these incidents are marked by considerable stealth on the part of the aggressors. Time, place, and situation may have influenced the provocation, but the time and place of the riposte or the violent act in question were in large part decided upon by the attackers who stalked their prey to a situation of suitable convenience and vulnerability. This control of the situation of violence by the aggressor also lent itself to the use of valets or of assassins and bully boys who could not be easily identified with or linked to their employers.

These premeditated attacks, while often demonstrating the same economy of violence as the spontaneous incidents, represent a different mental process. In cases where motivation can be discovered we find that there has been the same breach of dignity or civility, or the same threat to property as in others. But the offended parties did not react immediately with the careless public passion that was much admired by many (and more easily forgiven by judges). Instead they kept a bitter mental record of the offenses against them and carefully plotted the downfall of their enemies with a view to both the success of their project and their own safety.

Naturally, successful attacks of this sort leave little useful evidence. In April 1609 for example, François de Sistrières, attorney (*avocat*) in the Parlement of Paris and brother to the judge of Murat, was assassinated. Four horsemen, strangers to the country, stalked de Sistrières to a lonely spot on a high mountain road near the Bois de Lioran, a forest in the northern part of the province, and there murdered him. Records of the Présidial court reveal that the *vice-bailli* and his men conducted a very thorough investigation, questioning forty-five witnesses over a wide area surrounding the scene of the murder, but the results were paltry. One rider, it was said, was bearded, another rode a cob, and all rode hard with their faces concealed by their hats and coats, speaking very little to those they encountered in their travels.[68] The killers in this case chose a remote, secluded place for their work, like many others involved in similar projects. The highways, a special concern for the maréchaussée, were places of ambush, especially those highways near heavily wooded areas. These affairs did not usually erupt in public places such as the taverns, fairs, and populated fields. When such places were used, the incidents often took place at night. In other cases, the victims were attacked as they left or returned to their houses.

The only such attacks about which there is much evidence were either unsuccessful attempts or those in which there was a well-known grievance between well-known parties. Ambushes of this sort appear to have been particularly popular among nobles, and the records of the maréchaussée are full of accounts in which provincial nobles with their relatives, valets, and assorted henchmen lay in wait for their victims and attacked. In January 1610, for example, the Sieur de Cheylade managed to escape an attack near his house by Henry de Roche Montal and several of his troop, who pursued Cheylade with pistol and arquebus shots. This was only one of a half-dozen similar attacks known to the maréchaussée in that year.[69] The problem presented to the researcher by these attacks is that they seldom reached the local courts. The records of the maréchaussée usually indicate that the vice-bailli merely rode out and warned the parties to stop fighting and to use the channels of royal justice to resolve their differences, a piece of advice that was seldom heeded.[70] These police reports are useful therefore in bringing to light a "dark figure": that of noble violence.

When cases of carefully plotted attacks were brought forward, the evidence is often murky at best, as in the case against the Sieur de Perigniac who hired four strangers to attack Annet and Gaspard Dodet, brothers who were pursuing a civil case against the seigneur. Perigniac contrived to be absent from the area on 28 December 1650, and had

68. The case is found in Chevauchées 1609: 20 April. The vice-bailli also drew up an Information of forty-seven pages that is in Présidial d'Aurillac, A.D. Cantal 1B 1053. The Chevauchées reported five horsemen but the more extensive information revealed only four. De Sistrières had been accompanied by a lackey who fled into the forest to save himself and could give no useful information.

69. The attack of Cheylade in Chevauchées 1610: 2 January. Other similar incidents are in ibid.: September 4; July; 5, 6, March. Other years show similar attacks with heavy noble involvement.

70. As, for example, in the case of fighting between the Sieurs de Tremont and de Loudiere, Chevauchées 1611: 26 December.

hired four men to shoot the Dodets. The plan failed. The four men ambushed their victims in the evening as the Dodets were returning home from a fair. Annet managed to escape completely and Gaspard was wounded twice in the arm.

Several people had heard the seigneur threaten the Dodets before the attack. They were, he said, "bougres" and "rascals" he wished to see dead. When they attempted to have general summonses (*lettres monitoires*) published in the parish church, Perigniac suppressed them by threatening the parish priest. The harrassment continued along with the procedure against Perigniac, who admitted nothing under questioning. His own servants had been intimidated into silence about the four armed strangers he had received in his house, and his valet, who had stayed with the assassins to identify the Dodets, said that he had been traveling with his master on the day in question. The case itself became an offense added to the original impudence that Perigniac had attempted to punish with his own rough justice. The threats and harassment began in 1650 and continued at least until 1654 when the documents end inconclusively.[71]

In the cases before the courts of the Haute Auvergne, lethal passions were not usually deferred, perhaps because the immediate response to an affront was expected and more satisfying to honor. But when they were, the documents can give us some understanding of the situation, the provocation, and the riposte, as well as of many other behavioral characteristics. Such is the case with the murder of Jean Vilatte (also known as "Grand Jean") in 1664.[72]

Catherine de Tremoulhieres was a forty-year-old widow who kept a tavern and lodgings in the village of St. Just near the southeastern border of the province. She was in the difficult position of female innkeeper, an attractive, unattached woman prey to the unwanted attentions of males. The owner of a small business, she was doubly attractive in a society where as the proverbial wisdom had it, "women, like priests, never know where they will eat their bread." In 1664 she was enjoying the attentions of two men. One was a surgeon named Pierre Lacombe and the other was called Le Cadet, a guard in the house of a nobleman. Lacombe seems to have had the stronger claim, for he took rooms in the widow's house and began to take his meals and sleep there, "because of the said love trysts."

71. The most useful pieces in this case are the series of *interrogatoires* of the seigneur and his servants made on 12–13 January 1654, Bailliage of Salers A.D. Cantal 14B 227.

72. The case consists of fourteen pieces including a sentence, Juridiction of St. Just, A.D. Cantal 16B 1048. All the following pieces are found under the same number.

The soldier made love to Tremoulhieres as well, with hopes of marriage. When rebuffed, he became angry and called her, among other things, a "whore," abusing her and insulting her honor. The two suitors had quarreled openly several times and Lacombe was heard to say that he wanted to kill his adversary, and "that he had plenty of powder and lead for the belly of the said Cadet, his rival."[73]

On the evening of 14 April 1664, Le Cadet came to the widow's house to drink with a friend, Jean Vilatte. Lacombe the surgeon was not present. At one o'clock in the morning Vilatte stepped outside the house to attend to his "necessities." He had managed to walk four or five steps when he was hit by gunfire.[74] His killer or killers fled into the night. The alarm was raised in the village and the inhabitants ran to and fro with torches, searching for the murderers, who managed to escape.

Lacombe later told the parish priest that he had shot Vilatte in self-defense, although others claimed that Vilatte had been unarmed.[75] The strong suspicion was that the surgeon, aided by the widow's son, Bertrand Gourdon, stung by the insulting importunities of Le Cadet, and enraptured by the allure of the innkeeper herself, had intended to murder his rival in love. Unfortunately, the wrong man had been killed. This suspicion was reinforced by the allegation that the widow had removed all of Lacombe's possessions and many of her own furnishings from her house immediately after the murder.[76] Further, she was accused of having taken six livres from the dead man's pockets. Both Lacombe and Bertrand Gourdon fled after the killing, leaving Catherine Tremoulhieres to face accusation by the victim's widow. While she accused her erstwhile suitor, Cadet, of insults, the innkeeper persistently denied any part in the shooting and insisted that Lacombe had been nothing more than a lodger to her. She was, she said, a woman of honor and "good reputation."[77]

---

73. *Audition et Response de Catherine Tremoulhieres*, 21 April 1664. Le Cadet was not the only man to have insulted the widow. In a *confrontation* with Tremoulhieres, François Vinat admitted having called her *bougresse* and *gueuse* because he thought her responsible for the murder. *Cayer de Resumption* 12 May 1664.

74. *Audition . . . de Catherine Tremoulhieres*.

75. Deposition of "Gerard Delorme pretre et vicaire de St. Just," 18 June 1664.

76. *Audition*.

77. Ibid. While there was no sentence passed on Catherine Tremoulhieres, both Lacombe and Gourdon were sentenced to death in their absence. Lacombe was to be "put to death on the wheel with an iron bar." (The condemned person's bones were to be smashed with the iron bar while his body was stretched out on a wheel.) Gourdon was to be hanged. Their property was confiscated, one-third going to their wives and families and 1000 *livres* to the widow and children of the victim. If they could not be caught, both were to be executed in effigy "pour l'horreur des méchants" (to terrify the wicked).

"Good reputation" and honor were two points of universal sensitivity often repeated by Auvergnats in the courts, just as they were in Castan's eighteenth-century Languedoc. The violation of honor was a serious offense and like the transgressions against property it was often punished by violence. While honor knew no season, it was more likely to encounter offense in the sorts of situations described above, and its vindication was thus shaped by its environment. The feeble insistence, in the face of evidence or assertions to the contrary, that one was "a respectable man" (un homme de bien), or "an honorable woman" (une femme d'honneur), reveals a concern that one be accorded a certain respect and allowed a fundamental dignity. This was psychic property that if violated, would demand retribution and restoration, just as certainly as a violation of the closely divided space of the meadow required punishment.

Means to an End: Weapons, Their Use and Control

The "anonymous" attack was often a response to insults, threats, or other provocations, an action that punished the author of an affront without the satisfying immediacy and triumphant directness of a face-to-face confrontation; but it was also sometimes the only method by which any satisfaction could be achieved. Where single combat was not possible, or unlikely of success, or where a total vindictive destruction of one's enemy was the desired end, there were tools that promised success. The greatest equalizer among weapons was fire which, like nothing else, could ensure a tyranny of the weak.[78] Partly because of its combination of radical destructiveness and availability to those with no other possibility of attack or retaliation and little claim to honor, arson was regarded as a most serious offense.[79] It carried with it a suggestion of the demonic, the secret, the conspiratorial, and the subversive. Its authors usually worked by night, in secret, sometimes with wicked smelling substances, igniting the uncontrollable conflagration that would surely greet unrepentant sinners (such as arsonists) in the hereafter. Moreover the arsonist often had nothing to gain but the misfortune of others. Once well started, fire

78. Claverie and Lamaison, L'Impossible Mariage, 262.
79. Steven G. Reinhardt, Justice in the Sarladais, 262–63.

was remorseless and complete. It was the inexorable power of nature in the hands of evil, force against which there was little defense anywhere, and even less in rural areas.[80] Property-owners, at least, must have shared this demonic view of arson and arsonists.

Were the arsonists of Haute Auvergne in league with the devil, re-creating the fires of hell as medieval theory suggests? Were they insane, craving some sort of sexual or psychic release? Or was arson a form of social revolt by the underprivileged? A. Abbiateci in a study of eigh-teenth-century arsonists in the records of the Parlement of Paris found evidences of social revolt, extortion, robbery, and insanity connected with arson, which was practiced in the main by those from the lower orders of French society.[81] Abel Poitrineau mentions arson and the threat of arson in eighteenth-century Auvergne as types of blackmail favored by beggars;[82] and E. Le Roy Ladurie evokes the arsonist-shepherd as a familiar figure of Early Modern Languedoc.[83] Perhaps most striking of all is the plague of arson that became the principal weapon of vengeance and intimidation in the Gévaudan village of La Fage, brilliantly described and analyzed by Elisabeth Claverie and Pierre Lamaison.[84]

In the *Chevauchées* only six cases of arson occur, resulting in four deaths. Two of these cases were probably in reality multiple arsons that concerned the firing of villages, the final acts in a series of excesses by soldiers in the late sixteenth century.[85] In another instance of 1607, a house was burned to conceal the murder of its occupant.[86] Jehan Motet, a *valet*, was suspected of robbery as well as arson when he burned a house in 1631;[87] and in the early seventeenth century, local villagers were accused in two instances of burning the barns and stables of their neighbors.[88] No cases give evidence of any connection with mendicants

---

80. This still seems to be the view of insurance companies, judging from the fire insurance rates for houses in some areas of rural Canada, which are many times higher than rates in the cities.

81. A. Abbiateci, "Les incendiaires devant le Parlement de Paris" in *Crimes et Criminalité*, 13–32, first published under the same title in *Annales*, E.S.C. 25 (1970): 229–48.

82. A. Poitrineau, *La Vie rurale en Basse Auvergne*, 1:584.

83. E. Le Roy Ladurie, *Les Paysans de Languedoc*, 1:88–89. Both Poitrineau and Le Roy Ladurie are cited by Abbiateci. See also Iain Cameron, *Crime and Repression*, 136–94.

84. E. Claverie and P. Lamaison, *L'Impossible Mariage*.

85. *Chevauchées* 1587: 22 August; 1595: 20 May.

86. *Chevauchées* 1631: 5 December.

87. *Chevauchées* 1631: 5 December.

88. *Chevauchées* 1611: 3 September, 7 October; 1614: 3 July, 8 November.

or vagabonds although all arsonists were from the lower orders and one was a woman.

Arson was extremely difficult to detect because of its surreptitious nature and because fire often consumed evidence. Early Modern jurists tended to rely on evidence of threatening behavior before a fire. In any case, the *maréchaussée* do not seem to have concerned themselves much with arson in either the seventeenth or the eighteenth century, as the records for some other areas and periods are comparably small, either for want of succcessful detection, or because of the infrequency of the offense.[89]

Other weapons more controllable in their effect and more directly connected to the user included firearms, swords, sticks, stones, and subordinate human beings. In the records, the offense of carrying illegal weapons (*port d'armes*) was usually coupled with illicit assembly, with illegal troop activities (levying and lodging) and sometimes with rebellion. But in seven cases from the *Chevauchées*, all between 1610 and 1617, a period of unstable regency following the assassination of Henry IV, individuals alone were charged with carrying firearms. Despite the paucity of cases for this offense, however, the *Chevauchées* and court records give some evidence that the use of weapons, particularly of firearms was fairly widespread. While the *vice-baillis* did not always specify the weapons used in assault or homicide, when they did do so, firearms were most often mentioned and among firearms, pistols and arquebuses; then came swords, clubs, and knives.[90] However, the frequency of mention may have more to do with the unremarkable profusion of the weapons least mentioned than with the popularity of firearms.

The sword, light, deadly, and always at the ready, was more likely to be used in chance encounters; it could also be used to administer a beating as well as a lethal thrust. Firearms rather than swords seem to have been preferred weapons in planned attacks. Though effective, they required some preparedness, being heavy, awkward to load and prime, and often inaccurate. From their use one can often infer some premeditation, at least to the extent that the person so armed was expecting

89. Some examples: Iain Cameron found only six cases of arson in eighteenth-century Perigord (1720–90), *Crime and Repression*, 136; and Julius Ruff, seven in two *sénéchaussées* of southwestern France (1696–1789).

90. Of 76 weapons specified, 52 (68%) were firearms, 12 (16%) swords, 9 (12%) clubs, 3 (4%) knives. In the revolts of 1636–49 stones and firearms are also mentioned. Of firearms, 17 pistols and 15 arquebuses were specified.

trouble.[91] For all their limitations, they were sought after and indeed were the chosen weapons of feuding nobles. One could attack one's enemy at a distance and even with witnesses, avoiding many of the preliminary verbal exchanges between enemies so perilous to honor.

The evidence indicates that firearms could be bought in the ordinary way. Jacques Bastide, a merchant in Paulhac, displayed three pistols for sale in his stall in 1659. The judicial authorities did not trouble the seller on this point and passers-by were allowed to heft and examine the weapons. The case only came to light because a boy examining one of the pistols shot himself by accident. In the procedure against the accused merchant, the interrogator, the witnesses, and the other participants in the affair seem to have seen nothing unusual in the presence of firearms in a village merchant's stall, and Bastide was only questioned closely about the fact that the pistol was loaded.[92] In only one case was a merchant stopped carrying quantities of arms for sale.[93] The *vice-baillis* seem to have been concerned mainly with the provocative, public display of arms and there is little evidence of a general program of search and confiscation such as those conducted during the eighteenth century. Iain Cameron's research indicates that some villagers in eighteenth-century Auvergne continued to possess and use firearms in order to make festive noise, to protect themselves while traveling and to defy the cavaliers of the *maréchaussée*.[94]

As we have seen in our discussion of assault and homicide, the innkeeper Sales kept a sword and gave it to the peasant Ramond Laborie for protection while traveling at night.[95] In light of other cases such an incident is not surprising; both swords and firearms were owned and used by persons from all parts of the rural social order. One cannot therefore

---

91. The *Chevauchées* show that muskets, arquebuses, *pétrinals*, and pistols were used. Muskets were heavy, often weighing 15 to 20 pounds. Arquebuses were somewhat lighter and a *pétrinal* was a cross between a pistol and an arquebus. In loading, powder and ball had to be rammed into place, for cartridges did not come into use until Gustavus Adolphus of Sweden introduced them during the Thirty Years' War. In the case of a matchlock, a slow fuse had to be lit as well. Inventors of military weaponry in the seventeenth century concentrated on increasing the rate of fire and virtually ignored accuracy. See B. P. Hughes, *Firepower* (London: 1974) 8, 10, 11, 27, 80; and C. P. Russell, *Guns on the Early Frontier* (N.Y. 1957), 1–4, 7–8, 11, 14, 82–95.

92. Trenty v. Bastide *Interrogatoire* and the *Information* containing the deposition of six witnesses, 9 September 1659, Présidial d'Aurillac, A.D. Cantal IB 927.

93. *Chevauchées* 1616: 11 October.

94. I. Cameron, *Crime and Repression*, 79–88, 225–26 cites eighteenth-century examples.

95. *Information*, 23 July 1626 A.D. Cantal, 16B 432.

use weapons as a preliminary measure of social status,[96] although it is clear that carrying weapons was a greater misdeed when committed by non-nobles.[97] Certainly the privileges of nobles included the right to carry a sword, as Charles Loyseau noted in 1610, "everywhere," and the right to own and use arquebuses. The edicts and ordinances of the late sixteenth and early seventeenth centuries were more usually preoccupied with firearms, the most persistent concern being with pocket pistols (*pistolets à poche*). Nobles who had hunting rights could legally possess and use firearms in the chase; those who did not hunt could use them only within their houses. Loyseau pointed out that the nobility of the robe were excluded from the privileges of sword-carrying; but most edicts excepted soldiers and royal officers who used arms in the cause of their duties. At various times of national crisis, there were renewed attempts to control the proliferation of arms, such as the prohibition of 27 May 1610, two weeks after the death of Henry IV, and the various prohibitions declared during the Wars of Religion. But the continual issue of similarly phrased edicts is probably testimony to their ineffectiveness; our evidence shows a more widespread use of weapons than the traditional distinction of a sword-carrying nobility would indicate.[98]

It would be misleading, however, to leave the impression that ordinary rural inhabitants, when not traveling, usually went about their daily tasks

96. Twenty-two of 52 cases of firearms used were by nobles and 2 of 12 incidents of swordplay involved *gentilshommes*.

97. For example one Giraud caught traveling in company with firearms was hanged for the offense in Aurillac *Chevauchées* 1617: 2 August; 26 November, 14–15 December. A nobleman from Rouergue arrested in a fair at St. Antoine-les-Marcolès was fined 20 livres for carrying horse-pistols. Interestingly, his confiscated pistols were given to the *archer* who made the arrest.

98. Roland Mousnier, *Institutions*, 1:125. Charles Loyseau, *Traieté des Ordres et simples Dignités* (1610) (from *Oeuvres*, published Lyon, 1701), 1:29, paragraph 77, deals with the privilege of *gentilshommes* to carry swords. Mousnier's *Institutions* refers extensively to Loyseau. There are many ordinances and edicts that deal with arms, hunting, and the rights of the nobility. Mousnier uses the ordinance of 1601, article 4, to illustrate the noble right to fire arquebuses, although the text of that ordinance, in Isambert, *Recueil général des anciennes lois françaises*, 15:248, shows article 5 to concern the arquebus. The Ordinance of 25 November 1487, which forbade the bearing of arms, excepted the army and *gentilshommes* and it is referred to by the editors as the type from which subsequent ordinances derived. Examples closer to our period include Ordinance of January 1560, which gave *gentilshommes* the same rights outlined in the Ordinance of 1601, above, and forbade others to carry firearms; Ordinance August 1561, which allowed only *gentilshommes*, their servants, and soldiers to carry arms; 16 August 1563, "Defense du port d'armes;" 12 February 1566, "Nouvelle defense du port des armes a feu"; 4 April 1598, which prescribed a fine for first offenses and death for recidivists; as well as other regulations concerning the carrying, use, sale and manufacture of arms in 12 September 1609; 27 May 1610; 16 December 1611; 3 February 1617; 2 May 1618; December 1660; 25 June 1665.

armed with pistols or arquebuses, although these were often near at hand. In most incidents peasants probably used the weapons at hand: sticks, stones, tools, fists, and feet. Peasants carting hay or herdsmen moving animals commonly carried a cattle prod or staff, which could be a formidable weapon, as could the flail used in threshing cereals; travelers, most of whom moved on foot supported themselves with an all-purpose staff or walking stick.[99] Knives were necessary tools, the only means of cutting tough rye bread baked to last for months at a time, or of slicing the ubiquitous Cantal cheese. The victims of beatings usually tried in their complaints to make the offending weapon as menacing as possible, "a thick club," or "a huge stick."

Once a physical fight had begun, the rule often seems to have been a kind of pugilistic opportunism.[100] There was no particular pattern or etiquette to the brawls and beatings that took place. The fighters punched and tore and scratched each other; the unlucky person who fell was kicked where he or she lay. This is not to lessen the arguments that, first of all, the actual engagement of combat was the end of, or at least part of, a "ritual" of sorts; or second, that the concept of honor was closely tied to the body, concentrated, it has been argued, on the head and the face. But students should not draw too many elaborate inferences from, say, the target of a blow, when people may simply have hit their opponents on the head, rather than on the foot, for example, because that is where their blows were most effective. Knocking off the hat of an adversary, punching a pregnant woman in the stomach, beating an inferior with the cane rather than drawing the sword against an equal, could be choices of cultural significance or practical utility, as could the weapons chosen.[101]

As the metaphor of the duel suggests, however, there were distinct stages to confrontations like the ones we have seen in the examples above. One had a claim to certain psychic property; the claim was

99. Gregory Hanlon calls the stick or club, "the weapon of choice" in seventeenth-century urban Aquitaine, although he notes that city violence saw increasing use of the "canne bourgeoise" (bourgeois cane) toward the end of the seventeenth century. "Les Rituels de l'agression," 261–62.

100. This phrase was suggested to me by Professor James Tagg of the University of Lethbridge.

101. There has been a welter of speculation and theory on these matters, in much of the "honor" literature as well as that on mentalities, behavior, and the body. Steven G. Reinhardt takes a sensible, nuanced approach in *Justice in the Sarladais*, 172–73, when discussing violence against women, who were often struck in the belly rather than on the head as men were. This tactic accords with the style of insults to women, primarily sexual and physical.

challenged, rivaled, threatened in some way, and then defended. This pattern could be repeated several times within the same incident as each defense or response could be a new provocation. Moreover, at any point in the process, these aggressions and defenses could be verbal or physical, and could shift from one to the other. As we shall see when looking at some of the problems of women and then of social rank, the nature of verbal as well as physical weapons was sometimes laden with cultural significance, so that they could be used to greatest effect, in order to violate the most significant boundaries of the other person.

In the society of the mountains, police forces were small and distant; disputes were sometimes resolved by the private justice of combat. Many persons traveled in seasonal and annual migrations to strange places. It was not unusual—indeed, it was necessary—that some members of the rural community be armed for their own defense. The general lassitude of the *maréchaussée* toward weapons for most of the period may indicate that weapons were mainly offensive to the authorities when they were used. But in some ways the most feared weapon was the human body. More than anything the *maréchaussée* seem to have worried about the critical mass and temper of crowds that could overwhelm them, in a society where riot was for many the only powerful means of political expression.

Illicit assembly (*assemblée illicite*) was a term that could be applied to virtually any large gathering not sanctioned by royal authority. The Ordinance of 1670 concerning criminal justice placed such illegal gatherings within the competence of the *maréchaussée*. But the *vice-baillis* had been keeping watch over *assemblées* for three generations and previous declarations had exhorted *prévôts* and other royal officers to be vigilant in this regard.[102]

Usually crowds were cause for concern to the police of this period whether they were riotous gatherings at fairs, at church, or on festive days.[103] Although the most worrisome *assemblées* were armed, the term

102. Ordinance 1670, Titre 1 Art. 12.374. See for example "Declaration sur la défense du port d'armes et contre les assemblées illicites" 27 May 1610, Isambert et al., *Recueil général des anciennes lois françaises*, 16:6. Earlier ordinances forbade gatherings in cities without the permission of royal officers (8 February 1566) in ibid., 14:184, and assemblies of *gentilshommes* (August 1546). The latter prohibition was repeated in 1658, 23 June, ibid., 17:366.

103. See respectively, *Chevauchées* 1628: 11 January; 1652: 8 September; 1660: 28 June. The problem of riotous gatherings on feast days was such that both the *consulat* of Aurillac (A.C.BB¹⁵, 18 June 1642) and later the Grands Jours d'Auvergne in the *Registres* of Dongois saw fit to censure such goings-on.

was used on occasion to refer to unarmed crowds as well.[104] The motives could vary: attempts to exclude strangers in a time of plague; battles between rival parishes; resistance to taxes, or private quarrels among nobles. In the *Chevauchées* the *vice-baillis* used the term mainly to refer to assemblies of armed men and it was therefore an offense often closely associated with powerful rebellious men in fortified houses, with carrying weapons and with the unauthorized levy of armed men. In the period 1589–95 the province was full of such assemblies and the *vice-bailli* often wrote of them as part of the "schemes" and treasons of the powerful. When the term *assemblée illicite* reappeared in the reign of Henry IV, the new *vice-bailli* Jacques Lacarrière described scattered instances of groups of men preparing for private battles or feuds.[105] During the years of regency 1610–1617, Jacques Lacarrière reported 28 instances of *assemblées illicites*, most of which were also struggles and settlings of accounts between prominent local families. After 1617, while the same words were seldom used, the habits of collective violence in feuds and "querelles" continued.

The illegal levy of armed men was mainly a phenomenon of the regency of Marie de Medicis and the Ministry of Concini. The vigilance of the *vice-bailli*, especially during these years, was due in large part to the sensitivity of the royal government to the opposition of prominent nobles.[106] The levies in most cases achieved little. Some companies of arquebusiers were formed on the pretext of hunting; in others the leaders claimed to be raising bodies of troops for royal service in Savoy.[107] The latter alibi was easily disproved by the *vice-bailli*, who had knowledge of those permitted to raise companies. While illegal levies of troops were no longer mentioned in the *Chevauchées* after 1616, nobles continued the traditions established during the Wars of Religion and strengthened during the regency. While illegal levies do not bear directly on our study of violent crime, they point to military habits that will inform our examination of noble violence.

Offenses pertaining to the lodging and comportment of royal troops occur throughout the period and the *vice-bailli* wrote often of "ravaiges, rancons, extorsions et violences" (ravages, ransoms, extortion, and

---

104. *Chevauchées* 1594: 24 July.

105. For example, *Chevauchées* 1607: 25 April, 15 March; 1609: 5 May, 17 November.

106. For an account of the years of the regency and the revolt of the princes, see J. M. Hayden, *France and the Estates General of 1614* (Cambridge, 1974).

107. For example, *Chevauchées* 1615: 28 March; 8, 17 May; 15 June.

violence). Two particular offenses peculiar to soldiers were those of illegal halts or lodgings and desertion. By ordinance, communities were obliged to support royal troops by paying for their subsistence and allowing them to lodge in designated areas. No houses were exempt from these unpleasant duties save those of *seigneurs* with judgeships, and priests. Companies on the march were allowed only one night's halt and soldiers were theoretically forbidden on pain of death to force from their hosts any more than the required minimum of food and drink. When soldiers reached their area of jurisdiction, the *vice-bailli* was to ensure that they obeyed these rules and did not commit any offenses against the local populace.[108] In practice the *vice-baillis* usually escorted bodies of troops through the province and if sufficient force was available, compelled them to move when illegally lodged.[109] As for cases of desertion, they occur rarely in the *Chevauchées*,[110] although many of the troubles caused by soldiers seem to have been the work of men who had left their companies and were not under any legitimate authority.

Rebellion, as defined by French law, was simply resistance to authority, most commonly royal authority. In practice, specific cases involved some personal violence or physical struggle, although a simple refusal to obey the commands of royal officials could also be termed *rébellion*. Ordinances from the Early Modern period condemned various sorts of rebellion: outrages against *hussiers, sergents, commissaires* and other officers of justice (January 1475, February 1566);[111] holding châteaus or fortified houses closed against royal decrees (April 1472, May 1579);[112] resisting tax officials (January 1629);[113] and popular revolts in general (January 1640).[114] As it was identified by the *vice-baillis*, *rébellion* is the least satisfactorily quantifiable of the offenses in the *Chevauchées*. I have counted thirty-one specific acts of resistance called *rébellion*; but this figure corresponds little to the reality of the period. In August 1588, for

108. See the ordinance of January 1629, Isambert et al., *Recueil général des anciennes lois françaises*, 16:285–304.

109. *Chevauchées* 1595: 15 March; 1617: 8 May, 13 May; 1627: 29 October, 1628: 17 December; 1630: 20 October; 1631: 16 April; 1649: 3 January; 1636: 15 March, 30 April; 1652: 26 October, 15 August; 1659: 15 April.

110. Examples of desertion in *Chevauchées* 1629: 7 July; 1636: 2 June; 1647: 1 March; 1648: 24 April; 1659: 1 March.

111. Isambert et al., *Recueil général des anciennes lois françaises*, 14:198.

112. Ibid., 246–47, 426.

113. Ibid., 16:282.

114. Ibid., 525.

example, *vice-bailli* Jean Lacarrière reported a universal rebelliousness and a refusal to pay the *taille* in all the parishes of the Haute Auvergne, but described no specific acts of resistance.[115] Every year the *maréchaussée* assisted in the seizure of property for taxes; sometimes the resisters were branded rebels, sometimes not. For the massive tax rebellions of 1636 and 1647–49, the *Chevauchées* give an account of some of the most serious incidents; but they also record in detail an attack against a single minor official of the *taille* in September 1664.[116] The problem persists when one looks at the activities of those who held châteaus and defied the commands of royal justice. During the period 1587–95 when the province was rife with political-religious dissension and private bloodletting, Jean Lacarrière sometimes reported that nobles all over the province were defying royal authority from their strongholds; in February 1594, the culprits constituted much of the population of St. Flour, stronghold of the Catholic League.[117] During this period the words rebellion and treason came easily from the pen of the *vice-bailli*. In 1627, however, considerable detail was devoted to a single rebellion. François Dons, Sieur de la Grande, and some of his henchmen claimed and seized a château belonging to the Dame de Brezons, driving out her tenant farmer and servants. The *vice-bailli* pounded on the door and demanded entry in the name of the king, to which he received a stream of insults and the muzzle of a gun in reply.[118]

In light of their variety, counting rebellions is not the appropriate form of description. They do, however, fit into our pattern of provocation and riposte, both on the personal, face-to-face level, when the esteem of individual royal officers was involved, and in a wider sense of the defense of a collective psychic property from a greater entity. The taxonomy of historians has failed them when trying to identify this opponent: acculturation, the reform of manners, absolutism, modernization, Catholic reform. The list of terms for change is extensive and evolutionary.

Offended parties with a need for vengeance stood before a forked path. They could take an opponent to law or they could administer justice themselves. If they followed the latter course and the informal private

115. *Chevauchées* 1588: 17 August.
116. *Chevauchées* 1664: 3 September.
117. *Chevauchées* 1594: 12 February. An example of universal noble defiance is in *Chevauchées* 1589: March.
118. *Chevauchées*, 1627: 30 November.

"justice" reached the crucial threshold of blood, their vengeance sometimes became "crime," in which case the violence of the state and official
justice was brought to bear against them. In the case where the enemy
was officialdom itself, there could be no final satisfaction.

Women: Persons and Property, Honor and Shame

The idea of psychic property in some ways blurs the traditional distinction
between offenses against persons and those against property, with a
propensity both to "dehumanize" persons and to extend the purview or
the orbit of the human, in a way that I think may be faithful to the
sensibility of the period. This does not mean that such a clear distinction
between persons and property cannot be made where physical violence is
concerned, for such a confusion would lead to a preposterous reification
of symbols, and a negation of the clear evidence of our intellectual,
moral, and physical senses. But it does mean that although individual
persons might be deeply affected by some actions, the contemporary
regard for the offense (even by the victim) tended to be as anxious
concerning the "spoiling" of a human asset, as it was about human pain
and misery. Recall from Chapter 1 that the Haute Auvergne still favored
the use of the body of the debtor as security, even for small debts, and it
is less jarring to discover that this relationship of subordination in the
case of women and children, especially those of the lower orders, meant
that their suffering was often considered more in terms of "damages" or
"spoilage." This idea seems to be reinforced by the limited sense of
feminine honor, although it was not exclusively a way of viewing women.
In abductions, for example, the body, male or female, was valuable to
someone other than the immediate victim, and the offense was considered a violation of a kind of mutual psychic property.

Women, in the context of violent crime and honor, occupied a
particularly complex region of the early modern mindscape,[119] which

---

119. There is an immense and growing wealth of research on the history of women in France,
Europe, and the West in general, that cannot be summarized here, but must not be omitted
entirely. Three recent attempts in English to provide surveys are particularly accessible. R.
Bridenthal, C. Koonz, and S. Stuard, eds., *Becoming Visible: Women in European History*
(Boston, 1987), is the most historically coherent and integrated of the three. M. J. Boxer and
J. H. Quataert, *Connecting Spheres: Women in the Western World, 1500 to the Present* (Oxford,
1987), contains two essays on women in Early Modern France, S. Hanley, "Family and State in
Early Modern France," 53–63; and O. Hufton and F. Tallett, "Communities of Women, the
Religious Life and Public Service in Eighteenth-Century France," 75–85. B. S. Anderson and
J. P. Zinsser, *A History of Their Own: Women in Europe from Prehistory to the Present*, 2 vols.
(New York, 1988) is an ambitious attempt. For an early bibliography, see L. Frey, M. Frey, and

cannot simply be explained in a crude formulation of "women as property." Julian Pitt-Rivers has suggested that the concept of honor was firmly tied to the physical person, so that an assault on the body, despite the fact that some parts of it might be considered more inviolate than others, was always an assault on honor.[120] In the case of women, dishonor, insult, and offense tended to be more heavily confined to the sexual or physical. It might instead be more accurate to suggest that regarding women there was a more concrete sense of psychic property: the boundaries of honor were actual, physical boundaries of flesh. In woman, to the minds of our early modern people, there was therefore a

J. Schneider, Women in Western European History (Westport, Conn., 1982). New periodicals have also appeared, among them the Journal of Women's History from the United States and Gender in History from Great Britain. There are also valuable remarks on women in the various histories of the Western family, marriage, childhood, and sexuality, such as M. Mitterauer and R. Sieder, The European Family (Chicago, 1982). A solid basis for research is provided by J. A. Brundage, Law, Sex, and Christian Society in Medieval Europe (Chicago, 1987); Olwen Hufton, The Poor of Eighteenth-Century France; Jean-Louis Flandrin, Families in Former Times: Kinship, Household and Sexuality, trans. Richard Southern (Cambridge, 1979). The literature on Mediterranean honor, mentioned above, also contains pertinent comments, as do most of the recent works on criminality and violence. For France, two of the most interesting sources remain those by Natalie Davis: the essays in Society and Culture in Early Modern France (Stanford, Calif., 1975), and The Return of Martin Guerre, which deals with the nuances of early modern feminine mentalities in a remarkable way. French Historical Studies 16, no. 1 (Spring 1989) devoted a special issue to "Women and Gender in French History," which contains an excellent article by Sarah Hanley, "Engendering the State: Family Formation and State Building in Early Modern France," 4–27. M. Segalen, Love and Power in the Peasant Family: Rural France in the Nineteenth Century (Oxford, 1983) is also worthwhile, despite the period, and Claverie and Lamaison, L'Impossible Mariage is indispensable. Other useful works include: R. Forster and O. Ranum, eds., Family and Society (Baltimore, 1976) and Deviants and the Abandoned in French Society (Baltimore, 1978); R. Wheaton and T. Haraven, Family and Sexuality in French History (Philadelphia, 1980); the studies of mentalities and popular culture contain important research on the attitudes to and of women, for example, Y. Castan's magisterial, Honnêtété et relations sociales en Languedoc, and the work of Robert Muchembled, L'Invention de l'homme. For changes in the condition of and the attitudes to Frenchwomen, there are also a number of interesting studies, for example that of Carolyn C. Lougee, Le Paradis des Femmes: Women, Salons and Social Stratifications in the Seventeenth Century (Princeton, 1976), and a commentary on early modern sources in the feminist debate, M. Angenot, Les Champions des Femmes: Examen du discours sur la supériorité des femmes, 1400–1800 (Montreal, 1977). A useful essay is James B. Collins, "The Economic Role of Women in Seventeenth-Century France," French Historical Studies 16, no. 2 (Fall 1989): 436–70. One of the most important changes during the period, which was to have profound and widespread consequences for women is admirably treated in E. Rapley, The Dévotes: Women and Church in Seventeenth-Century France (Montreal, 1990). In some ways, those who wish to get a sense of Early Modern attitudes to women and of the historic change in viewing the lot of women would do best to read Simone de Beauvoir's The Second Sex, trans. H. M. Parshley (New York, 1952), Natalie Davis's "Women on Top," in her Society and Culture, 124–51, and then to look at primary sources such as Sprenger and Kramer's late medieval Malleus maleficarum, especially the sections explaining why women are more likely to become witches.

120. Pitt-Rivers, "Honor and Social Status," 25–26.

peculiar unity of the moral and the material. The distinction between persons and property was even less visible, the integity of psychic property even more complete. While many types of incidents bring the nature of this phenomenon into relief, abduction, to some degree, and rape, to a much greater extent, provide us with clearer examples of this attitude in action.

Abduction was a specialized activity in the Haute Auvergne, practised in the main by soldiers and the nobility. The former favored fairly indiscriminate kidnapping while the latter concentrated on more carefully selected targets.[121] Abductions mentioned in the *Chevauchées* took place between 1587 and 1660 with no concentration in any particular period.

In the cases involving soldiers, the taking of hostages was usually associated with other excesses of war and billeting: looting, arson, assault and sometimes murder. The victims, usually peasants, were simply taken and held hostage until a ransom or levy was raised by the local inhabitants. The object of the exercise was money. Other fruits of the countryside, unlike money, were not so easily hidden and women among these fruits had other temporary uses. One of the specific functions of the *vice-baillis* was to oversee the lodging and comportment of armies, but in the matter of abduction they often appear to have been particularly ineffective. Sometimes if the guilty parties had moved beyond the Haute Auvergne, the matter was simply forgotten.[122] In times of emergency the *vice-baillis* were frustrated by the lenient attitude of higher authorities when troops happened to be on the "right" side. When he complained of hostage-taking and ransoming by royal troops in 1588, *vice-bailli* Jean Lacarrière was told by the Governor de Missilhac that in times of peace one could prosecute such matters but, seeing as the forces of the enemy were close at hand with three cannon and two or three thousand men, such a prosecution would be out of place.[123] Confrontations with the soldiers themselves, though an undoubted show of police courage, often proved equally fruitless. In November 1592, royal troops on their way north seized for ransom a well-to do peasant named Bonnet Desboin. When the *vice-bailli* accompanied by only three *archers* demanded the

---

121. Nine abductions were by nobles and their domestics, six by soldiers, three by others.
122. For example *Chevauchées* 1636: 24 August; 1587: 22 August.
123. *Chevauchées* 1588, 3–5 January. The *vice-bailli* proceeded with his investigation despite the discouragement by the governor and he was still questioning peasants about military depredations in the parish of Raulhac in September 1588.

return of the hostage, the soldiers were ordered to turn their arquebuses and smaller firearms (*pétrinals*) on the *maréchaussée*. The *vice-bailli* was forced to pay 2 ecus for the return of Desboin, and took no further action against the soldiers.[124] The number of these military hostage-takings is no doubt much greater than the half-dozen incidents specifically identified by the *vice-bailli*, because in his vague reports of "ravages" by soldiers, unspecified "ransoms and excesses" are usually mentioned.

While some abductions by nobles were similar to those committed by soldiers and the holding of peasants in the prisons of châteaus for purposes of extortion occurred,[125] the abductions that caused more concern were those of wealthy or otherwise desirable victims. In several cases, plots by nobles to kidnap the daughters of merchants, bourgeois or prominent and presumably wealthy families of officials either failed or were resolved. The intent of the abductors was in some cases ransom, in others matrimony. The girls in question were young and were sometimes moved to a safe location under the care of a guardian.[126]

The victim of the abduction or her relatives were sometimes willing accomplices. In June 1592 the *vice-bailli* received a complaint from François de Caissacs that his fiancée Jeanne Palisse had been abducted by Pierre de la Tremolière and others. As the story unfolded, it appeared that the widowed mother of the victim had conspired to have her daughter abducted in order to avoid an undesirable marriage to Caissacs.[127]

The most notable case of abduction was that of Mademoiselle de Fontanges by the Sieur Colombier de la Volpiere. With three hundred men, the *vice-bailli* besieged the Château de Pierrefort to demand the return of the girl and to prevent a marriage to Colombier; no priest or

124. *Chevauchées* 1592: 30 November.
125. For example *Chevauchées* 1616: 28 November; 1617: 3 January; 1629: October. Among victims: 7 were women, 10 men; 3 nobles, 5 peasants, 6 bourgeois or merchants, 3 unknown.
126. See M. Cummings, "Elopement, Family, and the Courts: The Crime of Rapt in Early Modern France," *Proceedings of the Fourth Annual Meeting of the Western Society for French History* (1976): 118–25; G. Duby, *The Knight, the Lady and the Priest: the Making of Modern Marriage in Medieval Europe* (New York, 1983), 220; Hanley, "Engendering the State," 10–11; the first chapter of J. F. Traer, *Marriage and the Family in Eighteenth-Century France* (Ithaca, 1980). See also R. V. Coleman, "The Abduction of Women in Barbaric Law," *Florilegeum* 5 (1983): 62–75; the sections in Brundage, *Law, Sex, and Christian Society*, for a discussion of the origins of views of *rapt* (esp. 469–72). Brundage also notes that *raptus* could also refer to the theft of property, *Law, Sex, and Christian Society*, 311n.
127. *Chevauchées* 1592: 22 June; 27 August; 16 September. La Tremoliere was released and the girl Jeanne Palisse was told not to marry without the permission of her family.

legal official who could officiate at a marriage was allowed to enter. The girl was finally retrieved unmarried, but Colombier escaped and, although sentenced contumaciously to death, made other attempts over the next ten years.[128] It was partly cases such as this one that moved the French state in 1556 to forbid clandestine (secret, especially from the parents) marriages, demanding the presence of a priest in 1579, and then forbidding any parish priest to marry those from outside his parish in 1629. The exigencies of family and inheritance, and the power of the state, were to be above those of true love and the church.[129]

Perhaps the strangest abduction occurred in the parish of St. Cernin in 1660 and was the work of neither nobles nor soldiers. One Verdier, a forty-year-old bachelor from the village of Lagarde, was seized by a group of men from his village and taken to a parish priest who married him to Jeanne Jonquieres, a widow of the same village, on the allegation "that she had become pregnant by his works." The villagers said that they had proceeded against Verdier on the authority of a local judge because he was an adult (*major*) without mother or father, had made a verbal promise of marriage to the widow and then made her pregnant. The *vice-bailli* seems to have acquiesced in this community effort to remove two threats with one blow, an attractive widow and a mature and settled bachelor, and to force them to live "decently." Thus a collective restoration of a woman's honor by her fellow villagers.[130]

Abduction varied from a violent elopement or abduction (*rapt*) to a simple means of extortion (*rançon*) both of which were mentioned in royal ordinances of the sixteenth and seventeenth centuries. The former, although the subject of much later romantic excitement expressed in works such as Walter Scott's poem "Lochinvar," was a matter of concern to the church in its tension with the state on the matter of clandestine religious marriages and to families of substance, whose strategies of inheritance and succession it could ruin. Moreover, it demonstrated forcefully the liability of costly and vulnerable female children. But one must not overstate the violence of abduction. In no case is there any

---

128. *Chevauchées* 1607: 10 July–19 September; 25 September; 1614: 17 September; 1616: 8–11 August.

129. Hanley, "Engendering the State," 9–11.

130. *Chevauchées* 1660: 1 September. The case was investigated and then turned back to the local judge. It should be noted here that in the popular mind, widows were often attributed with a particular sexual avidity. See Claverie and Lamaison, *L'Impossible Mariage*, 222–23.

mention of sexual or other abuse; these were yet other dangers particular to "unattached" women.[131]

The vulnerability of "unattached" women is particularly evident in cases of rape, an offense whose study has engendered lively scholarly debates. There are several perspectives, some of which have existed for a long time, and are renewed with added scientific, historical, and statistical sophistication with each new period of controversy.[132] Rises in the frequency of rape have been regarded as the result of the sexual repression and frustration in some environments. Sexual desire in this view is a constant, explosive quantity that must come out in some form, and rape is one of the forms in which it emerges if there are not enough peaceful and consensual outlets such as prostitution, premarital sex, and so on.[133] This "hydraulic" view as Roy Porter has called it, is related to those that stress the biological imperative, the selection pressure that has made men more sexually aggressive than women. Like most crime, rape has also been "medicalized" and is thought by some to be a result of aberrant psychology, whether the latter is in turn environmentally or physiologically induced. In fact, rape has been attributed to most of the causes cited for other crimes.

Perhaps the most interesting recent theories have been those developed from the feminist perspective, which stresses the role of male-dominated societies or patriarchies in engendering rape. As a result of the work done from this perspective, rape has been seen as an increasingly important and revealing feature of such societies. Some would agree with Susan Brownmiller,[134] and indeed, there is currently quite widespread agreement, that rape has had more to do with power relations than with sexual desire per se (although this point of view need not exclude the theories mentioned above). But more than this, it has been argued by degrees that rape is functional to patriarchy, and that it is a typical expression, a

---

131. See especially "Declaration sur . . . le crime de rapt.," Isambert et al., *Recueil général des anciennes lois françaises*, 16:520–24.

132. Sylvana Tomaselli and Ray Porter have edited an interesting collection of essays in *Rape* (New York, 1986), the most pertinent of which for our purposes is Porter's "Rape—Does it have a Historical Meaning?" 216–36. For a brief discussion of some current perspectives on the problem see L. Ellis, *Theories of Rape: Inquiries into the Causes of Sexual Aggression* (New York, 1989). Ellis discusses "Feminist," "Social Learning," and "Evolutionary" theories of rape and then presents a "synthesized" theory.

133. This view of rape as an outlet for sexual desire seems the one most often implied in the sources dealing with early modern rape.

134. S. Brownmiller, *Against Our Will: Men, Women and Rape* (New York, 1975).

common aspect, even a necessity of patriarchal power, an act of which almost all men are capable and to which many are predisposed. Although admitting a place for sexual violence in the construction of the patriarchal edifice, Roy Porter contends that rapists are the "waste of patriarchy . . . not its life-blood but a diseased excrescence," and notes the disapproval with which patriarchal societies in the West have regarded rape.[135] The latter point of view may be defensible, but it minimizes a valuable point in the feminist argument. Rape can be functional without being approved, just as violence in general can. And in the context of honor and the defense of psychic property, it could also be seen as an assertion, a defense, and a violation of claims reinforcing the conception of women as those whose honor was attached to the hearth.[136]

The cases of rape that are documented have some interesting characteristics. All of the victims appear to have been either unmarried women, widows, or girls in the lower reaches of the social order.[137] Soldiers were among the chief culprits (although this may be a distortion natural to the *Chevauchées* because of the *vice-baillis'* role as military policemen) and the victims were often assaulted by more than one man, as often as not, strangers to the area. The only cases where a positive identification of the accused was made were those in which the victim knew her assailants or in which the rapist was caught in the act. In September 1612, for example, Anne Raube, a widow from the Rouergue was assaulted by Raymond Sarguaiot as she traveled alone on a road near the forest of Calvinet. Her assailant was caught "in the act" and imprisoned in the nearby Château de Longueverne after which he was brought to Aurillac for trial and sentenced by the *Présidial* to five years' banishment from the province.[138]

As the commonly used verb *forcer* suggests, rapes were sometimes accompanied by considerable brutality and by other crimes such as looting and arson, especially when soldiers were involved. One of many

---

135. Porter, "Rape," 235.

136. This is not to deny women the considerable domestic power that they could and often did wield, especially in the absence or the infrequent presence of migrant husbands. See Estadieu, "Journal," *Revue de la Haute-Auvergne* (1908): 245.

137. The vulnerability of these groups has been shown for the fifteenth century in southeastern France by Jacques Rossignal, "Prostitution, Youth and Society in the Towns of southeastern France in the Fifteenth Century," in *Deviants and the Abandoned in French Society*, ed. R. Forster and O. Ranum (Baltimore, 1978). The essay was originally published in *Annales E.S.C.* 31, no. 2 (March–April 1976): 289–323.

138. *Chevauchées* 1612: 16 September, 12 October.

reasons for a general lack of evidence on rape may be the possible brutal consequences of prosecution. In May 1609 Agnes Joubert was raped by "several" men in her house in the parish of Roussy. She notified the *vice-bailli* a few days later, but the investigation was postponed for several days because of other business. When the *maréchaussée* returned to her house, they discovered that she had received a punitive beating in the interim.[139]

The court procedure might have deterred some victims from seeking the compensation of royal justice, for a natural course of defense for the accused was to deny the act itself and to denigrate the honor of his alleged victim. The case of Gabrielle Maury against Jean Bordes illustrates some of the hazards and the indignities that could plague the accuser in a rape case.

On 19 July 1664 Gabrielle Maury, a twenty-six-year-old domestic servant appeared with her mother before the *lieutenant criminel* at Murat to say that on the day before Palm Sunday she had been raped ("violentee et forcee") by Jean Bordes, a thirty-year-old servant in the same house. According to Maury, she had been followed into a stable by Bordes who attempted to seduce her "with words and caresses." When she rejected his persistent advances, Bordes said that he would take her by force, to which she replied that he was a drunkard. At this, he punched her in the stomach and knocked her to the floor, where "the said Bordes took his pleasure and deflowered her." Now she found herself pregnant and feeling sick. Bordes had promised several times to marry her "provided that she did not turn him in to the Law."[140]

Arrested a week after the accusation, Bordes was brought to Murat for interrogation.[141] He denied any wrongdoing, stating that he knew Gabrielle Maury only as another servant and that he had had no relations with her "other than honorable ones." As to whether or not he knew of her pregnancy, Bordes said "that as far as he was concerned, he believed her to be an honorable girl and had not thought her pregnant." He also denied any promise of marriage and doubted that any of the accusations against him could be substantiated.[142]

---

139. *Chevauchées* 1609: 5 May, 14 May.

140. *Verbail de grossesse pour Gabrielle Maury*, 19 July 1664, marked "A," Bailliage de Murat, A.D. Cantal 7B 189. All subsequent references to this case are found under the same number.

141. *Verbail de la place de la personne de Jean Bordes*, 26 July 1664 marked "B."

142. *Interrogatoire* Jean Bordes, 27 July 1664. It should be noted here that the diminutive "girl" was not exclusively due to gender, but also to marital status and to social position. Bordes also refers to himself as "boy," in the documents, a designation that would have been socially accurate, and tactically wise, the latter for reasons of deference (he was not about to assert his

The next day a *confrontation* between plaintiff and accused was ordered.[143] Although both parties persisted in their claims, a certain
acrimony crept into the proceedings. Bordes's view of Gabrielle Maury,
the "honorable girl" had changed. When pressed to tell what he knew of
her life and morals, he declared that she had in fact a very bad reputation
and that in the city of Saignes she had been a prostitute. Maury, for her
part, insisted that she had never "known" any man other than Bordes.[144]

After this inconclusive but revealing meeting Gabrielle Maury was
examined by a physician who found none of what were regarded as the
signs of pregnancy: no pressure in the breasts, no swollen vessels, no
secretions of milk.[145] Three months after the alleged offense, Maury was
not yet officially pregnant, and Bordes pressed his advantage, demanding
through a lawyer that he be absolved and released. Gabrielle Maury was
after all a girl of unknown origins as far as he was concerned, who had
roamed far and wide, "a nameless, vagrant, roving person." She had only
been a chambermaid for a year whereas he, Bordes, was well known to
his noble employer for three or four years as a "lad of good repute"
(*garçon bien famé*).

Maury struck back, fighting for her honor. Her origins were well
known to Bordes she insisted; their native villages were close together,
and even if necessity had forced her to become a servant "this was only
in honorable houses and with the reputation of a girl of honor." In her
defense she began to play the game Bordes had begun with his slurs on
her honor. It is interesting that in attacking Bordes, Maury's major
weapon was his *qualité* or status rather than the reprehensibility of his
actions toward her. She said that while she had known no position other
than chambermaid, Bordes was only a "hired man . . . which is the
lowest rank and domestic service." In addition she demanded 100
livres damages.[146]

If the woman was indeed pregnant, time could only hurt Jean Bordes.
On 7 August he broke out of his prison in the *conciergerie* of Murat and
escaped. Two months later Gabrielle Maury was examined by a surgeon

---

manhood before the interrogating judge), and also because it was well known that jurists would
take into account the youth of the accused in moderating the harshness of sentences.

143. *Expedition de Sentence* 28 July 1664, marked "E."

144. *Accaration et confrontation pour Gabrielle Maury contre Jean Bordes*, 28 July 1664,
marked "F."

145. *Rapport du Chirugien*, 23 July 1664, marked "H."

146. *Requeste pour Jean Bordes contre Gabrielle Maury*, no date, marked "J." A subscript states
that a copy of Bordes's request was given to Gabrielle Maury. Her reply is appended to this copy.

and a midwife and finally declared pregnant.[147] She received 60 livres from the confiscated property of Bordes who was to be "pursued incessantly" and tried contumaciously if necessary.[148]

The rape of Gabrielle Maury was clearly different from those committed by soldiers or other strangers. In the rape committed by Bordes a brutal sort of transaction occurred between persons who knew each other and were approximate social equals. The degree of consent involved is a mystery, but one could infer that if Bordes had kept his word, the attack, although no less a rape to our minds, might have been considered little more than a rough courtship. The state was not called upon to intervene until it became clear that Bordes did not intend to redeem the honor of his victim. Her mother had to take the widow's revenge: official justice. Faced with the process of criminalization, Bordes first attempted to deny his actions and then to reduce the moral worth of his accuser. She was a loose woman; further she was aimlessly geographically mobile, a person without domicile, a vagabond. In contrast to his own solidity he tried to make Maury a social outcast: in time, with no honorable explanation for her twenty-six years; in space, with no long-standing connection to a village and parish; and in spirit, a person who ignored or flouted the accepted standards of behavior. She had no honor to violate, he as much as argued, no assets to steal.

The accusation of sexual immorality is interesting, because it was not only a natural defense for Bordes, it was also the most common frame of reference for calculating the honor and worth of women. In affairs of violence we can see the women in the various roles demanded by their situation. But whether they were aggressors, accomplices or, most often, victims, they remained distinctly women and their honor was usually calculated, insulted, and defended in sexual or physical terms. When insulting a woman, one normally began the string of epithets with "putain" (whore or slut), just as men were usually called *coquin* (rascal or knave). This sexual division of honor was one that persisted in most situations including those in which women quarreled with other women, those in which women were allied to a victim, and those in which women were the most convenient and vulnerable victims of violence. Other insults were usually variations on the physical-sexual theme, for example;

---

147. *Autre Rapport pour Gabrielle Maury*, 1 October 1664, marked "A." The report notes a swollen belly, dilated vessels in the breasts and "some secretions" coming from the right breast.
148. *Conclusions du Procur du Roy*, 1 October 1664 marked "Q."

bougresse (buggeress, hussy, bitch, jade), *garce* (tart, trollop, slut, coarse woman), *charron* or *charogne*.[149]

The defense against such verbal assaults was usually that of Gabrielle Maury: one was an honorable woman or girl, a *femme* or a *fille* "d'honneur." This limited meaning of feminine honor was consistent with the usual female role as the victim of violence both criminal and domestic, for even proverbial wisdom implied in a jocular way that the beating of women was part of the normal order of things:

You can always beat her arse: she won't go deaf.

A speechless woman is never beaten.

As the chimes of the Angelus rain
A girl not back in her own domain
Deserves to feel the caress of the cane.[150]

Marriage and the family were the major moral sanctuaries for women. Widows, spinsters, and other women without a family attachment were often in a vulnerable position and, as we have seen, were the likely victims of sexual assault as well as insult and moral suspicion. A seigneurial judge investigating the case of an abandoned infant in the jurisdiction of St. Urcize, for example, ordered that all the single women of childbearing age and all widows undergo a medical examination for signs of recent childbirth.[151] As in Castan's Languedoc, the activities associated with the women's world, of the hearth, were the most honorable, just as marital fidelity, sexual propriety, and modesty were the most important virtues. Attachment to a family through domestic service was

149. A useful reference to such terms is G. C. S. Adams, *Words and Descriptive Terms for Woman and Girl in French and Provençal and Border Dialects*, (Chapel Hill, N.C., 1949); *garce* signified "loose woman." The term that most shocked older patois speakers among my friends from the area of St. Santin Cantales was *charogne*, which they interpreted to mean a loathsome diseased corpse or body. Adams (66) gives it the meaning "hag, scornful shameless woman." Yves Castan (*Honnêteté*) found in the records of eighteenth-century Languedoc that "For a woman, essential honor lay in chastity" (165), and that "the insults directed at women . . . are almost always physical" (170).

150. Raynal, "Au jardin des Adages," *Auvergne*, 122 (1948): 139–40; Abel Beaufrère, "Confidences du Haut Pays," *Le Cobret* (April 1963): 8; (February 1963): 8–10. The brother of Marguerite Toubz took the last adage literally and beat his younger sister badly when she returned home late. The case of assault is in Jurid. Brezons A.D. Cantal 280 (12 June 1649).

151. Juridiction of St. Urcize, 1663 A.C. Cantal 16B 1075.

another possibility, but female domestics were vulnerable to the attentions of their masters and of male servants.[152] Another occupation in
which we find women was that of landlady of an inn or cabaret. While
this was a "hearth-related" position, it also put women into extensive
contact with the outside world. But the often unsavory associations of
innkeepers, as conveyers of information and gossip as well as receivers of
stolen goods and illicit lodgers, were sometimes transferred to women of
the profession, making them less than respectable. Herding and mountain
dairying activities are usually mentioned as male occupations, as are the
seasonal migrations of labor and transhumance, although the young
shepherdess was a common enough figure and, it has been argued by
other scholars of the Massif Central, one often subject to sexual predation
in lonely, isolated pastures.[153]

The role of woman as victim must be mitigated by evidence of feminine
assertiveness, for we do see aggressive women alongside the lists of victims
and accomplices. The murder of Pierre Cassans and other cases of
violence by women are some examples. Certainly women did not always
draw back when violence threatened. They assisted their husbands and
families, defended themselves and often suffered violent blows intended
for the men of the family, as well as for themselves. Their behavior in
instances of violence was not unlike that of men. A violent quarrel in
the Marmanhac area, for example, shows two village women exchanging
insults over a garden wall and finally coming to blows that ended with
one woman falling under the hail of stones.[154]

152. Jacques Depauw, "Illicit Sexual Activity in 18th-Century Nantes," in *Family and Society*,
ed. Forster and Ranum, (Baltimore, 1976), 145–91. See also the comments in O. Hufton, *The
Poor of Eighteenth-Century France*. Castan, writing of the role of women concluded that their
economic contributions to the family were ignored: "They were never thanked for their help,
but only for their conjugal and maternal virtue" (*Honnêteté*, 164). Le Roy Ladurie's discussion
of the problems of female laborers in *Paysans de Languedoc*, part 2, and Mousnier's analysis of
the status of wives (for example, *Institutions*, 67, 86–87) indicate a steady degradation of the
position of women in the "outside world" during the sixteenth and seventeenth centuries. It is
interesting to compare the rigidity of the seventeenth century with the relative freedom allowed
the wives and women in E. Le Roy Ladurie's *Montaillou* four centuries earlier.

153. See the brutal expectations of girls and boys who guarded the sheep, and of girls from
the lower orders in general, in Claverie and Lamaison, *L'Impossible Mariage*, 213–46.

154. Marguerite d'Allair v. Merille Foulhade, Juridiction Sedaiges, A.D. Cantal 16B 1078.
Julius Ruff, in his *Crime, Justice and Public Order*, for example, found that 15.5% of all defendants
(as against 21.7% of victims) in cases of physical and verbal violence, were women. Gregory
Hanlon, during the same period as that of our study, found a wide participation by women in
the violent encounters that took place in two towns in Aquitaine, "Les Rituels de l'agression,"
259–63. Note here that except in cases of arson, women did not usually use the weapons

One feature of the society and economy of the Haute Auvergne that may have countered the subservient "service" role of women was the traditional phenomenon of seasonal and long-term migrations of labour. While the impact of these migrations has never successfully been quantitatively assessed, where they occurred they were likely to affect the roles of women. The migrations were predominantly masculine and the migrants were usually married, sometimes leaving all property to their wives in case they were not able to return home. Women, children, and the aged in some communities were left to do at least the winter chores, if not much of the work altogether.[155] Whether or not this tendency toward feminine management of the family business led to a greater assertiveness by women in the Haute Auvergne is difficult to say, but it is certainly worth noting. Evidence of aggressive women considered however, the overwhelming weight of evidence from police records seldom shows them in the principal aggressive roles.

Even taking into account the above exceptions, the ideal of womanhood was thus a difficult model for ordinary women to follow, in the flux of economic and social circumstances. The physical boundaries of domesticity and the moral and physical barrier of chastity could be breached by economic necessity. Gabrielle Maury, the rape victim described above, used the second line of defense in both sorts of breach: she was a servant by necessity, but she was a good servant in a good house; she finally yielded to the importunate male, but he had at least been made to promise wedlock. (Yves Castan wrote the formula followed in such cases: "I am not dishonored, since I didn't give in until the promise of marriage.") Women, it is true, often enjoyed greater leniency under the law on account of what jurists saw as their "frailty" and "inferiority"; but this condescension was also reflected in their civil

---

designed by men and commonly carried for defense; rather, they made use of whatever was at hand.

155. The Intendant Lefèvre d'Ormesson estimated the number of migrants at five to six thousand; *Mémoire sur l'état de la généralité de Riom en 1697*, 174–75. The *Revue de la Haute-Auvergne* contains several articles on this phenomenon. The most useful are M. Trillat, "L'Émigration de la Haute-Auvergne en Espagne du XVIIIe aux XXe siècle," *Revue de la Haute-Auvergne* (1954–55): 257–94; L Bourrachot, "Les Immigrants saisonniers auvergnats en Haut Agenais," ibid. (1960), 173–80; M. Leymairie, "Emigration et structure sociale en Haute-Auvergne a la fin du XVIIIe siècle," ibid. (1956–57): 296–315. Louis Estadieu, a tax official in the mid-eighteenth century remarked that in several areas more than half of the men regularly emigrated to Spain, customarily leaving women and servants in charge of property. In the village of Barriac, he wrote, two-thirds of the men went to Spain every year. *Journal* in *Revue de la Haute-Auvergne* (1908): 245.

subservience to husbands, who usually controlled property and were virtually sovereign judges of their own domestic jurisdiction in the custom of the Haute Auvergne. Like the women of Normandy and other provinces, Auvergnates, should they assert themselves unduly, could expect physical "correction" from their husbands. No matter how fiercely women might fight among themselves, a woman's quarrel was a paltry thing. No matter how hard or honestly women might work, their contribution and their virtue lay for the most part within the prescribed domestic and sexual boundaries. Perhaps these attitudes explain more than anything else, the "invisibility," in police records of women, whose affairs were regulated largely within a restricted sphere.[156] The woman who left this sphere was a "disorderly" creature, and could be marginalized; those, like widows, who could not be fully integrated into it, clung fiercely to whatever marks of integration and protection they could claim. For outside the margins of the domestic rural existence, were those viewed constantly as threats to it: vagabonds and thieves.

Thieves, Fairs, and Vagabonds

Given the preoccupation of the maréchaussée with highways, commerce, and fairs, along with the competence of vice-baillis to try summarily the crimes of vagabonds, it is not surprising that theft was among the most common offenses reported in the Chevauchées. In most of the 246 cases of theft reportred, victims could not resort to out-of-court financial settlements; therefore it was natural that robberies were reported to the authorities and that robbers were vigorously pursued.

The forms of theft reported varied widely in style and purpose. Sneak thieves, cutpurses, pickpockets, bands of armed highway brigands and

---

156. Quoted words from Castan, Honnêtété, 165. See also Castan's comments on the "territories of the sexes" beginning in ibid., 174 and various comments on women's quarrels, 170–74. The reduced status of women in matters of property is commented on by Mousnier, Institutions, in discussions of women, dowries, wives, widows, and marriage. The light regard of the law toward women's offenses was naturally exploited by criminals. In the Chevauchées, a leader of the "Bohemians" Robert Guielmus, sent two women to pick a lock and steal some linens. The women enjoyed the expected impunity but their leader had his beard shaved and was beaten and banished. See Castan, Honnêtété, on the criminal division of labor that often took advantage of the legal status of women. O. Hufton, The Poor of Eighteenth-Century France, also remarks on this phenomenon in the section "The Crime of the Poor."

"rustlers" all appear to have troubled the Haute Auvergne. When the *vice-baillis* identified the objects stolen, these were varied as well: money, animals, food, and furnishings of various sorts. However, the exact objects of theft were not always reported; and furthermore, the act of theft itself was not always clear. Men were arrested as cutpurses (*coupeurs de bourse*) or "robbers" (*voleurs*) but it was not always stated whether the arrest was made on account of a specific recent theft or because of a history of thievery.

If we include the activities of pickpockets and cutpurses, money was among the most frequent objects of theft, mentioned specifically in 51 cases; it was probably also the goal of many robberies whose object was not specified. In any event, as the most convenient to handle and most desirable form of wealth in a cash-poor economy like that of the Haute Auvergne, money was naturally sought by thieves.

But there is also some truth to the expression "l'occasion fait le larron" (opportunity makes the thief). For the most frequently specified object of theft in the *Chevauchées*, mentioned in 87 cases, was livestock. In a province whose central mountain pastures alone had a capacity of some 20,000–30,000 head of cattle, such a trend is to be expected. The nature of the animals stolen also conforms, although less closely, to expectations. Most of the thefts (55%) were of bovines (*vache, boeuf, betail*); 40% were of horses and mules, and the remaining 5% were of sheep.[157] The high proportion of horses and mules is probably accounted for partly by the fact that they could be ridden and moved more quickly and hence were more immediately useful and rapidly disposed of than cattle or sheep. Moreover, the Haute Auvergne was celebrated as a source of fine horseflesh. Other sorts of dairy and agricultural products were also taken in a handful of cases that included thefts of cheese, grain, honey, bread, other food, linen, and other household furnishings.

There is no particular period distinguished by an absence or an abundance of thefts; nor was there any season of theft, although the period between November and January seems to have been somewhat of a "dead" season for thieves.[158] If the *vice-bailli* troubled to mention the time, it was usually night. Specific locations mentioned most frequently

157. Forty-eight cases involved cattle; 35, horses and mules; 4, sheep.
158. About 16% of thefts took place during the months of November, December, and January (35 of 214 cases). For a related discussion, see D. Martin, "Elevage et délinquance en Auvergne au XVIIIe siècle," in his *Elevage et la vie pastorale dans les montagnes de l'Europe: Colloque international* (Clermont-Ferrand, 1984).

were fairs, highways (especially near wooded areas), barns, houses, and fields. Very seldom were thefts from mountain pastures reported. Horses and cattle appear to have been stolen from barns, common pastures, and nearby enclosures.[159]

The incidence of violence in cases of theft is difficult to ascertain, but it was probably greater than the *Chevauchées* indicate.[160] Groups of experienced robbers were usually said to have been guilty of "vols et plusieurs autres excès," but injuries were not specified. And Auvergnats did not give up their property without a fight. A *laboureur* returning home on the road from Aurillac one February night struggled manfully with two thieves who finally beat him to the ground with sticks and stole his loaf of brown bread.[161] Thieves and robbers themselves were often well prepared for violence. The *vice-bailli* Jean Lacarrière surprised the "notorious robber" (*diffamé voleur*) Pierre Escarvachierès and his band of brigands as they lay in wait for passing victims, the fuses of their guns burning, ready for action.[162] Experienced robbers also put up a vigorous resistance when they had the chance to do so. Jean Longuecamp, another "diffamé voleur," was strolling the grounds at a fair in Salers in 1593 when he was spotted by men of the *maréchaussée*. As soon as he saw the *archers*, Longuecamp, favored by the press of the crowds and cattle, leaped over a wall and hid in a field beside the fairgrounds. The *maréchaussée* took up the chase on foot and when they reached their quarry, he stood and faced them, "his naked sword in his hand" (*son espée nue dans la main*). Somehow Longuecamp managed to hold them off; even after several thrusts to the arms and thighs, he ignored the "commands of justice," leaped over a precipice, and escaped into a nearby wood.[163] The *archers* of the *maréchaussée* did not deal lightly with robbers who resisted; for example, two "diffamé voleurs" were shot dead in October 1617 when cornered in a village near the highway.[164]

The surveillance of theft and thieves seems to have been haphazard. The *maréchaussée* generally responded to reports of theft or robber-bands;

159. Highways were mentioned in 25 cases; fairs in 35; barns and houses in 19; woods in 11; montagnes and pastures in seven.
160. Of 246 cases, 17 involved violence according to the *Chevauchées*.
161. *Chevauchées* 1587: 27 February.
162. *Chevauchées* 1617: 7 October.
163. *Chevauchées* 1617: 7 October.
164. Henri Durif, *Les Foires d'Aurillac* (Aurillac, 1873). The present importance of the fair on La St. Martin (November) was established in the eighteenth century.

but those who left the borders of Haute Auvergne were not usually pursued and there was no coordination amongst provinces.

Overall, theft in the Haute Auvergne was at least as likely to be stealthy as it was to be violent. Such property as there was, livestock, cheese, food, and rather spare furnishings, was closely guarded and Auvergnats were in the habit of defending or hiding it. In a society that put a high priority on "honor" and property, and where the protection of one was the defense of the other, the violation of property was a dangerous offense. However, the greatest violence pertaining to theft was, as we shall see in Chapter 4, the judicial violence used in the punishment of thieves and vagrants.

One of the magnets for both was the fair, a place of sociability, poverty, and plenty, where the destitute and the comfortable rubbed shoulders. At the market fair, acquaintances, enemies, friends, and strangers, from different parishes and even different provinces met face to face, drank, talked, and walked home on the evening roads. Whether drunk or not, many who had come a little distance felt the intoxication, daring, and release of "getting away" from the mental and physical circumscriptions of their communities.[165] This sense of psychological release and the freedom of space and movement did not, however, remove the vigilance of each person regarding psychic property. If anything, there was a combination of enhanced self-consciousness and claims to honor, along with a greatly increased number of occasions for confrontations with others. The potential for trouble, as the *archers* of the *maréchaussée* well knew, was boundless.[166]

The scale of this police duty was vast. Market fairs were the most frequent expression of economic and commercial life in the *Chevauchées*, and a constant preoccupation of the *maréchaussée*. Between 1587 and 1664 the *vice-baillis* reported 722 fair patrols. The frequency of patrols varied from a low of zero during some of the years of religious war to a high of 35 in 1655. The *vice-baillis* gave various standard reasons for this preoccupation: "to prevent robberies"; "to be on guard against vagabonds and evil-doers"; and above all, "to facilitate commerce." The numbers

---

165. Two fairly well known contemporary examples of the effects of this release from home constraints are, as might be expected in the age of Freud, sexual: the sex displays frequented by respectable Japanese men, and the remarkable activities of "exotic" dancers and male fairgoers at some rural American fairs.

166. The continued importance of the fair in the Massif Central is attested to by Claverie and Lamaison, *L'Impossible Mariage*, 250–56.

and importance of the fairs patrolled naturally followed the rhythms of transhumance, with the greatest frequency occuring in spring (April–June) and in October, the times when cattle were to be taken to summer pastures and when they returned from the mountains. Aurillac, the strongest center of economic life, held the most important fairs, particularly those near the end of May (Saint Urbain) and mid-October (Saint Géraud).

An economic necessity, fairs were also a source of unease to the forces of order. The money and the merchandise naturally attracted criminals, and the relatively large concentrations of people meant that, in addition to the arms many travelers carried, there was the uncontrollable weapon of the crowd. Over the years 117 offenses and arrests were reported by the *vice-baillis* as a result of fair patrols. Most were crimes relating to vagrancy and petty theft, but there were also affairs of violence or quarrels, the arrest of deserters, counterfeiters, and others.[167]

The assembled crowds and the exchange of goods between parsimonious Auvergnats and others sometimes erupted into violence. At the fair in Palleyrols, an irate sharecropper administered a beating to a goldsmith.[168] In Apchon, two merchants quarreled violently over the prices of cattle.[169] A "young man" from Aurillac wounded a peasant with his sword at the fall fair in Quezac in 1647.[170] Xenophobic peasants assembled at the fair in La Bastide to do battle with visitors from Quercy; groups from two neighboring parishes also assembled to fight at the fair in Quezac.[171]

While the *vice-baillis* frequently wrote that they were watching the fairs for counterfeit money, only two cases out of seven during the period arose at fairs. In one instance the accused escaped the *maréchaussée* completely.[172] In the other a man from Basse Auvergne was arrested in St. Flour for using in trade a gold coin marked with the fleur-de-lis, the like of which nobody had seen before in the region. He was held in prison for two months before the *vice-bailli* received information that the

167. The count from fairs: 73 vagabonds (35 with theft); 23 cases of violence or quarrels; 7 complaints of highway robbery; 2 of passing counterfeit money, 1 of carrying a pistol; 2 deserters; 1 abduction; in 8 other cases, the "crimes" were not specified.
168. *Chevauchées* 1654: 1 June.
169. Ibid., 9 September.
170. *Chevauchées* 1647: 22 October.
171. *Chevauchées* 1655: 10 May.
172. *Chevauchées* 1630: 5 May.

same coin was in use throughout Italy, Flanders, and other places.[173] The case supports the contention of Pierre Goubert, that the confusion of coinage during the Ancien Régime was so great as to permit only two men in a hundred the expertise to deal with money.[174] In chronically impoverished and isolated areas like the Haute Auvergne such knowledge was attained slowly and with great difficulty.

As far as the police were concerned, however, the greatest attention was usually reserved for those who had no money. Fairs were the scene of most arrests for vagrancy in the Chevauchées, 73 out of 81 vagabonds arrested during the period. Considering that vagabonds were the "quarry" (gibier) of the vice-baillis, the total is not impressive. But then the Haute Auvergne, with its hostile climate, difficult roads, and relatively sparse population, was not the sort of place one would expect to be a chosen destination of poor travelers.

That these few would come to fairs is understandable; for fairs were displays of property in its most portable forms: food, jewelry, weapons, utensils, and above all, money. The fairs at Aurillac, especially attractive, account for over half the arrests; and the largest numbers of arrests occurred during October, May, and June, following the periods of greatest activity in the commercial livestock and the grain-growing economies.[175]

Thirty-five of the vagabonds arrested were accused of being cutpurses. Some were arrested in the act while others were caught with the evidence. Jehan Castel of Gascony was found "putting his hand into a peasant's pocket."[176] Jean Sirgan from Languedoc was charged with taking the purse of Gilles Cassan, sharecropper for a bourgeois of Aurillac.[177] At the spring fair in Aurillac Jean Doyde of Limousin was captured with a purse containing eight livres.[178] A bourgeois of Aurillac lost his purse to a thief from Quercy at the St. Géraud fair in 1631.[179]

The benefit of the doubt seldom went to vagabonds. For example, Paul Lacarrière arrested three men at the St. Géraud fair in 1664 because they looked as if they were going to cut the purses of merchants.[180] Accusations of vagabondage itself also seem to have been based on rather vague

173. Chevauchées 1631: 22 May.
174. P. Goubert, Ancien Régime, 64.
175. Thirty-eight of 73 (52%) of vagrants were arrested at Aurillac.
176. Chevauchées 1654: 11 June.
177. Chevauchées 1611: 24 May.
178. Chevauchées 1629: 31 May.
179. Chevauchées 1631: 13 October.
180. Chevauchées 1664: 14 October.

criteria. If one was far away from home, with no money, merchandise, or discernible business at the fair, one could be considered vagrant. Indeed the geographic origins of vagabonds generally show them to have been native to other areas, but usually those bordering the Haute Auvergne: Basse Auvergne, Quercy, Rouergue, Limousin, and Lyonnais; one adventurous soul had come from Bordeaux. In any event, they were foreign enough to be considered intrusive and threatening strangers.[181]

Outside of fairs, vagabonds were probably not easy to recognize among the seasonal migrants and the humbler sorts of peddlers who traveled the roads during the spring and fall. Perhaps for that reason the eight cases of vagrancy that occurred away from fairs all involved more easily recognizable "Egyptiens" and "Boyemiens." Marcellin Boudet remarks on these cases and paints a portrait of "nomadic tribes of Slavs or other Orientals, with long, greasy black hair, swarthy complexions, living in tents and clad in sordid rags"—capable, of course, of unspeakable atrocities.[182] Boudet's remarks are probably more revealing of late nineteenth-century racial and ethnic attitudes than of seventeenth-century hygiene and coiffure. One wonders if gypsy hair could have been greasier than that of other "average" Europeans. Unfortunately the reports of the *maréchaussée* tell us neither the length nor the greasiness of gypsies' hair; nor do they give us any other exotic details. The *vice-bailli* and the locals indeed thought their presence alarming; but nothing more is said of their origins and they were accused of only two thefts. One company of "supposed families of Egyptians" lodged near Salers in 1612, were suspected of being mercenary thugs for hire; they moved out only after some resistance and the arrest of their leader Guielmus Robbert.[183] Two bands, also of "Egyptians," camping near the eastern and western borders of the province, were driven by the *maréchaussée* into Limousin and Gévaudan

---

181. Of 50 vagabonds for whom places of origin were given, Basse Auvergne was the home of 11; Quercy, 7; Haute Auvergne, 6; Limousin, 5; Rouergue, 5; Lyon, 4; Angoulême, 3; Albigoix, 2; Languedoc, 2; Gascogne, 1; Poitu, 1; Bordelais, 1; Brie, 1; Périgord, 1. On vagabonds, see also I. Cameron, *Crime and Repression*, 164–73; J. P. Gutton, *La Société et les pauvres: L'Exemple de la généralité de Lyon, 1534–1789*, (Paris, 1971); O. Hufton, *The Poor of Eighteenth-Century France*. Veronique Bucheron, in "La montée de flot des errants de 1760 à 1789 dans la généralité d'Alençon," *Annales de Normandie* (1971): 55–86, discovered that over half the vagrants in the *généralité* were native to it; and Nicole Castan, in "La justice expéditive," *Annales E.S.C.* 31, no. 2 (March–April 1976): 331–61, discovered that more than 76 of vagrants judged at Orléans came from areas that were close by.

182. Boudet, *Documents*, 63–65.

183. *Chevauchées* 1612: 12 February.

in September 1615.[184] In the autumn of 1630, a band stopping on the eastern border was called both "Egyptien" and "Boyemien." In 1647, 1654, and 1660 there were also reports of Bohemians and gypsies. In each case, the usual object of the *vice-bailli* was to drive them out of his jurisdiction.[185]

Vagabonds and gypsies, even to the relatively mobile population of the Haute Auvergne, were a threat. If not thieves, they were regarded as likely to become thieves, distrusted as much for what they might do as for what they had done. The range of most vagrants' travel was probably limited by cultural and linguistic boundaries more than any other factor. Nonetheless, even in a country of strangers, they could understand and make themselves understood.[186]

Perspectives on Crime

We cannot know the level of violence in the Haute Auvergne during our period. The *maréchaussée* on the average investigated four or five homicides every year, a half-dozen serious assaults and as many robberies; they kept an eye on passing troops and remained ever vigilant for signs of resistance to royal authority, unruly crowds, and vagabonds. No matter how frequent their patrols and investigations, the *archers* could not know of the strife in countless hamlets, fields, woods, and houses of the mountains. Nor would the local officials of justice, or the locals, necessarily have wanted them to know.

The *vice-baillis* give us a view, as it were, from the highway; but it is a view nonetheless. We can see that much of their time was spent in containing violence and the threat of violence. Violence was more common in the *Chevauchées* than theft, although theft was probably more likely to have been reported. Of violent acts homicides were surprisingly numerous by comparison with assaults. This proportion may reflect a tendency by the *maréchaussée* to respond only to serious violence; or it may be due to a tradition of out-of-court settlements for assault. At any rate it seems that some inhabitants of the mountains demonstrated a predisposition to violence.

When we leave the highway and take a closer look by means of the

184. *Chevauchées* 1615: 13, 25 September.
185. *Chevauchées* 1647: 22 May, 16 July; 1654: 19 June; 1660: 26 May.
186. N. Castan, "La justice expéditive."

records of the criminal courts, we can catch glimpses of violence in more detail. Living close together and of necessity sharing in each other's lives, the rural inhabitants of Haute Auvergne were alert and highly sensitive to any challenge that threatened the mental and material boundaries by which their lives were ordered. One must defend a necessary fund of self-esteem and be protected by a good reputation just as one defended the borders of real property. There was a body of psychic property to protect. When a person felt wronged or challenged, the most common threat was the threat of death: "you will pay for it." The payment was made in blood, in humiliation, in loss, whose necessary opponents were satisfaction, an enrichment of the blood, triumph, profit.

In many cases one can observe an internal pattern of provocation and riposte, the riposte being a violent informal "justice" administered by the injured party. When this punishment was disproportionate to the provocation or when serious violence occurred and blood began to flow, the agencies of official justice were brought into play. What had hitherto been a private matter became official and the violence of the state was brought to bear. The riposte, the informal justice, became crime. At this point the researcher enters, probably seeing only the peaks in a mountain landscape of crime or a single stage in an economy of violence: the court case. Sometimes the litigation itself acted as a provocation in a continuing cycle of vengeance. This pattern is not, of course, universally applicable. The victim of the initial offense might immediately turn to official justice for satisfaction, rejecting the option of a violent riposte. Or violence itself might be used in an attempt to prevent the discovery of theft or other crimes.

Incidents of violence were influenced by various factors. Alcohol could release one from the normal discretion. A compulsion to enhance one's own worth or, in a complementary way to reduce the worth of another might then find offensive expression in an insult or challenge. Similarly alcohol might exaggerate the offense taken and the riposte would be disproportionate to the provocation. Travel, which released one from the boundaries and constraints of a community was another sort of intoxicant that could lead to violence, a tendency often seen in the behavior of billeted soldiers.

The crowded months of summer, the festive release of holidays and gatherings of various sorts, in short, places of sociability, provided milieus for explosions of violence, spontaneous and public. In other cases a provocation occurred or a temptation presented itself but violence was deferred to a more suitable time and place. Duels proper were a prear-ranged, more ritual form of this "justice." But less formal duels, insults, challenges and combat, were occurring constantly at all levels among sensitive and violent men and women.

In the overview of particular crimes, we have ignored many of the social boundaries that formed a crucial part of the Auvergnat mentality. The subjects of weapons and abduction gave rise to a few comments on social differences. In our discussion of rape we examined a most basic division, the difference between men and women, a physical difference reinforced by social attitudes. But *qualité* or social identity further in-formed the dimensions of honor, the extent and nature of psychic property and their defense. In order to draw a fuller portrait, the documents must therefore now be allowed to describe some social charac-teristics of violence.

4 Violence and the Social Order

You didn't have the will to kill this rascal, you poltroons![1]
—Noble of Salers to his lackeys, who had refused to attack a notary

Violence and the threat of violence dominated the reports of crime in the Haute Auvergne. But who was committing these violent acts, and to whom? What can the documents of the courts and the *maréchaussée* tell us about the social characteristics and attitudes of violent men and their victims? What lines of solidarity and social divisions does the evidence describe? It is not the purpose here to provide a complete description of the social hierarchies of the Haute Auvergne. But having inspected some common behavioral boundaries of honor, sex, and property, it should be useful now to press on and examine the incidence and the style of violence within and between various social groups.

We shall first look at the problem of criminal violence within each of the three "estates" and between the members of different social groups. Having observed some of the geographical barriers, and the mental and physical enclosures within which an economy of violence seems to have held sway, we can turn to the boundaries of *qualité* or status and the limits of the rural community itself. In the last chapter, we touched only briefly on the crime of *rébellion*. Toward the end of this chapter, we shall

---

1. The French word here is *poltron* (poltroon), which during the period was applied in both French and English to a man who showed cowardice, baseness, and idleness. The punctuation is mine.

examine some forms of collective violence: as a riposte to the violation of forbidden territory; and as another example of the social alignments revealed by violence.

The Nobility

The violent and predatory behavior of the Auvergnat nobility, their bastards, and their lackeys is a phenomenon noted by seventeenth-century observers and recent scholarship alike. The Intendant Mesgrigny, who wrote in 1637 that the province abounded in *gentilshommes* more than any other in France, complained of the oppressive cruelty of seigneurs toward their peasants;[2] and the evidence assembled for the Grands Jours d'Auvergne of 1665 bears witness to the most spectacular and legendary examples of noble violence. Although his cultivated irony never failed him, the memoirist Fléchier was clearly shocked by the wantonness of mountain nobles such as Gaspard d'Espinchal, who was reputed to have poisoned his own wife, and castrated her manservant, having previously performed the same surgery on one of his own sons.[3] (The *greffier* Dongois felt moved by the same crimes to comment: "There would be enough to fill a book with the crimes of this man, one of the wickedest this earth has ever borne.")[4]

Commenting on the case of an impoverished noble murderer, Fléchier noted that the title of nobility "has long been a title of impunity for criminals" and that this particular nobleman, being without property, "didn't think himself able to prove his nobility except by some crime." While Fléchier's humble origins may have influenced his attitude, he nonetheless saw in the Auvergne a noble savagery unequaled elsewhere in France.[5]

2. Mesgrigny, *Relation de l'état de la province d'Auvergne en 1637* (Clermont-Ferrand, 1842), 183–84. For the problem of noble bastards, see Claude Grimmer, "Les bâtards de la noblesse auvergnate," *XVIIe Siècle* 29, no. 4 (1977): 35–48.

3. Espirit Fléchier, *Mémoires sur les Grands Jours d'Auvergne en 1665*, ed. A. Cheruel (Paris, 1865), 244–58. Although these stories were never proven, d'Espinchal was convicted of several murders and the mysterious disappearance of his manservant remains unsolved.

4. Dongois, *Registres*, Saturday A.M., 23 January 1966.

5. Fléchier, *Mémoires*, 213. Espirit Fléchier, the son of a merchant, entered the priesthood and became famous for his preaching, especially his funeral orations. In 1687, he became bishop of Nîmes. Arlette Lebigre, *Les Grands Jours d'Auvergne*, confirms my impression of the Auvergnat nobility, although she makes no reference to the *Chevauchées*, relying heavily on Dongois and Fléchier.

The *Chevauchées* depict the *maréchaussée* attempting rather ineffec-
tively to deal with a steady stream of violent feuds between noble families,
quarrels whose source or provocation might be honor, politics, or property, but as often as not had been forgotten, or unreported, but not
forgiven. If one examines cases of assault and homicide alone, more than
21% of the accused can be identified as nobles, seigneurs, and noble
bastards; and if one adds abduction and illicit armed assembly for noble
feuds (*querelles*), the proportions rise to more than 25%. Thus the
Chevauchées can give us some idea at least of the "dark figure" of
noble violence.

Each noble dispute had its own peculiar characteristics, but the
behavior of the fractious provincial nobility evinced a certain similarity
of style and spirit. In the case of the Sieur de Morèze, for example, the
issue was property, the château and *seigneurie* of Marmiesse; but the
actions of Morèze and his followers were typical of those taken by nobles
in other disputes. The property in question had been a fertile source of
legal disputes, and had already changed hands twice for the payment of
creditors when Morèze bought it in 1604. Unable to satisfy the vendor,
Morèze was himself forced out of the château a few years later, and the
struggle for control over the following fifteen years became violent and
troublesome enough to interest the *vice-bailli*. Morèze, after the fashion
of highland noblemen, committed his household and its hangers-on to
the enterprise of administering his own justice; his sons and his bastard,
along with various lackeys, took to beating and harassing the tenants and
allies of his enemy. Finally, in 1617, he assembled a substantial group of
armed men and seized the château by force, committing various outrages
on the incumbent farmer and his household. The complaints against this
gentleman in the spring and summer of the year could not be ignored;
and with Morèze in defiant command of the château, vice-bailli Jacques
Lacarrière was forced to act. But the six *archers* sent in the "name of the
king's justice" were contemptuously repulsed and Morèze continued to
enjoy his liberties at the expense of the local villagers.[6]

Such quarrels, seizures of noble houses, and "encounters" between

6. *Chevauchées* 1617: 24 April, May, 20, August 22, October. An account of the property
transaction and the dispute is also given in Deribier du Châtelet, *Dictionnaire* 5:263. Boudet,
Documents, 71n., also gives details of the legal dispute. The year 1617 was a particularly violent
one for nobles. See *Chevauchées* 1617: 20 June; 1 July; 4 August; 6 August; 2 October. The
figures from the *Chevauchées* record 109 (21.2%) nobles/seigneurs accused of assault and
homicide of a total of 515 accused, 6 accused of abduction (out of 17 cases) and 39 of 42
assemblées were led by nobles or groups of nobles. (See Appendix 1.)

nobles were not unusual, and nobles were usually the culprits in question when the *vice-baillis* investigated "illicit assemblies." The habits of *gentils-hommes* made noble violence a collective affair. They often traveled with groups of armed retainers, carried on their vendettas, and collected or extorted dues in groups. Their natural recourse for settling a dispute was private and their lackeys often enjoyed the same sort of freedom from community obligation as soldiers. Disputes in which nobles were involved naturally extended to family, servants, and sometimes to others associated with the noble patrimony, as well as some dubious characters hired to participate in an affray. Companies of twenty-five or thirty men were not unusual in noble disputes. For a feud with the Baron de Rossilhe, the Sieur de Fraisse gathered together his brother-in-law, his valet, several peasants from the area, and a score of others. The *vice-bailli* was especially concerned with this affair because "most of the accused were persons without domicile or abode."[7]

This group activity was to some extent a reflection of extensive noble households, which included relatives, domestic servants and, in a large household, various officers and armed retainers. The Wars of Religion may have impoverished some noble families but they certainly had done nothing to harm the tradition of noble violence in the Haute Auvergne; if anything, the wars strengthened the tradition of the extended household. While the analysis does not completely apply, one is put in mind of Peter Laslett's pre-industrial one-class society with its series of connected families and its large gentry households dominating the community. Lawrence Stone has also described the patterns of kinship among the English aristocracy, noting the decline in the sixteenth century of the vendetta, which pitted one clan against another, and under which families and households could be held responsible for the offenses of individual members. As Stone points out, this tradition of the "collective penal responsibility of the clan" persisted in France long after it had vanished in England.[8] As for the mountain nobility whose behavior we are discussing, their archaic regime cherished such customs. Hence the noble plea in 1614 for a lenient royal view of accidental violent "encounters." While we have seen that royal government took an

7. *Chevauchées*, 1654: 6 April. Other examples in *Chevauchées* 1616: 8 December; 1624: 30 May.

8. P. Laslett, *The World We Have Lost* (London, 1971) chaps. 2 and 3. L. Stone, *The Family, Sex and Marriage in England, 1500–1800* (London, 1977), 93–102, 125–26; *The Crisis of the Aristocracy* (Oxford, 1965), 228–29.

increasingly dim view of armed retainers during the seventeenth century, it must be remembered too that as recently as 1561, a royal ordinance had exempted the servants of nobles from prohibitions against carrying weapons. The attempt to assert royal power in the early seventeenth century was not particularly successful against the nobles of the Haute Auvergne, who followed an older tradition, and Richelieu's campaign to reduce the number of fortified châteaus fell mainly upon the Basse Auvergne.[9]

While it is true that *gentilshommes* were often the victims of attacks by rival families, generally they played the role of aggressor more often than that of victim. This disproportion suggests that there was considerable violence by nobles against non-nobles. We have already seen some cases of abduction and assault by nobles of those socially beneath them. Although our documents sometimes name nobles among the accused, they seldom contain complaints by commoners (*roturiers*) against nobles, unless the complaint was made by a protective seigneur on behalf of a tenant who had been a victim of the enmity between noble families.[10]

Gentilshommes often administered their own rough "justice" for an offense and they clearly held a more extensive sense of their own jurisdiction both socially and geographically, in this administration of vengeance. While lesser men could punish with impunity members of their own families and occasionally some members of their community, *gentilshommes* clearly enjoyed a wider competence that affected the members of all groups.

The most obvious level of jurisdiction was that of the seigneurs who had control of seigneurial high justice (*hautes justices seigneuriales*), whose courts could try criminal offenses; and there are scattered examples of these trials in criminal justice archives, involving for the most part thefts, assaults, insults, and other local disputes.[11] The Grands Jours d'Auvergne

9. Ordinance of August 1561: "It is prohibited to bear arms for all persons with the exception of military personnel, nobles and their servants." See also Manry, ed., *Histoire de l'Auvergne*, 290–91.

10. For example, see the case of the Sieur du Fayet v. Pierre Estienne Thoury, 2 December 1643, Bailliage of Salers, A.D. Cantal 14B 227. Nobles accounted for 13% of the victims of assault and homicide, as against 21.2% of aggressors or accused.

11. Examples: A theft of wood 1620, Juridiction de Lagarde, A.D. Cantal 16B 611; an accusation of seduction of a virgin, 1631, Juridiction de Saillans, A.D. Cantal, 16B 1010; a horse theft, 1638, Juridiction de Sedaiges, A.D. Cantal 16B 1098; a quarrel between women, ibid.; excesses by soldiers, 1622 Juridiction de Ruynes A.D. Cantal 16B 992; a beating, 1657 Juridiction de la Bessertte, A.D. Cantal 16B 212; a murder, 1615, Seigneur d'Anterroche, A.D. Cantal 16B 23; an assault and wounding, Juridiction du Seigneur de Lignerac A.D. Cantal 16B 670.

revealed more clearly that the seigneurial courts were sometimes used to exact vengeance. But the most common abuse of seigneurial justice in the Auvergne tells us more of avarice than of violence. Feudal obligations that had no basis in customary law were enforced through the courts, which fined the accused; in the most outrageous cases, the courts were simply a sure means of making money. For example, Charles de Montvalat not only imposed his own systems of weights and measures, he had an ingenious set of offenses through which he could extract fines at will: 460 livres for being found in a fight and 120 livres for separating those who fought; a fine for refusing to marry a girl, a tax for marrying, as well as a lucrative fine for "having made a girl pregnant" (30–200 livres).[12]

But seigneurial justice was only a metaphor for the sort of psychic property possessed by the nobility and marked at times by violence, a feeling, however insecure, that those of noble blood had a larger stake in the order of things. This sentiment had roots that can be supported by the most pedestrian observations about the facts of noble existence. Nobles were fewer than common folk. The greatest of their number could be called directly to an Estates General while the remonstrances of the vast Third Estate might undergo a distillation that muddied particularist sentiment.[13] The families and friends of seigneurs like Montvalat, or the infamous Espinchal, held land in several parishes if not provinces. Many *gentilshommes* traveled to Paris; indeed, the noble list of grievances in 1614 complained about the young Auvergnats who wasted their substance on the "pleasures of the Court and of Paris."[14] Even if he had little property, a poor *gentilhomme*, a humble d'Artagnan, enjoyed the superiority of the horseman over the pedestrian. To these physical facts we may add the theoretical superiority of "blood," *le sang pur*, of which so many nobles boasted, and which created the expectation of deference.[15] While

12. The case of Montvalat has received ample attention from A. Lebigre, *Grands Jours*, 102–6. The case is found in Dongois, *Registres*, 27 November 1665 and the damning depositions of his victims in A.N.X²B 1268. Montvalat was also accused of violence against peasants.

13. J. Russell Major. *Deputies to the Estates General in Renaissance France*, Madison, Wis., 1960) gives a detailed account of election and convocation procedures. J. M. Hayden, *Estates General*, 206 and "Deputies *et Qualités*: The Estates General of 1614," *French Historical Studies* 3, no. 4 (1964): 507–24, documents the "watering down" of peasant and other grievances.

14. "Le Cahier de la noblesse de Haute Auvergne aux Etats Généraux de 1614," 118.

15. Andre Devyver, *Le Sang epuré* (Brussels, 1973) is an interesting thesis on the genesis of "race" theory among the French nobility, 1560–1720. The author discusses the rise of the myths of "social racism" in the threatening period of social mobility of the mid-sixteenth century. These theories held the "true" nobility to be members of a separate and superior race; subsequent noble reactions to declining political and social power reinforced the concept of race. A number of historians support the theory of a declining "old" nobility in the late

honor was intrinsic, it had (in theory) been gained originally and was preserved by demonstrations of violence, whether on the larger battlefield or in the well-suited mountains of the Haute Auvergne, whose geography had set their inhabitants outside the major paths of commerce, and whose poverty had preserved their rural archaism. But before we offer any conclusions about noble violence, let us examine the *gentilshommes* in their violent interaction with the members of the First and the Third Estates.

The tensions between the rural nobility and the church were in some cases the natural antagonisms one might expect between competing landlords and between community leaders. The usual victims were the local priests, whose origins were often humble and whose incomes were frequently meager. The most fertile subjects for conflict were those that concerned disputed property and incomes: tithes and benefices, for in these matters nobles often had a sense of their own purview that far exceeded the letter of the law. Theoretically, all tithes impropriated by laymen after 1179 were the property of the church. But in the Haute Auvergne, impropriation seems, in some areas at least, to have been a yearly struggle. Similarly, benefices of which lay seigneurs might have the usufruct were hotly contested, as time sanctified "ownership." As might be expected, the outcome of these tensions in the Haute Auvergne was violent. Tithes felt to be burdensome on the domains of the nobility were resisted, sometimes with violence.[16] Those tithes whose impropriation was disputed were fought for[17] and debtors who expressed their belief

---

sixteenth and seventeenth centuries. Most prominently, Pierre de Vaissiére, *Gentilshommes campagnards de l'ancienne France* (Paris, 1925) portrayed the rural nobility in decline after a golden age in the early sixteenth century. G. d'Avenel, *La Noblesse française sous Richelieu* (Paris, 1901) and Lucien Romier, *Le Royaume de Catherine de Medicis* (Paris, 1922) described an agrarian nobility that suffered from a decline in income beginning in the sixteenth century. More recently Gaston Roupnel, *La Ville et la campagne au XVIIe siécle* (Paris, 1955) and Roland Mousnier have added to the impression of a declining nobility. Davis Bitton, *The French Nobility in Crisis, 1560–1640* (Stanford, Calif., 1969), saw the nobility as suffering from both economic decline and social intrusions. The research of James Wood on the nobility of Bayeux has shown however, that the pattern was not universal; "The Decline of the Nobility in Sixteenth- and Early Seventeenth-Century France: Myth or Reality?" *Journal of Modern History* 48, no. 1(1976): iii (abstract; complete article in offprint). The Haute Auvergne was particularly ravaged by the religious wars but James Goldsmith, "Agricultural Stagnation" and *Rural Nobles*, shows that the decline discussed by Boudet, *Documents Inédits*, and others was not universal. Certainly to my knowledge the individual violence of the *gentilshommes* of Haute Auvergne does not seem to find parallels outside the area of the Massif Central.

16. *Chevauchées* 1628: 9 October. Impropriation is the term used to describe the transfer of church revenue or property to laypersons.

17. *Chevauchées* 1609: 4 August.

that the amount of the impropriated tithes was excessive were dealt with brutally.[18] The Intendant Mesgrigny gave this brutality and unwarranted seizure of church property as one of the major complaints against the nobility: "Many of the gentlemen of the Auvergne make free with the tithes of their neighbours, the parish priests and ecclesiastics."[19]

The parish church of St. Saveur near the city of Pleaux was disputed by the Lignerac family who thought its benefice should be within their control. The conflict came to the attention of the *présidial* of Aurillac in 1634, when the Ligneracs, seemingly angered that they could not place their own candidate in the church, and already at law over the possession of the *curé*, took matters into their own hands. During a mass one Thursday in September 1634, two of the Lignerac brothers strode into the church, dragged the *curé* from the building and began to beat him with their swords. The following Saturday when the same priest met the Ligneracs, they began to insult him, shouting "rascal", "drunkard," and "ignoramus." Later that day they and several allies again drove him from the church. Even at the high mass on Sunday there was trouble. The Sieurs de Lignerac and the Sieur de Manhac again entered the church, took the mass book from the altar, dragged the priest outside, and threatened to kill him and to imprison any of his church found outside the city of Pleaux. They thus publicly prevented him from saying the mass "to the horror of the entire community."[20]

It is interesting to observe the disregard shown the church and the priestly office in this and other similar cases. Incensed over what was essentially a property dispute, the *gentilshommes* involved were willing to interrupt the high mass in front of the assembled community and to seize and outrage the priest in his vestments. They expressed their disdain with the flat of their swords, and with some insults that were traditional and stingingly modern: drunkard and ignoramus, respectively. In other cases the nobility showed a similar disdain for the lower clergy, assaulting, wounding, and even on occasion murdering them.[21] Only in one instance in the *Chevauchées* did a priest kill a seigneur and in that he was assisted by a noble bastard. Both men had committed several other outrages in the neighborhood of the homicide.[22] Even when they did not assault

18. *Chevauchées* 1611: 3 August.
19. Mesgrigny, *Relation de l'état de la province d'Auvergne en 1637*, 184.
20. *Requeste et Plaincte pour Mre Jehan Pages pbre et curé de Pleaux, Coups et Blessures*, 26 September 1634, Présidial d'Aurillac, A.D. Cantal 1B 922.
21. For example, *Chevauchées* 1649: 6 July; 1646: 3 January, 20 August; 1607: 17 March.
22. *Chevauchées* 1611: 7 November.

members of the clergy themselves, *gentilshommes* were known to have sent their lackeys to harass the tenants of church and monastic property, or to have seized control of monastic houses very much in the same manner they raided the house of other, secular nobles.[23]

Inevitably involved in affairs of noble violence were the servants of noble households, lackeys, guards, valets, and domestics of various sorts and stations. Servants participated and suffered in a number of ways. They were killed or wounded accompanying their masters, an unfortunate but not irreplaceable loss. Or if a *gentilhomme* could not find his intended noble victim he might make do with the harassment, assault, or murder of the domestics or peasants attached to his enemy. Such an act could inspire a reprisal in kind in which a servant attached to the enemy household would then be attacked.[24] Occasionally valets might carry on the affair and attack a *gentilhomme* on their own,[25] but the more usual situation was the death or wounding of a servant by the hand of his master's noble enemy.[26]

There is no evidence to suggest that *gentilshommes* killed their own servants, nor did a lackey ever complain to the courts or to the *maré-chaussée* about a beating from his master. Only one case brings to light the murder of a noble by her own servants, and the matter was treated with great seriousness and deliberate speed by the *vice-bailli*. On the evening of 15 March 1652, four masked men entered the château de Montlausy about 30 kilometers south of Aurillac and murdered the Dame de Montlausy. The *vice-bailli* Paul Lacarrière was notified at seven o'clock the following morning and immediately went to the scene of the murder where he spent three days in fruitless investigation. According to the domestics, no relatives of the Montlausy family had been in the house at the time of the murder and the disguise of the murderers prevented recognition. On the eighteenth, the *vice-bailli* returned to Aurillac.[27] Nine days later, at the request of the Sieur de Chaunac, father-in-law of the victim, *lettres monitoires*, or general summonses, were published in order to find witnesses.[28]

The Sieur de Montlausy returned home from military business in

23. For example, *Chevauchées* 1616: 31 December; 1631: 5 October.
24. *Chevauchées* 1617: 4 January; 1611: 7 October; 1593: 29 September, Lackeys, domestics, and servants of various sorts constituted 9.1% of the accused in cases of homicide and assault.
25. For example, *Chevauchées* 1616: 21 August.
26. For example, *Chevauchées* 1615: 25 December; 1616: 26 March; 1636; 6 May.
27. *Chevauchées* 1652: 16–18 March.
28. Ibid., 27 March.

Guyenne at the beginning of April and asserted that the Sieur de Lacassaigne had been staying at the château during his absence and was responsible for the murder of the dame. Again the *vice-bailli* traveled to Montlausy and questioned enough witnesses to throw suspicion on Lacassaigne, who was arrested and imprisoned at Aurillac. There he was interrogated and cross-questioned.[29] The result was inconclusive, however, and on a fair patrol to the nearby city of Montsalvy, the *vice-bailli* and his *archers* continued to search for clues to the Montlausy affair.[30]

Meanwhile the *lettres monitoires* seemed to have done their work in the parish of Ladinhac, for several witnesses came forward with an unusual story. The "masked men" who had so easily entered the château de Montlausy and murdered the dame were her own servants, who had conspired in the deed with the help and encouragement of some peasants and *emphitéotes* (holders of long-term leases that could be mortgaged) attached to the Montlausy family.[31] All of the servants who had previously been questioned were then reexamined and confronted with two other servants who had given the "revelation." It appears that the confrontation had some success, for the two female servants who had been accused in the information acquired (*révélation*) made counter-charges in an attempt to implicate their accusers.[32] The two women, Anthoinette Teyssedre and Anthoinette Sauret, were tortured and then confronted with the principal male accused, Simon Lapparra.[33] Both were then hanged and the body of Sauret, more strongly implicated, was burned to cinders.

Simon Laparra as the principal culprit was then tortured and afterward reexamined and confronted with his accusers.[34] On 11 May he was broken alive on the wheel. Two of his sons were banished forever and one of them had been forced to assist at the hanging of the two women. The two servants whose information had revealed the guilt of the others were forced to assist "with the noose around his neck" at the execution of Lapparra and both were then banned for ten years.[35] Finally on 15

29. Ibid., 2–6 April.
30. Ibid., 15 April.
31. Ibid., 21–23 April.
32. Ibid., 10 May.
33. Ibid., 3–4 May.
34. Ibid., 6 May.
35. Ibid., 11 May.

May, the Sieur de Lacassaigne, who had been languishing in prison for over a month, was acquitted and released.[36]

The servants in this case, perhaps the natural suspects to a late twentieth-century mind, appear to have been most unnatural suspects in the mid-seventeenth century. The burning of the maidservant's body is unusual in what remains to us of the annals of Auvergnat justice. It was a fate reserved for those condemned in "atrocious cases" (cas énormes), crimes that reversed or challenged the normal order of the universe: "parricide, heresy, witchcraft and sodomy."[37] The burning of a cadaver was viewed as "archaic" by the Parlement of Paris in cases of infanticide and incest as early as the late sixteenth century.[38] The murder of a master by a servant was clearly regarded as one of those "horror crimes" that required a stern deterrent example.

Servants were intimately involved then in the lives of the families they served, supporting them in many of the long-standing affairs of hatred and blood, complicit in their cruelties, avenging their injuries, bearing arms with them and perhaps sharing as well some of their power and glory. In most of the noble affrays, valets were present. Unfortunately, they were more likely to be captured and tried, and, if condemned, to suffer punishments their masters rarely shared. They were weapons, part of their masters' psychic property, but also, on occasion, sharers of it.

Peasants were at once more removed from noble households and more vital to nobles than domestic servants and henchmen. The general complaint of peasants against the gentilshommes of the Haute Auvergne was the same in 1665 as it had been in 1637 and as it is repeated throughout the Chevauchées. The Intendant Mesgrigny put it most concisely: "The most common complaint against the nobility is that they make use of the pretext of some vain rights that they have on their land to vex and overwork their peasants."[39]

Landlords, it was said, punished the failure to pay by violence or by sending armed men to occupy the houses of the reluctant. Further, they expected an annual payment in grain (devestis), which they sometimes deferred until prices were high, at which point they demanded the sum

---

36. Ibid., 15 May.
37. See, for example, Jean Bodin, De la démonomanie de sorciers (Paris, 1580), book 4, where burning of the cadaver is recommended for witchcraft. Quoted words from A. Soman, "Criminal Jurisprudence," 50.
38. A. Soman, "Criminal Jurisprudence," 51.
39. Mesgrigny, Relation de l'état de la province d'Auvergne en 1637, 183.

of the deferred payments in kind.[40] The *Chevauchées* and the court records are usually silent concerning these exactions, many of which were only fully disclosed in the *Grands Jours*, where almost all the nobles who appeared were charged with "the usual offense of the nobles of Auvergne" (*le délit commun des gentilshommes d'Auvergne*). But they do tell us something of the means by which nobles, their domestics, and their officers wrested what they wanted from peasants; shooting, beating, and general savagery against ordinary folk certainly existed.[41] But for the most part, complaints against nobles by their own tenants do not seem to have reached the courts, unless there was a real danger of death, an accumulation of clear-cut violence that had become unbearable, or, unless the offending seigneur clashed with another powerful interest. An example of the latter phenomenon was a case of the consuls of Aurillac against the Marquis de Conrot. Servants of the marquis erected several toll barriers on roads and bridges near Aurillac in 1660, and the consuls of the city fought a long battle in the *présidial* against the seigneur and his domestics, complaining that the barriers inhibited the flow of trade. Armed with pistols and swords, the servants of the marquis extorted livestock, money, and other possessions from passing peasants, beating and threatening those who refused to pay.[42] Situations like this one were the occasion of some gratuitous violence on the part of the servants in question who enjoyed the authority of their lord and release from the behavioral obligations a community ordinarily demanded.

There was, then, a certain tension between peasant and seigneur. But one is as likely to read complaints made by *gentilshommes* on behalf of their own peasants against other noble households as one is to find complaints by peasants against their own seigneurs. These distinctions, it must be remembered, are made against a background of general reluctance by peasants to report violence committed by their seigneurs. Why? The Intendant Mesgrigny complained that few cases of noble oppression of the peasantry reached court because of intimidation: "And the peasants, for fear of worse [treatment], dare not put any of this in writing."[43]

Is there also a suggestion of "vertical solidarities" here? Perhaps. As we

40. Ibid.
41. For example, *Chevauchées* 1610: September; 1646: 9 May.
42. *Information*, Consuls of Aurillac v. Marquis de Conrot, 1662, Présidial d'Aurillac, A.D. Cantal IB 928.
43. Mesgrigny, *Relation de l'état de la province d'Auvergne en 1637*, 184.

have already seen, interfamily rivalries among *gentilshommes* often extended to the servants and to the peasants of the two parties. If one could
not strike directly at his enemy, he made do with his enemy's dependents
or allies. Within his specific territory and among his own peasants, the
Auvergnat noble exacted outmoded obligations in many cases. But these
matters were disputes or disciplinary measures "within the family," so to
speak, imposed on individuals bound to the community of which the
noble seigneur was still the head. In conflicts with leaders of other rural
communities the whole extended "family" was implicated. These are
some of the boundaries marked by noble violence, and they suggest an
affinity with the opinions of Yves-Marie Bercé and Roland Mousnier.
One could eulogize with Marcellin Boudet or Pierre de Vaissières the
"bon seigneur" who kept one hand on the plow and the other on the
sword. But the tensions within the rural community, illustrated by the
flood of peasant grievances to the Grands Jours, hint too strongly that
the rural "family" was neither happy nor stable. Let us therefore leave
the discussion of "orders" and solidarities until we have seen more
examples of interaction among social groups, and can identify the lines
that will allow a fuller portrait of violence and its uses.

The attitudes and actions of the provincial nobility toward lawyers,
merchants, and the bureaucrats of royal fiscal and judicial institutions,
indeed toward those who dominated the towns in general and were not
so strongly tied to the rural communities, support the idea that some sort
of rural solidarity was at work. The cases of violence by rural nobles
against members of these groups abound. They involved disputes over the
payment of bills, over jurisdiction, and over matters of honor wherein
the sensitivity toward royal officers on the threshold of "true" nobility
was demonstrated.[44]

We have seen in some cases that the daughters of wealthy merchants
and bourgeois were natural prey for young noblemen in cases of abduction. For a merchant the collection of bills from an indebted *gentilhomme*
could be risky and unprofitable, as Jean Bleu, a bourgeois of Murat,
discovered when he attempted to collect thirty livres owed him by one
de Forges. Bleu had been carrying the debt for a year and so he went to
the house of Forges to demand payment. Reminded of the debt, Forges
flew into a rage, called Bleu "thief" and told him that he "was a man

---

44. Some examples: *Chevauchées* 1611: May, 22 February; 1614: October, 1617: 20 June, 1
July; 1630: 24 July; 1636: 16 June; 1650: 16 August; 1664: 23 July.

who was worth nothing," after which he set upon the unfortunate creditor and beat him about the head with his fists.[45]

Notaries or lawyers could meet with the same sort of rage when they found themselves in conflict with their betters. The family of a notary in the *bailliage* of Salers received rough treatment from a local noble in the absence of the notary himself. His wife was beaten, called "slut," and threatened with having her dress torn off. The vilification then centered on her absent husband, a "blackguard, rascal, cheat, moral defective" in the words of her assailant, who then excoriated his own valet and sharecropping tenant: "You didn't have the will to kill this rascal, you poltroons." He then promised to finish the job he had set them to, repeating the standard threat of death.[46] The notary's wife was placed in the category of all women to be insulted: "slut." The notary was first a "rascal" as was every male enemy, and a "blackguard"; but the insults then centered on the vices of the legal trade: cheating and a general lack of virtue. The family and servants of the notary, as in other cases, served as victims in the absence of the primary enemy.

The relations between rural nobles and the officers of the crown are interesting. They were by no means static relations, for they depended on the level of officialdom, the point at issue, and the size of the forces at odds. The *vice-bailli* would sometimes use the château of a local *seigneurie* to imprison a suspect, and he depended on châteaux for places of refuge in times of crisis such as the tax revolt of 1649 in the election of Salers.[47] Nobles would also occasionally report some grievances to the *maréchaussée* and in turn the *vice-bailli*, despite many jurisdictional quarrels, would turn prisoners over to the officers of a *seigneurie* if he thought a case could be handled there. There was therefore some cooperation among seigneurs and royal officers as representatives of the forces of order. It must noted as well that families of officials in justice and finance in the Haute Auvergne, such as the Lacarrières, the Senezergues, and the Laurens, also possessed *seigneuries* and attempted to acquire the marks of nobility—with some success, according to the *Nobiliaire d'Auvergne*, a sort of aristocratic *Who's Who*, or guide to the noble families of the region. They were therefore seigneurs as well as royal officials.

45. *Plainte* 25 November 1665, Bailliage of Murat, A.D. Cantal FB 204.

46. 1664. Bailliage of Sallers, A.D. Cantal 14B 230. For other examples of violence against *notaires*, see the murder of Guillaume Boudarys by the Sr. de Fraissines and his wife, *Chevauchees* 1630: 30 January; or the attack by Annet de Fontanges on the *notaire* of Raulhac.

47. *Chevauchées* 1649: October.

Against these evidences of cooperation and some identity of interests however, we must balance the more plentiful facts of antagonism and difference between the "old" rural nobility and the bureaucrats who aspired (*robins*). The strength of the families of the official class remained in the towns where theirs were the important houses and where they figured importantly in the consular elections recorded in the *archives communales*.[48] When *gentilshommes* were involved in a dispute, the *vice-bailli* usually accompanied his men. There seems to have been a certain delicacy about these affairs. In most quarrels, the *vice-bailli* merely remonstrated with the noble offenders. Seldom was he admitted to a fortified house, though he might stand before it and, in a humiliating ritual, demand entry in the name of the king. The reply was most likely to be a refusal, taunts, or even gunfire, and should the *vice-bailli* take a prisoner, *gentilshommes* allied to the prisoner might try to rescue him. Outright violence toward the lower ranks of the servants of the crown by *gentilshommes* and their families is common in the *Chevauchées*, whether it be the murder of a *sergent*[49] or a royal notary (*notaire royal*),[50] the assault of an *archer*[51] or a lawyer attached to the *présidial*.[52] On one occasion at least, the women of the nobility entered into this spirit of antagonism. A noblewoman in the *bailliage* of Salers went to see the wife of a prominent ennobled bureaucrat and with the help of servants, beat her enemy to the ground with punches and kicks.[53]

In collective violence by peasants against royal officers the influence and even the leadership of local nobles was suspected. In the frequent local rebellions against the *taille* and other levies and in other forms of resistance to royal decrees, *gentilshommes* were accused of complicity with the rebels, although proof was never offered. Even before examining some examples of collective violence, we can begin to agree with Mousnier that distinctions between the rural "old" nobility and the

48. All the prominent city families named by Mesgrigny in 1637 were officers of justice who reappear frequently in the records of both the courts and the *maréchaussée*. None of these is mentioned as being part of Mesgrigny's category of *gentilshommes*. The Lacarrières were at first part of the bourgeoisie of Aurillac and Jean Lacarrière the first *vice-bailli* began to sign himself *ecuyer* in 1587. *Chevauchées* 1587 preamble, *Nobiliare*. But any claim to nobility by the seventeenth-century *vice-baillis* Lacarrière was premature.
49. *Chevauchées* 1610: 6 December.
50. *Chevauchées* 1630: 30 January.
51. Ibid: 24 July.
52. *Chevauchées* 1636: 16 June.
53. *Chevauchées* 1611: 22 February.

aspiring prominent urbanites are necessary and real; and we can begin to say with Bercé that the *gentilhomme* "was incontestably a member of the rural solidarity."[54]

In his role as a leader of the predominantly rural Haute Auvergne, the provincial noble (*gentilhomme campagnard*) confronted a rival source of local authority. But the royal authorities of the Haute Auvergne were singularly unsuccessful in their prosecution of noble offenses. Most of the sentences passed by the *présidial* and the *vice-bailli* were not carried out and in many instances of serious assault there is no evidence of a sentence at all. Servants and henchmen were more likely than their masters to suffer for the sins of *gentilshommes*. This relative impunity, the fear of reprisal if charges were pressed, and the relative weakness of police forces gave nobles what was tantamount to a "right to assault" in our period. Perhaps when he wrote ironically in 1665 that crime was the Auvergnat method of proving nobility, Fléchier was not far off the mark. If one examines what we know of noble traditions and what we have observed thus far of the noble actions, violent crime does seem to have been in many cases almost an unconscious rite of social definition. First the long-standing tradition of arms, illustrated by the noble demand for military forces, reinforced the characteristic style of *gentilshommes*. The Early Modern military tradition was one of liberties, plunder, *excès*, and freedom from local control; of collective violence, ransom, and living off the land. These were also the characteristics of noble crime. Military office was the most honorable means of both proving nobility and of finding employment. This style of plunder and skirmish was continued in peacetime. Dueling, a more ritual form of combat had similar honorable associations; it was also a crime created by law rather than by communal revulsion. Second, nobility that served no productive function and that was threatened by base aspirants from among the rising bureacratic elite could in economic extremity compete for wealth in the only "honorable" ways: violent seizure and feudal chicanery; neither of these means traditionally threatened nobles with removal of their noble status (*déro-*

---

54. *Chevauchées* 1648: 11 February, 9 November; 1649: October. Y.-M. Bercé, *Croquants*, 2: 694. Roland Mousnier has developed this idea in much of his work including *Vénalité* and *Institutions*. For specific examples, however, see his *Peasant Uprisings*, 3–31 and his criticisms of "class" analysis in "Recherches sur les soulèvements populaires en France avant la Fronde," *Revue d'histoire moderne et contemporaine* 5 (1958): 81–113, an essay that has been translated in P. J. Coveney, ed., *France in Crisis, 1620–1675* (Totowa, N.J., 1977), 136–68. Mousnier provides a broader discussion of orders and classes in *Social Hierarchies: 1450 to the Present,* trans. Peter Evans (London, 1973).

géance).[55] Finally, the tradition of local liberties combined with the absence of strong local authority made such an arrogant statement of noble sovereignty both a possibility and an affirmation of traditional independence.

The Clergy

Since the early fourteenth century, the church had divided the territory of the Haute Auvergne between the diocese of St. Flour, whose 390 parishes constituted most of the upper province, and that of Clermont, which included a small area around Mauriac in the northwest. Some of the most venerable lines that recognized a distinction between Upper and Lower Auvergne had therefore been drawn by the church. The Haute Auvergne and especially Aurillac was (and is) proud of its religious tradition, given eminence by Saint Gerbert, a learned monk of Aurillac who founded an abbey there during the tenth century. After gaining renown as a teacher and an archbishop, he became Pope Sylvester II (999–1003); as Auvergnats are fond of saying, "the Pope of the year one thousand."[56] For the most part, however, criminal justice documents deal with clerics who were far removed from Rome. Aside from the occasional appearance of a noble canon or abbot, or a fracas involving the servants of the bishop of St. Flour,[57] it is usually the humble village *curés* and *vicaires*, the parish priests, whom one encounters in the reports of violent conflict.

Within the ranks of the lower clergy the question of social status is somewhat complex. While members of the First Estate, the local priests were clearly not *gentilshommes* by virtue of their orders (although they could have noble origins). They were "notables," however, in village and parish; literate, sometimes leaders, privy to the secret sins of their

55. Y.-M. Bercé, "Beyond the influence of ideology, it is necessary finally to mention, at the origin of this noble criminality, material motives, the difficulties of the nobility impoverished by the fixed nature of its income and, above all, by the barrier of *dérogéance*, which obliged it to look for fraudulent ways of enrichment" (*Croquants* 1:137).

56. Gerbert was a master in the school at Reims, archbishop of Reims in 991, patriarch of Ravenna in 998 and pope in 999. See in F. L. Cross and E. A. Livingstone, eds., *The Oxford Dictionary of the Christian Church* (Oxford, 1974), the entry under Sylvester II, 1329–30; and Manry, ed., *Histoire de l'Auvergne*, 106.

57. *Chevauchées* 1617: 1628: 19 August.

parishioners and the only dispensers of God's grace. Even within the ranks of village priests, the social gradations could be considerable. First of all, there were two sorts of *curés*. *Curés decimateurs* were those who enjoyed all of the revenues of a parish, which could include various rents as well as tithes. *Curés congruistes* were chosen by a patron, either an ecclesiastical or temporal seigneur, or a *curé décimateur*, who paid them an income (*portion congrue*). The *portion congrue* varied from place to place, partly according to wealth of the parish, but largely according to the generosity of benefactors. *Curés décimateurs* were more likely to be well-to-do than *congruistes* although the disparity between parishes was so great that this was not always the case.[58] Attempts to reform the clergy in the period 1629–34 included a minimum *portion congrue* of 300 livres of which the actual pastor of the flock was to receive at least 100 livres.[59]

As village notable, the priest could have a decent income; but numbers might diminish his importance. Some parishes in the Haute Auvergne contained a *curé* and several subordinate *vicaires*. Furthermore, there was yet a lower caste of priests, *prêtres communalistes* or *filleuls* who lived in community and were supported by their families as well as by the income from the services they performed.[60] In a tour of seventeen parishes during the mid-seventeenth century the bishop of St. Flour wrote assessments of seventy priests;[61] and a historian of the diocese of Clermont has estimated that in the mid-seventeenth century about 20% of parishes held substantial communities of *prêtres filleuls*. Abel Poitrineau, in a study of ten parishes northeast of St. Flour, estimated the ratio of priests to parishioners at 1:150. *Chanoine* Joubert of Aurillac, who has studied the lower clergy for most of his life, seems convinced that they were numerous and poor. And these estimates are for the secular clergy, which does not

58. Mousnier, *Institutions*, 333–36; Joubert, "Quelques notes sur le bas clergé d'Ancien Régime en Haute Auvergne," *Revue de la Haute-Auvergne* (April–June 1979): 105–7; L. Welter, *La Réforme ecclésiastique du diocèse de Clermont au XVIIe Siècle*, (Clermont-Ferrand, 1956), 7–8.

59. "An ordinance of 1620 fixed the *portion congrue* at 300 livres. In 1634, parish priests without a subordinate were to receive 200 livres and those with a subordinate 300 livres, the *curé* or *vicaire* subordinate to the *congruiste* was to receive 100 livres. Mousnier, *Institutions*, 333, Joubert, *Notes*, 105.

60. A. Poitrineau, "Avant la réforme catholique du XVIIe siècle: Un échantillon du clergé paroissal au diocèse de St. Flour sous le régne de Louis XIII, "*Almanach de Brioude* (1975): 207–13. G. de Léotoing, d'Anjony, *La communauté des prêtres filleuls de l'Eglise Notre Dame*, (Aurillac, 1954). L. Welter claimed that *filleuls* were often employed to say masses for the dead, *Réforme*, 7–8. Elsewhere, this job was sometimes taken by priests called *habitués*.

61. The parishes were in the southeastern corner of the Haute Auvergne in the area of Chaudesaignes and Ruines, A.D. Cantal, 346 F33.

include the monasteries, convents, and priories located in the Haute Auvergne. Although his count may have been high, the bishop of St. Flour claimed in the mid-seventeenth century to have in his diocese 6000–7000 "ecclesiastiques," which was about 4–5% of the population.[62]

The attempts to secure a better living for priests were part of a more general Counter-Reformation effort to improve the character of the lower clergy. The pastoral visits (*visites pastorales*) by the bishops of Clermont and St. Flour were in themselves evidence of reforming zeal; the information they gathered was evidence of the need for reform. The bishop of St. Flour found the first *curé* he interviewed in the parish of Espinasse a scandalous drunkard; and the inspection continued to uncover similar problems. Some priests could not say mass properly; libraries were small and poor. One priest had intimate relations with a widow, another wore colored clothes and reveled in village festivities. Drunkenness, adultery, and frequent merrymaking, as well as ignorance and sloth were discovered in several parishes. In Salers, a rough city where the *procureur du roy* was reported to have carried two pistols under his long robe, the priests carried on in high mountain style. The bishop of Clermont found that in addition to the more common sins of the dances and taverns, some Salers priests "carry firearms and commit every sort of insolence in the midst of the city." It must be added that there were also competent pastors and even good theologians among poor *curés*; many at least were considered satisfactory. As a result of the pastoral visits in the period 1620–50, the worst offenders were suspended from their functions, and others were admonished and ordered to study their catechism.[63] These reforms were accompanied by other efforts, to establish colleges in St. Flour and

62. Welter, *Réforme*, 7. Poitrineau, "Avant le réforme," 209. Joubert, "Notes." R. Mousnier estimated that male clerics, regular and secular, constituted about 1% of the population of France. L. Perouas in his study of La Rochelle found that in the mid-seventeenth century the ratio of priests to Catholics was much higher, *Le Diocèse de La Rochelle de 1648 à 1724* (Paris, 1964), 486–87. Although we do not have exact figures for the regular clergy, it is worthy of note that L. Welter, discussing only the most "important" establishments mentions 18 abbeys and more than 100 priories as well as "numerous" convents and monasteries in the diocese of Clermont alone. The dense population of priests seems to have been a perennial problem in the Haute Auvergne. In a case between the consuls of Aurillac and the church of Notre Dame d'Aurillac in 1547, the Parlement of Paris ruled that the number of priests attached to the church should be *reduced* to 100 or 120 "or whatever other number of them can be maintained completely and without indigence *et absque penuria*" A.D. Cantal 13 G5. See also Manry, ed., *Histoire de l'Auvergne*, 294.

63. The *visites* in the diocese of St. Flour are contained in A.D. Cantal 346 F33 and 346 F13. Joubert, *Notes*, used selections from the former, and Poitrineau, "Avant la Réforme," is based on the latter. Salers quotation from L. Welter, *Réforme*, 36.

Aurillac, to improve the maintenance of hospitals and monasteries and to encourage more decorous conduct among both regular and secular clergy.[64]

When assessing the evidence surrounding the lives of clerics, students must carefully take account of the sources and their historical milieu. These descriptions of parish priests were written when the last great effort to "clean up" parish religion and its clergy was probably just getting under way, and it was an effort that would bear fruit in the late seventeenth and early eighteenth century. The result of these reforms was, in many ways, the Tridentine Catholicism that would characterize the church until the 1960s. The ideal cleric was to be a member of a separate, elevated caste: chaste, seminary-trained, an educated ritual expert who devoted himself to the tasks of performing the sacraments, confessing his parishioners, educating them, and admonishing them with sermons. He was to be affable but not overfamiliar, stern but not oppressive, at once separate from profane village culture and yet influential in its reform. In addition to the new seminaries, which were to be constructed in every diocese, the parish clergy gradually acquired a series of aids in their appointed round, such as diocesan catechisms to instruct the faithful more clearly, confessional boxes to allow privacy in the increasingly personal and interior matter of "directing conscience," and regular meetings of clerics, "ecclesiastical conferences," where priests could discuss and clarify more abstruse matters of the faith and their application to the pastoral calling. In short, the French rural clergy in the seventeenth century was in the throes of professionalization—or perhaps "upgrading" would be a more fully appropriate term for this process. The discipline of the clergy was to be the first step in the reform of popular religious practices. Because most festive events had a religious signifi-

64. The Jesuits, who had been expelled from Aurillac in 1594, reestablished their college in 1619, Manry, ed., *Histoire de l'Auvergne*, 284, 293–95. Several historians have recently taken an interest in pastoral visits as sources for the study of parish religion in early modern France. See R. Sauzet, *Les Visites pastorales dans la diocèse de Chartres pendant la première moitié du XVIIe siècle* (Rome, 1975), and *Contre-Réforme et Réforme catholique en Bas-Languedoc: Le Diocèse de Nîmes au XVIIe siècle* (Paris, 1977). The C.N.R.S. has recently produced a four-volume guide to pastoral visits, *Répertoire de visites pastorales de la France* (Paris, 1977–85), which is large enough to have inspired an analytical guide, Froeschlé-Chopard and M. Froeschlé-Chopard, *Atlas de la réforme pastorale en France* (Paris, 1986). One project centered around a rich archive of pastoral visit records is described in M. Greenshields, "An Introduction to the Pastoral Visit Project: Between Two Worlds, 1560–1720," *Proceedings of the Annual Meeting of the Western Society for French History* 15 (1988): 51–60, and J. M. Hayden, "The Pastoral Visit Project Phase I: The Dioceses of Coutances and Avranches," ibid., 61–70.

cance, or at least interfered with a religious service, the scope of such a reform was immense, ideally amounting to a reordering of rural life and a transformation of behavior and attitudes. This importation of new standards of "decency" to rural France was, moreover, an idea to which the temporal authorities were attracted, both personally and politically, for it promised an orderly, deferential countryside from which resources could be extracted.[65]

For the moment, however, most of these changes were in the future, and the parish clergy of the Haute Auvergne were often in the difficult position of men whose "job description," as it were, was changing. In many cases native sons, familiar with the local idiom, their training had often been haphazard, perhaps even an informal sort of apprenticeship; and their pastoral duties conformed to the customs of their region. But now, with change in the air, they were beset with ecclesiastical reformers, judging them by a different, and perhaps a more rigorous, standard. It is well to keep in mind, too, the mentality of the reformers who composed many of the catalogues of local clerical misdeeds. They often brought an urban, elite sensibility to their task, which demanded that they discover and root out local misbehavior and the "superstitions" of popular belief and practice that, they claimed, had grown up in isolated rural parishes.

65. For accounts of the changes in early modern Catholicism, see Jean Delumeau, *Le catholicisme entre Luther et Voltaire* (Paris, 1971), translated as *Catholicism between Luther and Voltaire* (Philadelphia, 1977); F. Lebrun et al., *Histoire des Catholiques en France du XVe siècle à nos jours* (Toulouse, 1980). Another perspective on religious reform is provided by the essays in K. von Greyerz, ed., *Religion and Society in Early Modern Europe, 1500–1800* (London, 1984) and by the examinations of the cultural context in P. U. Burke, *Popular Culture in Early Modern Europe* (New York, 1978), and R. Muchembled, *Popular Culture and Elite Culture in France, 1400–1750*, trans. Lydia Cochrane (Baton Rouge, La., 1985). The study of religious life and attitudes had also been the subject of several important monographs on specific regions of France. Notable examples include L. Pérouas, *Le diocèse de La Rochelle de 1648–1724;* J. Ferté, *La Vie religieuse dans les campagnes parisiennes, 1622–1695* (Paris, 1962); A. N. Galpern, *The Religions of the People in Sixteenth-Century Champagne* (Cambridge, Mass., 1976); P. Hoffman, *Church and Community in the Diocese of Lyon* (New Haven, 1984) and Michel. Vovelle, *Piété baroque et déchristianisation en Provence au XVIIIe siècle* (Paris, 1976). John Bossy's *Christianity in the West, 1400–1700* (Oxford, 1985) is among the most fertile and thought-provoking monographs on the overall meaning of religious reform to ordinary Europeans. For a recent discussion of some of the implications of the Catholic Reform in the rural community, see M. Greenshields, "What Happened in Quibou? The Catholic Reformation in the Village," *Proceedings of the Annual Meeting of the Western Society for French History* 18 (1991): 80–88, and J. M. Hayden, "The Catholic Reformation at the Diocesan Level: Coutances in Normandy," ibid., 89–97. The most telling objection to the idea of the urban acculturation process reforming the countryside is in J. Wirth, "Against the Acculturation Thesis," in Greyerz, *Religion and Society*, 66–78.

Despite this caution to the student of pastoral visits and other documents of the Catholic Reform, however, it must be said that the parishes of the Haute Auvergne did provide the reformer with some stirring examples of the "bad old ways" of unreformed Catholicism.

The lives of the clergy show no monstrous hypocrisy; rather the *curés* and *vicaires* seem to have been fallible men, attracted to the same sins enjoyed by their parishioners. In other ways they seem to have been very much "of the people" a part of the communities they served, in whose wealth or poverty they often shared, whose violence they suffered or committed. Like peasants they were sometimes the victims of customary extortion by seigneurs. But like *gentilshommes* they were also leaders and sometimes landlords, collecting their own dues. The incidents of violence illustrate the relations between priest and parishioners quite vividly.

The records of the courts and the *maréchaussée* provide evidence of priestly involvement in affairs of violence both as victims and as aggressors. Priests were attacked and beaten or murdered by individuals and groups among their parishioners[66] and as we have seen, by *gentilshommes*.[67] They in turn struck out at their parishioners, committing offenses that ranged from mild assault to homicide.[68] While their assailants came from all groups, their victims were usually peasants. Like other members of the community, clergymen formed alliances against enemies, stood by their families, traded insults, and defended their dignity and property.

Witnesses offered this account of a quarrel between two well-to-do peasants and a priest near Aurillac. On the evening of Monday, 3 August 1654, Martin Bonnal, priest in the Church of Notre Dame d'Aurillac, had just finished dining in the village inn of Laboigue and was taking his ease with several other diners, a notary from Aurillac, a priest from nearby Arpajon, and Marguerite Courbaisse, the keeper of the inn, who also helped Bonnal collect the tithes on the adjacent domain of Chambon. One of the local inhabitants entered the room and told Bonnal that the Laborie brothers were in a field adjoining the village, leading sheep into a cart to take them away without paying tithe. The landlady told Bonnal that in previous years the produce and livestock on that piece of

66. Examples *Chevauchées* 1615: 15 January; 1630: 30 September. In the *Chevauchées* clergy accounted for 2.3% of the accused and 5.8% of the victims in cases of homicide. Whether these proportions are due to the Christian forebearance of priests or to their greater boldness in making complaints is impossible to say.

67. *Chevauchées* 1607: 17 March; 1646: 3 January; 1649; 6 July.

68. *Chevauchées* 1628: 6 June; 1629: 25, 30 May.

land had been subject to his tithe.[69] Father Bonnal, the innkeeper, and her daughter immediately went to this field to prevent this evasion of the tithe. The Laborie brothers and a helper were busy loading the sheep when the priest approached and said that they couldn't transport any sheep without first paying tithe. Ramond Laborie replied that there was no tithe owing on the field, to which the priest countered that, "au contraire," the field was not exempt. After several more exchanges of this sort, Father Bonnal demanded that the sheep be put into the care of someone in the village until the affair could be settled. Laborie said that he would do nothing of the kind, that the sheep could be counted in his own village of Chambon. Meanwhile, the peasant helping the Labories had continued to lead the sheep, prodding them with a hayfork. Bonnal grabbed the fork and stopped the work.[70] The Laborie brothers leaped forward and seized the priest by the collar, to which insolence he replied by knocking off Ramond Laborie's hat. (This an instructive exchange for the student of honor and psychic property, for the priest's reproof included both an insulting cuff and the demand that the head of a parishioner be uncovered in the presence of a clergyman.)[71] Anthoine Laborie and his helper began to struggle with Bonnal, tearing his shirt and doublet.[72] Holding one another, the three men fought to the edge of the field, tumbled over a high bank and onto the road. Meanwhile the landlady was grappling with Ramond Laborie, her hair and clothes in disarray.[73] When the three men rolled into the road, they separated. Ramond Laborie left the woman and together both brothers shouted at the priest: "Rascal! Robber! Leper! Damned greedy guts! You'll pay for this!"[74]

So went the tale of witnesses provided by the priest Martin Bonnal. But according to the same witnesses, Bonnal then counted out the sheep for the tithe and took them away. The priest's initial complaint had

69. Deposition of Jean Coffin, priest, 7 August 1654, *Information*, Présidial d'Aurillac, A.D. Cantal IB 924. All pieces hereafter (notes 69–76) refer to the same number.

70. Deposition of Estienne Bonhomme, 7 August 1654.

71. Deposition of Coffin. The head is thought to be the most important part of the body in the bestowal and denial of honor. Julian Pitt-Rivers has discussed the relation between the head and honor, noting the importance of bowing the head, covering and uncovering it, slapping the face, and beheading. See the *Fate of Schechem*, 4–5, and Reinhardt, *Justice in the Sarladais*, 165.

72. All witnesses.

73. Deposition of Jean LaRibe, 6 August, 1654.

74. Depositions of Coffin, Bonhomme, and LaRibe.

depicted the Laborie brothers more savagely. They had hit and kicked him, threatened his life with a hayfork and promised to kill him.[75] The Labories, ordered to appear before a *présidial* judge, said that in fact they had been attacked on their own land by the priest. Bonnal, they said, had since been intimidating and threatening many persons to prevent a response to a general summons for information (*lettres monitoires*) published in the parish where the attack had occurred.[76] The cases continued for a year, with charges and countercharges after which there is no evidence.

Leaving questions of guilt or innocence aside, the evidence is nonetheless informative. Martin Bonnal, a forty-five-year-old priest, acted in any event, with a great deal of confidence and self-assertion. However the struggle began, he succeeded in wresting the disputed tithe from two reluctant peasants. Although they had overpowered him, the Labories gave way to the priest and his portion. Bonnal, it seems, had a loyal flock in the village as well as in the field, for he was able to line up favorable witnesses. The local inhabitants informed him of the evasion and even one of Laborie's helpers showed no resentment of the tithe and was willing to testify against his employers. In the heat of the moment the Labories offered an interesting array of insults: rascal, thief, leper, and damned greedy guts, words appropriate to the offense they had taken and perhaps to the offender. "Rascal" and "thief" would have been the standard epithets attached to the actions in question, no matter who the actors had been. But greed and drunkenness were vices popularly attributed to the clergy, whose peculiar "deadly" sin was usually said to be gluttony.[77] The most interesting and instructive insult of all in this case, however, was "leper," because it provides an apt metaphor for some aspects of the priest's position in the rural community. The obverse of his eminence and leadership was isolation and separateness. Separateness was also a traditional aspect, even a definition, of holiness, whose pejorative possibilities included accusations of unnaturalness and disease, characteristics that separate with an element of disgust. In a sense, therefore, the distinctive marks of holy orders could, at times of trouble, take on the nature of stigma.[78]

75. *Plainte* of Martin Bonnal, 4 August, 1654.
76. Response of Labories, no date.
77. In addition to gluttony, the traditional seven deadly sins are pride, covetousness, lust, envy, anger, and sloth.
78. For an examination of the phenomena associated with the stigma, see E. Goffman, *Stigma: Notes on the Management of Spoiled Identity* (Englewood Cliffs, N.J., 1963).

Resentment and resistance to priestly power, and self-assertion and leadership by priests, were not unusual. Priests often showed the same propensity for violent solutions to their quarrels and the violent repression of challenges to dignity as did their parishioners. In the *bailliage* of Salers we find a village *curé* disputing with a prosperous peasant over the course of a stream that the priest wanted to divert to his own meadow. Armed with a cattle-prod, a hatchet, and a hoe, the *curé* and his valet entered the field of the peasant and ordered the peasant's helpers to depart. Priest and valet then proceeded to beat their enemy bloody, the *curé* adding (in the rustic touch of one deposition) a few kicks with his wooden clog (*sabot*) for good measure. Their foe vanquished, the two men set about diverting the stream.[79]

While priests jealously asserted their fiscal rights, they could also stand in solidarity with members of their flock when outsiders threatened the community. When a bailiff and guards were sent by a *bailliage* court to seize some cows from a peasant in the parish of Fontanges, they faced just such a priest in Anthoine Dufour. They alleged that as they led the cows away, the priest, "totally seized by fury," led an attack against them. Grabbing the bailiff by the collar and ejecting him from the village, he rescued the animals from the official grasp.[80] The attitude of the parish priest toward the interventions of official justice in this case was little different from that of the rest of the rural community, except that he behaved as a leader.

In addition to leading village resistance against such interference, the parish priest can be seen sharing the xenophobic and suspicious reaction to the relatively harmless presence of strangers. On Saint Bartholomew's Day (24 August) 1646, two legal officials from a nearby town entered the village of Jugolles near Carlat in order to collect a debt. Anthoine Martin and Anthoine Montion approached the village "about the time of vespers" and encountered a group of men and women threshing grain, among them a priest named La Ribe and his nephew. Martin asked the group if anyone knew where one could find Pierre Laboize. The priest's nephew replied that he had no dealings with either Martin or Laboize and that if the two strangers had some business with Laboize, they would know where he was. At the house of Laboize they were told that he was

79. *Information pour Antoine Meynial*, 13 April 1660, Bailliage of Salers, A.D. Cantal, 14B 229.

80. Dufour denied any wrongdoing. *Interrogatoire*, 12 December 1658, Bailliage of Salers 14B 229.

not at home. Walking back down the road, the two men passed by the threshers again and it was there that Anthoine Martin made his mistake. Assuming a priestly role, he stopped before the group and told them, "that they were doing wrong to thresh grain today because of the solemn occasion of an Apostle's day," and that they could be taken to court for doing so. The immediate reaction to this unwelcome piety was anger. One of the threshers replied that it pleased them to thresh, feast day or no feast day. This piece of defiance seems to have emboldened the hostility of the peasants into rage. They began to shout insults at the strangers, calling them rascals, drunkards, and forgers. Using their flails and staffs, they rained blows upon the unfortunate Martin and Montion. The priest participated lustily, beating Montion with a bar. Had it not been for the arrival of two officers from the château de Carlat, the two men said, they would have been killed.[81]

The most common role of the priest in court documents was that of witness. Often he was unusual in being the only literate person among the witnesses called, and as something of a community leader, he was frequently asked to testify in an affair, even if his knowledge of the particular incident was slight. He was generally knowledgeable about the business of his parishioners and probably little cowed by the official procedure and the mysterious jottings of the clerks. Acting as a witness could be dangerous, especially if the accused was a prominent person, for by doing so one became implicated in a cycle of vengeance, taking one side or another in a dispute. His position was made more sensitive and powerful by the knowledge he gained in the confessional. The priest Jean Vergnes testified against the daughters of a bourgeois of Murat and was soundly beaten for his effrontery.[82]

We see the parish clergy participating in the economy of violence. Their reactions to provocation, their imposition of "justice" are the sorts of violent ripostes with which we have become familiar. This violence outlines several aspects of the behavior and position of priests. Within the community, the priest participated in village life, sharing many of the rural agricultural concerns of his parishioners. But he also tried to assert a position of leadership and to ensure a measure of respect as well as the protection of his property. Violence within the community by

81. Bailliage of Vic, August 1646, A.D. Cantal 15B 675.
82. *Plainte* of Jean Vergnes, 22 July, 1665, Bailliage of Murat, A.D. Cantal 7B 204. Pierre Charryre, the accused, claimed that the priest had abused him, *Interrogatoire*, 23 July 1665. In ibid.

priests was usually directed downward, most often toward peasants, in a process of control. When the community was threatened or interfered with from without, the coalition of priest and people was closer and the priest stood in solidarity with his parishioners or simply participated, in violence directed outward, toward the alien threat.[83]

Because of the ambiguities of his position, it is difficult for historians to do justice to the complexities surrounding the role of the parish priest. However degraded one may think his position to have become, the priest was an important figure and a cultural mediator between external elites and the rural populace, and the impulse to reform religion newly emphasized his importance. He was a man, but he was to be more than a man as well. In traditional Catholic theology, he stood astride the chasm between God and humanity, a creature of earth and heaven both. This lonely, half-human position was undergoing reinforcement as the seventeenth century progressed. In the insults of some parishioners, we can see not only traditional anticlerical sentiments, but also a telling analysis of the postion of priest: "leper, drunkard, damned greedy-guts"; a figure separate from the rest of humanity and yet prey to human vices.[84]

The Third Estate

In a sense, there was no Third Estate. The vast and rambling category outside the juridical limits of the first two orders, defined by what it was not, comprehended an array of groups and individuals, a myriad of estates, and what we might call identities (qualités), families, and communities. In the Haute Auvergne the tendency toward settlement in small

83. The scant evidence in our records of the activities of the higher clergy makes their behavior more difficult to interpret. But the impression is that they acted very much like gentilshommes, especially in cases involving abbés, sometimes leading bands of armed men, fighting for their dues and tithes, seizing disputed properties and doing violence to their enemies and to the servants, allies, and relations of their enemies. In 1656, for example, the abbot of Lodieu led a band of armed men in the seizure of the château de Pesteils, Bailliage of Salers, 1656, A.D. Cantal 14B 228. In another case, a canon of the Church of St. Amant severely beat a curé because of litigation with the curé's brother. Bailliage of Salers, 1657 A.D. Cantal, 14B 228. See also Chevauchées 1628: 29 April.

84. See Greenshields, "Pastoral Visit," 52–53. For a discussion of the changing views of the priesthood during the seventeenth century, see J. M. Hayden and M. Greenshields, "The Clergy of Early Seventeenth-Century France: Self-Perception and Society's Perception," French Historical Studies 18, no 1 (Spring 1993): 146–72.

hamlets and the tradition of family communities must be taken into account when one looks at the rural hierarchy. Because settlements were less concentrated or nucleated in the mountains than for example in the Limagne or Basse Auvergne, each settlement was even less likely to contain inhabitants belonging to the full range of rural *qualités*. Added to the mountain customs of seasonal emigration and the employment of agrarian and pastoral workers in part-time trades, this lack of concentrated populations may have been responsible in part for the continuing image of the Auvergnat *débrouillard* (survivor), capable of turning his hand to many different sorts of tasks. Family communities emphasized the importance of attachments to family and place, both components of *qualité*, over the convenient sorts of sociological generalizations used to "place" individuals in the rural hierarchy. Indeed in the *Chevauchées*, more than half of those accused of assault and homicide were identified only by place and names.[85] Descriptions of individuals were spare: "Jean Combelles, inhabitant of the place called Combelles," or "Jean Combelles, son of Anthoine, inhabitant of the place called Combelles." The *vice-baillis* were faithful in recording the *qualité* of nobles, seigneurs, bastards of nobles, domestics, priests, *officiers* and sometimes *bourgeois*, merchants or "professionals"; but when it came to distinctions among peasants, artisans, herdsmen, and other populous groups of the countryside, the *Chevauchées* are often silent. This impression persists to a lesser degree in court records, where the demand for name, age, *qualité*, and residence sometimes elicited only a statement of residence, name, age, place of birth, and family relations. The tendency is not unique to the Haute Auvergne. Arlette Lebigre was similarly frustrated by the records of the Grands Jours d'Auvergne, kept by the clerks of the Parlement of Paris.[86] But despite these drawbacks, enough evidence exists for us to identify some of the social characteristics of the rural hierarchy of the Haute Auvergne.

Aside from the parish clergy and from the *gentilshommes*/seigneurs and their officers, there were several sorts of rural inhabitants whose status was not directly related to agricultural or pastoral pursuits. As Abel Poitrineau has suggested, there was a rural "bourgeoisie" but its members were not found in every village of the Auvergne,[87] and most certainly not

85. Of those accused in cases of homicide and assault, 258 or 50.1% were identified only by name and place or family; 39.1% of victims were described in the same terms. (See Appendix 1).

86. A. Lebigre, *Les Grands Jours d'Auvergne* (Paris, 1976).

87. A. Poitrineau, *Basse Auvergne*, 1:608–9.

in all the hamlets and villages of Haute Auvergne. While merchants, bourgeois, and "professional" men are rare in the *Chevauchées*, they were identified as such by the *vice-baillis* and more fully described by the documents of the criminal courts. One can find "notaires," "practiciens," whom we would probably call lawyers or solicitors, as well as barristers, surgeons, and apothecaries among the professions; merchants and the occasional villager called bourgeois also appear, although all of these types were more usually from towns and cities.

There was considerable variation in status within the designated professions. "Pierre Lacombe, *chirurgien*" (surgeon) at St. Just[88] was really an artisan, in a modest position compared to "Honnorable homme Maistre Jean Grolat docteur en medicine" of Aurillac."[89] The term *bourgeois*, normally associated with larger towns and cities can also be found in more rural cases like that of "François de Vereuze, Sieur de Laborie, bourgeois."[90] *Marchand* (merchant) was a term even more fraught with peril in the Auvergne, for it could refer to a substantial trader or to a *colporteur* or peddler.[91] Merchants were therefore not necessarily *bourgeois*, although in the *Chevauchées* they were usually simply referred to as merchants; Jean Goudriatte by contrast realistically called himself "marchand porte panier" (literally, "basket carrrier").[92]

It should be added that the nonpeasant non-noble elite of the country-side was usually closer to the soil than professional titles or *qualités* would suggest. Its members sometimes held land that they leased in sharecropping contracts; or a legal professional for example might act as leasing manager (*fermier*) of a seigneurial *domaine*. They were usually associated with larger villages and towns, and sometimes regarded as intruders to the smaller rural settlements rather than as social superiors.[93] In the *Chevauchées*, those designated by honorable professional group

---

88. Audition, 21 April 1664, Juridiction de St. Just, A.D. Cantal 16B 1048.
89. Deposition, 1608 in Présidial d'Aurillac, A.D. Cantal IB 920. An excellent brief list of *qualités*, professions, etc., and their relative position in the social order is found in the appendix of Ruff, *Crime, Justice and Public Order*. For the distinctions within the medical professions, see Mousnier, *Institutions*, 1:458–63. Mousnier contrasts the relatively important social position of physicians with that of barber-surgeons who were usually allowed to perform only minor operations, the removal of boils and the treatment of open wounds.
90. Deposition, 1656, *présidial d'Aurillac*, A.D. Cantal IB 926.
91. Poitrineau, *La Vie rurale en Basse Auvergne*, 1:608.
92. Deposition, 20 April 1609, Présidial, Prêvoté d'Aurillac, A.D. Cantal IB 1053.
93. Poitrineau, *La Vie rurale en Basse Auvergne* 1:610. For proportions of bourgeois and merchant land ownership, see Léonce Bonyssou, *Montagnes* and James Goldsmith, "Agricultural Specialization."

formed a very small percentage of the accused in homicide and assault cases and were much more likely to be victims than aggressors. In cases of abduction, more than one-third of the victims were *bourgeois, marchand, apothecaire*, or *notaire*.[94]

The hierarchy of peasants, herdsmen, and rural artisans extended from positions of relative economic ease to those of indigence, and the thresholds of independence and subsistence moved with the economic flux of the period. The *vice-baillis* rarely described peasants or artisans at all, but when they did, the terms were those familiar to students of peasant France: *paysan* (peasant), *emphytéote* (lease holder), *laboureur* (ploughman or husbandman), *métayer* (sharecropper), *tenancier* (tenant), and a list of trades and positions of agricultural service.[95] As with other such descriptions, we must leaven our acceptance of them with some respect for the ambiguities of language. At the top of peasant society was the *laboureur aisé* (the peasant or ploughman in easy circumstances), who sometimes rivaled the *bourgeois* in importance, an "independent" agriculturalist who cultivated relatively extensive lands and could sometimes afford to hire others to work for him.[96] But as Poitrineau noticed in Basse Auvergne, "The term *laboureur* is quite ambiguous and frequently applied by a generous concession to some pretty miserable peasants."[97] When Jean Lacarrière wrote in January 1587 that the *laboureurs* of Bonnac had massed to attack and rob royal troops, he probably intended the word to mean peasants in general.[98] There are also cases in which peasants referred to themselves as both *laboureur* and *métayer*, or *domestique* and *laboureur*; and, as in Goubert's Beauvaisis or Lefebvre's Nord, *laboureurs* in the Haute Auvergne could be those who were prosperous enough to own oxen and cultivate the fields of others.[99] The group of *laboureurs* who were truly well off was probably quite small.

Emphytéote could refer to any peasant who held long-term rights to

94. As accused 1.2%; as victims 6.8%. In cases of abduction 6 of 17 victims (35.3%) and none of the accused were part of this group. Merchants were particularly vulnerable to highway robberies, sometimes accompanied by violence.

95. It is probable that the large "other" category among the accused and victims in the *Chevauchées* was occupied in significant part by peasants, who were only specifically named as such rarely: 1.2% of the accused and 7% of victims in cases of assault and homicide.

96. For the ownership of peasant lands in Haute Auvergne, see M. Leymairie, "La Propriété et l'exploitation foncières au XVIIe siècle dans la Planéze de St. Flour," *Revue de la Haute-Auvergne* (1965): 482–86.

97. Poitrineau, *La Vie rurale en Basse Auvergne*, 1:611.

98. *Chevauchées* 1587: 1 January.

99. For example, Interrogatoire, 27 July 1664. Bailliage de Murat A.D. Cantal 7B 189.

land, and it could indicate a great range of prosperity as well. *Métayers*, who held short-term, sharecropping leases were usually among the poorer and less secure peasants, in a continual struggle with debt during the seventeenth and eighteenth centuries: "The Auvergnat sharecroppers are always poor, impecunious devils."[100] In court records and in the *Chevauchées* both *métayers* and *emphytéotes* by contrast with *laboureurs*, were identified with reference to the *rentier* or seigneur,[101] as in "métayer of a bourgeois of Aurillac," or "emphitéotes of the Sr. Marquis."[102] It should be added that those who participated in the pastoral economy could also be called *métayer* or *laboureur*. The level of persons involved with livestock varied a good deal as well. For along with skilled dairymen, *vachers*, and *messages*, were boys who worked as *bouviers* (cowherds); and girls such as Anthoinette Bonafé, a twelve-year-old who described herself as both a "domestic maid" and "shepherdess" for her bourgeois master.[103]

Those who worked as domestics, lackeys, valets, and other servants of the higher orders were frequently well identified in the *Chevauchées*, probably because of the importance of their masters. And in court records we can find those who served in humble wineshops, inns, and more modest houses, sent to work because their families could not support them at home.[104] There was also a group of day-laborers (*journaliers*) who did occasional or seasonal tasks for others, taking any sort of work to keep family and residence together, trying to maintain themselves above the threshold of subsistence and living at the margins of stable rural society.

Rural artisans and craftsmen of the Haute Auvergne are occasionally mentioned in both *Chevauchées* and court records: shoemakers, spinners, weavers, tailors, tinkers, blacksmiths, masons, charcoal burners, and others. But these were not always the master tailor, "maistre tailleur d'habitz de Marmanhac," or the master shoemakers, "Maistre Cordonniers," seen in the larger towns and villages. Auvergnats often lived by a combination of rudimentary skills and marginal agricultural pursuits, "working out" for another family or leaving their residence and small plot of land to work in other provinces or in Spain during the winter. A trade

---

100. Poitrineau, *La Vie rurale en Basse Auvergne*, 1:181–82, 196–97. See also Goldsmith, "Agricultural Specialization."

101. *Chevauchées* 1611: 24 May.

102. *Chevauchées* 1652: 4 May.

103. For example, *Plainte*, 29 November 1646, Seigneurie de Peschans, A.D. Cantal 16B 902.

104. Deposition, 23 July 1626, Juridiction de Conros, A.D. Cantal 16B 432.

or other work of some sort was often supplementary to an insufficient bit of land, or to a necessitous family community. During the eighteenth century, the connection with permanent residences and with extended or multiple family communities weakened and the mountains became a source of various permanent emigrant workers: cobblers and tinkers from the region of Aurillac to Spain; sawyers and knife-grinders from the northwest; water-carriers, bootblacks and street porters from the impoverished Aubrac; hawkers, peddlers, and agricultural workers from every part of the province.[105] The poorest agricultural workers and part-time craftsmen, the "gagne-petits," itinerant knife-grinders and so on, were never far from begging; vagabonds, when arrested, sometimes gave an occupation with their place of residence: pinmaker, weaver, *métayer*, soldier. One young man, accosted at the fair of St. Géraud in Aurillac, even claimed to be a merchant.[106]

Thus the rural hierarchy of the Third Estate was richly varied. At the top, a few could keep themselves free of physical toil. Below this threshold of complete independence were the many in varying degrees of security and dependence who clung to their slight property and attempted to preserve it. Charles Estienne, writing on agriculture in 1601, discussed the Auvergne as a labor pool for the new landlord: "The Auvergnat [is] skilfull, laborious and enduring of time and chance but if he knows of your profit, he will share in it if he can."[107]

The social directions of violence within the Third Estate form an interesting series of behavioral vectors. First, there was the violence between those who were approximate social equals. Second, there was "downward" violence used in the repression or punishment of social inferiors. A third phenomenon was violence "outward" in defense of the rural community against an alien threat. Only in the third case do we see many attacks against those who could be considered social superiors.

As we have seen in Chapter 3, those not *gentilshommes* displayed an acute sensitivity to challenges to dignity, honor, and property. Their psychic property depended upon the recognition that others accorded their claims. Conflicts between social equals abound in court and police

---

105. See Poitrineau, *La Vie rurale en Basse Auvergne*, particularly the sections on "l'artisanat campagnard," 1:572–79 and on emigration, 1:560–72, as well as the references to emigration in Chapter 1 above. The most notable recent study of early modern artisans is Farr, *Hands of Honor*, which concerns Dijon, but is widely applicable concerning the activities, sensibilities, and comportments of the urban artisanat.

106. *Chevauchées* 1652: October.

107. Charles Estienne, *L'Agriculture et la maison rustique* (Paris, 1601), 27.

records. In October 1648 during a fair at Brezons in the southeast of the province, a merchant from Chaudesaigues demanded from a defiant butcher the repayment of a disputed debt. When the money was not forthcoming, the creditor seized a stone and broke open his debtor's head.[108] In nearby Cezens in August 1654, after a heated and drunken game of dice, a local bourgeois seized a club and administered a severe beating to a notary and members of his family.[109] A bourgeois landowner and a notary, brothers-in-law in the northern *bailliage* of Murat exchanged insults and menaced each other with firearms in 1662 over the grazing of a few pigs in a disputed meadow.[110] Two village women in the jurisdiction of Sedaiges, seemingly long-standing enemies, exchanged insults and finally one of them injured the other physically with stones thrown from the top of her garden wall.[111]

The unpaid debt, the insult, the violation of one person's space by another, gave rise to various degrees of violent behavior, frequently at the times and places we have already observed. The persons involved were connected by the very indebtedness, the long-standing enmity or the juxtaposition of their property. They were also connected by the fact that the social distance between them was not so great as to preclude violent contact.

In addition to these confrontations of equals, a second phenomenon was the downward violence within the rural community. We do not see examples of a *gentilhomme* attacked by a peasant or a merchant. If there is any social direction to the incidents of violence, it is toward social inferiors. Attacks on rural inhabitants by their betters, as in some cases of *gentilshommes* already discussed, could be attempts to punish merely the representative of an enemy closer to one's own social position. When Pierre Cassang, the *métayer* of Monsieur Antoine del Sol, attempted on the instructions of his employer to cart a load of hay across the meadow of Marguerite Doux, he met the owner and her son-in-law Antoine Jourde, blocking his path. Jourde, with "a naked sword in his hand," would have liked to confront the master del Sol directly but decided to make do with the peasant Cassang:

> "God's Death, rascal! Who told you to pass through my meadow? If you ever try to go through there any more, it'll cost you your

108. 10 October 1648, Juridiction of Brezons, A.D. Cantal 16B 280.
109. 19 August 1654, Brezons, ibid.
110. March 1662, Bailliage of Murat, A.D. Cantal 7B 189.
111. Juridiction of Sedaiges, A.D. Cantal 16B 1098.

life. . . . Why doesn't the one who ordered you to pass through there come here himself, because if he does by the death of God I'll kill him!"[112]

So saying, he threw himself on the unfortunate Cassang, who was beaten, thrown into a nearby river, and finally stoned into unconsciousness by the formidable Marguerite Doux.[113]

Punishment of this sort was also a feature of "labor relations" among peasants. Simon Vergnes, a shepherd in the parish of Chavagnac, requested wages owed him for the previous year by Claude Teissedre, a well-to-do peasant from a neighboring village. According to Vergnes, Teissedre came to his house about five o'clock in the evening and "having flown into a rage" split his head open with a hoe. Both man and wife then seized Vergnes's brother by the hair and dragged him out of the house. When the shepherd intervened, he was hit on the head with a stone.[114] Two witnesses, a widow and her daughter, who were neighbors of the victim, supported this account of the incident. The injuries were verified by a physician who found two wounds on Vergnes's head made by an instrument "such as a hoe, stone or crow-bar."[115] The case never received a sentence, although to all intents and purposes the release of the accused after interrogation was tantamount to the closing of the affair. The attack is an interesting show of self-assertion on the part of the peasant and his wife. By all accounts they entered the shepherd's house to punish him. Such an entry was most often accomplished by social superiors and cases in which a social equal or a subordinate made so bold as to enter the house of another uninvited are rare.[116] Such violence downward on the social scale was not uncommon. A sharecrop-

112. *Plainte*, 27 July 1632, Bailliage of Salers, A.D. Cantal 14B 307.
113. *Plainte and Information*, 27 July–4 August 1632.
114. *Plainte*, 11 May 1661, marked "A" Bailliage of Murat, A.D. Cantal 7B 189.
115. *Rapport du Chirugien*, 12 May 1661. After the case had lain in abeyance for four years, the accused finally submitted to interrogation and a different story emerged. According to the Teissedres, the shepherd was in debt to them for land worked by Claude Teissedre. Vergnes, along with his brother, had come to Teissedre's sheepfold and taken a ewe. When pursued by the Teissedres to their own village, they had turned and attacked their pursuers. While Teissedre admitted fighting to protect his wife, he said that it was not he but his opponent's own brother who had wounded Vergnes by mistakenly hitting him with the hoe in the heat of battle. *Interrogatoires* of Jeanne Roche and Claude Teissedre, 13 November 1665.
116. The house was especially inviolable in the absence of its head. See Castan, *Honnêtété*, 174–76. In this case, however, the intruders may have owned the house.

per might punish an insolent gleaner,[117] just as one landlord might punish the workers and peasants of another.[118] There is no strong evidence to suggest that the flow of violence was ever directed upward, except in the cases where the servants of a feuding family were involved in an attack on the masters of a rival clan. From the standpoint of violence at least, the "vertical solidarities" of rural society seem to have been quite firm.

Another exception to the trend of downward violence was the third phenomenon, attacks on intruders who threatened the rural community or some of its member families. In a province of small hamlets, many of them family communities,[119] there were also many strangers and intruders. The evidence for this xenophobic tendency varies, from the troubles that arose between rural inhabitants and billeted soldiers, to the impediment of travelers from an area of plague. One consistently repeated note was that of resistance to the officers demanding various fiscal levies. The violence inspired by these clashes is evident in both court records and the reports of the *maréchaussée*, the latter source bearing witness to incidents ranging from a single clash between a peasant and a bailiff to large rebellions that persisted for months.

The traditional historical interest in politics is, from one perspective, simply a matter of scale, and we can move fairly directly from the personal politics of face-to-face negotiation, conflict, and violence to a politics that contained the same elements, but has attracted historians, because the mass of "little" men and women attained a magnitude sufficient to alarm the "great."Although we are not concerned in the main with large-scale rebellions, when examining the resistance of the rural community to alien threats, we must follow, in a cursory way at least, the progression from individual acts of resistance to large-scale conflicts. As well as demonstrating the xenophobia that greeted the intrusive stranger, this progression demonstrates in macrocosm the economy of violence and the collective sense of psychic property that characterized the rural community. Under the rubric of "outward" violence, therefore, we shall also look briefly at the implication of the collectivity in these incidents.

117. 16 August 1662. Bailliage of Murat, A.D. Cantal 7B 204.
118. 9 July 1643, Bailliage of Salers, A.D. Cantal 14B 227.
119. For a discussion of family and community types and their development, see Flandrin, *Families in Former Times.*

Alien Threats: Soldiers, Taxes, and Collective Violence

The phenomenon of violence in groups would probably escape this study altogether were it not for the *Chevauchées* and the concern of the *vice-bailli* with "illicit assemblies" and "rébellion." Indeed, it could be argued that a study of criminality should not include collective action; for as the number of persons involved in an incident grows, the quantitative change engenders a qualitative change. Widespread collective acts of violence become popular revolt; when the scale of such acts becomes sufficiently large, they are cleansed of the taint of criminality and become war. The same sorts of premeditated murders and thefts by large numbers of heavily armed men gain a sanctity they could not enjoy as discrete events. Men are rewarded for committing enormities for which they would in different circumstances have been punished. The premeditation and the responsibility are the province of princes and kings, who release their countrymen from the constraints of decency in a festival of violence. Just as the release of festive occasions sometimes led to expressions of criminal violence therefore, soldiers who had been gathered, removed from their domiciles, and released from obligations enforced by the community, took great liberties in the home country as well as on the battlefield. The haphazard stationing and provisioning of troops in the early seventeenth century aggravated this tendency to domestic military disorder and, as we have seen in the cases of ransom and rape, their urgent business of war allowed them to ignore or defy attempts to make them behave peaceably. Soldiers in groups as well as individually often committed crimes that escaped the censure of institutions and their arms usually allowed them to escape the censure of the community as well. Usually, but not always: witness the discovery of murdered soldiers and the occasions on which the *vice-baillis* were called upon to protect troops from the local populace.[120]

Soldiers meant nothing but trouble for almost every member of the community. Town- and countryfolk alike were forced to provision them, and taxes for their maintenance were levied in addition to the normal impositions.[121] In their opposition to the ravages of men at arms there-

---

120. *Chevauchées* 1649: 3 January; 1629: 6 June; 1587: January. This last incident actually dates from December 1586.

121. For example, meetings of consuls in January and February 1646 contained complaints about the ruinous cost of maintaining men at arms which was entirely in this case the responsibility of the *élection* of Aurillac. A.C. Aurillac, BB[15].

fore, a wide range of social groups often made common cause. When a company of cavaliers lodged without permission began to pillage the parish of Mandailles in 1652, the *vice-bailli* and his *archers* gathered together a group of the local inhabitants and chased the intruders from the area; this was only one of a number of similar confrontations in that year.[122] In April 1659 *vice-bailli* Paul Lacarrière sent the peasants written permission to attack and drive out a group of light-horsemen who were passing slowly and expensively on their way to Rouergue.[123] Local nobles also joined in the defense of the countryside against armed outsiders. In 1659 for example, the Comte de Malause went to the aid of his tenants and neighbors in the district of Mauriac against marauding soldiers from the Régiment de Carignan. Mounted on horseback and accompanied by other local noblemen, Malause led a victorious army of peasants equipped with iron bars and tools.[124] In the parishes near Aurillac, the light-horsemen of the Duc d'Orléans met a wall of local solidarity in 1658 when the *maréchaussée*, local nobles, and other inhabitants of all sorts gathered and pursued them with gunfire and sickles.[125] While the bourgeois of Aurillac were not willing to go outside their city walls to join these expeditions, action against soldiers was clearly in their interest.[126] There were occasions then when the coalition of rural forces comprised all groups.

The individual and the army are two extremes. We can also see the extension of violence to the collectivity as a matter of degree. Even in the case of a dispute between individuals, the community often became involved, first as observers of the event in question that took place in the close confines of village life. They might then become further involved in an intervention to keep the matter below the crucial threshold of blood, and perhaps later in a legal case if official justice had been sought. In the case of an external threat, members of a rural community might take a more clearly partisan position and help to administer retributive justice to the "outsider." The collectivity thus often became involved in affairs between individuals; when a bailiff or tax collector came to seize property for arrears in taxes or dues, or if a stranger otherwise interfered

---

122. *Chevauchées* 1652: 26–29 October; 3–7 November, 19 November.
123. *Chevauchées* 1659: 15 April.
124. Bercé, *Histoire des Croquants*, 2:555.
125. Boudet, *Documents*, 113.
126. A.C. Aurillac BB 15 1649.

in the business of a village, he might find himself facing an entire family or even a community.[127]

The habitual rural way of doing things increased the likelihood of group confrontations. One preferred to travel in company, to eat with others, and often to work in groups. When a man heard about a seizure of his livestock or illegal passage through a field, the natural course for him was to seize whatever weapon he had, call to his aid servants and family members and go out to confront the invader, often with bloody results.[128] It behooved everyone to have allies, whether for a dispute between priests over a benefice, for a struggle over pasture rights, or to extract a more telling vengeance from an enemy.

We can see quite clearly the progression from individual to collective acts of violence in the resistance of members of the rural community to the external threat posed by tax officials. Members of the *maréchaussée* were often assigned to the escorting of tax collectors, the protection of tax monies, the assistance of officers at tax auctions, and the investigation of tax revolts. In these unpopular functions they naturally encountered resistance and duly recorded it. From the beginning the *Chevauchées* show a pattern of numerous small incidents occasionally erupting into large-scale rebellions. The incidents were usually precipitated either by attempts to collect the tax or by the auction of the property of those who could not or would not pay. The levy most frequently at issue was the *taille*, but there was also resistance to the taxes levied directly for the maintenance of billeted armies and even occasional resistance to the collectors for a seigneury who entered a village to collect dues. For the most part the officials involved were lower level types, bailiffs and court guards, usually alien to the communities and families whose property and persons they threatened. Such violence did not always center directly on fiscal matters; the mutual dislike and disrespect as well as the liberties of authority extended into other areas of life as well.

The seizure of livestock was a common means by which seigneurial officials exacted payment, not always unaccompanied by violence. When the manager of the seigneury of Brezons went with three others to the village of Frescollanges to collect arrears in the *cens* from a peasant named Jean Gibral, he was, he claimed, attacked by Jean Belgus, son-in-law of the debtor, who beat and wounded him. But bailiffs and stewards

---

127. Examples in December 1664, Juridiction of Brezons, A.D. Cantal 16B 280; 1637 Présidial of Aurillac, A.D. Cantal IB 1056; 1646 Bailliage of Vic, A.D. Cantal 15B 675.
128. See 27 July 1632, Bailliage of Salers, A.D. Cantal 14B 307.

were as likely to use force in their duties as they were to receive it. Belgus's story under interrogation was that the manager and bailiff had beaten him. They had, he said, refused his offer of partial payment of the fifteen livres owing and insisted on taking instead a pregnant mare that was about to give birth.[129] Another case of violence against a *sergent* in the jurisdiction of St. Urcize shows a similar ambiguity, when the *sergent* attempted to seize some sheaves of grain and claimed he was beaten by the accused, a daughter-in-law, and two sons. Both parties made complaints on the same day, each claiming the other had been guilty of violence against him.[130] Interestingly the peasants involved in incidents like these did not attack the seigneur himself; only his subordinates.

Rebellions against seigneurial dues were characteristically small in scale and related only to conditions on individual domains or to the circumstances of individual families. The *taille* and other royal taxes were a more widespread problem and the forces associated with them more distinctly alien to the village community.[131] The *Chevauchées* depict both aggression by the collectors and resistance by local inhabitants. Discrete incidents involving small numbers of individuals appear in diverse areas and at different times.[132] It was in these incidents that persons could be singled out for accusation and charges laid. The bailiffs, local constables, and other officers were also accused of brutality in the collection of funds and the auction of property.[133]

The natural defense of property and livelihood by individuals sometimes grew into something more widespread in which whole communities, parishes, and finally whole regions participated. The danger of revolt accounts partly for the preoccupation of the *vice-baillis* with illicit assemblies. From the very beginning of the *Chevauchées* and during the tenure of all three *vice-baillis*, the *maréchaussée* tried to prevent small isolated blazes of revolt from turning into large conflagrations. In the summer of 1588, Jean Lacarrière rode to numerous cities and rural areas all over the province warning the inhabitants who had refused to pay the

---

129. *Interrogatoire*, 10 December 1664, Jurid. Brezons, A.D. Cantal 16B 280.

130. Two *Plaintes* both from 13 August 1665, Juridiction St. Urcize, A.D. Cantal 16B 1075.

131. The Haute Auvergne was a *pays d'élection* (which meant, perversely, that it was under the sway of appointed officials called *élus*) and an area of *taille personnel* (which meant that the tax was based on persons or villages rather than land) comprising three *élections*: Aurillac, Mauriac, and St. Flour.

132. *Chevauchées* 1590: February; 1595: 26 December; 1647: 18 March, 5 October; 1659: 21 July, 13 August, 2 September; 1660: 28 April, 1664: 3 September, 26 October.

133. *Chevauchées* 1654: 1 July, 1660: 28 April; 1630: 25 June; 1660: 13 February.

taille.[134] In 1594, large assemblies of armed inhabitants in several parishes in the southeastern part of the province were told by the *vice-bailli* to disperse, even though they assured him that they had only gathered to elect deputies who would petition the king to relieve them from the onerous *tailles* and other levies on account of their poverty and misery.[135] As the amount of the *taille* increased steadily until 1649, so did its unpopularity; the violence provoked by these increases was not always so easily contained by the *maréchaussée*.

Although family and village rebellions against taxes and *officiers* occurred throughout the period 1587–1665, the crucial years of more widespread revolt in the Haute Auvergne were roughly 1630–49. During this period, France, the Massif Central, and particularly the Auvergne suffered from a harsh conjuncture of circumstances that placed a heavy load on the rather threadbare economic structures sustaining mountain communities. With economic pressure came social upheaval; and the revolts, like lightning on a dark night, illuminate in different postures the social groups and the social boundaries that are of interest to our study of rural violence.

While it is outside the immediate range of this study, a few brief observations are in order about some problems that preceded the revolts and that persisted during much of the period of revolt. Taxes demanded cash and the increase in taxes coincided with a growing monetary shortage in the area. Two major sources of specie in the Haute Auvergne were the sale of cattle and the money earned by emigrants to Spain. By 1630 the income resulting from emigration was diminishing fast. Economic problems in Catalonia, civil strife, and eventual revolt in 1640 aggravated the problem of enmity with France. During the previous ten years, Spanish wages had begun to fall; and as France deepened in her opposition to Spain's allies in the Thirty Years' War, emigration itself was severely diminished. As for the rest of the economy, a high royal official (*maître de requêtes*) assessed the situation of Auvergne as a source of royal revenue and trouble:

> The country produces neither grain nor wine except for the needs of its own people who have no means of making money other than the sale of livestock, their principal possession, that

134. *Chevauchées* 1588: 17 August.
135. *Chevauchées* 1594: 24, 30 July.

is also the principal thing that the collectors can seize for payment, without which they would be poorly paid, because the furnishings of the houses in these parishes are cheap and difficult to sell. Grain and wine are rare this year and imprisonment is not money, there being many imprisoned here for a year because of the *taille*.[136]

In addition to shortages of grain and money, nature itself, never particularly kind to the Haute Auvergne, conspired against the suffering population. The capricious weather of the period was very hard on crops; but the most devastating enemy of the provincial welfare was the plague, which began to infest the mountains in 1627–28. In Aurillac alone at least a third of the population died, and the pestilence seems to have afflicted most other areas of the province as well.[137]

It does not take much imagination to envisage the reception accorded officers of the royal fisc and the *maréchaussée* by rural communities beset with such problems and predisposed to a certain violent xenophobia at the best of times. At the very least, as we have seen, the response to

136. Vautorte to Séguier, 10 September 1643, in R. Mousnier, ed., *Lettres et mémoires adressées au chancelier Séguier* (Paris, 1964) 1:545. For an overall assessment of the economic situation in rural Auvergne during the period of mass revolt, see Bercé, *Croquants* 1:38–39, 245. See also Trillat, "L'emigration de la Haute Auvergne en Espagne" in *Revue de la Haute-Auvergne* (1954–55): 257–94; J. Meuvret, *Etudes d'histoire économique*, 127–37; L. Trénard, "Images d'Espagne au temps de l'émigration auvergnate," *Actes du 88e Congrès des Sociétés Savantes* (Clermont-Ferrand, 1963), 731–62. Bercé, *Croquants* also refers to A. Girard, "La saisie des biens français d'Espagne en 1625," *Revue d'histoire économique* (1931): 297–315. The problems of the Haute Auvergne to which I refer are only a small sample of the "crises" that affected much of Europe during the period, a time of widespread war, unstable prices, unpredictable weather, revolt and constitutional instability. For discussions of climate, see Le Roy Ladurie, *Times of Feast, Times of Famine*, which discusses the Little Ice Age; and John A. Eddy, "The 'Maunder Minimum': Sunspots and Climate in the Reign of Louis XIV," in *The General Crisis of the Seventeenth Century*, ed. G. Parker and L. M. Smith (London, 1978), 226–69. The latter contains several other interesting essays on crisis. In the same vein, T. H. Aston, ed., *Crisis in Europe, 1560–1660* (New York, 1965) contains several essays basic to the debate on the seventeenth century, including H. R. Trevor Roper's "The General Crisis of the Seventeenth Century," 59–97, which enlarges Aston's thesis that European Renaissance monarchies, which had ambitiously expanded their activities of the state, but without a sufficient fiscal base to sustain the expansion, came into conflict with a recalcitrant "country" population. Most useful for an overview of the debate as it regards France, is P. J. Coveney, ed., *France in Crisis, 1620–1675* (Totowa, N.J., 1977). For the economic and social problems of various regions, the results of regional researches are summarized in Labrousse and Braudel, eds., *Histoire économique et sociale de la France*, vol. 2; and Duby and Wallon, eds., *Histoire de la France rural*, vol. 2.

137. *Chevauchées* 1628: June. The plague at Aurillac, St. Flour, and elsewhere was part of a major epidemic in France and Europe. See Bercé, *Croquants* 1:24–37.

property seizures for taxes had always been sullen; but as the situation of the rural community grew more desperate, the resisters grew more aggressive and numerous. In January 1628, a band of officers was sent by the tax collector to enforce the payment of the taille in the countryside around St. Flour. As they passed by the village of Falasac, a small army of the inhabitants of the parish attacked them, and after "excesses" and humiliations of various sorts, chased the intruders from their area. Jean Delort and Pierre Dupont, the two officers who had suffered most of the abuse, reported the incident to the lieutenant of the *vice-bailli* at St. Flour, and a party of *archers* went to Falasac to investigate. Those villagers who could be found explained that the villages had assembled to prevent the spread of the plague that had recently ravaged St. Flour.[138]

It seemed an ordinary sort of incident, except for the aggressiveness of the attack, and the *maréchaussée* had no trouble with the accused. But the following twenty years make it seem like the opening shot in a long struggle for possession of scarce revenues and for local independence from representatives of royal authority. Scattered incidents, which involved "popular riots" and resistance to tax collections and to property seizures, continued through 1630 and 1631. Aurillac felt much of the effect of these disorders, but the local authorities despaired of reestablishing order, saying to the consuls "that they had done their utmost," but "the evil was discovered to be so great that it is impossible there to employ the necessary solutions."[139] The presence of any tax official was sufficient to arouse popular suspicion that "extraordinary subsidies" were about to be levied. The *vice-bailli* Jean Lacarrière could not leave the district of Aurillac in April 1631 because of the uproar surrounding the Sieur de Teilhard, treasurer general of France, and the *maréchaussée* provided protection to Teilhard, "who was in some danger,"[140] while he assessed the contribution of the city. Widespread popular violence in Haute Auvergne prompted the governor d'Effiat to express concern in October 1631 that the problem was growing serious, and that "officers" and "people of quality" had done nothing to prevent disorder.[141] The scale of disturbances sometimes grew to immense proportions. In 1635 the Planèze de St. Flour erupted into virtual war. Popular resistance was fueled by the rumor of a new tax on livestock, the "pied fouchu"

---

138. *Chevauchées* 1628: 11 January.
139. A.C. Aurillac BB¹⁴, 5 April, 1630.
140. *Chevauchées* 1631: 20 April.
141. A.C. Aurillac BB¹⁴, 20 October 1631.

(literally, "the cloven hoof") and a massive rising ensued, the "guerre des esclops" (war of the *sabots* or clogs worn by peasants) during which royal troops were massacred.[142] Disorder spread throughout the mountain villages and in October 1636, the *vice-bailli* rode north with a force to rendezvous with the *prévôt général* of Auvergne at Riom-es-Montagnes. Everywhere he went on the way Laccarrière found that "even the most pious . . . are not at all willing to pay"; and many peasants had said they would rather die than pay. The *vice-bailli* never completed his journey. As he rode through a narrow valley approaching Riom, the tocsin was sounded and peasants lined the cliffs to attack the *vice-bailli* and his men. Faced with constant musket fire and avalanches of boulders, the *maréchaussée* retreated, losing one man.[143] The following year saw disturbances spread further in the area around Salers and Apchon. Mesgrigny administered a military defeat to a large group of rebels on the Planèze de St. Flour and boasted in June 1637 that "this region is now submissive." His comments on the rebellion, even taking into account seventeenth-century statistics and victor's exaggeration, give some idea of the scale of the disturbances on the Planèze: "As for the Haute Auvergne, there is no longer any danger and of six or seven thousand men who took up arms . . . to prevent the levy of the King's taxes there is not one stirring, the only trouble is that they are still among the crags and woods and have abandoned their houses to escape punishment."[144]

During the 1640s resistance was again troublesome and widespread. Many of the abandoned lands were reoccupied, but conditions were such that there was great difficulty in recovering taxes. In July 1641 a severe frost wiped out the ripening grain in the upper province and the decade that followed was to be one of continual strife.[145] One observer wrote that at the very mention of the word "gabelle" the people of the region "are so agitated . . . that they seem to be beside themselves."[146] In Aurillac itself there was considerable disorder and early in 1643, the house containing the lodgings of a royal tax official was set afire. While the rebel *croquants* besieged Villefranche in Rouergue that autumn, the consuls of Aurillac could find few Aurillacois willing to go to the aid of the besieged;[147] in any event, the countryside of the Haute Auvergne

142. A.C. Aurillac II⁷; Manry, ed., *Histoire de l'Auvergne*, 288–290.
143. *Chevauchées* 1636: October.
144. Mesgrigny to Séguier, 19 June 1637, in *Lettres*, 1:389; Bercé, *Croquants*, 1:440–41.
145. A.C. Aurillac, BB¹⁵, 17 September 1641.
146. D'Epernon to Séguier, 21 November 1645 in Mousnier, *Lettres*, 2:760.
147. A.C. Aurillac, BB¹⁵, 4–5 October 1643.

itself was by no means secure as the disturbances from Rouergue spilled over its borders. A dozen soldiers and officers were killed at St. Constance in Auvergne as their defenses crumbled at the onslaught of the rebels.[148] Troubles persisted to the end of the decade and beyond. In the parishes near the southwestern city of Maurs, no tax at all was paid from 1649 to 1652[149] and in October 1649, three *archers* were killed in an attack by several hundred peasants near Salers. The aggressiveness of the rebels around Salers had increased markedly since the incidents of the 1630s. When the *vice-bailli* and his *archers* saw the assembled force, they retreated across a river; but the peasants pursued and attacked them, chasing them into the sanctuary of a nearby château. The area was considered unsafe for most of the following year.[150] While there is little evidence of disturbances after 1650, the truculence of Auvergnats did not disappear. In October 1652, *vice-bailli* Paul Lacarrière reported that the *élection* of Salers still refused to pay the *taille*; and the area around Maurs was still resisting any attempts at collection. By 1654, however, the incidents involving the *taille* seemed to have resumed their pattern of occasional resistance by individuals or families; collections of taxes and seizures of property continued, often with the *maréchaussée* in attendance.[151] The last instance of resistance in the records of the *maréchaussée* occurred in September 1664, when two inhabitants of the election of Salers assaulted a *huissier* who had come to execute a property seizure for arrears in the *taille*. The response was heavy: Fortia, the Intendant of Auvergne himself, ordered Paul Lacarrière to find the culprits. When he arrived at the village of Besse, the *vice-bailli* found that both the accused and their relatives had fled and justice was satisfied with the seizure of furnishings from their houses.[152]

What do the revolts tell us about social alignments and social divisions? Were these popular uprisings by the poor against the rich (bourgeois, nobles, and the crown) as Boris Porchnev has suggested? Or were they reactions against a centralizing intrusive monarchy by the provincial "vertical society," described by Roland Mousnier and elaborated upon for the revolts in the southwest by Yves Bercé?[153] While we are not embark-

148. Charreton to Séguier, 30 December 1643, *Lettres* 1:576–77.

149. Bercé, *Croquants* 1:473.

150. *Chevauchées* 1649, 19–30 October; November; December 1650: 29 June; July.

151. *Chevauchées* 1652: 10 October, 6 October; 1654: 15 April, 18 March, 18 January, 1 July.

152. *Chevauchées* 1664: 3, 14–16 September.

153. A central point of contention between Mousnier and Porchnev lies in the analysis of what the revolts before the Fronde revealed about French social structure and about the interaction of different elements within the social order. Porchnev in his *Les Soulèvements*

populaires en France de 1623 à 1648 (Paris, 1963) contends that the revolts were popular uprisings in which peasants and the urban poor faced a united front. This class front included nobles, the monarchy, and the bourgeoisie, the last group having been "feudalized" away from its revolutionary role and attached to a "feudal-absolutist" power structure by the purchase of offices during the sixteenth and seventeenth centuries. Porchnev's book is valuable because it provides at least a partial chronology and a geographic analysis of seventeenth-century revolts (661–76) based on the Russian collection of the Séguier papers. His idea of a "feudalized" bourgeoisie is also useful because, although his case is somewhat overstated, it emphasizes the social aspirations of officeholders and the social fluidity of the period. Roland Mousnier's objections to the Porchnev theory are based on his extensive research into the anatomy of the Ancien Régime, beginning with his classic *Vénalité des offices* and followed by his *Institutions de la France* as well as numerous essays and books; see for example: "L'evolution des institutions monarchiques et ses relations avec l'état social," *XVIIe Siècle* (1963): 42–43; "Problems de stratification sociale" in *Deux cahiers de la noblesse pour les Etats Généraux de 1649–1651*, ed. J.-P. Labatut and Y. Durand, (Paris, 1965), 9–49; "French Institutions and Society," in *New Cambridge Modern History* (Cambridge, 1971), 4:474–502. His arguments with regard to peasant revolts are given ample documentation in *Lettres et mémoires adressées au chancelier Séguier* and more specific delineation in 'Recherches sur les soulèvements populaires en France avant la Fronde," *Revue d'histoire moderne et contemporaine* 5 (1958): 81–113 and in *Peasant Uprisings in Seventeenth-Century France, Russia, and China*, (New York, 1970) a translation by Brian Pearce of *Fureurs Paysannes: Les Paysans dans les révoltes du XVIIe Siècle* (Paris, 1967). According to Mousnier, Porchnev's thesis contains several important flaws, the most general being the narrow base of documentation. He also takes issue with Porchnev's view of horizontal layers of classes in French society, finding instead a "vertical society" in which seigneurs encouraged peasants in their opposition to royal impositions and bourgeois were aligned with the urban poor in the same cause, against the impositions of a monarchy essentially above class and against royal *commis* created to circumvent the obstacle of venal *officers*. Mousnier further rejects Porchnev's use of the term *feudal*, which implies servile rather than legally free peasant labor, although he admits that under the inchoate capitalism of the seventeenth century, seigneurs were still dominant (hence the persistence of noble dynasties and *clienteles*). The definition of nobility is another major point of contention. Porchnev's criteria admit both ennobled *officers* and *noblesse d'epée*. Mousnier, while he allows that *robins* could be legally noble, emphasizes the gulf between *noblesse de robe* and the *gentilshommes* of the traditional *noblesse d'epée*. The rise of the former at the expense of the latter, shown by the increased presence of *robins* in the king's council during the seventeenth century, was both an illustration and a cause of the conflicts between the two groups. A valuable addition to the debate is the detailed and fascinating work of Yves-Marie Bercé, *Croquants*, which investigates seventeenth-century popular uprisings in southwestern France. Bercé examines the social and economic conditions of the period, the taxes, and their effect on various social groups. He then provides a chronicle of the revolts followed by an analysis of the motives and behavior of rebels. In relation to the debate on social alignments, his clearest evidence is of a rural or vertical solidarity between peasants and *gentilshommes*, and generally his analysis of rural society could be said to support that of Mousnier. Among the numerous essays which have appeared, some of the most useful are J. H. M. Salmon, "Venal Office and Popular Sedition in Seventeenth-Century France: A Review of a Controversy," *Past and Present* 37 (July 1967): 21–43, and the collection edited by P. J. Coveney, *France in Crisis, 1620–1675*, which includes, as well as articles by Mousnier and Porchnev, some useful overviews of the debate and its problems: H. Methivier, "A Century of Conflict: The Economic and Social Disorders of the 'Grand Siècle,' " 1–63 and P. Deyon, "The French Nobility and Absolute Monarchy in the First Half of the Seventeenth Century," 231–46.

ing on a full-fledged inquiry into revolts, the question can still tell us much about the boundaries marked by violent criminality.

In the Haute Auvergne it is clear that peasants were the most important source of energy for revolt. They were the immediate victims of hard times and of tax collectors, and they formed the critical mass that changed individual rebellions into revolts. The uprisings were therefore popular, but how wide a community did they embrace? We have seen peasant families and then villages involved in resistance to the officers who threatened their property and persons. But the *Chevauchées* and other documents also give examples of lawyers, priests, and *gentilshommes* involved in resistance.[154]

Local nobles were often suspected of providing military leadership and sometimes arms for rebels, and the suspicion was always there that the nobles of Auvergne were exciting their peasantry to resist the agents of the crown.[155] One statute of the period went so far as to hold *gentilshommes* responsible for revolts of their peasants.[156] The letters of intendants and other royal agents were clear in their view of *gentilshommes* as leaders and fomenters of revolt. The Intendant De Sève near Aurillac, writing to Séguier in 1643 was also somewhat prophetic: "I have as much trouble over the *taille* in fighting against the gentlemen who thwart the payments as I do with the ill-will or the impotence of the taxpayers and I maintain that this province is more the place for a court of Grands Jours than for an Intendant of Justice."[157]

Another correspondent wrote that the nobles with their constant feuding and brigandage were setting a bad example for ordinary folk who then thought "that it is also permitted for them to shirk their duty." The Sieurs d'Estaing and Canillac had gone so far as to throw a tax official into a barrel of quick lime; and de Chaulnes, *maître de requêtes*, wrote, "I dare not go outside the walls of this city," for fear of d'Estaing and Canillac.[158] *Vice-bailli* Paul Lacarrière blamed *gentilshommes* for inciting the peasants to revolt in the Salers area and the Sieur de Senezergues was implicated in the deaths of several *archers*, when his lackeys along with other local inhabitants rescued a tax evader from the clutches of the

---

154. For example, *Chevauchées* 1642: 5 October; 1648: 11 February; 1659: 2 September, 21 July.

155. See, for example De Sève (Intendant) writing to Séguier from St. Flour, 26 February 1645, *Lettres* 2:757.

156. Ordinance of 8 January 1640, Isambert, *Receuil* 16: 525.

157. 18 October 1643 in *Lettres* 1:603.

158. De Chaulnes to Séguier, November (?) 1643, ibid., 1:558–59.

maréchaussée, killing the policemen in the process.[159] Whether or not *gentilshommes* were leaders in revolts, it seems highly improbable that they formed a "class front" with the crown and the officers of finance. As landlords, their interests lay with the peasantry, whose financial stress under taxation could only diminish their ability to pay seigneurial dues. Nobles defended the rural community upon which they depended and in which their interests lay against a rival power. Likewise we have seen the rural clergy acting in defense of their community against outsiders, and although they seldom appear in accounts of revolt, when they did, their allegiance was clear. De Chaulnes complained in 1643 of their subversive role. "There are even priests who have declared in the midst of the marketplace . . . that there should be no more payment of subsidies or arrears in *tailles*." There were only two parishes in the entire *élection* of Aurillac that had made an attempt to pay the *taille* in that year.[160] When the tocsin rang in the village, the priest was with his parishioners.

The experience of the city of Aurillac indicates that many within its walls were ready to resist the *taille*. But in general, the fortified towns, especially St. Flour and Aurillac, were still the safest places for tax gatherers, although the consuls along with other bourgeois and officers were bitterly opposed to the increase in taxation.[161] Trade was already suffering and many bourgeois were also seigneurs. The *vice-baillis* and their men were in a rather difficult position. Essentially a part of the community by birth and upbringing, in their role as protectors of the tax collectors, they found themselves the objects of abuse and sometimes of murderous attacks. For purposes of recovering taxes they could expect no help from the community and had to use their own resources as well as soldiers from royal regiments to suppress tax-related disorders. The local assistance they enjoyed when challenging disorderly regiments or sounding the alarm to chase out "Bohemians" vanished completely when they became reluctant agents of royal taxation.[162]

The "vertical solidarities" seem therefore to have demonstrated them-

---

159. *Chevauchées* 1636: October; 1649: October. In July 1650, Lacarrìere was warned away from the fair at Puy St. Mary in the election of Salers because a group of rebels had gathered there, and stirred up by "gentilshommes," were preparing to attack the *maréchaussée* and "tear them to pieces." For the rebellion at Senezergues and the trial of rebels, see *Chevauchées*, 1647–48.

160. *Lettres* 1:558.

161. See A.C. Aurillac, esp. 1636, 1642–43.

162. Their reluctance was probably particularly great in 1649 because the *maréchaussée* had not been paid for 1649, 1648, and half of 1647. *Chevauchées* 1649: November and December.

selves when the rural community was threatened by outsiders and the scale and social composition of the resistance widened with the magnitude of the threat. In the large-scale disturbances we can see that the violation of communal boundaries and the threat to the well-being of the community occasioned a massive riposte against the intruder, in which all members of the rural hierarchy participated. This solidarity does not deny the antagonism that peasants might feel toward the oppressive exactions of the *gentilshommes*, or the conflicts we have remarked between clerics and various other members of the community (for these were conflicts that would surface again very soon). Nor does it deny the normal deference to social superiors. It simply demonstrates the universal rural perception of the threat.

Common interest, tradition, and geographic location were strong cohesive forces. But this violent cohesion against outside threats was not necessarily a permanent structure; like many other sorts of violence, it represented a particular response to a particular situation. Solidarities arose and dissolved according to interest or necessity, albeit conditioned by traditional mentalities. So the "social order" was briefly reordered to meet the threat and a unanimity of fear or anger enabled a violent refutation of anyone who threatened the rural community.

The economy of violence during the period 1587–1664 displays certain social characteristics. The nature of the provocation and the riposte depended to some extent on the social characteristics of their authors. In the behavior of the rural elites we can see both assertions of leadership and attempts at social control. *Gentilshommes* were in an ambiguous position as both a source of authority and a major source of disorder. Their sense of a broad social jurisdiction, their tradition of collective and military action, and the impunity with which they could act gave them virtually a "right to assault." Violence itself was in some cases almost a proof of nobility, a useful tool in the administration of justice to inferiors and in the vindication of honor among themselves. As we shall see more clearly, however, the extent and the defense of noble psychic property were both extravagant in the perception of the central, reforming forces of a different order. The local clergy were very much "of the people" and shared in the life of their flock. They also exercised a local leadership and on occasion displayed a certain power and dignity that they jealously defended, often in the violent style of the region. But the penetration into the parish priesthood of Tridentine demands for a separate, elevated, and expert clergy would slowly effect a change in the attitudes of priests and of parishioners to priests, as the church tried to divide the traditional promiscuity of the sacred and the profane. Not only were priests to teach resignation to the humble, they had also to instill, and to learn, "decency."

Whether or not we can detect the beginning of elite withdrawal from the endemic combat of rural life, we can discern some vectors in the midst of the fray. The direction of violence was generally downward or lateral; violence upward, toward social superiors, was rare. *Qualité*, or identity, was therefore an important determinant in the direction and style of violence. But on occasion, social rank was not a prime consideration in the administration of the riposte. Just as an individual defended himself and his own worth, the protection and the honor of families and family communities were all-important. Just as a threatened family might forget its internal antagonisms[163] in order to confront an intruder, so did the rural communities, when faced with dangers from the outside, forget for a moment internal community problems and unify to repulse a threat to their perceived interests. For the moment, and for some time to come, ordinary rural dwellers would demonstrate remarkable resilience in the face of external influences. Solidarities were familial, local, and regional.

---

163. While not commonly reported, family disputes and violence are in evidence. Men murdered their wives (for example, *Chevauchées* 1588: 16 August; 1610: 1 January); on one occasion a young man killed his father (*Chevauchées* 1629: 18 August) and there were also murders of brothers-in-law and uncles (*Chevauchées* 1593: 27 March, 3 May; 1631: 5 April; 1647: 10 January).

5 The Process of Criminalization

A man disgraced is already half hanged.
—Proverb of the Haute Auvergne

In some struggles, the requirements of honor, and the defense of property, or simply the interest of the authorities, brought Auvergnats into the criminal courts. The combat then involved a new and less controllable belligerent: the crown or the state. Its purposes were similar in that it wanted vengeance for an affront. Like others dishonored, it wanted to teach the offender a public lesson, and to restore the honor or the order that its self-regard demanded, to demonstrate to all that its extensive claims were justified and must be recognized. Furthermore, as is often argued, during the period we have been examining, the monarchy was attempting more than ever—and more successfully—to enforce these extensive claims, overcoming obstacles to royal power, trying to extend its purview and its authority throughout France. Although it is not an all-sufficient description, one could say in the terms we have been using that the psychic property of French kings in our period was vast and growing, and given the insufficiency of force available, the crown could not in every case satisfy its honor with the violent immediacy that honor demanded. It could not quickly restore the productive decorum over which good kings were supposed to preside. The emphasis of the authorities was placed instead therefore on the publicity and dramatic solemnity of the lessons of justice, which unfolded from the arrest of a delinquent to shame, repentence, apology, and and a well-rehearsed, highly public death. It was to be clear to everyone that this was punishment, the fate of the wicked, not combat, that kings had no worthy adversaries within their own kingdoms. If the honor of ordinary subjects was not satisfactorily restored by unwitnessed vengeance, how much more publicity did the satisfaction of royal honor require?[1]

What did an accused person face when brought to justice? In the preceding chapters, we have seen the sorts of violent offenses for which inhabitants of the Haute Auvergne were pursued by the forces of order. Some of these acts of violence were forms of private justice, ripostes administered to those who challenged the dignity, honor, property, social leadership, or well-being of others. The recourse to official justice could be made at any stage in this economy of violence, and private justice thus made public. Having seen some of the evidence documented by the criminal courts, it remains to us now to examine the procedures that gave birth to those documents.

What did an accused person face? He or she faced a series of procedures that often challenged dignity and property as much as any private threat could do. In the case of the humbler sort of defendants, the alien, literate French-speaking world they feared and mistrusted was present in the officers of the court and the accused had to defend themselves in a hostile environment. Accusers could vilify them with no immediate fear of reprisal. Finally, they faced physical or financial punishment. Let us now discuss what were sometimes the last stages in the economy of violence.

French criminal procedure in our period depended heavily upon an expert judiciary, on secrecy, and upon written evidence. The process through which the accused passed was in the main a series of attempts to collect proofs of the offense in question; as the documents usually tell us, these were considered proofs "against" the accused. As each stage of procedure was completed, another piece was added to the *dossier* of the case. The accumulated written evidence was then examined and the fate of the accused decided. The system was supposed to be precise and mathematical, so that an expert judge could examine the written evidence and calculate the guilt of the accused.[2] There was, however, no

1. Perhaps what some regard as the disproportionate severity of official, as compared to popular, justice was due to the disproportion between the large claims and the small effectiveness of royal justice, the necessity of a political lesson. See Reinhardt, *Justice in the Sarladais*, 161–63, and the horrific opening of Michel Foucault, *Surveiller et punir: Naissance de la prison* (Paris, 1975), which is backed by this sort of argument. A most incisive study of the didactic and of the theatrical lessons of early modern punishment is Pieter Spierenberg, *The Spectacle of Suffering* (Cambridge, 1984).

2. Full proof was the statement of two "reputable" eyewitnesses under oath or a full confession by the accused. While in straightforward cases this standard made for admirable

precise code by which the officers of the courts could be guided. The oft-quoted ordinance of Villers-Cotterets (1539) enjoined "judges diligently to attend to the expedition of criminal proceedings,"[3] and referred to the various stages of procedure, constantly admonishing the tardy and the slipshod; but it never spelled out what exactly a judge was supposed to do, nor did it define or explain many of the terms and procedures to which it cryptically referred. In short, neither in this ordinance, nor in any of those that succeeded it, was there the sort of precise description that would have allowed a newcomer with no experience of the courts to understand the processes of French criminal law. For this reason, the criminal justice system required a high degree of expertise in its officers. One can also speculate that the existence of an expert bureaucracy and the need for a mass of written evidence must have given the courts a particularly daunting aspect to those who, unschooled in its ways, became its victims.[4]

More than royal statutes, the commentaries of noted jurists were a source of detailed information on how to proceed in criminal cases. They usually provided footnotes with classical Roman examples; sometimes the author also stated his views on the virtues and defects of the system. While some recent works have relied heavily on these commentaries and manuals, the value of such works is difficult to ascertain.[5] It may be that

---

dispatch in the proceedings, in cases that provided neither of these means of decision-making, the system broke down and judges tried to find partial proofs or resorted to torture to elicit confessions. Pierre Liset scorned the practice of allowing the deposition of one reputable witness to stand as "semi-full . . . because the truth is indivisible and that which is not fully true, cannot be half true." *Practique judiciaire pour l'instruction et décision des causes criminelles et civiles* (Paris, 1603), book 1, fol. 63. See also John Langbein, *Torture and the Law of Proof* (Chicago, 1977), 6–8, 50–55; and *Prosecuting Crime in the Renaissance* (Cambridge, Mass, 1974), 129–39 and 210–251, for a general discussion of the theory behind French legal procedures, a discussion that is primarily an elaboration of statutes.

3. Article 139.

4. Judges of the Ancien Régime, after a long period of "liberal" disrepute, are being rehabilitated, and it is increasingly common to find, or at least to be able to infer qualified admiration for their professional expertise. See, for example: Langbein, *Torture* and *Prosecuting Crime*; A. Soman, "Criminal Jurisprudence"; C. Plessix-Buisset, *Le Criminel devant ses Juges en Bretagne aux 16e et 17e siècles* (Paris, 1988), L.-B. Mer, "La procédure criminel au XVIII siècle: L'Enseignement des archives bretonnes," *Revue historique* 274 (1985): 9–42.

5. The two commentaries most frequently consulted for this chapter have been Pierre Liset, *Practique Judiciare*, and Jean Imbert, *La pratique judiciaire tant civile que criminelle* (Cologny, 1615), especially the former. J. Langbein, *Prosecuting Crime* is useful only as a general guide. He has relied on A. Esmein, *Histoire de la procedure criminelle en France et spécialement de la procédure inquisitionelle depuis le XIIIe siècle jusqu'à nos jours* (Paris, 1822), and especially on Imbert. The basic points of reference for this section are the dossiers of criminal records in the departmental archives.

they were simply glosses of procedural detail for the cultivated persons of their day. At any rate these works, if only because they were usually written from Paris, could not escape error in some parts of a diverse and far-flung bureaucracy. As Alfred Soman has suggested, most jurists' commentaries of the sixteenth and seventeenth centuries were not particularly accurate or useful for the Parlement of Paris,[6] let alone the outlying regions.

Compiling the Dossier in a Criminal Case

The complete dossier of a criminal case in the Haute Auvergne could range in size from a few separate pieces of paper up to thirty or more *cahiers*, depending on the survival of documents, the nature of the case, and the extent to which it was pursued. After the case had been introduced, either by a private party or by public prosecution, the two officials most extensively involved were the judge and the *procureur*. The former, along with his subordinates, was the author of the major documents we shall discuss, while the latter, whether a *procureur du roi*, which might be translated crown attorney, or his counterpart in a seigneurial court of criminal justice, reviewed each of the documents and recommended the next step in the proceedings; his recommendations were usually implemented by the judge. At various stages throughout, the accused or a representative of the accused petitioned the court for release from prison, or to have the charges dropped, usually (as far as the Haute Auvergne is concerned) with little result.

The documents in a complete criminal dossier were the following:[7]

6. See A. Soman, "Criminal Jurisprudence in Ancien-Régime France," 43–44. Soman's work is based on most extensive research in the criminal cases from the Parlement of Paris in the sixteenth and seventeenth centuries, and he found jurists' commentaries to be "not merely conservative but downright misleading" (44). While this is often true of the text of Liset, *Practique Judiciare*, his notes sometimes discuss accurately the divergence between practice and theory that took place in the Haute Auvergne. Soman's basic conclusion that only familiarization with more archival evidence will enable us to assess the value of these commentaries is, however, sound, and his work displays an enviable tenacity and intelligence in discovering the idiosyncrasies of actual practice.

7. Lists similar to this one have been published in several different places. The best supported of these are for the eighteenth century. See André Lachance, *La Justice criminelle au Canada au XVIIIe siècle* (Westport, Conn., 1981), 195–200. For the period under study here,

1. *Plainte or Dénonciation*   A complaint or accusation by the injured party or his representative, received by a judge.
2. *Information*   Depositions of witnesses, usually against the accused, gathered by a judge.
3. *Rapport du Chirugien*   A report of the medical examination undertaken in cases of physical abuse, carried out by a surgeon.
4. *Lettres Monitoires*   A summons to the general public to reveal information, published when the number of witnesses was insufficient.
5. *Décrets de prise de corps*[a] or *ajournement personelle*[b]   Decrees demanding the arrest[a] or appearance[b] of the accused.
6. *Interrogatoire or interrogation*   The examination of the accused by a judge.
7. *Conclusions du Procureur*   Procureur recommends either:
   (a) Conclusions préparatoires and   **or**   (b) Conclusions définitives

PROCÈS EXTRAORDINAIRE	PROCÈS ORDINAIRE

8. *Récolement*   Confirmation or Alteration by witnesses of depositions in *Information*
8. *Sentence by Judge*

END OF CASE 1

9. *Confrontation*   The accused meets witnesses to test their credibility.
10. Conclusions du Procureur   Either:
    (a) Conclusions préparatoires   **or**   (b) Conclusions définitives
11. *Faits Justificatifs*   *Torture*   Sentence by Judge
    evidence or witness   to produce
    in favor of the accused   confession

END OF CASE 2

12. Conclusions Définitives du Procureur
13. Sentence by Judge.

END OF CASE 3

The *Plainte:* Reporting Crime

The foundations of a criminal case were the complaint or denunciation and the *informations* or investigations against the accused, recorded by a judge or one of his subordinates.[8] In most cases the complaint is the first document, the initial exposure of an incident to official scrutiny; it launched the complex proceedings that constitute the dossier. While the complainants could be virtually anyone affected by an offense, they were usually either victims or their relatives, close friends or, occasionally,

---

the best lists remain the *inventaires* that accompanied complete dossiers in the archives: for example, Bailliage Royal de Murat, Procureur du Roy contre Jean Meyran, 18 September 1665, A.D. Cantal, 7B 204, which lists fourteen separate documents.
   8. Liset, *Practique Judiciare*, book 1, fol. 2.

servants. In some cases judges were simply alerted to an occurrence and then went to the scene of the crime to receive the statement of a complainant if one could be found.[9]

One major obstacle to the pursuit of justice by a victim was the cost, which in the royal courts was usually borne by the accuser. Whenever possible, victims or their relatives attempted to recover damages and conducted a civil suit parallel to the criminal case being pursued by public prosecution. The complainant thus also became a civil party (*partie civile*). While *plaintes* are usually found in the criminal archives being considered here, the place of the private complainant in criminal justice had become less important during the sixteenth century; by the period under study public prosecution was well developed.[10] A private complainant choosing to pursue a case also took on the responsibility of paying the expenses of the case. There is the suggestion in the court records of the Haute Auvergne that, in a case where the complainant did not have sufficient means to undertake the expense of seeking damages, and the *procureur* thought the case warranted public prosecution, the *procureur* became a joint complainant with the private party, who was not for the moment considered a paying *partie civile*. Damages could still be awarded to the plaintiff in the sentence against the accused and expenses subsequently collected by the court.[11] Effectively, then, whether prosecution was public or not, the *partie civile*, where such existed, paid the bills. In the event that the accused was permitted to call defense witnesses, the expenses of this part of the procedure could be charged to the defendant rather than the *partie civile*.[12] But that was much later in the proceedings. In any event the forces of order and "justice," were clearly more available to those who could pay, and others depended on the interest of the *procureur* in the gravity or importance of their case. In addition to poverty, rural seekers after justice in many cases had to contend with other obstacles. The distances to the appropriate courts were often long and the mountain paths difficult, and if one had to pay the expenses of witnesses, court officers, and court procedures, these

---

9. For example, Plainte du 17 Juillet, 1659, Présidial d'Aurillac, A.D. Cantal 1B 927.

10. Langbein, *Prosecuting Crime*, 224.

11. Sentences deffinitives contre Anthoinette and Francoize Quier, 26 September 1659, A.D. Cantal, 1B 927. The "Epice au conseil" of twenty-three livres was taken from the property of the contumacious accused. Because of the poverty of the homicide's widow in this case, the judge had earlier (17 July 1659) taken her "declaration" as a "plainte."

12. Plessix-Buisset, *Le Criminel devant ses Juges*, 488.

physical obstacles could make the cost prohibitive. The recourse to private vengeance therefore had attractions not directly related to honor.

The amount of information given in *plaintes* varied along with the form in which it was given. Some complainants simply told their story with a minimum of detail about themselves,[13] while others gave their name, age, *qualité*, and residence, and then swore to the truth of narrative, which was copied, read back to them, and signed.[14] The officer who received the *plainte* was usually a judge (although this was not necessary) and the *plaintes* bear their signatures and offices.

The *plaintes* themselves usually demonstrate a paucity or at least a similarity of imagination in the narrator. The accused was often said to have committed the offense without any reason at all, and in cases of violence, the murderous rage of the offender was given an unlikely suddenness by the aggrieved party. Sometimes a clue to the motives of the accused was given, but the general rule even in these cases, is of a transparent attempt to paint a portrait of virtue defiled by unmitigated evil. The guilty were usually said to have committed their crimes swearing and blaspheming all the while, striking "great" or murderous blows. Much was made of the sex, age, or disabilities of the victim if they helped to make him or her appear more pitiful. In the case of assault brought by Catherine Chareyres against Antoine Rougier, for example, Catherine's pregnancy was dwelt upon in the *plainte*, in the witnesses' depositions and even mentioned in the inventory of the dossier.[15] The *plaintes* as a result of these characteristics often present a simple moral drama.

Complaints were not always necessary. In particularly grave criminal cases or those which were discovered "in the act" (*en flagrant délit*), the judge simply went ahead with the information, collecting the depositions of witnesses. But most crimes in the documents from the Haute Auvergne were discovered by persons close to the victim and reported to royal or seigneurial authorities. In the cases involving actions of the *maréchaussée*, when crimes were often learned of by rumor (*bruit commun*), by public outcry (*clameur publique*) or interrupted in progress, the complaint proper was dispensed with and the *vice-bailli* immediately proceeded with his investigation.

13. Plainte pour Anthoine Tremoliere contre Jean Gibral, 9 October 1648, Juridiction de Brézons, A.D. Cantal 16B 280.
14. Plainte pour Guilhaume Lesset Denoniant contre Guilhaume Monieres, accuze, 24 July 1646, Juridiction Royal of Vic, A.C. Cantal 15B 675.
15. Bailliage of Murat, 1665, A.D. Cantal 7B 204.

With the official recording of a complaint that portrayed the accused in the worst possible light, an incident was elevated from a village crisis into formal litigation and the intervention of the state and of outsiders was, in most cases, virtually assured. Uneasy neighbors had become plaintiff, accused, and witnesses. For the accused, the process of criminalization, as we shall call it, had begun.

The Information

It was now the duty of the judge to investigate immediately the matter raised in the *plainte*. Royal ordinances and jurists' commentaries use the same language to express the necessity of a careful investigation; the *informations* from royal courts, *procès verbaux* and reports of the *maréchaussée* all imitate religiously their language of diligence and urgency.[16] If he took their claims seriously, the reader of *informations* would be convinced that all across the Haute Auvergne, judges were constantly and energetically springing into the saddle and riding to the scenes of crimes before breakfast or in the middle of the night, for judges make a habit of stating that they started out "incontinent après," or "immediatement" or "soudain" to commence the compiling of the *information*. The complainant needed to name witnesses if he wished the case pursued effectively, and it was to these witnesses that the judge went for depositions, as it was duly noted, "against" the accused; these depositions constituted the *information*. When witnesses were not immediately available or forthcoming, the judge would issue a decree requesting their appearance.[17]

In the ideal *information* the judge himself examined the witnesses, and in cases of serious crime or those which involved *gentilshommes*, this procedure seems usually to have been followed as decreed by law. But the jurist Liset recognized that in less important cases or at times when the appropriate officer was absent or indisposed, subordinates might take depositions. This might mean that *sergents royaux* at times questioned witnesses. Liset recommended that the *sergent* seek the assistance of a

16. Liset says "incontinent et sans delay" (at once and without delay), *Practique Judiciare*, book 1, fol. 2.
17. For example, "Exploit d'assignation des tesmoings," July 1659 marked "B," Présidial d' Aurillac, A.D.C. 1B 927.

senior court clerk or a *notaire* "whom he knows to be knowledgeable and experienced."[18] Preambles and signatures in cases from courts of the Haute Auvergne indicate that most depositions were recorded by a clerk in the presence of a judge but there are enough departures from the proper order of things to suggest a certain latitude of practice. In cases pursued by the *maréchaussée*, examinations were usually conducted by the *vice-bailli* or his lieutenant and recorded by the company recorder, sometimes in the presence of an assistant judge, or *assesseur*. In any case, the literacy of some *sergents* must be placed in doubt and it is improbable that all would have been capable of conducting much of an inquiry so heavily dependent upon written evidence.

The examination of witnesses followed a fairly consistent procedure: witnesses were to give their depositions separately and in secret; and the depositions in our dossiers often make reference to the fact that the witnesses had indeed been examined "in secret."[19] This secrecy referred not only to the accused, who might not know of the charges against him but also to the complainant or *partie civile* pursuing the case. Common sense tells us that the preservation of secrecy was in many cases restricted only to the exact words the witness had used in his deposition. In cases that involved a spectacular or long-standing dispute in a close-knit village community where the witnesses, the victim, and the accused were all well acquainted, the likelihood of secrecy was small. Some cases even reveal that witnesses had witnessed very little and were in fact repeating the same story heard from a single witness or, it is probable, from the complainant. Information was nonetheless being gathered against the accused and certainly the secrecy and the hostile nature of the proceedings thus far served to give even plagiaristic depositions a rather frightening aspect. This in a country, as Fléchier wrote in 1665, "where false testimony is not so forbidden as it is elsewhere."[20]

18. The Ordinance of Villers–Cotterets 1539, Art. 144 inveighed strongly against the practice of allowing subordinates to conduct examinations, while the Criminal Ordinance of 1670 allowed for illness or absence, Titre 6, Art. 6. That Pierre Liset made similar allowance indicates that in this matter the Ordinance of 1670 was probably recognizing existing practice. *Practique Judiciare*, book 1, fol. 2.

19. *Practique Judiciare*, book 1, fol. 3. See, for example, Information, 30 May 1662. Présidial d'Aurillac, A.D. Cantal, IB 928. Information, 19 October 1654, Présidial d'Aurillac, IB 925.

20. E. Fléchier, *Mémoires sur les Grands Jours d'Auvergne en 1665*, ed. A. Cheruel (Paris, 1856), 179. Indeed, we have found no cases in which subornation of witnesses was punished. In nearby Gévaudan, false witness seems to have been almost part of a litigious way of life, according to Claverie and Lamaison, *L'Impossible Mariage*.

The ritual in the *information* also added solemnity to the business at hand. First of all the witness gave the vital aspects of identity: name, age, *qualité*, and place of residence. In the case of married women, the maiden name was given and then the name of the husband. For the most part, the ages were approximate, as was other quantitative information given in the deposition: the witness was "about thirty years old," for example.[21] Often, before stating a dwelling place, the witnesses gave their place of birth, which seems to have been almost a part of the family name. The *qualité* was sometimes given as distinct from the occupation and witnesses were specific about both. For example, one stated that he was a *laboureur* (husbandman or ploughman) employed as a *palefrenier* (groom).

When their identity had been established, witnesses swore an oath in one of a number of styles. In the Haute Auvergne there was considerable variation from place to place. Some held one hand "raised to heaven,"[22] others "on the Holy Gospels"; a clergyman was to swear "a hand placed on his chest."[23] Witnesses then declared their knowledge of and relationship to the parties involved. In the Haute Auvergne the *informations* were often slipshod in this regard, although it was common for witnesses to declare themselves neither enemies, nor allies nor (if applicable) relatives of the parties involved.[24] Thus showing an awareness of the strength of alliances and households, the Ordinance of 1670 also required that they state whether or not they were "servants or domestics," but this requirement had usually been taken care of in the original oath.[25]

Witnesses were reminded of the incident in question by a reading of the *plainte* and then began to tell their tale. At this point the editorial effect of the clerks was probably highly important, for the depositions often read like the pared-down minutes from a long meeting. First of all, clerks wrote in the third person, not a verbatim record of the interview. Second, the deposition was probably spoken in Occitan but written in French, further eroding the original expression of the witness. Third, a naive reader might conclude that Auvergnats, despite their reputation for taciturnity, spoke in paragraphs. This is a point on which one can find

21. Information C, 10 April 1966, Juridiction de St. Urcize, A.D. Cantal 16B 1075.
22. Information, 9 April 1647, Juridiction de St. Chamont, A.D. Cantal, 16B 1015 and Bailliage Royal de Salers, 30 April 1633, A.D. Cantal 14B 307.
23. Information, 10 October 1648, Juridiction de Brézons, A.D. Cantal 16B 280.
24. Information, 23 July 1626, Juridiction de Conros, A.D. Cantal 16B 432.
25. Titre 6, Art. 5.

no definite proof, but it is an important point, not only for the *information* but also for the subsequent interrogation of the accused. Invariably statements take paragraph form. The *informations* show only that the witnesses stated their identity, and took the oath; these preliminaries are then followed by a well-ordered and continuous relation of the matter in question. The witnesses carefully established the time and date, the vantage point from which they watched the incident and then proceeded to tell in logical order, and sometimes in precise detail, what had happened.

The similarities of depositions in matters of order, vocabulary, and form suggest that there must have been considerable composition done by the clerks. What is probably missing is the evidence of prompting or interruption by the examiner. In a natural interview with witnesses, many of whom were reluctant or imprecise, one would expect the examiner to stop the story and ask for greater exactitude and better order in the telling. While this likely editorial influence undermines the usefulness of the documents, they are nonetheless valuable. Variations do occur in testimony, and there are details about weapons, actions, times of day, relationships and motives; in addition, insults, expletives, and ejaculations of various sorts are often included in probably close to their original form.[26]

When the deposition had been completed, it was read back to the witness who then signed the statement. Most ordinary folk in Haute Auvergne could not sign, and the subscript "did not know how to sign" is common in the case of peasant witnesses, sometimes accompanied by a mark. The dossier was then given to the *procureur du roi* or that of the seigneurial court, who could recommend several different courses of action. If the case against seemed to have substance, he could suggest a summons or an arrest; or if the number of the depositions of witnesses were insufficient, the next step might be the publication of *lettres monitoires*.

The *Monitoires*

The accuser who could not produce enough witnesses to support an accusation might ask the judge for permission to have *lettres monitoires*,

---

26. Judging from the work of others, such as L.-B. Mer, S. Reinhardt, and J. Ruff, the eighteenth-century depositions contain more in the way of direct speech.

literally "monitory letters," posted and read in the parish where the crime had occurred. The *curé* of the parish and sometimes those of neighboring parishes were then required to read clearly the document at mass on three consecutive Sundays. The *monitoire* demanded that all those who knew anything about the incident in question come forward and bear witness, enjoining them "to come to tell and reveal what they know from having seen, heard tell or otherwise within a week [eight days] on pain of excommunication."[27] Those words were in a *monitoire* issued by the Abbé of Aurillac, who ordered it read in several parishes, which was duly done and the document was signed by the parish priests. Such a document would seem to have added a sudden gravity to the proceedings with its threat of ecclesiastical and hence of divine censure, leading to the suggestion that it was used for only the most serious of crimes.[28] While this may have been so elsewhere, there are examples such as the *monitoire* requested in 1644 by the Sieur Lescure, an Aurillacois who had recently purchased land at St. Martin de Jussac and wanted to know who had cut down some of his trees "in abhorrence of his purchase."[29] While the seriousness of the crime was no doubt relevant to the decision to use a *monitoire*, one must conclude that crimes of a solitary, surreptitious nature, which were often less important but also less likely to have been witnessed, were the natural subjects for such a procedure.

The reason for the reluctance by the complainant to use the *monitoires* was more probably related to the dangerous unpredictability of their results. Up to this point, the complainant had managed to oversee the case quite carefully, relating only those facts that strengthened it and relying on witnesses who would support the accusation. The *monitoire* was a disinterested summons that could not designate specific witnesses[30] and that might ultimately reveal more than the complainant wanted. It could only be used at risk in contentious matters or in cases like that above of Lescure, who could not be damaged by some errant truth.[31]

27. For example, from Monitoire obtenu par Francois de Vernhes, Aurillac, 14 June 1655, Présidial Aurillac, A.D. Cantal 1B 926. The Ordinance of 1670, Titre 7, contains eleven articles on *monitoires* but there seems to have been nothing earlier in the way of statutory guidelines elsewhere, although *monitoires* were used throughout our period. See also A. Lachance, *La Justice Criminelle*, 67, C. J. Ferrier, *Dictionnaire de droit et de practique*, 2:306.

28. A. Lachance, *La Justice Criminelle*, 67–68.

29. *Monitoire*, 9 March 1644, Présidial d'Aurillac, A.D. Cantal 1B 1057. The *monitoire* had a mixed success, yielding six witnesses, who named different culprits. Another similar *monitoire* of 1642, A.D. Cantal 1B 923, was posted to discover who had stolen some food.

30. See Ordinance of 1670, Tit. 7, Art. 4.

31. See Yves Castan, *Honnêtété*, 95–96, an authority on the subject, who describes the

The Medical Reports

Sometimes a physical examination of the accused or, more usually, of the victim, was relevant to a criminal case. While in many instances of assault, this sort of evidence was observed and reported by the official who received the complaint, in others, especially toward the end of the period under consideration, the dossier contained the report of a surgeon. Such evidence might be required at any one of a number of points in the proceedings. The body of the accused might be inspected for brands that indicated a previous conviction, or in cases of murder or assault, the body of the victim was inspected to discover the extent of wounds and divine the types of weapons used.[32] Women were examined for evidence of rape, signs of recent unrecorded childbirth, or signs of pregnancy.[33] If a case involved injury, the surgeon was sometimes called by the onlookers or the complainants and then made his report while the issue was still alive.[34] In other cases, medical expertise was called upon considerably after the fact and the surgeon examined the corpse or bedridden victim.[35] The doctor then wrote the report to say that he had "diligently" examined his patient and finished his description with a date and a signature.

The examinations themselves were quite rudimentary and commonsensical, describing visible wounds and bruises as to their size and location along with other symptoms, such as fever, the inability to speak, and so on. The physician's cant was usually reserved for the naming of bodily parts. The corpse of Pierre Cassans for example bore a wound "on the left part of the parietal bone, having compressed the brain."[36] In the measurement of wounds and bruises the doctors usually resorted to rather

---

monitoire as "a remedy against the confinement of the inquiry . . . the way freely open to all witnesses" (96).

32. For example, Surgeons' Reports: 7 November 1648, Juridiction de Brezons, A.D. Cantal 16B 280; 4 November 1654, Présidial Aurillac, A.D. Cantal 1B 925; 9 April, 1661, Juridiction de St. Urcize, A.D. Cantal 16B 1075.

33. At La Roche-Canillac in 1663, a judge ordered the local midwives to carry out the examination of women suspected of child abandonment, 20 August 1663, Juridiction St. Urcize, A.D. Cantal 16B 1075.

34. For example, Rapport de Chirugien D, 17 July 1659, Présidial d'Aurillac, A.D. Cantal 1B 927; Francois Lasalle contre Ramond Laborie et Ser. Pradel, 23 July 1626. Juridiction de Conros, A.D. Cantal 16B 432.

35. For example, an assault was committed on Jean Tourdes, 1 September 1654, but the Surgeon's report was not made until 4 November 1654, Présidial d'Aurillac, A.D. Cantal 1058.

36. Rapport de Chirugien D, 17 July 1659, Présidial d'Aurillac, A.D. Cantal 1B 927.

homely imagery that was clearly recognizable to all, using expressions such as "the size of the palm of the hand," or "the length and width of three fingers," or in one case, "a wound the size and roundness of a five-sol coin."[37] The description of the likely weapons was usually so imprecise as to be useless, often suggesting both blades and blunt instruments in a list including swords, stones, clubs, daggers, and so on.[38] In cases where recent or current pregnancy was suspected, the signs were again obvious and external: swelling of the belly, tension or turgor in the breasts and nipples, or secretions of milk.[39] These examinations were not only performed by surgeons; in one case of infanticide before the *Grands Jours d'Auvergne*, a local judge had ordered that the breasts of all young women in the village be examined, leading Fléchier to imply in his *mémoire* that the interest of the judge was as much prurient as it was professional.[40]

Decrees and Arrests

When the *procureur* received the dossier containing the *plainte* and witnesses' depositions, he had then to present his conclusions. These were usually brief, only a sentence or two scrawled at the bottom of the *information*, and the ideal was that the conclusions be presented to the judge no later than two days after the *information* had been completed.[41] While *procureurs* often complied in the Haute Auvergne and presented their brief advice within the same day (if we are to believe their dates),[42] there were also cases in which the conclusions were late and the advice

37. Rapport de Chirugien B, 9 April 1661, Juridiction de St. Urcize, A.D. Cantal 16B 1075, and Rapport de Chirugien E, ibid, Rapport du Sr. Vaissiere Chirugien H, 2 November 1648, Juridiction de Brezons, A.D. Cantal 16B 280.

38. Rapport du Sr. Vaissiere Chirugien H, 2 November 1648, Juridiction de Brezons, A.D. Chantal 16B 280.

39. Report H, 29 July 1664, Bailliage of Murat, A.D. Cantal 7B 189.

40. Fléchier, *Mémoires*, 124. The judge was described as "un vieux raffineé."

41. Liset, *Practique Judiciaire*, book 1, fol. 11, gives two days as the maximum delay between the receipt of *information* by the *procureur* and the presentation of the *procureur's* conclusions. Unfortunately in some of our cases the *procureur* did not date his conclusions and therefore it is impossible to say how expeditiously the case was moved along.

42. Often the *procureur* simply dated it, as did the *procureur* Trenty in a case before the Présidial at Aurillac in 1659: "The procureur ex-officio, considering the investigations made in the number of five witnesses requires it to be ordered that the accused be arrested . . . and the whole to be communicated as required and as is fittingly arranged the said day and year as above"; A.D. Cantal 1B 927.

lengthy. One Giral Delchie for example, complained to the local court of St. Urcize on 9 April 1661 that he had been attacked in his own house. He was examined by a physician the same day and a long, interrupted *information* was completed on 20 April. The conclusions of the deputy *procureur* did not appear until 30 April and they came in a separate *cahier* together with a decree of arrest (*prise de corps*). Furthermore, the conclusions were not the usual brief message but a two-page summary of the case thus far, including the complaint, the medical report, and a detailed *précis* of all the evidence given.[43]

In his conclusions, the *procureur* recommended the means by which the accused could be brought in for examination. We have few cases in which the judge did other than what the *procureur* recommended; therefore it is safe to assume that when he issued a decree, the judge generally agreed with the *procureur* as a matter of form.[44] Justice officials used three different levels of decrees or *arrêts*, the *assignation a être oui* (summons to be heard), the *ajournement personnel* (personal summons) and the *décret de prise de corps* (writ of arrest). The three documents essentially represent different degrees of constraint upon the accused, the first two being summonses of varying weight and the last, physical capture and imprisonment. The *assignation a être oui* was the least threatening of the three orders, simply a summons that seems to have been almost in the nature of a request. If resisted, however, the judge could decree an *ajournement personnel*, or summons with fixed periods of time, after which the defaulting accused could be arrested with a decree of *prise de corps* and have his property seized by the court.[45] The deliberations of the *procureur* took into account the gravity of the offense, the completeness of the proofs and the *qualité* of the persons involved. The last factor is particularly important to our study: it not only shows the wide discretion

43. Décret de prise de corps, 30 April 1661, G, Juridiction de St. Urcize 16B 1075. Unfortunately the actual decree was in the second half of the *cahier*, which was badly damaged.

44. This seems generally to have been the case elsewhere. Liset did not mention the possibility of a disagreement between *procureur* and judge. See also A. Lachance, *Justice Criminelle*, 67–68. Exceptions did take place. In the case of assault against a *notaire royal* at Murat, the judge did not decree against the accused as the *procureur* had wished, but simply attached a note to the conclusions saying that the accused should be informed of the "suspicions" against him and should come to see the judge at three o'clock that afternoon. Subscript to *information*, 30 June 1665, Bailliage of Murat, A.D. Cantal 7B 189.

45. The Ordinance of 1670 codified the practice very clearly in Tit. 10, Arts. 3 and 4, saying that (3) The *assignation pour être oui* will be converted into a *décret d'ajournement personnel* if the party does not appear and (4) The *ajournement personnel* will be converted into a *décret de prise de corps* if the accused does not appear within the time set by the *décret d'ajournement personnel.*

allowed judges in the vital matter of bringing the accused to justice; it also betrays the social attitudes of the inquisitor toward the accused. Liset in this, as in other procedural matters, never lets his readers forget that Justice must approach her subjects with due regard for their standing in society:

> And in all cases, injuries as well as others, in enacting the said investigations, the Judge will be attentive to the quality of the persons charged: because one can and must more easily issue writs of arrest against those of low estate, or although they be of noble quality, nevertheless lead a wicked life than those of noble quality and who have always lived well before without blame or reproach.[46]

In the Haute Auvergne the administration of justice found little ambiguity in the words *noble* and *qualité*; both referred exclusively to social rank in matters of this sort. In relatively unimportant matters an ordinary person might receive an *assignation* or an *ajournement*,[47] but in more serious cases only those who held noble or at least notable rank could expect to walk with some measure of dignity as they approached the royal judiciary. *Assignations* and *ajournements personnels* in our documents were used frequently therefore to call to justice *gentilshommes* and other influential persons.[48] Indeed, part of the "shock value" of the extraordinary Grands Jours d'Auvergne of 1665 was in the perfunctory fashion with which some members of the most eminent families in the province were arrested and imprisoned.[49]

While a summons allowed more dignity to the person in question, there was a second, even more likely, reason for its use in cases involving

46. Liset, *Practique Judiciare*, book 1, fol. 12.

47. For example, case of *excès*, *décret d'ajournement personnel* v. Marguerite Doux and Antoine Jourde, 4 August 1632, Bailliage Royal de Salers, A.D. Cantal 14B 307; Décret d'Ajournement personnel v. Charles Segret, 21 August 1662, Bailliage de Murat, A.D. Cantal 7B 204; Ajournement, 11 March 1648, Juridiction de Brezons, A.D. Cantal 16B 280.

48. Assignation, *Chevauchées*, 1659: 19 August; Ajournement Personnel, ibid., 1655: 12 February; Ajournement personnel, ibid., 1664: 28 July. In fairness to the *vice-baillis*, while they generally followed Liset's attitude in these matters, they all seem to have pursued accused noblemen more valiantly than did the other royal officers.

49. The Vicomte de la Mothe de Canillac was so sure of his immunity on an old charge of murder that he stayed in Clermont at the opening of the Grands Jours. He was startled in bed by the *prévôt* d'Auvergne and was taken prisoner, tried, and beheaded, Fléchier *Mémoires*, 51–53, Dongois *Registre*, 23 October 1665.

the wealthy and powerful. In a province inhabited by families with armed retainers and fortified houses, the task of prising a *gentilhomme* from his lair or of defeating him in a skirmish was daunting; a summons was easier and probably as liable to succeed. In any event, the dignity of royal officers often suffered in the affair, no matter which procedure was followed.

While judges had great latitude in the matter of arrests and could and did issue writs of arrest with less than a complete *information*, they were constrained by simple force of arms and by the social distance between the arresting officers and their quarry. Liset gave some of his best advice on this point: in cases that involved "influential and mighty people of noble rank" the arresting officer must be as high ranking as possible and must take with him "a good number of constables and other folk."[50] For the rest of the accused, writs of arrest were used liberally in cases ranging from simple theft to murder.[51]

The *Interrogatoire*

Accused persons appearing at the court were to be examined immediately, properly, and diligently. The judge was to conduct the examination personally; it was never to be done by a subordinate official.[52] The accused were to answer the questions directly, "from their lips" and without counsel,[53] and the questions were based on the contents of the *plainte* and the *informations*.

The *interrogatoire* was a pivotal point in any case and aside from the pronouncement of the sentence, it was also probably the most solemn for the accused. Liset used the most ancient and unassailable precedent he could find in his notes on the subject, writing that God himself had used the same system, having conducted interrogations of both Adam and

50. Liset, *Practique Judiciare*, book 1, fol. 12.

51. Arrests for theft, for example, *Chevauchées* 1630: 1 June; 15 June; 1636: 19 April; 1646: 16 May; 1647: 3 April.

52. Both the Ordinance of 1539 (Villers-Cotterets), Art. 146 and that of 1670 Titre 14 emphasized the urgency of prompt questioning, at most twenty-four hours after the accused appeared or was arrested. The matter was also taken up by Liset, *Practique Judiciare*, book 1, fol. 45, who referred to the 1539 Ordinance.

53. Liset, *Practique Judiciare*, book 1, fol. 48, Ordinance of 1670, Titre 14, Art. 8.

Cain before he condemned them.[54] This parallel is altogether felicitous, for the accused in Early Modern France must at times have felt themselves in the position of the first two biblical accused. But the fear many may have felt could at least be mitigated by the hope that at this stage defendants finally had a chance to defend themselves.[55]

Alone, in secret, and sometimes without much knowledge of the evidence against them, the accused faced officials who were part of another world and who had considerable discretionary power vested in them. Not only would these circumstances have been somewhat daunting; defendants at this point also participated for the first time in their own case. The accused were only given hints to the accusations they faced in some cases, through the content of the examiner's questions, but their fate depended in large part on the outcome of this interview. Here they could for the first time "raise defenses,"[56] although they had no lawyer and the trial was heavily dependent on their aptitude for answering questions. Here also it would be decided whether or not a case was sufficiently serious and the proofs convincing enough for the matter to be pursued further, perhaps to the point of torture. With so much attached to the *interrogatoire*, it is not surprising that Langbein perceives it as something imbued with stark drama and excitement referring to "leading players" and the "supporting cast."[57] In some *interrogatoires* these qualities were indeed present and the jurist Jean Imbert advised judges to record the fear, changeability, and nervous mannerisms of the accused.[58] Liset did not hope for much in the way of detail, but he did advise judges on how they should conduct an examination:

> It is the duty of the judge to examine the criminal in which great prudence and discretion are required, especially in heinous crimes, of which it is proper to search out and discover the truth, and the criminal must respond from his own lips to the questions put to him. Because I wish a certain adroitness in a judge, to question the accused subtly, precisely and diligently: I cannot also condone the deceitful tricks used by some who are driven more by emotion than by the mandate of justice.

54. Liset, *Practique Judiciare*, book 1, fol. 48.
55. Genesis 4:9, 10, authorized version.
56. Langbein, *Prosecuting Crime*, 230.
57. Ibid., 228.
58. Imbert, *Practique*, chap. 10, 628–29 quoted in Langbein, *Prosecuting Crime*,

While he did not want judges to surrender to passionate browbeating, Liset did recognize the fact that the judge was nonetheless an actor:

> Commensurate with the nature of the crimes the judge should be more severe or more moderate and benign in questioning the criminal: but in all cases and deeds he must maintain the restraint and prudence of a judge.[59]

In contrast to these stage directions, our *interrogatoires* seem rather pedestrian documents relating questions and answers. The hand of the recorder may have been at work again, compressing, translating the dialect, converting statements into the third person and deleting evidence of prompting, as seems to have been the case in the *information*. But *interrogatoires* still retain a good deal of the dramatic contest between the judge and accused; they also illustrate varying levels of subtlety and care employed in the examinations. The accused swore an oath to tell the truth, gave their name, age, *qualité*, and place of residence. Then the judge began. The differences among examiners appear almost immediately. A common first question was whether or not the accused knew his victim, which was usually answered more elaborately than with a simple yes or no: "I know him to see him," or "I know him because we both come from the same village."[60] Another common question was the stock phrase of courtroom drama: "Where were you on the night of . . . ?" specifying a time and date.[61] After initial questions like these, the styles of the *interrogatoires* show considerable variation. Gerauld Fabry, judge in the royal court at Vic, asked only two questions after the initial response, the first of which occupied about three pages. Clearly here the judge was simply reading from notes on the case, for his first question went through all the details of the matter at hand; or the clerk may simply have ignored the series of questions and made the entire document into one long question followed by one long answer. The accused Ramond Jarrige denied his guilt but then gave his version of the incident in question in a response that occupies a page and a half.[62]

---

59. Liset, *Practique Judiciare*, book 1, fol. 48.
60. For example, Interrogatoire, 11 August 1646, Bailliage of Vic, A.D. Cantal 15B 675; Interrogation, 26 July 1664, Bailliage of Murat, A.D. Cantal 7B 189.
61. For example, Interrogatoire, 12 March 1648, Juridiction de Brezons, A.D. Cantal 16B 280.
62. Interrogatoire, Royal Courts at Vic, 11 August 1646, A.D. Cantal 15B 675.

Although some judges seem to have been lazily content to give the accused all the details of the accusations against them right away, others approached the prisoner more gradually and attempted to elicit his version of the incident in question. In a case of assault and wounding (1616), Jacques Lacarrière, *vice-bailli*, began by asking Pierre La Salle if he knew the victim, Laurent Delboin, and if he had ever had any disagreements with Delboin. When La Salle denied ever having "had a dispute with him," the examiner then narrowed his questioning to the specific incident.[63] Judge du Laurens used similar tactics when questioning his first two accused in a case of communal resistance to tax officials in January 1644.[64] But the next day in questioning the third defendant, he used the other tactic of repeating the entire accusation before awaiting a response.[65]

In the most serious cases, the examining magistrates seem to have approached the matter much more carefully and the *interrogatoires* were more elaborate, even where the case itself was not necessarily more complicated. While in every case the judges wanted to find out what was done and by whom, in some cases of murder, or cases that involved the more socially eminent, there seems to have been a more elaborate attempt to set up the situation and the motivations surrounding the crime, and a good deal more effort to lead the accused toward confession that constituted proof. When Jacques Ruat examined a woman accused of conspiring in the murder of an unwelcome suitor (1664), he first tried to establish that she was a "loose" woman who had had rival lovers; he then attempted to question her about the growing acrimony between the two men, and about how she had formed a "conspiracy and plot" with one lover. The judge concluded with the actual murder and then tried to get an admission of guilt by forcing the accused to recount her incriminating behavior after the murder had taken place.[66] An *interrogatoire* of 1659, in which a merchant was questioned about the death of his customer, was about seven pages, the same length as the case above. The judge Boigues began by asking the accused why and by whose order he

---

63. Audition, 2 December 1616, Coups et Blessures, Présidial d'Aurillac, A.D. Cantal 1B 921.

64. Interrogatoires of Marguerite de Sallectz and Catherine de Courbasse, 25 January 1644, Présidial d'Aurillac 1B 1057.

65. Interrogatoire of Jeanne de Sallectz, 26 January 1644, ibid.

66. Audition et Response, 21 April 1664, Juridiction de St. Just., A.D. Canal 16B 1048.

was imprisoned. Then he proceeded to reconstruct events, mainly with the testimony of the accused.[67]

Two final observations should be made about the behavior of judges evident in most *interrogatoires*. The first regards the general refusal to pursue interesting lines of inquiry raised by the accused. The questions asked often give the impression that examining magistrates were virtually deaf to the responses of the accused. Even after the defendants denied the truth of the examiner's statements, the latter usually continued to pound away at the basic facts he was trying to verify, with little show in most cases of attempting another approach.[68] The other outstanding characteristic is the final severity of the judge's remonstrances at the close of the examination. A typical case in point is the series of three *interrogatoires* by Jean André de la Ronade, *lieutenant général, civil et criminel,* in the *bailliage* of Salers. The judge at the end of each examination repeated what seems to have been a common final assertion among the examining magistrates: "We remonstrated with him that he had not told and confessed the truth at all." Others were more forceful: "We remonstrated with him that he was perjuring himself,"[69] while at other times, the clerk merely recorded something like "Summoned to tell the truth he said that he had told it."[70] Usually after giving this stern admonition, the judge repeated the basic accusation and the accused denied it. The purpose was to show that the accused knew what he was saying, after which the record would show that he had heard the repeated questions and confirmed his answers before signing, or declaring that he was unable to sign the document.

As for the accused, the most remarkable characteristic of the detailed *interrogatoires* from the Haute Auvergne is their lack of confessions. All defendants, by their own account, were innocent. Even in cases that contain a substantial body of proof against them, the accused protested their innocence to the end.[71] While many would admit to having been on the scene at the time in question, the crucial admission of guilt was

---

67. Interrogatoire, 9 September 1659, Présidial d'Aurillac A.D. Cantal 1B 927.

68. Interrogatoires of Pierre Noel, Gabrial Rodde and Pierre Chalier, 12–13 January 1654, Bailliage of Salers, A.D. Cantal 14B 227.

69. Interrogatoire, 11 August 1646, Royal court at Vic, A.D. Cantal 15B 675; Interrogatoire, 17 October 1648, Juridiction de Brezons, A.D. Cantal 16B 280.

70. Interrogatoire, 26 January 1644, Présidial d'Aurillac, A.D. Cantal 1B 1057.

71. This despite Langbein's quoted opinion from Imbert that some judges frightened or tricked their prisoners into confessing. *Prosecuting Crime,* 229–30.

not given. It was in many ways second only to flight, the most sensible course of action for the accused. Judges were interested mostly in the discovery of the incriminating physical facts of the case; and the court officers in the inquisitorial system acted as both accusers and defenders of the defendant.[72] With no counsel available in the *interrogatoire*, the accused could only hope to convince the judge that there was enough doubt in the matter to allow further defenses to be raised. Even though they had been able to discover the main points of the accusation from the questions asked, the accused still had no idea of the weight of evidence in their own favor, although they did not yet have the right to name witnesses in their own defense.[73]

Reglement À L'Extraordinaire

When the *interrogatoire* had been completed, it was given to the *procureur*, who reviewed the dossier and then presented his conclusions. If the *procureur* thought the case only a light criminal matter he would present *conclusions définitives*, recommending a specific sentence from the judge;[74] or he could request that the case be converted to a civil procedure, through which the *partie civile* could receive damages if willing to pursue the matter further.[75] The *conclusions définitives* at this point indicated that procedures were following *règlement ordinaire*. If, however, the *procureur* thought the matter serious enough to warrant further prosecution of the case and heavy punishment, and if a confession had not been obtained, he presented *conclusions préparatoires* and recommended that the judge pursue the case following *règlement à l'extraordinaire*. The latter course was a serious step. It meant that the judge would proceed to the *récolement* and *confrontation* of witnesses, and beyond.[76] In the most complete *conclusions*, the *procureur* enumerated the various documents of the dossier and then made his request that the accused "[would] be tried

72. Liset, *Practique Judiciare*, book 1, fol. 8.

73. Langbein, *Prosecuting Crime*, 230.

74. For example, "Conclusions Definitives," 12 September 1659, Présidial d'Aurillac, A.D. Cantal 1B 927. See also Liset, *Practique Judiciare*, book 1, fol. 56, 46–47.

75. Example of a case converted to civil procedure, 12 January 1654, Bailliage de Salers, A.D. Cantal 14B 227. For example, Conclusions du Procureur and Sentence of Extraordinary Procedure, 29 August 1608, Présidial d'Aurillac, A.D. Cantal 1B 920.

76. Ibid.

by the reexamination of previous evidence and the confrontation of witnesses." The judge signified his agreement either with a simple subscript or in some instances, with a fully documented sentence.[77]

Récolement and Confrontation

The *récolement* was simply a confirmation by the witnesses of their testimonies taken during the *information*. Witnesses appeared separately before the judge and his clerk. The proceedings were still secret, and theoretically neither the evidence nor the identity of the witnesses was known to the accused. Witnesses swore to tell the truth and heard their depositions read to them by the clerk. They were then asked if they wished to deny, amend, or persist in their original deposition. When the witnesses had indicated and carried out their desire, they were then asked to sign the record of the *récolement*.[78] In no case do we find a denial of previous testimony.[79] This is not surprising, for false witnesses could face criminal proceedings and, once they had testified, were obliged to appear. The *récolement* therefore, took on a rather perfunctory air, with truths and lies confirmed by the witnesses.

When the *procureur* had received the *cahier* containing the *récolement*, he could request that the judge order a confrontation between the accused and principal accusers. This was the second chance for the accused to defend themselves verbally, and in some cases, the last chance.[80] In the *confrontation* the witnesses each appeared separately with the accused. Both then swore an oath before the judge. The witness then identified the accused as the person referred to in the deposition; and the accused was immediately asked if there was any objection to the witness. Not having heard the deposition, the defendant could only make state-

---

77. For example, Sentence marked "N," August 1659, Présidial d'Aurillac, A.D. Cantal 1B 927.

78. For example, Récolement 12 May 1664, Juridiction de St. Just, A.D. Cantal 16B 1048. The standard phrase was usually something like the following: "After his deposition has been read to him word for word he says and affirms by means of the oath he swears . . . that he wants neither to add to nor to diminish it and that he will support it fact for fact."

79. A. Lachance, *La Justice criminelle*, had similar findings in his eighteenth-century documents (76).

80. The Ordinance of Villers-Cotterets 1539, Arts. 152–57 contains provisions concerning confrontations.

ments in the way of personal objection to the witness: a mutual dislike, long-standing enmity, or perhaps a previous legal conflict.[81] When the objections had been recorded, the witness's deposition was then read aloud and the accused was allowed to object to any of the facts therein and to question the witness.

After the deposition had been read, the accused had supposedly lost the chance to object to the witness per se, but the confrontations by their very nature led to an excitement that did not always follow the prescribed forms. In the royal prison at Murat, witness François Pounhet was brought before the prisoner Jean Meyran. In the initial phase of identification there was no objection to the witness, known only to accused by sight; but when Meyran heard the damning deposition, the record shows that he immediately attacked Pounhet and "Staring at him intensely, told him angrily that he was an old witch."[82] Confrontations did not take place merely between the accused and witnesses, but also between the accused and the complainant; or, in cases that involved more than one accused, the defendants might be brought together.[83]

Faits Justificatifs

During the phases of *interrogatoire* and *confrontation* the accused could not only object to the witnesses, but could also give an alibi or some other strong defensive objection, "justificatory facts," to the accusation. These *faits justificatifs*, recorded by the judge, could be the basis for a move by the prosecutor to request the designation of defense witnesses by the accused. In the case that such defenses were raised, the *procureur*, who had been organizing the prosecution of the accused, was suddenly involved in organizing the defense. The ordinance of Villers Cotterets demanded that the designation of witnesses be done immediately and much has been made of the injustice of such a harsh and peremptory

81. Langbein, *Prosecuting Crime*, 234.
82. Confrontation marked "K" undated (probably August 1665), Bailliage de Murat, A.D. Cantal 7B 189. All four of the witnesses in this case upheld their depositions and the accused discredited none of them, nor did he produce any evidence to warrant the examination of defense witnesses. See also a series of confrontations, 3–10 June 1656, Présidial d'Aurillac, A.D. Cantal IB 926.
83. Confrontation, 28 July 1664, Bailliage de Murat, A.D. Cantal 7B 189.

demand.[84] But the notes of Liset contradict the ordinance, noting that this haste, because of its injustice, was seldom enforced, and the accused, according to the circumstances of the case, was usually allowed a delay,[85] after which witnesses for the defense were examined in much the same way as those for the prosecution had been.

Torture

If the *procureur* received a dossier that contained strong evidence of guilt, but not full proof against the accused, he could recommend torture. While the subject of torture has inspired recent interest, not much is known about the extent to which it was practised during this period. Liset's manual has fairly extensive notes on the matter, cautioning judges to use torture carefully, only to use it once on the accused, and to avoid torturing persons of quality or decent folk of good reputation. As if to emphasize the nature of those being tortured, he always uses the word "criminal" instead of "accused."[86]

Unfortunately, there are no complete minutes of tortures in the dossiers of the royal courts in Haute Auvergne and so I cannot describe in detail the tortures that, as Liset encouraged, followed the "style of the region."[87] But the records of the *vice-baillis* indicate that torture was used on prisoners of the *maréchaussée* although they do not describe the methods used. Prisoners were tortured in Jean Lacarrière's vivid phrase "to extract from their mouths the truth of the case."[88] These tortures

84. Arts. 157 and 158. Langbein holds to this view of promptness of the ordinance and quotes J. Imbert, *Practique*, in support of his view, *Prosecuting Crime*, 235.

85. Liset, *Practique Judiciare*, fol. 57, note e. There are not enough examples of *faits justificatifs* in the A.D. Cantal records for me to comment upon them.

86. Liset, *Practique Judiciare*, fol. 64. See also fols. 58–59, 63–66. The most extensive archival work on torture is being done by Alfred Soman. See his "Criminal Jurisprudence in Ancien Régime France," 54–61. Soman particularly emphasizes the ineffectiveness of torture as a means of obtaining a confession. Julius Ruff provides a brief clear discussion of torture in his *Crime, Justice and Public Order in Old Régime France: The Sénéchaussées of Libourne and Bazas, 1696–1789* (London, 1984), 55, 61, 63.

87. Liset, *Practique Judiciare*, fol. 66.

88. *Chevauchées*, 1592, 30 April. There seems to have been no particular period for torture. In cases of theft, for example, there are 18 sentences of torture spread evenly throughout the period, the last three in 1659. In 717 cases, J. Ruff found only one case of torture as a means of eliciting a confession, *Crime, Justice and Public Order*, 55. His evidence is, however, for a later period.

took place after the *interrogatoire* but before the definitive sentence, and their object seems to have been a full confession, although there is no indication that the desired evidence was obtained;[89] in some cases the accused were even released after torture.[90] But there were also cases in which torture was used on those already condemned in order to find out about accomplices.[91] While Liset cautioned that only those thought to be guilty of grave crimes should be tortured,[92] thieves as well as murderers were submitted to the *question* (torture).[93] In other cases such as that of the murder by servants of their mistress, it seems that torture was used as punishment.[94]

The Sentence

In his *conclusions définitives* the *procureur* recommended the final course of action for the judge, based on a review of the dossier, and then the judge passed sentence on the accused. In the *sentences définitives* of the Haute Auvergne, the judge listed again the separate documents of the case before rendering a verdict. He listed them but did not really explain, usually writing of the accused, for example, "We have declared and declare them sufficiently guilty and convicted of having killed and beaten to death by stoning the deceased."[95] An exception was Judge Guillaume de Travesse in the *bailliage* court at Murat, who in a murder case not only listed the pieces of evidence but gave a sentence that occupied one *cahier* and then listed his proofs in another, describing in detail the strength of each piece of evidence: (1) a deathbed confession (2) eyewitnesses; (3) surgeon's report; (4) vacillation of the accused during the *interrogatoire*. All of which made it "very just and reasonable" to hang the murderer.[96] This sort of scrupulous accounting was closer to the ideal of the day than

89. For example, *Chevauchées* 1593: 13 April; 1593: 30 May; 1595: 13 March; 1607: 7 June; 1608: 23 February.
90. *Chevauchées* 1592: 23–30 April; 1593: 31 May.
91. *Chevauchées* 1593: 18 June; 10 August.
92. Liset, *Practique Judiciare*, fol. 64.
93. *Chevauchées* 1627: 10 August; Estienne Esclause was not given credit for a specific crime, but simply called "diffame volleur" and tortured 13 March 1595.
94. *Chevauchées* 1652: 4 May.
95. *Sentence Deffinitive*, 26 September 1659, Présidial d'Aurillac, A.D. Cantal 1B 927.
96. *Sentence Definitive*, 18 September 1665, Bailliage de Murat, A.D. Cantal 7B 204.

most sentences: the matter of assigning penalties was probably the stage of procedure requiring the most erudition among judges; "because in France," as Liset had it, "the penalties are arbitrary."[97]

It is interesting that despite the impulse to codify criminal procedure that found expression in the Ordinances of 1539 and 1670, the Ancien Régime never produced an official criminal code. The more extensive of the two ordinances (1670) contains punishments in descending order of severity: death, torture *avec réserve de preuves*, life in the galleys, perpetual banishment, torture *sans réserve de preuves*, limited terms in the galleys, and banishment for a limited time.[98] But nowhere in the ordinance were judges told in what circumstances to apply the penalties. They had the accumulation of royal statutes to give them instances of the maximum penalty for some specific crimes, but the calculation of guilt was a chore for the legal mind with no statutory guidelines. This arbitrary power of the judge therefore lay in the attenuation or the augmentation of punishments; for the principles by which to use this power, judges had to rely on ancient tradition and the words of the learned doctors of laws.[99]

Theoretically there was a great range of circumstances that could affect the severity of punishments, all of which were the subject of learned debate. Interestingly, they were in many cases the sorts of issues debated in courts of law operated on the adversary system. What were the

97. *Practique*, book 1, 64.

98. Ordinance, August 1670, Titre 25, Art. 13. There is some debate as to the meaning of the words *réserve de preuves* attached to torture sentences. B. Schnapper, in a study of sixteenth-century sentences from the Parlement of Paris seems to believe that torture *avec réserve de preuves* referred to sentences in which partial proofs were retained and the prisoner punished despite the lack of confession during torture. See, for example, "La Justice criminelle rendue par le Parlement de Paris sous le regne de François 1er," *Revue historique de droit français et étranger* 52, no. 2 (1974): 252–84, esp. 262–68. A. Soman ("Criminal Jurisprudence in Ancien-Régime France," 55) has raised serious questions about Schnapper's interpretation, citing cases in which a similar phrase was used (*les indices ne seront purgés*) but which nonetheless resulted in the release of the accused. A similar phrase (*sans purgation d'indices*) occurs in the *Chevauchées* (for example, 1652: 4 May), but unfortunately there is not enough regularity in the use of the phrase to allow speculation on its meaning; in most torture cases it was not used at all and there seems to have been no difference in the fate of the prisoners afterward. Certainly Schnapper's theory seems logical enough and the judges may have been unwilling to let a strongly tainted suspect free simply because he had resisted torture.

99. André Laingui's thesis on the considerations that affected the severity of sentences used more than one hundred of these works to discuss the traditional criteria by which judges were to operate. The striking characteristics of the authors he cites are their immense learning and the polemical nature of some theorists, leading one to think that judges with such a welter of precedents, some of which were contradictory, had great liberty of choices in their assignment of penalties; see *La résponsabilité pénale dans l'ancien droit, XVIe–XVIIIe siècle* (Paris, 1970).

intentions or motivations of the accused? Had they intended to achieve the results obtained? If there had been an accident or an extreme provocation, or if the accused had been motivated by a creditable impulse, responsibility and thus penalty might be diminished. If, however, the accused had been motivated by greed, intentions of fraud, hatred, or had simply shown contempt for the law, a judge might be more severe.

According to the learned jurists, judges were also to examine the characteristics of the accused: age, sex, social rank, previous reputation. Youth might be some excuse, whereas persons who abused public office or positions of authority might be dealt with more harshly; vagabonds too would be automatically suspect, while the mentally defective could not be considered fully responsible for their actions. Some jurists also thought women should be less severely punished than men, citing their "natural" fragility, infirmity, and suggestibility. Similarly, judges were enjoined to consider the nature of the victim per se, and also in comparison to that of the accused. The young, defenseless victim was to excite the wrath of justice against the accused, who would also suffer more severely if he were a servant who had transgressed against his master or if his victim had been a representative of the king.

The time and place of the crime were also important, as was the manner of its execution. If the deed had been done in a church for example, or on a saint's day or during religious services, it might go harder with the accused. If the accused had broken into a locked house or committed an outrage in a public place causing scandal, or if the scene of the crime was known to be a place of low repute, judges might also sentence more harshly. On the other hand, one who confessed readily, one who had done the country a patriotic service, an outraged cuckold, or the old and infirm might be spared the worst retribution of justice. If, however, the accused had committed previous offenses or had committed an offense that was currently particularly troublesome, they could expect little mercy.[100]

The learned doctors' works can tell us what was supposed to have gone

100. Pierre François Muyart de Vouglans, *Institutes du Droit Criminelle* (Paris: 1768) 1: 281–83, contains a frequently cited list of circumstances that could rightfully affect the judge's decision. Laingui's thesis remains most valuable because of its extensive discussion of conflicting views on each point. (*Résponsabilité Pénale*). See, for example, book 2, "Les causes de non culpabilité," which contains sections on madness, 173–96; drunkenness, 199–203; youth, 219–40; old age, 248–51; females, 251–54; book 3 has a particularly good discussion on provocation. A. Lachance, *Justice Criminelle*, 87–88 also uses Muyart de Vouglan's criteria.

on in the minds of judges but they cannot tell us what deliberations actually occurred; and the judges of the Haute Auvergne did not leave us enough enumerations of their proofs for an assessment of the reasoning behind the penalties assigned. In all of the criminal justice archives for the Haute Auvergne in our period there remains only a handful of sentences, and most of those are bereft of details.

Why is there a shortage of sentences? Several likely reasons can be advanced. Among the most plausible are carelessness on the part of officials, willful destruction, and *accommodement* (settlement). The same laziness that characterizes some of the *interrogatoires* was no doubt carried over into the sentences, which were no more than footnotes or which were lost if they had ever existed; in addition to carelessness there were intentional omissions. The register of the *Grand Jours* occasionally brings to light such practices in the Haute Auvergne. Judge du Laurens, of the Aurillac family of notable *robins*, was accused of charging 300 livres in fees for a trial he had never seen;[101] a *receveur* named "Debort" (most likely Delort) was charged with falsifying his registers[102] and a bevy of other justice officials was charged with malversations ranging from the failure to acknowledge appeals by the accused to the destruction of court documents.[103] Unfortunately, as Alfred Soman has remarked, "Lynchings and summary executions seldom leave written traces";[104] therefore we must not place too great a reliance upon numbers of sentences as an indication of the way in which crimes were penalized, although they can be useful for discussion.

Another factor, that of private *accomodement* or settlements out of court must also be considered; while official prosecution was common-place it is probable that many of our abbreviated dossiers and unanswered *plaintes* represent cases where the principals made some sort of financial agreement that put an end to prosecution. This procedure was probably the course followed in many cases of assault or *excès* which, in the event of official prosecution, would have often resulted in fines to "pay for the wounds" of the victim. The extensive work of Steven Reinhardt on

101. Dongois, *Registres*, Tuesday A.M., 24 November 1665.
102. Ibid., Friday A.M., 23 October 1665.
103. Ibid., Wednesday A.M., 13 January 1666; ibid., Saturday A.M., 16 January 1666. See A. Lebigre, *Grands Jours*, for a discussion of these problems, many of which are illustrated by cases from the Haute Auvergne, 82, 94–95 in general, 81–96. For the condemnation of the Sieur d'Espinchal, see *Registre*, 23 January 1666. D'Espinchal was said to have destroyed much of the justice archives at Massiac.
104. "Criminal Jurisprudence," 49.

settlements in eighteenth-century Sarladais suggests that *accomodements*, both informal and notarized were common practice in cases of both theft and violence.[105]

The absence of sentences is the most acute lack in the trial papers of the judicial archives; they are less numerous than *interrogatoires*, which are fewer in turn than *informations*. One must also consider the possibility that the judges of the Ancien Régime were more careful about proceeding in uncertain cases than their critics would have us believe. Perhaps many dossiers end with the *information* simply because in some of these cases, judges thought the evidence insufficient to warrant further proceedings against the accused. This supposition is not unreasonable when one considers the sober care in procedure recommended by all jurists' commentaries.[106]

While we cannot enter the minds of judges, we can still gain some idea of the sentences that were pronounced in particular cases, for the *procès verbaux* of the *vice-baillis* contain reasonable numbers of sentences, some of which were pronounced by the same judges who have left us so few in the dossiers of their courts.[107] The records of the *vice-baillis* report the use of most major types of penalties available to French judges, as well as a few that are somewhat unusual, such as the duel to which the governor and lieutenant general de Missilhac sentenced Captain Rouerguas in 1591.[108] Generally, however, the types of sentences documented in police records are those mentioned in other sources of the period. While these sentences represent only a fragment of the penalties assigned during our period, they can at least give us a glimpse of the fate that awaited the condemned prisoner, and of the style of repression and deterrence in the

---

105. For example, *Chevauchées* 1647: 10 January; 1617: 3 December. Iain Cameron cites administrative correspondence to show that such *accomodements* had long been common and even encouraged in the Auvergne; *Crime and Repression*, 192–93. The most thorough scholarly analysis of the process of dispute settlement is in Reinhardt, *Justice in the Sarladais, 1770–1790* (Baton Rouge, La., 1991), 118–60. See also Fléchier, *Mémoires*, 52–53. Alfred Soman has told me of notarized *accomodements*, although I was unable to find any such documents in the *archives notariales* at Aurillac. For the eighteenth century, Nicole Castan, *Justice et répression en Languedoc à l'époque des Lumières* (Paris, 1980), documents the shallow penetration of official justice into the process of settling disputes.

106. This is one of the strong suggestions of L.-B. Mer, "La procédure criminelle."

107. In some most serious cases the *vice-baillis* was in the habit of acting as *juge d'instruction*; after he had completed all the preliminary procedures, he handed the dossier to the *présidial* or *bailliage* judges, who then deliberated together and produced a sentence.

108. *Chevauchées* 1591: 16, 17, 22, 18 September. Rouergas, although defeated, managed to survive the duel with Captain Viollatte, but Missilhac then sentenced him to be hanged.

Haute Auvergne when the procedure was carried through to its conclusion.

Death

The death sentence was used frequently to punish both crimes against
property and those against persons; 59 out of 96 sentences for homicide
and 75 of 190 for theft ordered the ultimate penalty. Hanging was the
most common means of execution for notorious thieves, usually described
by the *vice-baillis* as "infamous robbers" (70 sentences) and for murders
(35 sentences).

For particularly offensive crimes or for great numbers of flagrant crimes,
the condemned man might be sentenced to be stretched on a wheel and
have his bones broken "with an iron bar." This sentence was used only
rarely, on four thieves and five murderers. A subdeacon named Bellet for
example, betrayed his trust in 1607 by stealing religious objects from his
church; for his crime he was tortured, made to give a public apology, and
then broken on the wheel.[109] The penalty of the wheel was a relatively
recent punishment, imported from Germany in 1535 specifically for the
punishment of highway robbers, "in order to inspire dread and terror and
give an example to all others," as the edict described it.[110]

In some sentences for crimes thought particularly repulsive, the judges
emphasized the exemplary terror of the execution, ordering that a hand
be severed, or that the corpse be publicly burned after death, or in one
case that the prisoner have his body broken while hanging from a scaffold
and then be allowed to expire on the wheel.[111]

Beheading was reserved for the nobility until the honor was democratized during the revolutionary period. Although eighteen such sentences
were handed down in homicide cases, it is worthy of note that none of
them was ever executed, all the murderers having fled and been condemned in absentia. The weakness of local royal justice against the
nobility is clearly visible from sentences alone.

109. *Chevauchées* 1607: 17 February.
110. The edict of January 1535 in Isambert, *Recueil*, 12:400–402 is cited in A. Soman,
"Criminal Jurisprudence," 51 and note. Some of Soman's sentences from the Parlement of Paris
also contained merciful *retenta* that allowed for the strangulation of the prisoner soon after his
limbs were broken.
111. *Chevauchées* 1652: 4 May; 1629: 18 August; 1616: 9 August.

The accomplices of the condemned were sometimes condemned to *la peine accessoire de la hart*, which meant that they had to stand near the place of execution and watch while the principal malefactor was punished. Usually the *vice-bailli* added the phrase *assister la hart au col* which meant that the observer also had to wear a noose around his neck while watching the execution. The effect of this was supposed to be an instant reformatory; it must have been especially brutal for one like Jean La Vilhe, a young man who was forced to watch his father hang for theft in 1659 before he himself was whipped and banished from the province.[112]

The Galleys, Banishment, and Corporal Punishment

Sentences to the galleys were infrequently used to punish homicide (1 sentence) and theft (3 sentences) and only slightly more common in cases of serious assault and *excès* (10 sentences). Banishment from the Haute Auvergne was a more popular means of getting rid of thieves (42 sentences) and of those with a persistent tendency to fight (16 sentences); but men convicted of homicide were only rarely banished (6 sentences). Those convicted of violent assaults were usually banished for terms ranging from one to ten years, while thieves were most often banished for life. Although banishment was usually upon pain of death, there is no evidence to suggest that the threat was taken seriously.[113]

Whipping, branding, and mutilation were usually reserved for thieves and vagabonds. The *procès verbaux* contain two terms that seem to have been used interchangeably: "fustiger de verges" (beaten with rods or switches) and "fouetter," (whipped) both of which were used most frequently in cases of theft (38 sentences). It is impossible to discover the duration or intensity of these whippings, although occasionally the sentence in the police records would specify that a prisoner was to be whipped twice around the public fountain or up one street to the crossroads.

Branding (19 sentences) involved putting the stamp of the fleur de lis on one shoulder or, in some more serious cases, on both shoulders. In no case was the archaic practice of branding the forehead used in the Haute Auvergne. The brands were a sort of crude filing system that enabled the

112. *Chevauchées* 1659: 4 June.
113. A. Soman found in the Parlement of Paris that in cases of a broken ban the culprits "were seldom punished with anything worse than flogging"; "Criminal Jurisprudence," 53.

authorities to identify recidivists; because those branded knew they were liable to severer penalties should they be caught in another offense, branding was also a deterrent.

Mutilation by our period had almost gone out of use and only two cases, both of ear-cropping, both from the year 1615, appear in the records.[114] As a means of identifying thieves, ear-cropping was far superior to branding, for the shoulder brands could be burned into unidentifiable, albeit suspicious, marks. Perhaps the humane instincts of the Parlement of Paris, which had ceased using ear-cropping in the mid-sixteenth century, had worked their way down to lesser courts.[115] Practically speaking, ear-cropping had the disadvantage that it placed the convict permanently in the netherworld of Early Modern crime.

Fines and the award of confiscated property to victims were employed to punish offenders in acts of violence (23 sentences). For those condemned persons who were thought to have profaned the sacred in some way there was *amende honorable* (full apology), in which the condemned man, usually holding a burning candle and wearing a placard describing his sin, made a public apology to God, the king, and whatever other person or institution the judge thought fitting.

Acquittals, Contumace, and Plus Amplement Informé

Recorded acquittals were relatively rare, occurring in only 18 of 286 sentences for theft and homicide. More common was the release of the accused with the statement that there was need for further investigation, "pour être plus amplement informé" (to be more fully investigated). The phrase most often referred to in other works concerning such cases is *plus amplement informé*, but in addition to these words the *vice-baillis* used other expressions, such as *plus amplement enquis* (more fully inquired into), or the admonition that the accused was released, but must be ready to comply with further demands from the judge on the case. In most cases, the effect of these pronouncements was the same; the accused was released and the case never arose again. John Langbein has cited jurists'

114. Caught by the *maréchaussée* in Ruynes on 23 July, Pierre and Estienne Chaliaguet guilty of thefts and other "excès" were flogged, had their ears cropped, and were perpetually banned from the Haute Auvergne; *Chevauchées* 1615: 23 July.

115. A. Soman, "Criminal Jurisprudence," 54. Soman's research indicates that in the Parlement of Paris branding had replaced other forms of visible mutilation by 1565 (53–54).

commentaries to show that during the sixteenth century *plus amplement informé* became a sort of punishment rather than the intention literally expressed by the words, and that in some cases it was a means of imprisoning someone against whom there were indications of guilt not yet strong enough to justify torture.[116] While the matter of imprisonment is in some cases borne out by the police reports, the prisoners were often held for several months *before* the sentence, and then released; as for the argument that in cases of *plus amplement informé* there was insufficient evidence for torture, there are instances for the Haute Auvergne in which the sentence of *plus amplement informé* was given *after* the accused had been tortured.[117] Despite Langbein's inference that *plus amplement informé* had some shame attached to it, in the fifty-three sentences that used it in cases of theft and violence, it seems to have been for the most part simply a form of release without absolution.

In the event that the accused failed to appear or be caught, they were tried in "deffault et contumace" (nonappearance and contumacy). Contumacy signified not only absence, but rebellion against justice or what we might call contempt of court. In the place of the confrontation of witnesses with the accused, the *récolement* or rereading of depositions was to have the same weight of evidence as confrontation.[118] With nothing but the depositions and other evidence against them, the accused were condemned, usually to death, and executed in effigy; in many cases, their property could be seized and eventually sold. Sentences against the contumacious accused were particularly numerous for homicide (30 sentences) and other violence (25 sentences) but were not used so frequently for theft (14 sentences); as we have seen, they were consistently used against nobles accused of homicide.

Was justice growing harsher in the Haute Auvergne during this period?

116. J. Langbein, *Torture and the Law of Proof,* 52–54.

117. *Chevauchées* 1592, contains three cases of suspected thieves who were released on sentences of *plus amplement informé* after torture. Jehan Rixen, Louys Robberte, and Jehan Passelanque, who had been languishing in prison at Mauriac for an indeterminate length of time, were taken by the *vice-bailli* Jean Lacarrière to Aurillac in April and tortured on 1 May. Four days later they were released because the evidence was insufficient and a fuller investigation was needed. A similar case appears in *Chevauchées* 1608: 30 April, 13 May. Liset seems to have been aware of this practice, *Practique Judiciare,* book 1, fol. 59.

118. As Liset put it in the case of contumace: "récolement vaudra confrontation" (recolement is equal to confrontation); *Practique Judiciare,* book 1, fol. 28. Liset disagreed with Imbert, who in *Practique Judiciare,* book 3, chap. 3 said that if the accused appeared a confrontation proper would then take place. But Liset insisted that the procedure would continue giving the *informations* the same weight as *confrontation.*

On the evidence of death sentences for theft and homicide, one would have to say no: although 46% of offenses occurred in the period 1627–64, only 30% of the death sentences occurred during the same period. Throughout our period, violence remained less effectively punished than theft. Violent men more often received sentences by *contumace* and they were more apt to challenge the competence of the *vice-bailli*, although it could be argued this last difference was due to the preoccupation of the *maréchaussée* with theft, and to the jurisdictional difficulties attending to crimes of violence.[119]

We have examined the forces of order and the procedures they employed in the courts. It has been argued by others that the image of "a relentless inquisitorial process" must be softened by the facts; that defensive measures could be taken; that lawyers were used by some defendants; that acquittals did occur and that *plus amplement informé* allowed for leniency in cases of uncertainty.[120] It is also true that the criminal justice system in the Haute Auvergne, examined through the fragments it left behind, was not a smoothly running machine; its officers often seem to have been jurisdictionally confused and its procedures sometimes slipshod. But to a defendant of humble origins who actually faced those *officiers* and their complex procedures, the process must have seemed relentless, and it was certainly, for the most part, inquisitorial. The accumulation against them of written evidence of which they might be ignorant, followed by the often hostile questioning of a judge to whom protestations of innocence might be perjury, and the general lack of counsel for the poor, must have left many ordinary defendants feeling powerless. If dishonor and humiliation were as important as they seem to have been, then the terrors of justice lay in the process as well as the outcome.

Finally, there was the sentence, pronounced by a judge. In theory, he

119. Only 11 thieves were transferred to other judges while 69 prisoners accused of violence successfully asked to be transferred. The difficulty of showing that murder and assault cases were within the competence of the *maréchaussée* is admirably discussed by Iain Cameron, *Crime*, 135, who notes that *assassinat premedité* (premediated murder) was the most prolific source of jurisdictional conflicts; the severity of murder penalities, along with the ambiguities of the criminal ordinance of 1670, was to blame. *Assassinat premedité* was therefore removed from prevotal competence in 1731.

120. A. Soman, "Criminal Jurisprudence," 60–61; A. Lachance, *Justice criminelle*, 103. For defensive pleas by lawyers, see, for example, the supplications on behalf of Antoine Fabre, 25 and 29 June 1608, Présidial d'Aurillac, A.D. Cantal 1B 920, or those in the case of Meynials v. Romeufs from 1654, Juridiction Brezons, A.D. Cantal 16B 280.

was to be learned in the law, basing his decisions on exquisite calculations of guilt; in fact he had the considerable arbitrary power that could only safely be given to an erudite being. Rather than on regular and effective penalties, justice relied on the violent and the exemplary; the secret accusations and interrogations were followed by public shame, the parade of corpses or of effigies, the whippings, all "to terrify the wicked." If one of the surest affronts to honor was the physical attack, then the full weight of the law could amount to an obliteration of psychic property—perhaps the most cruelly logical thing for the state to do when the lessons it taught were to compensate for the delinquents who escaped its grasp. From the beginning the system seems to have been designed to set the accused apart from the community, as a criminal. The mark of the fleur-de-lis, the banishments, and the sentences by *contumace* seem as much a prescription for outlawry as a response to it. In other cases, the behavior of official justice was not unlike that of private retribution, an example that cannot have escaped those who watched its demonstrations. Unfortunately, as the *Chevauchées* indicate, the powerful often escaped official retribution and continued to live as it pleased them. A ditty that appeared on the occasion of the Grands Jours d'Auvergne of 1665–66 summed up the habits and attitudes of the mighty:

> Le noble qui doit
> Tout ce que sa race
> a mangé de boeuf
> Tout le vin qu'il boit
> Et quelque habit / neuf
> Payer
> Ne veut, ni plaider
> Mais de chez lui il chasse le marchand,
> Il cadenasse son magot
> Sans rien payer du tout,
> Ni denier, ni jeton:
> Pour tout payement, il le menace
> De coups de bâton.[121]
> (Laborieux, "Noel des Grands Jours")

---

121. Loosely translated: "The noble who owes / All that his kind / Has eaten of beef / Or swallowed of wine / And his suits of new clothes, / Does not care to pay nor make a legal case / But drives the merchant from his hall / And keeps his treasure locked in place / Without paying anything at all, / Not a penny nor a tick, / In lieu of payments all he gives / Are threats of beating with a stick." My thanks to John Greenshields for his suggestions in the translation of these verses.

6 The Grands Jours d'Auvergne, 1665–1666

Crime, which is always accompanied by shame and naturally seeks the shadows, has never found a surer or more secret repair than these steep crags that nature seems not to have made for reasonable persons, but rather has appointed only to be the habitation of animals.[1]

Ordinary people here are so hopeful about the Grands Jours and the nobility fear them so.[2]

—Abbé Fléchier

Paris was well aware of the unconquered mountains of central France. Jean-Baptiste Colbert, the king's minister, did not lack informants, and their letters told of a defiant lawlessness unchecked by the agents of justice. In fact as one correspondent complained in 1661, *officiers* were part of the problem: "Disturbances are so frequent in Auvergne, and are committed so commonly by every sort of person, that I thought it my duty to warn you that everybody, and particularly the officials, each in his own jurisdiction, shelters the guilty instead of punishing them."[3]

1. Fléchier, *Mémoires sur les Grands-Jours d'Auvergne en 1665,* ed. A. Cheruel (Paris 1856), 203.

2. Ibid., 162.

3. La Ribe to Colbert, 1661, in G. B. Depping, ed., *Correspondance administrative sous le règne de Louis XIV,* 2:9–10. Quoted words are from 9. Jean-Baptiste Colbert (1619–83) entered the service of the crown in 1651 under Mazarin. In 1661 Louis XIV made him *Intendant des Finances* and in 1665 he became *contrôleur général des Finances.* A creature of the king, he became an influential minister, with access to the most powerful councils of the state privy to the intelligence gathered by the network of royal *commissaires* throughout France.

This note of urgency continued through the early 1660s, and although the offending incidents changed from letter to letter, the themes were similar. De Pomereu, *intendant de la justice, police et finances* in the *généralités* of Moulins and Riom, wrote from Aurillac in October 1663 about the scandalous impunity of Gaspard d'Espinchal, Sieur de Massiac "whom everyone knows to be sullied by crimes," and who had managed to remain at liberty with the compliance of the local authorities and the complicity of other nobles.[4] Later the same month, de Pomereu felt moved to describe more generally the problem of unfettered noble power in the Auvergne: "one of the principal abuses I have witnessed consists in the vexation of the ordinary inhabitants of parishes by *gentilshommes*, most of whom have lands and collect huge dues in grain as a consequence." He then went on to reveal the chicanery by which *gentilshommes* enriched themselves in grain speculation, violently enforced illegal *corvées*, usurped the common lands, and appropriated ecclesiastical revenues.[5] One of the most persistent offenders mentioned in these matters was the Comte d'Apcher, whose dependent peasants near St. Flour in Haute Auvergne had made many complaints about injustice and oppression.[6]

Colbert could not long have ignored the mountains of Auvergne. A month after Pomereu's letter yet another informant was decrying disorder and official malversations, this time in the high-mountain *élection* of Salers, whose inhabitants were crushed by excessive and fraudulent taxation. The cause of problems in Salers was clear to the writer: "The source of this disorder arises from venality, and from the fact that the collectors-general have subcontracted the takings with the people holding contracts exceeding the amounts in the returns sent to the king."[7] Included in the accusations was the suggestion that the Intendant Pomereu was himself guilty of complicity in corruption.[8]

One of the most concise descriptions of problems in the Auvergne came to Colbert in 1664 from an anonymous Auvergnat who outlined

---

4. De Pomereu, Intendant, to Colbert, 2 October 1663, in ibid., 2:18.

5. De Pomereu to Colbert, Clermont, 29 October 1663, in ibid., 1:688. The same letter is also in ibid., 3:51–52.

6. Ibid., 1:689.

7. Joly to Colbert, Riom, 27 November 1663, in ibid., 3:57–58.

8. Ibid., 3:58. Interestingly, Pomereu later accused Joly of the same thing in December 1663 and an anonymous letter of 16 December 1664 pointed to Fortia, the Intendant of Auvergne. Ibid., 3:372. Boudet, *Documents*, 115.

"the wrongs most in need of reform." According to this letter there were three types of persons responsible for the most serious problems: "nobles, revenue collectors and officials . . . both royal and those of ecclesiastical lords." While the greatest and most violent nobles were well known and somewhat pacified, there were many lesser men whose nobility "is based only on the sword they carry," and "who have a free hand to exercise liberally their violent ways on H.M. subjects."[9]

The lawless particularism of the mountains was an open provocation to the vigorous young monarchy of Louis XIV; and the royal riposte was not long in coming. Letters patent of 31 August 1665 announced that an extraordinary court, "commonly called the Grands-Jours,"[10] was to be held that year in Clermont. The need for this court and its purposes were explained:

> . . . the first and principal object that we intend and that on which, after the consolidation of our conquests, after the safety

9. Lettre d'un auvergnat anonyme à Colbert, 21 June 1664, in ibid., 3:123.

10. The criminal cases of the Grands Jours d'Auvergne are fairly well documented in manuscript, printed sources of the period, and several recent interpretations. The register and journal of the *greffier* Dongois are found in A.N. U750 and a longer version in A.N. U749. A printed version that excludes the historical introduction to *grands jours* is U. Jouvet, ed., "Les Grands Jours d'Auvergne de 1665: Le Registre du greffier Dongois," published in the series L'Auvergne Historique Littéraire et Artistique (Riom, 1905). Fléchier's *Mémoires* provide the most entertaining and incisive look at the persons involved in the Grands Jours; and the Cheruel edition of 1856 contains an appendix in which some of the letters patent, trials, condemnations, verses, and genealogies of notable families are preserved (302–423), most having been taken from the journal of Dongois. Some of the pieces from the trials of Auvergnats are contained in A.N. series X²B 1267–69. Collections of the *arrêts* of the court, reports on the trials and some minutes are in A.N. XB 9699–9703. Letters on the Grands Jours and the Auvergne are found in all the volumes of G. B. Depping, *Correspondence administrative*. A recent study by Arlette Lebrigre, *Les Grands Jours d'Auvergne* (Paris, 1976), provides an interpretation of the Grands Jours as one of the first great incursions into the provinces by the centralizing absolute monarchy of Louis XIV. It includes a quantification of crimes and sentences. Albert H. Hamscher, "Les réformes judiciares des Grands Jours d'Auvergne, 1665–1666," *Cahiers d'Histoire* 1, no. 4 (1976): 425–32, concentrates on the positive aspects of legal reform rather than the sensational evils of the great nobles. R. Mousnier, *Institutions*, vol. 2 provides a brief summary based on Lebigre. Other important references include the essay by Abel Poitrineau, in Manry, ed., *Historie de l'Auvergne*, and Boudet's discussion in *Documents inédits*. The main sources for this brief essay are the work of Arlette Lebigre; the *Registres* and *Journal* of Dongois; Fléchier, *Mémoires*; the administrative correspondence of Colbert in Depping and documents from A.N. X²B 1267–69; as well as the secondary sources cited above. The *lettres patentes* are found in Dongois, *Registres*, and in Cheruel's appendix 2 to Fléchier's *Mémoires*, "Lettres Patentes pour l'establissement des Grands-Jours," 316–21.

of the public peace, after the restoration of our finances and the re-establishment of commerce, we have fixed all our attention, has been to have justice reign and to reign with her in our State.[11]

Central France was clearly a place where neither the king nor justice reigned:

> We are informed that the problem is greater in the provinces distant from our court of parlement; that the laws are scorned there, the populace exposed to all kinds of violence and oppression; that weak and wretched persons can find no succor in the authority of justice; that the noblemen often take advantage of their standing to commit actions unworthy of their birth, and that moreover, the weakness of officials is so great, that, unable to withstand their vexations, the crimes remain unpunished.[12]

The area of the court's jurisdiction was immense, including "bas et haut Auvergne, Bourbonnois, Nivernois, Forez, Beaujolais, Lyonnois, Saint-Pierre de Moutier, Montferrand, Montaignes d'Auvergne (Salers), Combrailles, la haute et basse Marche, Berry and all their jurisdictions."[13] Its authority and competence were no less impressive. With the full weight of the Parlement of Paris, the judges of the Grands Jours had the power to judge without appeal all cases, either new matters or those that had fallen into abeyance; to resolve all manner of civil disputes; to review the cases and procedures of local *officiers*; to prescribe and enforce ecclesiastical discipline; to fix the prices of commodities and regulate weights and measures; and to examine illegal or oppressive seigneurial practices.[14]

While the Parlement of Paris had traditionally been more influential than the crown in deciding on the composition of *grands jours*, the Grands Jours d'Auvergne were a creature of the monarch. Nowhere was this royal predominance clearer than in the nomination of members to the court, all of whom were named by Colbert.[15] Near the end of 1663,

---

11. Cheruel, appendix 2 to Fléchier's *Mémoires*, 316–17.

12. Ibid., 317.

13. Ibid.

14. Ibid., 318–21 and Cheruel, "Notice sur les Grands Jours," 303–16.

15. In a marginal note the *greffier* Dongois wrote of past *grands jours*: "Of all the officers comprising the Grand Jours, the King named only the President." He went on to cite instances where entire courts had been elected by the *conseillers* of the Parlement of Paris. Other examples include the Grands Jours of Poitu (1531), Tours (1533), Troyes (1535), Angers (1539), Moulins (1540), Potiers (1541), Riom (1547), Poitiers (1634). See also Lebigre, *Grands Jours*, 7–20 and

the king's minister had received at his request secret assessments of the "personnel" in the *parlements* of France. Their honesty, wealth, or poverty, circle of friends or noteworthy relations, their devotion to duty, intellectual capacity, and soundness of judgment were set before Colbert by his intendants.[16] All but one of the judges in the Grands Jours were chosen from among the members of the Parlement of Paris listed in this secret file.

A perusal of the characteristics ascribed to the *président*, sixteen *conseillers* and the *procureur général* of the Grands Jours reveals much. Nowhere was there a hint of mediocrity or dishonesty. Most were described as disinterested men of ability, devoted to their duty, and well regarded by their fellows. They were also men of wealth and importance, part of a close-knit group that dominated the judicial hierarchy where much intermarriage and common interests prevailed.[17] Only two had important relations in the Auvergne: Denis Talon, the *procureur général*; and Nicolas Potier de Novion, the *président*. The latter had connections with the Ribeyre family of officials in Clermont and with the de Canillacs, who were wealthy noble villains, particularly renowned in the Haute Auvergne.[18] The nobles and officials of the Haute Auvergne now faced in the Grands Jours an insular group not unlike their own, albeit on a grander scale.

The court with its entourage of family, servants, and aides must indeed have made an impressive party when it arrived in the Auvergne that September and began its business. The abbé and memoirist Fléchier claimed that all Clermont and Montferrand came out to meet them and that little groups of officials stood along the road every few hundred paces. At each group the carriages stopped, even "in the midst of the countryside" and listened to long "speeches . . . filled, for the most part, with sun and moon, with broad daylight [*grands jours*] and with daybreak [*petits jours*]." This was only the beginning of Clermont's attempt to

Cheruel, "Notice," 303–16. A discussion of previous *grands jours* is also found in A.N. U 750, fols. 1–65 and A.N. U749, fols. 1–203.

16. "Notes secrèttes sur le personnel," in Depping, *Correspondance administrative*, 2:33–132. At various points Fléchier, *Mémoires*, also describes the members of the court. Lebigre, *Grands Jours*, as well relies on these sources throughout.

17. Cheruel, "Nomination des commissaires chargés de tenir les Grands Jours," in Fléchier, *Mémoires*, appendix 3, 321–24. See also Lebigre, *Grands Jours* and Mousnier, *Institutions*, 2:492–93.

18. His son-in-law's sister, Catherine de Ribeyre, was married to a Canillac. Lebigre, *Grands Jours*, 33.

impress Paris: "After having endured these unpleasant encounters, we entered the city, where it was again necessary to hear some speechifiers who wished to omit nothing of all their past studies, and who intended to make their reputations with an extremely tiresome display of their wretched eloquence."[19]

Among the greeters was the Marquis de Canillac Pont-du-Château, sénéchal of Clermont, with fifteen or twenty gentilshommes, all of whom dismounted and approached the visitors. The commissioners of the Grands Jours left their carriages. The marquis with his greeting "protested every sort of respect and obedience." De Novion, président of the court, prophetically "assured him that the company had a particular regard for the nobility of the district."[20]

And so the Grands Jours began their tenure at Clermont. After the first day, the judges would deliver the speeches, and even the abbé Fléchier would have his chance at eloquence, from the pulpit. The aldermen of Clermont had received a lettre de cachet from the king on 6 September, ordering them to give lodgings to the visitors, to welcome them and treat them with due respect. These officials fulfilled their commission well and Fléchier's mémoires recount many of the delights of local society, including the rather violent Auvergnat dances which (to the alleged disgust of the abbé) involved a good deal of kissing and indecent shaking and joining of the bodies.[21]

On 25 September, the eve of the court's opening session, the président de Novion and the procureur de Talon made their first bold move. The Vicomte de la Mothe-Canillac was arrested in his bed, to the surprise and alarm of the Auvergnat nobility.[22] The Canillac family was among the greatest in Auvergne and la Mothe-Canillac was considered in Fléchier's words, "the most innocent of all the Canillacs."[23] But he was innocent only by comparison with the rest of his family, and his crimes included murders and woundings in affrays with other gentilshommes and their henchmen.[24]

According to Fléchier, this first notable arrest struck fear into the

19. Fléchier, Mémoires, 36.
20. Dongois, Registres, 25 September 1665.
21. "Lettre de Cachet" in ibid. Descriptions of the bourrée and goignade in Fléchier, Mémoires, 241–44.
22. Dongois, Registres, 3 October 1665. Fléchier, Mémoires, 50–51.
23. Fléchier, Mémoires, 51.
24. Ibid., 51–52 and Dongois, Registres, 23 October 1665.

hearts of the Auvergnat nobility: "the terror was universal. The entire nobility was put to flight."[25] All were examining their past sins and making restitution to forestall peasant complaints to the new court.[26]

Terrified or not, the quarry of the Grands Jours were not brought to bay so easily as the court had hoped they would be. Before arriving in Auvergne, the *procureur général* de Talon had sent a long and detailed *monitoire* to be read in the parishes of the court's jurisdiction. It demanded information on virtually every possible crime and disorder except vagrancy: murder, theft, rape, and other violent crimes; simony, usury, usurpation of tithe; extortion and illegal tax collection; illegal rents, *corvées* and grain pricing; false weights and measures; illegal tolls on roads and bridges; as well as a host of judicial malversations such as imprisonment without trial and other improper procedures. Significantly the longest section pertained to seigneurial chicanery of various sorts.[27] But the response to this impressive document was disappointingly small. Apparently it was seldom read in the parishes, and where read it seemed to have been ignored.[28] Vigorous commands had been issued to "baillifs, sénéchaux, vice-baillifs, vice sénéchaux, prévosts des maréchaux," demanding the pursuit and capture of accused persons and the execution of all orders given by the Grands Jours, to no avail.[29]

Demands for court records[30] went unheeded, both because local officials resisted them and because the records themselves were either nonexistent or in a lamentable state of neglect. There was a general reluctance among witnesses, some of whom had been intimidated or bribed; there were also false witnesses. The problem of the contumacious accused, with which we have become familiar in the course of this study, was of immense proportions. Long and inconclusive procedures testified to the weakness and the corruption of the lower courts. But evidence in these matters was, naturally, scarce. The Grands Jours by 6 October

25. Fléchier, *Mémoires*, 50.
26. Ibid.
27. Dongois included the *monitoire* in his journal AN U750, fols. 65–68 and AN U749, fols. 203–12. There is also a copy of a similar *monitoire* in Fléchier, *Mémoires*, appendix 4, 324–29. A.D. Cantal IB, Présidial d'Aurillac contains printed *monitoires* that are remnants of the Grands Jours; they are forms with blank spaces in which could be placed the particulars of a crime under investigation.
28. A. Lebigre, *Grands Jours*, chap. 2.
29. The original letters patent contain such an injunction, 31 August 1665. Another more specific order was issued 28 September 1665; Dongois, *Registres*.
30. "Arrest de renvoi des procédures, 12 September 1665," Dongois, *Registres*, 2 October.

1665, had concluded only two criminal cases and neither was of much significance.[31]

At the beginning of October, the judges of the Grands Jours adopted measures that challenged the inaction of local justice, the reluctance of witnesses, and the allies of the accused. First, the court published decrees that identified problems and proposed solutions. Accused persons had often used the weakness of neophyte judges and the jurisdictional jealousies of local courts to create "procedures immortelles" and thus remain unpunished; judges of the Grands Jours were therefore given the power to ignore all such disputes, previous royal ordinances notwithstanding.[32]

Local officers had neglected to pursue cases against the accused, had suppressed evidence in return for money; or they had fulfilled the letter of the law by sending to the Grands Jours "only simple procedures for inconsequential cases," with the result that the court was inundated with minor cases, unable to secure evidence for scandalous crimes. In reply the court demanded that *officiers* comply with its requests on pain of dismissal, and decreed that suppression of evidence was a crime; delays in sending evidence would also be punished.[33]

To deal with the problem of *contumace*, especially among noble offenders, the crown gave the Grands Jours a wide-ranging series of powers. The accused who had been judged contumacious were obliged to appear before the Grands Jours by mid-October. Failing an appearance, the *seigneur* in question could expect a garrison of royal troops or constables of the *maréchaussée* in his house and the revenues of the seigneury could be seized for the maintenance of the garrison. Those seigneurs who refused entry to the forces of law or who resisted the decrees of the court could have their houses razed. Seigneurs who had several houses were obliged to reside in the house nearest to Clermont. Having struck a blow against noble strongholds, the decree then attacked the noble system of family alliances. Any *gentilhomme* who harbored a fugitive could be arrested, have his château razed, his noble title removed, and his property auctioned. Pardons, or *lettres de grâce* protecting offenders had to be examined by the court.[34]

31. A Lebigre, *Grands Jours*, 70–71. Dongois, *Registres*, 8 October. The *conseillers* were Hébert and Le Pelletier.
32. "Règlement sur le fait des conflicts de jurisdiction," Dongois, *Registres*, 1 October 1665.
33. Ibid., 1, 2, 3, October 1665. Lebigre, *Grands Jours*, 55–79.
34. "Declaration du Roy portant rèlement pour l'instruction des proxès qui se traitteront aux Grands Jours," Dongois, *Registres*, 1 October 1665.

Armed with these extensive powers, the judges then decided on a course of action that rendered their legal power more effective. Because local justice resisted their demands for records, judges of the Grands Jours would themselves go to the most troublesome districts. The decision seems to have been taken in the wake of a visit by two judges to religious houses in Auvergne on 8 October.[35]

On 26 October, the delegates were chosen and their task defined. The description of their duties was a summary of criminal procedure. They were to be sent:

> in order to receive complaints that will be delivered to them there, to issue warrants against the guilty; have them arrested, question them, read their evidence to them, confront the witnesses to the accused present, and proceed against the contumacious after they have defaulted . . . who will be judged by them, with the *récolement* of witnesses to serve as confrontation, and with all the necessary inquiries.

One judge was to be sent to Bourbonnais, another to La Marche, and a third to Lyonnais, Forez, and Beaujolais. The Haute Auvergne became the burden of the fourth judge, Hiérome (Jérome) Le Pelletier.[36]

In accepting his commission, Le Pelletier had drawn the most difficult lot, "the greatest source of abuses."[37] The Haute Auvergne for its part was to receive a formidable visitor: "honest man, intelligent, devoted to his profession, disinterested," according to Colbert's files.[38] He left Clermont on 3 November 1665, when snow already covered the mountain passes and did not return until 12 January 1666. The Grands Jours were to have ended on 30 November 1665 but, partly because of Pelletier's travails, they were extended to the end of January 1666.[39] His trip was apparently arduous as Fléchier wrote, "in such a disagreeable season," and his work was done "in such great danger." Arlette Lebigre imagined him picturesquely riding a mule across the Planèze de St. Flour in winter's rudest months.[40]

---

35. A Lebigre, *Grands Jours*, 70–71. Dongois, *Registres*, 8 October. The *conseillers* were Hébert and Le Pelletier.
36. Dongois, *Registres*, 26 October 1665.
37. Boudet, *Documents*, 123.
38. "Notes Secrettes" in Depping, *Correspondance administrative*, 2:44.
39. Dongois, *Registres*, 13 January 1666. "Lettres de Cachet" in ibid., 12 November 1665.
40. *Grands Jours*, 72.

Crime

Whatever the uncomfortable details of his sojourn, by all accounts, Le Pelletier did well in the Haute Auvergne. On his return to Clermont, "bringing back an infinity of investigations against the nobility living in the mountains," he immediately pressed to have the Grands Jours extended further lest his labors be in vain.[41] While his register does not give us the number of cases related to the Haute Auvergne, Dongois speculated that had they dealt with all of Pelletier's affairs, the Grands Jours would have lasted another four months.[42] Certainly Fléchier's account describes a tireless, determined, and successful agent of the king's justice:

> It is true that he accomplished deeds which showed well the absolute authority of the king in his kingdom and the awe that justice had imprinted on the spirit of the people. He alone was seen turning upside down this entire mountain country; making the law known where it had never been known, and bringing respect into places that had always been inaccessible to justice. They saw him do just violence where so much criminal violence had previously been done; enter the most secret châteaus and send the proudest and most powerful men of the province under the guard of a police officer to Clermont to account for their conduct.[43]

Whether or not Le Pelletier reformed the entire upper province in two months, he certainly brought home his share of trophies and inspired respect if not terror. The account of the *greffier* Dongois, though less colorful than that of Fléchier, attests to his success.[44] Among his notable cases were those against the Comte d'Apchon, the Marquis de Malauze, the Comte d'Apcher, the old Marquis de Canillac, the Sieur de Lignerac, and a clutch of *officiers* from the *bailliage* of St. Flour. Two of the five notorious and elusive Combalibeuf brothers (a gang of noble brigands)

41. Fléchier, *Mémoires*, 277.
42. Dongois, *Journal*, October 26.
43. Fléchier, *Mémoires*, 227.
44. Dongois, *Registres*, 13 January 1666.

were also captured under Pelletier's direction and brought back to Clermont where they were tried and executed.[45]

The investigations of Le Pelletier and the other judges of the Grands Jours opened the closed rural society of the mountains to scrutiny by alien legal minds; the documents bear witness to an isolated brutality that seems almost to have been one of the normal expectations of Auvergnat life.

The dominion and unbridled liberties of Auvergnat *gentilshommes* were probably the phenomena most remarked upon by contemporary observers; the most prominent, violent, and outrageous nobles naturally received the fullest attention. The Canillac family for example had left an arrogant trail of evidence and previous futile condemnations. They were proud of their ancient lineage, which included two popes and which had given them extensive land holdings throughout the Auvergne.[46] Jacques de Timoléon, Marquis de Canillac, seventy-two years old (popularly called "le Vieux Marquis") was the leader of the clan and known to be the greatest sinner. For a generation, he had spread terror in the mountains, committing violence and extortion with the help of a group of lackeys and allies known as "the Twelve Apostles," men with names like "Brise-Tout," "Sans-Fiance," and "Bastard."[47] Ignoring several death sentences, he had always managed to enjoy liberty, and great profit through feudal chicanery and extortion, the "usual offense of the nobles of Auvergne." He was emulated by two sons and three nephews. All had been responsible for homicides and all had mistreated their peasants, traveling in strength and relieving tenants and neighbors of their goods and sometimes their lives.[48]

The Marquis de Salers and his entourage had avenged themselves, it was alleged, by attacking a lone enemy, putting out his eyes, and then stabbing him to death.[49] The Combalibeuf brothers were locally renowned thugs who assisted a friend in the murder of a prominent official and then retired to the high mountains of Haute Auvergne. They

45. Ibid., 13 January, 29 January 1666.
46. The popes were Clement VI (1342–52) and Gregory XI (1370–78). See the *Concise Oxford Dictionary of the Christian Church*, ed. Elizabeth A. Livingstone (Oxford, 1978) for biographical entires.
47. Dongois, *Registres*, 26 January 1666. Fléchier, *Mémoires*, 261. Lebigre, *Grands Jours*, 108–9.
48. Dongois, *Registres*, 6 October, 19 October, 22 October, 23 October 1665; 15 January, 26 January 1666. Lebigre, *Grand Jours*, 108–11.
49. Fléchier, *Mémoires*, 230. Dongois, *Registres*, 21 January 1665.

were captured by a nameless "prévôt qui etoit fort vigilant."[50] Ranking with the Canillacs in notoriety and surpassing them in cruelty was Gaspard d'Espinchal, accused of murders as well as the usual seigneurial injustices.[51]

The tales of these prominent men of violence were but the most glaring examples of a widespread hostility to judicial officials and a seigneurial indifference to the customary rights of tenants, problems about which intendants had complained for thirty years. All of the Canillacs, d'Espinchal, and the others were expert at profitable extortions, usurpation of common lands, and various other means of taking the goods and lands of others.

Inquiries into the violence of the most prominent revealed a tradition, almost a regional structure of habitual chicanery. The Marquis de Merville was charged with extorting money, imposing excessive *corvées*, usurping common pastures and demanding seigneurial "rights" that extorted goods of every sort from peasants in the country near Laroquebrou.[52] Robert, Sieur de Lignerac, from northwestern Haute Auvergne, had made profits both from excessive seigneurial dues and from the usurpation of the *cure* of St. Chamant.[53] The latter charge is particularly interesting because the Ligneracs had been embroiled in a violent struggle over the benefice for at least thirty years; the case entered the records of the Présidial d'Aurillac in 1634, when they were charged with assaulting a priest who disputed their possession of the *cure*.[54] Louis de Bourbon, marquis de Malauze, had enjoyed the fruits of a *cure* at Chalvignat in collusion with a priest, despite the fact that Malauze was a Huguenot.[55] In the tradition of the old Marquis de Canillac, the Comte d'Apcher had extorted money and extraordinary levies with the help of nineteen "apostles."[56] Charles de Montvalat was notorious in Chaudesaigues and in St. Flour, for his series of unusual illegal and profitable exactions which have been described earlier.[57]

50. Fléchier, *Mémoires*, 276.
51. Dongois, *Registres*, 23 January 1666, Fléchier, *Mémoires*, 245–358. The accusations are also in the "lettres d'Abdition" in Fléchier, *Mémoires*, appendix 26, 398–411.
52. Dongois, *Registres*, 13 January 1666, 29 January.
53. Ibid., 24 January 1666.
54. A.D. Cantal IB 922 Coups et Blessures.
55. Dongois, *Registres*, 29 January 1777.
56. Ibid., 30 January 1666. Dongois notes that Apcher was an "imitateur" of the Marquis de Canillac.
57. Ibid., 27 November 1665. See also Interrogation of Montvalat in A.N. X²B 1268.

While these cases may have been unusual in the wealth of the accused and the amounts of money at issue, the nature of the offense was generally known and until the Grands Jours, one might suppose, generally accepted. For all his fraudulence, Charles de Montvalat for example was regarded locally as a peaceful person, certainly not a violent man, although he had rather brutally punished one of his peasants. Fléchier even suggested that Montvalat's timidity and leniency had been the reason why more than sixty of his peasants felt little fear in bringing complaints against him.[58] A wise peasant would indeed have taken pause before publicly challenging the likes of d'Espinchal or Canillac.

But witnesses were found and challenges did arise, in ever greater numbers.[59] The increasing boldness of the peasants was noticed by Fléchier: "It is said . . . that the peasants were very bold, and that they voluntarily gave depositions against the nobles when not restrained by intimidation." Failure to greet a peasant civilly could earn the threat of punishment by the Grands Jours, claimed Fléchier, who related stories of peasant impudence: of peasants who had begun to wear gloves and of one who kept his hat on his head while threatening his seigneur with legal retribution. One peasant asserted "that the time of restitution had come," and that the king was sending men who would not fear his seigneur, "and who would dispense good justice." The peasants, according to Fléchier, had become the lords of their own seigneurs.[60]

Apocryphal though these stories may be, one could infer from them and others like them that the Grands Jours had opened a wound in the "vertical solidarities" of rural society. As such rumors sometimes will, they show a visceral fear of the order broken, the world turned upside down, of peasant malevolence, and peasant revenge. There is also a corresponding hint of peasant hopes that a good ruler, protector of the poor, would restore the rural world to an ancient state of justice and freedom from oppression.[61]

As for the officials of local justice, they too came under the scrutiny of

58. Fléchier, Mémoires, 155–59.
59. On 15 December 1665, Dongois wrote of the flood of minor cases: "Ce vint à un si grand excès que plusieurs procureurs recurent chacun plus nombre d'affaires, il yen avait trois quarts et demi qui étaient pour des sommes très legères." But the number of criminal cases was such that for the most part, civil cases were ignored.
60. Fléchier, Mémoires, 160–61.
61. The best general description of these mentalities is in Y.-M. Bercé, Révoltes et révolutions dans l'Europe moderne (Paris, 1980). His chapter 1 deals with "les mythes fondateurs," which include the presentation of peasant grievances and the return to a "golden age."

the Grands Jours. The *bailli* and *substitut du procureur* of the Bailliage des Montagnes at Salers were charged with irregularities in procedure: a suggestion of complicity in the case of a woman who was condemned for arson and then simply released after she had decided to appeal her case.[62] Delort, a collector in the *élection* of Aurillac, was charged with minor fraud and the falsification of his registers.[63] One judge in the présidial was accused of having sold a letter of remission without ever having read the evidence of the case and[64] another was given an *ajournement personnel*.[65] The *bailliage* of St. Flour was particularly productive of cases. The recorder of the *maréchaussée* the *procureur du roy*, the *lieutenant général*, and the *substitut du procureur* were charged with unidentified malversations.[66] Justice officials at the seigneurial level fell with their masters whenever *justices seigneuriales* had collaborated in the vices of their *seigneurs*.

What of the *vice-bailli* of Haute Auvergne? He is never mentioned by name in the documents of the Grands Jours. There are, however, two references to a "prévôt" in Haute Auvergne and the only *prévôt* at that time was Paul Lacarrière, third *vice-bailli*: Fléchier and Dongois both recorded that the *prévôt* who delivered Le Pelletier's prisoners from St. Flour was then arrested himself, and Fléchier also mentions that a "prévôt . . . fort vigilant" (a most vigilant prevot) assisted in the capture of the Combalibeuf brothers. Whether or not Paul Lacarrière was arrested, he continued in his office after the Grands Jours, which had taken their toll of other *prévôts* and their constables. In the absence of any sentence or specific condemnation we can assume that whatever the charge, he emerged unscathed.[67]

The other readily identifiable group in the documents of the Grands Jours was the clergy, and here Arlette Lebigre's study confirms the earlier impression left by the documents of the local courts: "the complete and regrettable conformity in the mentality and behaviour of these priests with the very rough surroundings in which they were supposed to lead."[68] Le Pelletier and Amable de l'Ort, lieutenant general of Aurillac, were

62. Interrogation of Pierre André de la Ronade, Lieut. Criminel, 30 October 1665. A.N. X²B 1267. Dongois, *Registres*, 17 October, 12 November 1665.
63. Dongois, *Registres*, 23 October 1665.
64. Ibid., 24 October 1665.
65. Ibid., 16 January 1666.
66. Ibid., 13 January, 30 January. The cases were transferred to Paris.
67. Fléchier, *Mémoires*, 222, 276. Dongois, *Registres*, 13 January, 30 January 1666. Boudet, *Documents*, 124–25.
68. Lebigre, *Grands Jours*, 123.

commissioned to examine the state of ecclesiastical establishments in the Haute Auvergne.[69] The clergy were found to be too numerous for their revenues, the hospitals insufficient, monasteries and convents guilty of "libertinage"; divine services often lacked dignity and benefices were difficult to maintain. Significantly in its treatment of the clergy, the court gave reform precedence over condemnation and the strongest recommendations were for a return to the truly cloistered religious life and for an adequate portion paid to parish priests.[70] A decree of 27 January 1666, for example, called for a reduction in the size of the community at Chaudesaigues, "because of the paltriness of the chapter."[71]

Although the cryptic nature of the registers frustrated attempts to discern the social rank of those who were not nobles, *officiers*, or clergy, the incidents described indicate crimes familiar to a student of violence in the Haute Auvergne: tavern insults and brawls, assaults with farm implements, stones and other weapons ready to hand; struggles over small violations of property and honor. Arlette Lebigre, whose study of the Grands Jours d'Auvergne is the only recent work devoted entirely to that subject, unfortunately found the offenses of the majority "inevitably less interesting."[72] But it must be said that the expressed purpose of the Grands Jours was after all to attack the powerful oppressors, corrupt officials and notorious, unpunished offenders.[73]

Punishment

When the Grands Jours closed at the end of January 1666, the judges from the Parlement of Paris had received a rapid and extensive education in mountain violence. Although it is impossible to discover the precise nature and number of crimes encountered by the Grands Jours, Arlette Lebigre attempted to count the remaining records, warning that quantitative studies were "hazardeuse" because of the paucity of specific informa-

---

69. Dongois, *Registres*, 3 November 1665.
70. Lebigre, *Grands Jours*, 121–32. Dongois, *Registres*. The recommended portion was 300 livres.
71. Dongois, *Registres*, 27 January 1666.
72. Lebigre, *Grand Jours*, 134–38, quoted words, 135.
73. Dongois gives this purpose (undated) in A.N. U750, fols. 64–65.

tion.[74] While Fléchier claimed that the court had dealt with 12,000 cases,[75] Lebigre found 1350, of which 202 were new cases; of the 1350 cases only 283 identifiable offenses could be found. Violence dominated the register and there were 107 murders among the crimes recorded, 19 committed by gentilshommes and one by a priest. Among the more numerous offenses were 34 assaults, 14 rapes, 9 kidnappings, and 13 slanders or insults.[76]

The sentences, recorded by Dongois and counted by Lebigre and Depping, reveal a busy court: 692 condemnations, 370 of them death sentences, and over 600,000 livres in fines. The impressive total of death sentences gave the conseillers a fiercer aspect than they deserve, for only 23 of the condemned were executed, 6 gentilshommes and one priest among them. Royal justice thus continued to rely upon stern example rather than effective police work.

The pecuniary penalties, however, were more thoroughly applied and therefore probably more effective than the execution of effigies.[77] Châteaus were garrisoned and then demolished in the absence of their owners, the materials sold to pay fines and damages. Ornamental trees were cut to three feet high—a sign of dishonor. Gaspard d'Espinchal, the various Canillacs, and the Sieur d'Apcher all suffered substantial losses, as did the Marquis de Malause, the Marquis de Merville, and the Comte d'Apchon. Common lands and lost revenues were returned to peasants.[78]

The Combalibeuf brothers and the Vicomte de la Mothe-Canillac paid

74. Ibid., 139. In this chapter Lebigre makes some very good points regarding the unreliability and difficulty of court records.

75. Fléchier, Mémoires, 292. Depping, Correspondance administrative, vol. 2, xi also used the total figure of 12000 "affaires."

76. Lebigre's totals were as follows: Meutres (murders): 107; Violences graves (serious violence): 34; Duels: 14; Portes d'armes et rébellions (arms offenses and rebellion against authority): 2; Vols (thefts): 37; Concussions (extortion, bribery): 24; Fausse monnaie (counterfeiting): 8; Délits assimilés à l'escroquerie (fraud, swindling, and related offenses): 2; Incendies volontaires (arson): 2; Viols (rapes): 14; Enlèvements (abductions): 9; Infanticides: 8; Adultères (adulteries): 3; Mauvaise conduite (malversations): 3; Injures (insults): 13; Blasphème (blasphemy): 3. Total: 283–Total offenses v. persons: 202; Les Grands Jours d'Auvergne, 139.

77. Depping, in his Correspondance administrative, made much of the impressive total of death sentences without mentioning the small number of corpses and the larger ones of effigies; cf. Lebigre's findings in Grands Jours, 153–57. Fines totaled 607,064 livres.

78. See references to Dongois, Registres, for individual sentences. Some examples include Charles de Montvallat, 27 November 1665; Jacques de Beaufort-Canillac, 12 January 1666; Guillaume de Beaufort-Canillac, 15 January 1666; Jacques Timoléon (old) Marquis de Canillac, 26 January 1666; Robert Sr. de Lignerac, 26 January; Marquis de Malauze, 29 January; Marquis de Merville, 29 January; Comte d'Apchon, 30 January. The old Marquis de Canillac, for example, was treated quite severely. He was sentenced to death (by contumace). His Auvergnat

with their lives for the behavior of many others of their kind, and clearly the deaths of the powerful seem to have impressed contemporary observers more than the monetary sanctions. This impact was especially strong with the execution of La Mothe-Canillac. All of Clermont was shocked with grief according to Fléchier.[79] Three days before the execution of his relative, de Novion, *président* of the court, virtually exulted to Colbert, "The Auvergnats have never known so clearly as they do at present that they have a king." Although the connection was remote (his son-in-law's sister was married to a Canillac), it seems a resoundingly clear rejection of family solidarity in favor of loyalty to the king and his law. In the same letter, Novion wrote that the rural *prévôts* had gained heart from the boldness of the court; he then recounted a tale much like those of Fléchier, concerning the new insolence of peasants toward *gentilshommes*. His conclusion: "Never was there so much dismay among the mighty and so much joy among the weak."[80]

What did the Grands Jours d'Auvergne achieve? At the time, neither the *greffier* Dongois nor the abbé Fléchier foresaw anything quite so extensive as a pacification of the rural nobility, but both were hopeful about the influence of the court. Fléchier, speaking through the character of an unnamed "friend," thought that the Grands Jours had given hope to decent folk in a province where crime had been so rife "that one was ashamed to be a respectable man (*un homme de bien*)."[81]

Dongois, as befitted a chief clerk or registrar, was more cautious in his conclusions. Considering the short duration of the court and the long duration of the problems it came to solve; the opportunities for the accused to flee justice; the reluctance of subordinate judges to execute the orders of transient courts and the habit of those condemned in absentia to return after the court's departure, he judged that extreme measures had been necessary and effective: "the provinces derived some real benefit from them through the terror that they inspired in the guilty, and the example that they left for those who would emulate them."[82]

Recent scholars seem to have accepted the utility of the Grands Jours

---

properties were to be confiscated, 32,000 livres to go to the crown and 48,000 to those seeking damages. His châteaus in Auvergne were to be razed and all his lands were deprived of the rights of seigneurial justice. The Marquis de Malauze was to pay 58,000 livres both fine and restitution of the fruits of the *curé* he had enjoyed, retroactively to 1630.

79. Fléchier, *Mémoires*, 72.
80. Novion to Colbert, 20 October 1665, in Depping, *Correspondance administrative* 2:165.
81. Fléchier, *Mémoires*, 292–93.
82. Dongois, *Registres*, conclusion after 30 January 1666.

as well. Abel Poitrineau referred to the court as part of a "great restoration of order," a chastening of the Auvergnat nobility, that was made more effective by the removal of 200 false noble titles in the *preuves* of 1666–68 and that ended a period of "under-administration" by royal government.[83] Likewise Arlette Lebigre decided that the mountains "were severely purged of their disorders," a step toward the taming of the aristocracy and the strengthening of royal authority.[84] It has also been argued that the Grands Jours initiated many useful reforms in legal procedure, ecclesiastical, and seigneurial practices and the standardization of weights and measures.[85]

As an experience and an experiment for the future of criminal procedure, the Grands Jours were of great importance, although their influence is of the sort that is not really measurable. The greatest reform of criminal law during the period was to be the Criminal Ordinance of 1670, and four of the judges from the Grands Jours, including the president de Novion, were instrumental in drawing up the final version of the ordinance. It seems likely that some of its provisions were informed by the mountain experience of the jurists. Some of them could be interpreted as an attack on the tradition of "private justice." Public prosecution was to be strengthened, with the *procureur*, whether royal or seigneurial, bringing charges in every case. Complainants did not need to become *parties civiles* and pay the costs of procedure, so that it was theoretically easier for the humbler sort of victim to have charges brought against the author of an offense. The taking of depositions was to be more strictly regulated, and if the evidence justified an arrest, the warrant required the conclusions of the *procureur*. The cases in which arrest warrants could be issued are interesting, because they seem to indicate a concern with violence and private vengeance, emphasizing among other things that the person to be arrested must have been responsible for serious offenses, "involving possible loss of life [or] liberty."[86]

The attack on local chicanery was evident in some of the provisions of the court that also affected the rest of France, in a series of decrees between October 1665 and January 1666. The "measures of Clermont," were to become standard, with some exceptions. Weight was to be measured in units that were "sixteen ounces of the king's weight of the

83. A. Poitrineau in Manry, ed., *Histoire de L'Auvergne*, 297–306.
84. A. Lebigre, *Grand Jours*, 137 and 177–91.
85. A. H. Hamscher, "Les réformes judicaires."
86. Ibid., and Mousnier, *Institutions* 2:403–5.

city of Paris," and an ell of cloth was to measure three feet, eight inches. Seigneurs were naturally under scrutiny and several decrees specified what they could and could not demand from their tenants and others. The *corvées* or work obligations were regulated by laws that limited their frequency and severity. There were also new rules forbidding the extralegal levy of fines and seizure of tenant's goods and livestock, the levy of dues and tools above customary levels and the demand for unreasonably high quality of payments in kind. How effective these decrees really were is a matter for debate, but they were, in any event, public statements of a new standardization of behavior that had been accompanied by some dramatic enforcement.

Despite their renown for administering exemplary justice to the mighty, the Grands Jours did pay attention to the needs and the behavior of the general populace. Some "profane" celebrations, songfests, and dances were prohibited on holy days, and there were legislative attempts to control the obscene, the blasphemous, the drunken, and the pugnacious. The dates of fairs and markets were changed, so that they did not coincide so explosively with Sundays or holidays, when many folk were at liberty with no good purpose, and so that the holy days were not profaned. For the indigent there was to be increased order and decency as well: confinement, training, and "manufactures," with the accompanying severity for those "undeserving" poor who broke the new law against begging.[87]

These visions of an orderly state were sympathetic to those of religious reformers and to the champions of a newly powerful state. Although not without effect, they remained visions in many cases where the regulation of ordinary life required a state more intrusive than the seventeenth century could devise. Whatever else it may have done, however, the court revealed the system of private retribution amongst Auvergnats and intervened in the rural world of violence whose brutal isolation has been summarized by Roland Mousnier:

> The members of this rural society looked upon urban judges and their agents as enemies to their world and viewed their interference as an intolerable form of aggression and coercion. They preferred to settle their affairs by themselves, in their own way. The man who took his case to the courts of the state was

87. Mousnier, *Institutions*, 2:498–501.

violating at least a tacit social pact and infringing certain traditional liberties. Among *gentilshommes* these sentiments were reinforced by the pride of belonging to a superior race. Disputes between *gentilshommes* were supposed to be settled sword in hand; disputes between *gentilshommes* and one of his inferiors were supposed to be settled by beatings or thrashings, or occasionally with a pistol or musket.[88]

The Grands Jours dealt a massive riposte to those whose provocations local justice could not or would not punish. The unruly nobles of the highlands were by 1665 probably more an affront to royal honor than a threat to the crown; in fact, that is probably partly why the Grands Jours enjoyed such success. It was possible to criminalize and punish these nobles because they no longer posed a political or military danger, but merely constituted a vestigial disorder, some *gentilshommes* not having learned that their "liberties" had now clearly become criminality. The lesson seems to have penetrated the shield of noble self-regard. In 1697, a generation after the last case had been heard, the Intendant Lefèvre d'Ormesson even wrote that "the tribunal to reform justice known as the Grands Jours . . . was beneficial, having corrected the excessive power of the *gentilshommes*, who are currently very submissive and far removed from all troubles with their vassals and their neighbours."[89] Royal justice had given a dramatic demonstration, using the most prominent actors, to show that no one was above the king's law.

We must balance this portrait of judicial success and this triumph of the rule of law with the persistent deference to and allure of nobility. Fléchier was uneasy with the harsh interrogation of prominent *gentilshommes* by the judges and he questioned the justice of the court. In the case of the Vicomte de la Mothe-Canillac, he noted that the accused had after all killed someone of inferior rank after some provocation to his honor. Despite his calling, Fléchier was a man of his time and did not confuse honor with virtue. In the matter of honor, in the enforcement of claims, it was more important to be dangerous than to be good.[90] The memoirist was also enraptured with the handsome good manners of Gaspard d'Espinchal who seemed to enjoy a good deal of local esteem,

88. Ibid., 2:496.
89. Lefèvre d'Ormesson, *Mémoire sur l'état de la généralité de Riom en 1697*, 164.
90. See Pitt-Rivers, "Honour and Social Status," for the observation that "the reputation of a dangerous man assures him precedence over a virtuous man," 23–25.

and whose villany aroused as much fascination and respect as ire. His bravery was as legendary as his cruelty; his resourcefulness and stamina in evading justice combined with his good family name made him a worthy opponent of the crown. In the winter of the Grands Jours, it was said, he retreated to the most inaccessible regions of the Haute Auvergne, where he survived with the aid of a single peasant and was not betrayed, although his phantom was seen everywhere. For various homicides and seigneurial oppression d'Espinchal was condemned and executed in effigy in January 1666, his house razed, and the revenues he had taken returned to the inhabitants of Massiac.[91]

But his story did not end with the Grands Jours. Having served as a commander of troops for the elector of Bavaria, d'Espinchal was pardoned by Louis XIV in 1678; his ancestors' faithful service to the crown, his own previous military service, and the fact that "youth played the greatest part in his criminal actions" were among the reasons given for the favor of the king.[92] After more than a decade of exile, he returned to his lands and, near the ruin of his razed château, built a house that is now the town hall of Massiac. It is said that he performed many penitential good works in his old age and died at peace. Something, at least, was left of the noble right to assault. D'Espinchal's flight, his ancestry, and his military prowess were ultimately able to overcome the censure of the Parlement of Paris. But by then, of course, he was more virtuous than dangerous. Noble violence had begun to be controlled and vertical solidarities to erode.

91. Sentence in Dongois, *Registres*, 23 January 1666. Fléchier's remarks on d'Espinchal in *Mémoires*, 244–58; Lebigre, *Grands Jours*, 116–19. For a sympathetic view of d'Espinchal, see Alfred Douet, "Un Gentilhomme d'Auvergne au XVIIe siècle: Gaspard d'Espinchal," *Revue de la Haute-Auvergne* (1931–32): 133–61.

92. "Lettres d'Abolition" in Cheruel's appendix 25 to Fléchier, *Mémoires*, 398–411; Lebigre, *Grands Jours*, 191. See also "le Grand Diable," in A. Lauras-Pourrat, in *L'Auvergne mystérieuse*, 341.

7 Conclusion: The Economy of Violence and the Haute Auvergne

This experiment with the terse and fragmented criminal justice documents of the seventeenth century has enabled us to see some seventeenth-century people at close range and permitted us to watch and listen to them in action. A close reading of individual cases revealed a world of "justice" outside the official courts. For while official justice did not usually intrude very deeply into the life of the community, its occasional penetration, documented in court records, allows us to see some aspects of rural violence and rural life. What we have found is an economy of violence.

The people of the Haute Auvergne, contained by the mountains and by their internal borders of property and honor, struggled for advantage and repelled threats, illuminating the territories of the interior with explosions of violence. The endless, small-scale economy of provocation and riposte was also overshadowed by a larger violent response to the exigencies of rural life and royal finance in the period 1628–54, when the energies of rural Auvergnats, perhaps led or encouraged by their "betters," were directed against the representatives of the increasingly intrusive royal government.

The mountains enclosed a private world of tough, taciturn people used to settling their affairs on their own. This was a collective, but not a personal, privacy, one that shunned outsiders, but was also "public" in the sense that its ledgers of affront and vengeance were well known, and the settling of accounts was often witnessed by others in the community. Within the upper province was a series of smaller worlds formed in part by the dissected topography of the mountains. Southern in much of its cultural orientation, the province was far from the source of judicial power to the north, a fact that reinforced the tendency to private local justice. Aggravating this isolation was the tradition of escape: escape to the mountains as a place of refuge for outlaws; escape away from their poverty by the migrations of transhumance and the movements of those in search of trade or employment; and the sedentary festive escapes of alcohol and celebration. Violence itself could be a personal escape from some internal desperation, a vital self-expression and a sort of mute vocabulary in a society where words were inadequate at some of the most important points in interpersonal relations.

Facing the world of private justice were the official forces of order: the *maréchaussée*, led by the *vice-baillis*, *prévôts des maréchaux*; the royal and seigneurial criminal courts, mostly headquartered in the larger towns. The significant officials of justice were a literate French-speaking élite, often interrelated by blood and marriage, jealous of their jurisdiction, judging and repressing the offenses of a rural patois-speaking commonality. The true police force, that is, the *maréchaussée*, was much smaller than the body of court officials. All these official "forces of order" taken together were puny compared to the pervasive vigilance of the rural inhabitants who punished each other's infractions of the common behavioral code with private retribution.

Characteristics of Crime

By the measure common to earlier studies of crime, reported offenses against persons were more common than those against property in the Haute Auvergne and violence was very much a part of rural life, the natural response to many different sorts of threats and the basis, more or less veiled, of power.

In the more detailed scenes of violence documented by the courts, there was often a pattern of provocation and riposte. In the provocations—challenges, attacks, threats, and insults—lie some interesting clues to the sensibilities of rural inhabitants. Honor, reputation, property, dignity, and worth, not easily separable, were usually the possessions most closely guarded. They were not discrete elements of character and well-being, but rather different facets of the whole person. Self-worth and dignity were part of the psychic property of each person and their borders were marked as clearly as the individual hay meadows necessary to the survival of the cattle herd in winter. Moreover, these properties were asserted and defended dramatically in the theater of public life where moral qualities and their defense were expressed.

One should not, and this is an important point, make too great a distinction between persons and property. In the Haute Auvergne a violation of either posed the same sort of challenge and could meet with the same sort of violent response. This unity of the material and the moral was epitomized in women, for whom the boundaries of honor and the basis of good repute were physical, actual boundaries of flesh. Thus women were insulted with attacks on, among other things, their sexual propriety, chastity, and physical beauty, while for men the attacks concerned a wider range of qualities: honesty, courage, and worth. A woman, for example, could be called slut, prostitute, tramp; a man, rascal, cheat, poltroon, blackguard, good-for-nothing and so on. This sexual division of honor reflected the circumscribed hearth-related world of women in contrast to the relative liberty of males, who could also be insulted with epithets appropriate to their status or profession: a notary as forger or shifter of boundary stones; a priest as leper, drunkard, or glutton. But the aim of insults was usually similar: the devaluation of the worth of another; humiliation and separation from the community, the destruction or seizure of psychic property. Challenges and threats had the same underlying promise: you will pay for it, the threat usually of physical violence or ultimately of death.

The verbal defenses were weak: one was an honorable woman or a respectable man; therefore one sought satisfaction and recompense in the violent physical riposte. In response, one might nurse wounded pride and plan a future attack, usually in well-armed stealth; or in the unendurable fury of the moment, a challenge might meet with an instant retaliation. This most vital theater demanded an audience for fullest satisfaction and the public administration of an affront or response to an affront was most satisfying to honor. But insofar as rational calculation was concerned, it might be enough that others in this public arena knew of the vengeance and its author, the latter escaping official punishment by settling accounts more stealthily.

All levels of rural society participated in this economy of violence, usually either in attacks against social equals or inferiors. The nobility of the Haute Auvergne with their households and retainers carried on feuds between clans, avenged slights, and enforced their authority and chicanery over dependents and neighbors. Nobility said to have been won in the past by feats of battle was sometimes maintained by rites of violence: duels, "rencontres," and sometimes simple brigandage. Theirs was a military office, and in the absence of war and of effective police, nobles continued to enjoy military liberties and the habits of conquest. The absence of effective royal authority gave them a right to assault and the extensive nature of their psychic property made them a source of disorder.

The local clergy were in an ambiguous position, still leaders in the rural community, literate and privy to the secrets of the confessional but often numerous and poor. They participated more fully in the intimate details of parish life and had an important economic stake; but they were not usually noble, and therefore played a dual role: at some times the good protectors of their flock; at others a separate caste identified as useless, greedy, or drunken. They were not so socially distant as to be immune from challenges by their parishioners and their interest as *rentiers* sometimes brought them into dispute with *gentilshommes* jealous of ecclesiastical benefices and revenues. Priests could reflect the violent behavior of their parishioners and sometimes exercised their authority with the common violence. In our period, reformers were attempting to control the excesses of priests and parishioners and to instill Christian orthodoxy and self-restraint. One could see this tendency as a divorce between Christianity and honor that had to be effected among the parish clergy before it could apply to their parishioners. The separation and elevation of the rural clergy from its surroundings may have begun to make clerical mores more consistent, and it may have encouraged a new kind of piety among some of the laity. But the stricter separation of the sacred and the profane may also have ultimately divided the parish and ensured that religion would no longer inform all of human activity, withdrawing it from village life and in turn taking much of the "profane" vitality from religion. This social rupture and diminution of vitality not only make more understandable the religious indifference of the eighteenth century, but also clarify some of the conditions that permitted the criminalization of violence and, to some extent, of poverty.

The rest of the rural hierarchy was not always clearly identified by the documents, but on the existing evidence it appears that violence was employed either between social equals, or by social superiors against those beneath them. There is seldom evidence of attacks by ordinary folk against those significantly superior to them within their rural world. Attacks could cross a broad social gulf upward, however, when the threat came from outside the rural community. Peasants would resist urban *officiers*, marauding soldiers, or others threatening the well-being of the household, village, or parish. Furthermore, if the scale of the threat became great enough, all the orders of the rural community might band together in self-defense or outrage at the intrusion. Thus *gentilshommes* turned their predatory skills into protective ones, and the clergy used whatever authority they had in defense of the parish. There was a deep-seated xenophobia that grew in scale depending upon the community threatened, beginning at the village level and extending to the antipathies between the town and country and between the outlying regions and the center of power. It was a xenophobia that operated in time as well as space as it were, in that much of the violence of the struggles we see derives from a resistance to "modern" innovations, whether religious, absolutist, fiscal, or judicial. The position of the *maréchaussée* and the *vice-baillis* depended upon the nature of the disturbances. They might be the threat incarnate when assisting in the collection of taxes or suppressing rebellion; or they could lend their authority to the rural defense against bands of soldiers or brigands.

There is also evidence of the vertical rural solidarities proposed by Mousnier and Bercé. This social cohesion began to be weakened, or perhaps its weakness was revealed, by the intrusion of the Grands Jours d'Auvergne, which elicited peasant complaints about seigneurial oppression. We must recognize too that these solidarities changed according to the changing nature of threats to the community. As for those on the social margins of the community, vagabonds and habitual thieves, the violence that most often concerned them was judicial violence. In the case of vagabonds, their very existence was a provocation to the forces of order and the official riposte was either corporal punishment or further separation in the form of banishment.

The Judicial Riposte

If violence within the community was excessive or came to the notice of the authorities, then accused persons might find themselves in the alien world of official justice; there village antagonists could find themselves officially criminalized. Illiterate patois speakers faced a complex process full of daunting demands for precision and an accumulation of written evidence. The judicial officials, very like those outsiders distrusted by the rural community, copied their statements and challenged their dignity with impunity. The accuser was unseen; the accused, with few defenses, faced a "relentless, inquisitorial" system. The judge, seemingly deaf to the defensive nuances of the accused, had substantial arbitrary powers and solemnly pronounced a sentence based on the "proofs" accumulated during the trial. The sentences indicate that thieves were more frequently punished than the violent and that the courts used violence to punish thieves and vagrants. Acquittals were few and punishments were public and meant to be deterrent.

But appearances covered the fact that the system was gentler than it has often been portrayed. Moreover, justice did not grow harsher during our period; if anything, it grew less so according to the reduced frequency of death sentences for both theft and homicide after 1627. The reaction of official justice to many crimes was, however, similar to private retribution. The secret trial, the public shame, the parade of corpses, whippings, mutilations were meant to terrify the wicked. Along with the banishments, branding, and death sentences in absentia, these procedures separated some offenders from the community and probably made them outlaws in their pride, defiance, or desperation.

Faced with this alien inquisitorial process, it is little wonder that the accused usually chose either flight or protestations of innocence. They were facing yet another outside intervention by the sorts of officials against whom rural communities had banded together in the past. Their property, life, and integrity were threatened, and at this point, the only weapons they possessed were silence, escape, and denial. Official justice, in its general weakness, used its moments of strength to dispense exemplary punishments to those unfortunate enough to be caught and weak enough to be punished without danger to officialdom. *Gentilshommes*, on the other hand, seldom among its victims, could only be punished locally by their peers. The Grands Jours would change that.

Exemplars of Violence

If the rural society of the Haute Auvergne in the period 1587–1664 was indeed characterized by vertical solidarities, could it be argued that to some extent those at the top of the hierarchy were models of violent behavior? Peter Burke has noted in his work on popular culture that the role of the nobleman as warrior-hero was common to many parts of Europe during the early modern period. Certainly the legendary violence and bravery of the most prominent Auvergnat nobles such as the Canillacs and the "Grand Diable" Gaspard d'Espinchal was a well-known phenomenon throughout this period, from the righteous violence of the religious wars to the final revelations and repressions of the Grands Jours. The origin of the *gentilshommes* lay in the same soil as that of other rural inhabitants. The broader sense of boundaries, the identification with the clan and territory, the refined sensitivity to slights against honor, the violent defense of dignity, the tradition of collective activity, and the enviable liberty of *gentilshommes* in these matters were not lost on the population of the mountains. The privileged material and social ease of the nobility were no doubt admired by those others, including even the censorious *Abbé* Fléchier. Nobility itself seems to have been the goal of *officiers* and *bourgeois* who bought seigneuries. Certainly the grand passions of the most evil were a subject of romantic and terrified gossip. Could not similar passions inhabit the hearts of lesser folk? As we have seen, such emotions were not the exclusive preserve of the nobility.

What of official justice itself? Perhaps in its violent revenge upon "trespassers" it was also exemplary, but not always deterrent. It often replied to offenses in the same style as private retribution, with violent revenge, separation from the community, humiliation, and seizure of property. Similarly, the clergy as local leaders were not immune to the contagion of violence in the defense of dignity, authority, privilege, and property. Aspirations toward economic ease and respect were nearly universal, whether it meant the hope of the peasant to acquire enough wealth to hire others for the heavy work, or the desire of an *officier* to acquire a seigneury and other marks of privilege. Was violence then in part an imitation of nobility and of "justice"?

The stubborn violence of the Haute Auvergne would not have been unfamiliar to the inhabitants of other regions, although it may have persisted longer; it had recently enough been a part of ordinary life everywhere in the West. While often associated with leisure, the tavern, and the festival, it could also be, as we have seen, an element of working life in the Haute Auvergne, of daily self-assertion, a way of preserving the order of the world around one, and of making sure that others did the same, whether they were members of the closer community or

Intruding strangers, a way of preserving, as we have proposed, the psychic property of individuals and the collectivity. Research in other areas suggests that this common violence was declining, that the ideologies of self-restraint, the internalization or interiorization of feelings and passions, of religious and other sentiments, and the complementary imposition of public order, were bringing about this retreat of "private" violence. While these developments may have operated at certain levels in the Haute Auvergne, such as those of the large peasant revolt, the formal duel, and judicial violence, which seem to have followed the trends in evidence elsewhere, there is little evidence of such a decline in the day-to-day lives of ordinary folk. The seventeenth-century diagnosis, that the areas least accessible from the metropolis were the most troublesome in this regard, seems to have been fairly accurate. The regulation, or more properly, the redistribution of the power of violence and vengeance, came dramatically, from the outside. The Grands Jours deliberately chose drama, attacking first the problems among elites: noble violence and chicanery, official, judicial malversation, and ecclesiastical disorder. The region required such an exercise because it was remarkable (although perhaps not unique) in its disorders. Such imported drama was an attempt to overwhelm the local theater, but only the beginning of a strong response to the violent theatrics of ordinary life. Something so profound as the sense of psychic property must be altered by a long attrition, almost by erosion as well as by a great didactic shock. The thunderclap of exemplary punishment that demonstrates power and submission must give way to the droning of regular catechism that inculcates them.

The strengthening of royal justice and the movement toward the seizure and centralization by the state of the power of vengeance helped to tip the precarious balance between private and public justice, but it also revealed antagonisms of future importance in the rural social order. Moreover, as the crown attempted to assert a more extensive purview, it encountered the resistance of all those whose means of defending their psychic property was at risk. The attempt to modernize power relations confronted obsessions that were closely related to essential fears: honor to the fear of infamy, and social death; property to the fear of indigence. To some in the traditional rural theater, bound by the requirements of subsistence, the exigencies of xenophobia and, above all, by the eyes of others in the community, physical extinction was not too high a price to pay to avoid deaths such as these.

Appendixes

Appendix 1

Qualité and Violence in the Chevauchées, 1587–1664: Cases of
Assault and Homicide According to Social Status or Occupation

Status or Occupation	No. of Accused	%	No. of Victims	%
Noble/seigneur/noble bastard	109	21.2	53	13.0
Officier	9	1.7	21	5.3
Sergent, huissier, or archer	7	1.4	18	4.5
Merchant, bourgeois, and "professions"	6	1.2	27	6.8
Soldier	18	3.5	22	5.5
Artisan	3	0.6	7	1.8
Hoste	4	0.8	1	0.3
Lackey, servant, domestic	47	9.1	17	4.3
Peasant (laboureur, métayer, etc.)	6	1.2	28	7.0
Clergy	12	2.3	23	5.8
Women	8	1.6	16	4.0
Named but no status given (usually "habitant du lieu")	258	50.1	156	39.1
Unknown	34	6.6	17	4.3
Total	**521**	**101.7**	**405**	**101.7**
Counted twice*	6	1.2	6	1.5
Total	**515**	**100.5**	**399**	**100.2**

SOURCE: Archives départementales du Cantal, Fonds de Comblat, Procès Verbaux des Vice-baillis.
*Accused: 4 noblewomen, 2 female domestics.
  Victims: 2 robines, 1 noblewoman, 1 bourgeoise, 1 maid, 1 wife of merchant.

Appendix 2
Penalties for Homicide in the *Chevauchées*

Punishment	1587–95 (9 yrs)	1606–17 (11 yrs)	1627–47 (8 yrs)	1648–64 (9 yrs)	Totals 1587–1664 (96 sentences)
Hanging	9	16	5	6	36
Wheel	0	3	1	2	5
Beheading	6	7	3	2	18
Total death	**15**	**26**	**9**	**9**	**59**
Assisting "la hart au col"	0	0		2	2
Torture	1	0	2	3	6
Galleys					
Life	1				1
Limited term					
Total	**1**				**1**
Banishment					
Life				2	2
5–10 years				2	2
1–3 years			2		2
Total			**2**	**4**	**6**
Whipping				1	1
Branding					
Mutilation		1		1	2
Amende honorable					
Fines and property confiscation		4		3	7
Plus amplement informé		0	6		6
Transferred to other courts	3	4	3	4	14
Contumace	8	14	4	4	30
Acquittals and unconditional releases	1	2	6	1	10
Lettres de grace	0		1	1	2

SOURCE: Archives départementales du Cantal, Fonds de Comblat, Procès Verbaux des Vice-baillis.

Appendix 3
Penalties for Theft in the *Chevauchées*

Punishment	1587–95 (9 yrs)	1606–17 (11 yrs)	1627–47 (8 yrs)	1648–64 (9 yrs)	Totals 1587–1664 (190 sentences)
Hanging	27	21	10	13	71
Wheel	2	2			4
Beheading					
Total death	**29**	**23**	**10**	**13**	**75**
Assisting "la . . . hart au col"			1	2	3
Torture	6	3	5	4	18
Galleys					
Life		1	1		2
Limited term				1	1
Total		**1**	**1**	**1**	**3**
Banishment					
Life		13	15	2	30
5–10 years	2	3	2		7
1–3 years		2	3		5
Total	**2**	**18**	**20**	**2**	**42**
Whipping		20	12	6	38
Branding		15	3	1	19
Mutilation		2	1		3
Amende honorable		1	1		2
Fines and property confiscation	2				2
Plus amplement informé	10	5	7		22
Transferred to other courts	3	2	1	5	11
Contumace	8	6			14
Acquittals and unconditional releases	5	2	1		8
Lettres de grace					0

SOURCE: Archives départementales du Cantal, Fonds de Comblat, Procès Verbaux des Vice-baillis.

Select Bibliography

PRIMARY SOURCES

Manuscripts

Archives départementales du Cantal
    Series B
        1B Bailliage, siège Présidial d'Aurillac

1	Edit de création, Présidial d'Aurillac
2	État des épices en Haute Auvergne
9–15	Livre du roy en consequence
31–32	Edits, déclarations et ordonnances
920–929	Dossiers Criminels
1053–1059	Minutes Criminelles

        3B Bailliage d'Andelat
            25 minutes criminelles
        5B Bailliage de Calvinet
            36 Dossiers Criminels
        7B Bailliage de Murat

189–202	Dossiers Criminels
204	Minutes Criminelles

        10B Bailliage de St. Flour

90	Dossiers Criminels
103	Minutes criminelles

        14B Bailliage de Salers

227–230	Dossiers criminels
307	Minutes criminelles

        15B Bailliage de Carladez à Vic

583–586	Recueil de procédures et plaintes criminelles
599–600	Dossiers criminels
675	Minutes criminelles

        16B Juridictions Seigneuriales (criminal)

23	Anterroche
25	Apchon

212	La Besserette
280	Brezons
283	La Broha
399	Cheylanne
432	Conrot
460	La Dailhe
611	La garde (Leu camp)
670	Lignerac
902	Peschans
992	Ruynes
1010	Saillans
1015	St. Chamant
1048	St. Just
1075	St. Urcize, La Roche-Canillac, La Trinitat
1098	Sedaiges

Series E: Fonds Delmas dossiers 163–167
 Officiers of Aurillac
 Fonds de Comblat, Procès Verbaux des Vice-baillis
Series F: 346F 33 Catalogue des curés prêtres des paroisses
 Calendrier de Festes
 Évêché de St. Flour
Series G: Évêché de St. Flour 11G9 paroisses
Archives Communales d'Aurillac
 Mainly series AA and BB meetings of consuls, police, disturbances relating to the city of Aurillac
Archives Nationales
Documents pertaining to the Grands Jours d'Auvergne
 U 749–750
 X1B 9699, 9701, 9702, 9703
 X2B 1267, 1268, 1269
Bibliothèque Nationale
 Manuscrits français
 3328, 4083, 4782, 11916
 Manuscrits français nouvelles acquisitions
 2808, 5714
 Collection Clairambault
 742
 Collection Dupuy
 658
Other Archives
 A.D. Côte d'Or 3473
 A.D. Dordogne 6C1
 A.D. Maine-et-Loire I Mi II (R1)
 A.D. Puy-de-Dôme 5C Aa 3rr
 A.D. Saône-et-Loire BB78, C505
 A.C. Nevers BB21

Printed

Basmaison, Jean de. *Paraphrase sur les Coustumes du bas & hault pays d'Auvergne.* Clairmont, 1628.

Bodin, Jean. *De la démonomanie de sorciers.* Paris, 1530.

"Le Cahier de la noblesse de Haute Auvergne aux Etats Généraux de 1614." Edited by Pierre-François Fournier. *Revue de la Haute-Auvergne* (1947–49): 117–21.

Cellini, Benvenuto. *Autobiography.* Translated by G. Bull. Toronto, 1956.

Chabrol, M. *Coutumes générales et locales de la province d'Auvergne.* 4 vols. Riom, 1786.

Depping, Georges B., ed. *Correspondance administrative sous Louis XIV.* 3 vols. Paris, 1851.

Dongois, Le Greffier. *Les Grands-Jours de Clermont, Registres tenus par le Greffier Dongois (1665–1666).* Printed as *Les Grands Jours d'Auvergne,* edited by Ulysse Jouvet. Riom, 1903.

Estadieu, Louis. *Journal.* Published by Gabriel Esquer as "La Haute Auvergne à la fin de l'Ancien Régime, Notes de géographie économique." *Revue de la Haute-Auvergne* (1905): 381–97; (1906): 90–108, 150–68, 256–278, 395–428; (1907): 125–58, 278–313, 384–432; (1908): 237–76; (1910): 209–35; (1911): 84–94.

Estienne, Charles. *L'Agriculture et la maison rustique.* Paris, 1601.

Fléchier, Espirit. *Mémoires sur les Grands Jours d'Auvergne en 1665.* Edited by A. Cheruel. Paris, 1856.

Imbert, Jean. *La Pratique judiciaire tant civile que criminelle.* Cologny, 1615.

Isambert, André, et al., eds., *Recueil général des anciennes lois françaises depuis l'an 420 jusqu'à la révolution de 1789.* 29 vols. Paris, 1822–33.

Lefèvre d'Ormesson, Antoine. *Mémoire sur l'état de la généralité de Riom en 1697.* Edited by Abel Poitrineau. Clermont-Ferrand, n. d.

Liset, Pierre. *Practique judiciaire pour l'instruction et décision des causes criminelles et civiles.* Paris, 1603.

Loyseau, Charles. *Oeuvres (1610).* 5 vols. Lyon, 1701.

Mesgrigny, Jean de. *Relation de l'état de la province d'Auvergne en 1637.* Clermont-Ferrand, 1842.

Mousnier, Roland, ed. *Lettres et mémoires adressées au chancelier Séguier.* 2 vols. Paris, 1964.

Muyart de Vouglans, Pierre F. *Institutes du droit criminel.* 2 vols. Paris, 1768.

SECONDARY SOURCES

Abbiateci, André, François Billacois, Yvonne Bongert, Nicole Castan, Yves Castan, and Porfiry Petrovitch. *Crimes et criminalité en France sous l'Ancien Régime 17e–18e siècles.* Paris, 1971.

Achard, André. *Une Ancienne Justice seigneuriale en Auvergne: Sugères et ses habitants.* Clermont-Ferrand, 1929.

Adams, George C. *Words and Descriptive Terms for 'Woman' and 'Girl' in French and Provençal and Border Dialects.* Chapel Hill, N.C., 1949.

Anderson, Bonnie S., and Judith P. Zinsser. *A History of Their Own: Women in Europe from Prehistory to the Present.* 2 vols. New York, 1988.

Angenot, M. *Les Champions des Femmes: Examen du discours sur la supériorité des femmes, 1400–1800.* Montreal, 1977.

Anglade, Jean. *Histoire de l'Auvergne.* Paris, 1974.

Arbos, Philippe. *L'Auvergne.* Paris, 1932.

———. "L'Emigration temporaire en Auvergne." *Revue d'Auvergne* (1931): 41–45.

Aston, Trevor H., ed. *Crisis in Europe, 1560–1660*. New York, 1965.

Avenel, Georges d'. *La Noblesse française sous Richelieu*. Paris, 1901.

Beattie, John M. *Crime and the Courts in England 1600–1800*. Princeton, 1986.

———. "The Pattern of Crime in England, 1660–1800." *Past and Present* 62 (February 1974): 47–95.

Beaufrère, Abel. "Confidences du Haute Pays." *Le Cobret* (April 1963): 8; (February 1963): 8–10.

Beauvoir, Simone de. *The Second Sex*. Translated by H. M. Parshley. New York, 1952.

Becker, Marvin. "Changing Patterns of Violence in Fourteenth- and Fifteenth-Century Florence." *Comparative Studies in Society and History* (1976): 281–296.

Bercé, Yves-Marie. "Aspects de la criminalité au XVIIe siècle." *Revue Historique* 239, no. 1 (1968): 33–42.

———. "De la criminalité aux troubles sociaux: La noblesse rurale du Sud-ouest de la France sous Louis XIII." *Annales du Midi* (1964): 41–59.

———. *Histoire des Croquants—Études des soulèvements populaires au XVIIe siècle dans le sud-ouest de la France*. 2 vols. Geneva, 1974.

———. *Révoltes et révolutions dans l'Europe moderne*. Paris, 1980.

Bergin, Joseph. *Cardinal Richelieu: Power and the Pursuit of Wealth*. New Haven, Conn., 1985.

Billacois, François. *The Duel: Its Rise and Fall in Early Modern France*. Edited and translated by Trista Selous. New Haven, Conn., 1990.

———. "Pour un enquête sur la criminalité dans la France d'Ancien Régime." *Annales E.S.C.* 22, no. 2 (March–April 1967): 340–49.

Bitton, Davis. *The French Nobility in Crisis, 1560–1640*. Stanford, Calif., 1969.

Bloch, Marc. *Les Caractères originaux de l'histoire rurale française (1931)*. 2 vols. Paris, 1961.

———. *French Rural History*. Translated by Janet Sondheimer. Berkeley and Los Angeles, 1966.

Bonnefons, Edouard. *Étude sur les anciennes juridictions du Haute Pays d'Auvergne*. Paris, 1874.

Bossy, John. *Christianity in the West, 1400–1700*. Oxford, 1985.

Boudet, Marcellin. *Documents inédits sur la justice et la police prévôtales*. Riom, 1906.

———. *La justice et la police prévôtales*. Riom, 1902.

Bourrachet, L. "Les Immigrants saisonniers auvergnats en Haute Agenais." *Revue de la Haute-Auvergne* (1960): 173–80.

Boutelet, Bernadette. "Etude par sondage de la criminalité dans le bailliage du Pont-de-l'Arche (XVIIe–XVIIIe siècles)." *Annales de Normandie* (1962): 235–62.

Boutillet, Jean Baptiste. *Nobiliaire d'Auvergne*. 10 vols. Clermont-Ferrand, 1846–53.

Bouyssou, Léonce. "Étude sur la vie rurale en Haute Auvergne. La région d'Aurillac au XVe siècle." *Revue de la Haute-Auvergne* (1939–44): 101–54, 224–33, 271–89, 336–49; (1945–46):47–63, 74–86.

———. *Les Montagnes cantaliennes du XIII au XVIIIe siècle*. Aurillac, 1974.

Boxer, Marilyn J., and Jean H. Quataert. *Connecting Spheres: Women in the Western World, 1500 to the Present*. Oxford, 1987.

Bowler, Gerald Q., et al. *Europe in the Sixteenth Century*. London, 1989.

Braudel, Fernand. *The Mediterranean and the Mediterranean World in the Age of Philip II*. 2 vols. Translated by Sian Reynolds. London, 1972.

Brennan, Thomas. *Public Drinking and Popular Culture in Eighteenth-Century Paris*. Princeton, 1988.

Bridenthal, Renate, Claudia Koonz, and Susan Stuard, eds. *Becoming Visible: Women in European History.* Boston, 1987.

Brownmiller, Susan. *Against Our Will: Men, Women and Rape.* New York, 1975.

Brundage, James A. *Law, Sex, and Christian Society in Medieval Europe.* Chicago, 1987.

Bucheron, Véronique. "La Montée du flot des errants 1760 à 1789 dans la généralité d'Alençon." *Annales de Normandie* (1971): 55–86.

Burke, Peter. *Popular Culture in Early Modern Europe.* New York, 1978.

Cameron, Iain. *Crime and Repression in the Auvergne and the Guyenne, 1720–1790.* Cambridge, 1981.

Castan, Nicole. *Justice et répression en Languedoc à l'époque des Lumières.* Paris, 1980.

———. "La Justice expéditive." *Annales E.S.C.* 31, no. 2 (March–April 1976): 331–61.

Castan, Yves. *Honnêtété et relations sociales en Languedoc (1715–1780)* Paris, 1974.

Champin, Marie-Madeleine. "La Criminalité dans le bailliage d'Alençon de 1715 à 1745." *Annales de Normandie* (1972): 47–84.

Chapman, Terry L. "Crime in Eighteenth-Century England: E. P. Thompson and the Conflict Theory of Crime." *Criminal Justice History* 1 (1980): 139–55.

Chaumeil, Abbé. *Biographie des personnes rémarquables de la Haute Auvergne.* St. Flour, 1867.

Claverie, Elisabeth, and Pierre Lamaison. *L'Impossible Mariage: Violence et parenté en Gévaudan.* Paris, 1982.

Clout, Hugh. *The Massif Central.* Oxford, 1973.

———. *Themes in the Historical Geography of France.* London, 1977.

C.N.R.S. (Centre National de la Recherche Scientifique). *Répertoire des visites pastorales de la France.* Paris, 1977–85.

Cockburn, J. S., ed. *Crime in England, 1550–1800.* Princeton, 1977.

Coleman, Rebecca V. "The Abduction of Women in Barbaric Law." *Florilegeum* 5 (1983): 62–75.

Collins, James B. "The Economic Role of Women in Seventeenth-Century France." *French Historical Studies* 16, no. 2 (Fall 1989): 436–70.

Cooper, J. P., ed. *The New Cambridge Modern History.* Vol. 4. Cambridge, 1971.

Coveney, Peter, ed. *France in Crisis, 1620–1675.* Totowa, N.J., 1977.

Crépillon, Paul. "Un Gibier des prévôts: Mendiants et vagabonds entre la Vire et la Dives (1720–1789)." *Annales de Normandie* (1967): 223–52.

Croix, Alain. *Nantes et le pays nantais.* Paris, 1974.

Cross, F. L., and Elizabeth A. Livingstone, eds. *The Oxford Dictionary of the Christian Church.* Oxford, 1974.

Cummings, Mark. "Elopement, Family, and the Courts: The Crime of Rapt in Early Modern France." *Proceedings of the Fourth Annual Meeting of the Western Society for French History* (1976): 118–25.

Curtis, Timothy C. "Explaining Crime in Early Modern England." *Criminal Justice History* 1 (1980): 117–37.

Darnton, Robert. *The Great Cat Massacre and Other Episodes in French Cultural History.* New York, 1984.

Davis, John. *People of the Mediterranean.* London, 1977.

Davis, Natalie Z. "On the Lame." *American Historical Review* 93, no. 3 (June 1988): 572–603.

———. *The Return of Martin Guerre.* Cambridge, Mass., 1983.

———. *Society and Culture in Early Modern France.* Stanford, Calif., 1975.

Dawson, John P. A History of Lay Judges. Cambridge, Mass., 1960.

Delumeau, Jean. Catholicism between Luther and Voltaire. Translated by Jeremy Moiser. Philadelphia, 1977.

———. Le catholicisme entre Luther et Voltaire. Paris, 1971.

Depauw, Jacques. "Pauvres, Pauvres, mendiants valides ou vagabonds?" Revue d'Histoire Moderne et Contemporaine 21 (July–September 1974): 349–418.

Deribier du Châtelet, M. Dictionnaire statistique ou histoire du département du Cantal. 5 vols. Aurillac, 1852–57.

Derrau-Boniol, Simone, and André Fel. Le Massif Central. Paris, 1963.

Devyver, André. Le Sang Épuré: Les Préjugés de race chez les gentilshommes français de l'Ancien Régime. Brussels, 1973.

Deyon, P. "The French Nobility and Absolute Monarchy in the First Half of the Seventeenth Century." In France in Crisis, 1620–1675, ed. P. J. Coveney, 231–46. Totowa, N.J., 1973.

———. Le Temps des prisons. Paris, 1975.

Dion, Roger. Essai sur la formation du paysage rural français. Tours, 1934.

Donahue, Roy L., Raymond W. Miller, and John C. Schickluna. Soils: An Introduction to Soils and Plant Growth. Englewood Cliffs, N.J., 1971.

Doucet, Roger. Les Institutions de la France au XVIe siècle. 2 vols. Paris, 1948.

Douet, Alfred. "Un Gentilhomme d'Auvergne au XVIIe siècle: Gaspard d'Espinchal." Revue de la Haute-Auvergne (1931–32): 133–61.

Duby, Georges. The Knight, the Lady and the Priest: The Making of Modern Marriage in Medieval Europe. Translated by Barbara Bray. New York, 1983.

Duby, Georges, and Armand Wallon, eds. Histoire de la France rurale. Vol. 2. Paris, 1975.

Dupont-Ferrier, Gustave. Les Officiers royaux des bailliages sénéchaussées et les institutions monarchiques. Paris, 1902.

Durand, Alfred. La Vie rurale dans les massifs volcaniques des Dorés du Cézallier du Cantal et de l'Aubrac. Aurillac, 1946.

Durand, Yves, ed. Deux cahiers de la noblesse pour les États Généraux de 1649–1651. Paris, 1965.

Durif, Henri. Les Foires d'Aurillac. Aurillac, 1873.

Durkheim, Émile. The Rules of Sociological Method. Translated by Sarah A. Solway and John H. Mueller and edited by George E. G. Catlin. New York, 1964.

Eddy, John A. "The 'Maunder Minimum': Sunspots and Climate in the Reign of Louis XIV." In The General Crisis of the Seventeenth Century, ed. Geoffrey Parker and Leslie M. Smith, 226–68. London, 1978.

Elias, Norbert. The Civilizing Process. Vol. 1, The History of Manners Translated by E. Jephcott. New York, 1982.

———. The Civilizing Process, Vol 2, Power and Civility. Translated by E. Jephcott. New York, 1982.

Ellis, L. Theories of Rape: Inquiries into the Causes of Sexual Aggression. New York, 1989.

Esmein, Adhémar. Histoire de la procédure criminelle en France, et spécialement de la procédure inquisitionelle depuis le XIIIe siècle jusqu'à nos jours. Paris, 1882.

Farr, James R. Hands of Honor: Artisans and their World in Dijon, 1550–1650. Ithaca, N.Y., 1988.

La Faute, la répression et le pardon. Actes du 107e Congrès national des sociétés savantes, section de philologie et de l'histoire jusqu'a 1610. Vol. 1. Paris, 1984.

Fel, André. *Les Hautes Terres du Massif Central.* Paris, 1962.

Felgères, Charles. "L'Auvergne sous Richelieu." *Revue d'Auvergne* (1928): 72–98.

————. "Contrebandiers et faux sauniers en Haute-Auvergne aux XVIIe et XVIIIe siècles." *Revue de la Haute-Auvergne* (1927–28): 187–209, 251–72.

Ferro, Marc, ed. *Social Historians in Contemporary France.* New York, 1972.

Ferté, J. *La Vie religieuse dans les campagnes parisiennes, 1622–95.* Paris, 1962.

Finlay, Robert. "The Refashioning of Martin Guerre." *American Historical Review* 93, no. 3 (June 1988): 553–71.

Flandrin, Jean-Louis. *Families in Former Times: Kinship, Household and Sexuality.* Translated by Richard Southern. Cambridge, 1979.

Forster, Robert. *The Nobility of Toulouse in the Eighteenth Century.* Baltimore, 1960.

Forster, Robert, and Orest Ranum, eds. *Deviants and the Abandoned in French Society.* Baltimore, 1978.

————. *Family and Society.* Baltimore, 1976.

Foucault, Michel. *Surveiller et punir: Naissance de la prison.* Paris, 1975.

Fournier, Pierre-François. "Emigrants auvergnats en Espagne au XVe siècle." *Revue d'Auvergne* (1924–27): 230–41.

Franiatte, Jean-Baptiste. *Tableau des poids et mésures en usage dans la ci-devant Haute Auvergne.* Riom, 1802.

Frey, Linda, Marsha Frey, and Joanne Schneider. *Women in Western European History.* Westport, Conn., 1982.

Froeschlé-Chopard, M.-H., and M. Froeschlé-Chopard. *Atlas de la réforme pastorale en France.* Paris, 1986.

Gachon, Lucien. *L'Auvergne et le Velay, La vie populaire d'hier et d'avant hier.* Paris, 1975.

Galpern, A. N. *The Religions of the People in Sixteenth-Century Champagne.* Cambridge, Mass., 1976.

Gatrell, V. A. C., Bruce Lenman, and Geoffrey Parker. *Crime and the Law: The Social History of Crime in Western Europe Since 1500.* London, 1981.

Gégot, Jean-Claude. "Étude par sondage de la criminalité dans le bailliage de Falaise (XVIIe–XVIIIe siècles): Criminalité diffuse ou société criminelle?" *Annales de Normandie* (1966): 103–64.

Geremek, Bronislaw. "Criminalité, vagabondage, pauperisme: La marginalité à l'aube des temps moderns." *Revue d'Histoire Moderne et Contemporaine* 21 (July–September 1974): 337–75.

Gilmore, David D. *Honour and Shame and the Unity of the Mediterranean.* Washington, D.C., 1987.

————. *Manhood in the Making: Cultural Concepts of Masculinity.* New Haven, Conn., 1990.

Girard, A. "La saisie des biens français d'Espagne en 1625." *Revue d'histoire économique* (1931): 297–315.

Goffman, Erving. *Relations in Public: Microstudies of the Public Order.* New York, 1971.

————. *Stigma: Notes on the Management of Spoiled Identity.* Englewood Cliffs, N.J., 1963.

Goldsmith, James L. "Agricultural Specialization and Stagnation in Early Modern Auvergne." *Agricultural History* 47, no. 3 (1973): 216–34.

————. "The Rural Nobles of Auvergne under the Old Régime: The Seigneurs de Salers and Mazerolles and Their Domains." Ph.D. diss. Harvard University, 1971.

Goody, John, Joan Thirsk, and Edward P. Thompson. *Family and Inheritance: Rural Society in Western Europe, 1200–1800.* Cambridge, 1976.

Goubert, Pierre. L'Ancien Régime. 2 vols. Paris, 1969–73.
———. The Ancien Régime. Translated by S. Cox. New York, 1971.
Greenshields, Malcolm R. "An Introduction to the Pastoral Visit Project: Between Two Worlds, 1560–1720." Proceedings of the Annual Meeting of the Western Society for French History 15 (1988): 51–60.
———. "The Relations of Sentiment between the Peasants and the Rural Nobility in the Cahiers to the Estates General of 1614." M.A. thesis, University of Saskatchewan, 1978.
———. "What Happened in Quibou? The Catholic Reformation in the Village." Proceedings of the Annual Meeting of the Western Society for French History 18 (1991): 80–88.
———. "Women, Violence, and Criminal Justice Records in Early Modern Haute Auvergne (1587–1664)." Canadian Journal of History / Annales Canadiennes d'Histoire 22 (August 1987): 175–94.
Greyerz, Kaspar von, ed. Religion and Society in Early Modern Europe, 1500–1800. London, 1984.
Grimmer, Claude. "Les Bâtards de la noblesse auvergnate." XVIIe Siècle 29, no. 4 (1977): 35–48.
———. Vivre à Aurillac au XVIIIe siècle. Aurillac, 1983.
Gutton, Jean P. La Société et les pauvres: L'exemple de la généralité de Lyon 1534–1789. Paris, 1971.
Hale, John R. Renaissance Europe, 1480–1520. London, 1971.
Hammer, Carl I. "Patterns of Homicide in a Medieval University Town: Fourteenth-Century Oxford." Past and Present 78 (February 1978): 3–23.
Hamscher, Albert H. "Les Réformes judiciaires des Grands Jours d'Auvergne, 1665–1666." Cahiers d'Histoire 1, no. 4 (1976): 425–32.
Hanley, Sarah. "Engendering the State: Family Formation and State Building in Early Modern France." French Historical Studies 16, no. 1 (Spring 1989): 4–27.
Hanlon, Gregory. "Les Rituels de l'aggression en Aquitaine au XVIIe siècle." Annales E.S.C. 40, no. 2 (March–April 1985): 244–68.
Hauser, Henri. Notes et documents sur la Réforme en Auvergne. Paris, 1909.
Hay, Douglas, Peter Linebaugh, John G. Rule, Edward P. Thompson, and Cal Winslow. Albion's Fatal Tree: Crime and Society in Eighteenth-Century England. New York, 1975.
Hayden, J. M. "The Catholic Reformation at the Diocesan Level: Coutances in Normandy." Proceedings of the Annual Meeting of the Western Society for French History 18 (1991): 89–97.
———. "Deputies et Qualités": The Estates General of 1614." French Historical Studies 3, no. 4 (1964): 507–24.
———. France and the Estates General of 1614. Cambridge, 1974.
———. "The Pastoral Visit Project Phase I: The Dioceses of Coutances and Avranches." Proceedings of the Annual Meeting of the Western Society for French History 15 (1988): 61–70.
———, and Malcolm Greenshields. "The Clergy of Early Seventeenth-Century France: Self-Perception and Society's Perception." French Historical Studies 18, no. 1 (Spring 1993): 146–72.
Hess, Albert G. "Hunting Witches: A Survey of Some Recent Literature." Criminal Justice History 3 (1982): 47–79.
Hobsbawm, Eric J. Bandits. London, 1969.
———. Primitive Rebels. London, 1959.

Hoffman, P. *Church and Community in the Diocese of Lyon*. New Haven, 1984.

Hufton, Olwen. *The Poor of Eighteenth-Century France*. Oxford, 1974.

Hughes, B. P. *Firepower*. London, 1974.

Imberdis, André. *L'Auvergne depuis l'ère gallique jusqu'au XVIIIe siècle*. Paris, 1863.

————. *Histoire des guerres religieuses en Auvergne pendant les XVIe et XVIIIe siècles*. Riom, 1846.

Imbert, Jean, ed. *Quelques procès criminels des XVIIe–XVIIIe siècles*. Paris, 1974.

Joubert, Edouard. "Quelques notes sur le bas clergé d'Ancien Régime en Haute Auvergne." *Revue de la Haute-Auvergne* (April–June 1979): 105–7.

Jouvet, U., ed. "Les Grands Jours d'Auvergne de 1665: Le Registre du greffier Dongois." L'Auvergne Historique Littéraire et Artistique. Riom, 1905.

Juillard, Marcel. "Le Brigandage et la contrebande en Haute Auvergne au XVIIIe siècle." *Revue de la Haute-Auvergne* (1935–36): 441–92.

Klimath, Henri. *Travaux sur l'histoire du droit française*. Paris, 1843.

Knafla, Louis A., ed. *Crime and Criminal Justice in Europe and Canada*. Waterloo, Ontario, 1981.

Labatut, J.-P., and Y. Durand, eds. *Deux cahiers de la noblesse pour les Etats Généraux de 1649–1651*. Paris, 1965.

Labrousse, Ernest, and Fernand Braudel. *Histoire économique et sociale de la France*. 2 vols. Paris, 1971, 1977.

Lachance, André. *La Justice criminelle au Canada au XVIIIe siècle*. Québec, 1978.

Laingui, André. *La Responsabilité pénale dans l'ancien droit, XVIe–XVIIIe siècle*. Paris, 1970.

Langbein, John H. *Prosecuting Crime in the Renaissance*. Cambridge, Mass., 1974.

————. *Torture and the Law of Proof*. Chicago, 1977.

Laslett, Peter. *The World We Have Lost*. London, 1971.

Lauras-Pourrat, Annette. *Guide de l'Auvergne mystérieuse*. Paris, 1976.

Lebigre, Arlette. *Les Grands Jours d'Auvergne*. Paris, 1976.

————. *La Justice du Roi: La Vie judiciaire dans l'ancienne France*. Paris, 1988.

Le Blant, R. "L'Evolution sociale d'auvergnats parisiens aux XVIIe siècle." *Actes du 88e Congrès des traités savantes* (Clermont-Ferrand, 1963): 696–707.

Lebrun, François. *Histoire des Catholiques en France du XVe siècle à nos jours*. Toulouse, 1980.

Lecuir, Jean. "Criminalité et moralité: Montyon, statisticien du Parlement de Paris." *Revue d'Histoire Moderne et Contemporaine* 21 (1974): 445–93.

Le Goff, T. J. A., and Douglas M. G. Sutherland. "The Revolution and the Rural Community in Eighteenth-Century Brittany." *Past and Present* 62 (February 1974): 96–119.

Léotoing, d'Anjony, Georges de. *La communauté des prêtres filleuls de l'Eglise Notre Dame*. Aurillac, 1954.

Le Roy Ladurie, Emmanuel. *Montaillou, village occitan de 1294 à 1324*. Paris, 1975. Translated by Barbara Bray as *Montaillou: The Promised Land of Error*. New York, 1979.

————. *Les Paysans de Languedoc*. 2 vols. Paris, 1966.

————. *Times of Feast, Times of Famine*. New York, 1971.

Leymairie, Michel. "Émigration et structure sociale en Haute Auvergne à la fin du XVIIe siècle." *Revue de la Haute-Auvergne* (1956–57): 296–315.

————. "La Propriété et l'exploitation foncières au XVIIe siècle dans la Planèze de St. Flour." *Revue de la Haute-Auvergne* (1965): 482–86.

Livingstone, Elizabeth A. *The Concise Oxford Dictionary of the Christian Church*. Oxford, 1978.

Lougee, Carolyn C. Le Paradis des Femmes: Women, Salons and Social Stratification in the Seventeenth Century. Princeton, 1976.

Machiavelli, Niccolò. The Prince. Trans. R. Adams. Introductory essay by Sheldon S. Wolin. London, 1977.

Mackrell, John. "Criticism of Seignorial Justice in Eighteenth-Century France." In Essays in Memory of A. Cobban, edited by J. F. Bosher. London, 1973.

Major, J. Russell. Deputies to the Estates General in Renaissance France. Madison, Wis., 1960.

Malmezat, Jean. Le Bailli des Montagnes d'Auvergne et le Présidial d'Aurillac comme agents de l'administration royale. Paris, 1941.

Mandrou, Robert. Introduction à la France moderne, 1500–1640. Paris, 1961.

———. Magistrats et Sorciers en France au XVIIe siècle: Une Analyse de psychologie historique. Paris, 1968.

Mannheim, Hermann. Comparative Criminology. Boston, 1965.

Manry, André-Georges, ed. Histoire de l'Auvergne. Toulouse, 1974.

Margot, Alain. "La Criminalité dans le bailliage de Mamers 1695–1750." Annales de Normandie (1972): 185–224.

Marion, Marcel. Dictionnaire des institutions de la France aux XVIIe et XVIIIe siècles. Paris, 1968 (Originally published 1923).

Martin, Daniel. Elevage et la vie pastorale dans les montagnes de l'Europe: Colloque international. Clermont-Ferrand, 1984.

———. "La Maréchaussée d'Auvergne face aux autorités administratives et judiciaires aux XVIIIe siècle 1720–1780." Cahiers d'histoire 18, no. 4 (1973): 337–49.

Mer, Louis-Bernard. "La procédure criminel au XVIII siècle: L'Enseignement des archives bretonnes." Revue historique 274 (1985): 9–42.

Methivier, H. "A Century of Conflict: The Economic and Social Disorders of the 'Grand Siècle.' " In France in Crisis, 1620–1675, ed. P. J. Coveney, 1–63. Totowa, N.J., 1973.

Meuvret, Jean. "Circulation monétaire et utilization économique de la monnaie dans la France du XVIe et du XVIIe siècles." Études d'Histoire Moderne et Contemporaine 1 (1947): 15–28.

———. Études d'histoire économique. Paris, 1971.

Miramon-Fargues, Bernard de. Le Métier de gendarme en Auvergne pendant la première moitié du XVIIe siècle. Aurillac, 1900.

Mitterauer, Michael, and Reinhard Sieder. The European Family. Chicago, 1982.

Mousnier, Roland. L'Evolution des institutions monarchiques et ses relations avec l'état social." XVIIe Siècle (1963): 57–72.

———. "French Institutions and Society." In New Cambridge Modern History, 4: 474–502. Cambridge, 1971.

———. Fureurs paysannes: Les Paysans dans les révoltes du XVIIe siècle. Paris, 1967.

———. Les Institutions de la France sous la monarchie absolue, 1598–1789. 2 vols. Paris, 1974, 1980.

———. The Institutions of France under the Absolute Monarchy, 1598–1789. 2 vols. Translated by Arthur Goldhammer and Brian Pearce. Chicago, 1979–84.

———. Peasant Uprisings in Seventeenth-Century France, Russia and China. Translated by Brian Pearce. New York, 1970.

———. La Plume, la faucille et le marteau. Paris, 1970.

———. "Problems de stratification sociale." In Deux cahiers de la noblesse pour les Etats Généraux de 1649–1651, ed. J.-P. Labatut and Y. Durand, 9–49. Paris, 1965.

———. "Recherches sur les soulèvements populaires en France avant la Fronde." *Revue d'Histoire Moderne et Contemporaine* 5 (1958): 81–113.

———. *Social Hierarchies: 1450 to the Present.* Translated by Peter Evans. London, 1973.

———. *La Vénalité des offices sous Henri IV et Louis XIII.* Paris, 1971.

Muchembled, Robert. *L'Invention de l'homme moderne: Sensibilités, moeurs et comportements collectifs sous l'Ancien Régime.* Paris, 1988.

———. *Popular Culture and Elite Culture in France, 1400–1750.* Translated by Lydia Cochrane. Baton Rouge, La., 1985.

———. *La Violence au Village: Sociabilité et comportements populaires en Artois du XVe au XVII siècles.* Turnhout, 1989.

Parker, Geoffrey. *Europe in Crisis, 1598–1648.* New York, 1979.

Parker, Geoffrey, and Leslie M. Smith, eds. *The General Crisis of the Seventeenth Century.* London, 1978.

Peristiany, John G., ed. *Honor and Shame: The Values of Mediterranean Society.* Chicago, 1966.

Perouas, Louis. *Le Diocèse de La Rochelle de 1648 à 1724.* Paris, 1964.

Pfohl, Stephen J. *Images of Deviance and Social Control: A Sociological History.* New York, 1985.

Pinchemel, Philippe. *France, a Geographical Survey.* Translated by C. Trollope and A. J. Hunt. London, 1969.

Pitt-Rivers, Julian. *The Fate of Shechem, or the Politics of Sex: Essays in the Anthropology of the Mediterranean.* Cambridge, 1977.

———. *The People of the Sierra.* Chicago, 1961.

———. "Social Class in a French Village." *Anthropological Quarterly* 33 (1960): 1–13.

Plessix-Buisset, Christiane. *Le Criminel devant ses Juges en Bretagne aux 16e et 17e siècles.* Paris, 1988.

Poitrineau, Abel. "Aspects de l'émigration temporaire et saisonnière." *Revue d'Histoire Moderne et Contemporaine* 9 (1962): 5–50.

———. "Avant la réforme catholique du XVIIe siècle: Un échantillon du clergé paroissial au diocèse de St. Flour sous le règne de Louis XIII." *Almanach de Brioude* (1975): 207–13.

———. "Propriété et société en Haute Auvergne à la fin du règne de Louis XV: Le cas de Vic." *Cahiers d'histoire* 6 (1961): 425–55.

———. *La Vie rurale en Basse-Auvergne au XVIIIe siècle (1726–1789).* 2 vols. Paris, 1965.

Porchnev, Boris. *Les Soulèvements populaires en France de 1623 à 1648.* Paris, 1963.

Potter, Jack M., May N. Diaz, and George M. Foster. *Peasant Society: A Reader.* Boston, 1967.

Pourrat, Henri. *Le temps qu'il Fait.* Paris, 1960.

Rabb, Theodore K. *The Struggle for Stability in Early Modern Europe.* New York, 1975.

Rapley, Elizabeth. *The Dévotes: Women and Church in Seventeenth-Century France.* Montreal, 1990.

Raynal, François. "Au Jardin des Adages, 1016 proverbes en dialecte de Haute Auvergne." *Auvergne* 122 (1948): 67–140.

Reinhardt, Steven G. "Crime and Royal Justice in Ancien Régime France: Modes of Analysis." *Journal of Interdisciplinary History* 13, no. 3 (1983): 437–60.

———. *Justice in the Sarladais, 1770–1790.* Baton Rouge, La., 1991.

Ribier, René de. *Les Paroisses de l'Archiprêtre de Mauriac: Notices historiques.* Paris, 1920.

Rigaudière, Albert. *La Haute Auvergne face à l'agriculture nouvelle au XVIIIe siècle* Paris, 1965.

Rivière, H. F. *Histoire des institutions de l'Auvergne.* 2 vols. Paris, 1874.

Romier, Lucien. *Le Royaume de Catherine de Medici.* Paris, 1922.

Roupnel, Gaston. *La Ville et la campagne au XVIIe siècle.* Paris, 1955.

Rousselet, Marcel, and Jean-Michel Aubouin. *Histoire de la justice.* Paris, 1943.

Ruff, Julius. *Crime, Justice and Public Order in Old Régime France: The Sénéchaussées of Libourne and Bazas, 1696–1789.* London, 1984.

Russell, C. P. *Guns on the Early Frontier.* New York, 1957.

Saby, Marcel. "L'Âme paysanne et la vie rurale en Haute-Auvergne au XVIIe siècle." *Almanach de Brioude* (1975): 157–78.

Salmon, John H. M. "Venal Office and Popular Sedition in Seventeenth-Century France: A Review of a Controversy." *Past and Present* 37 (July 1967): 21–43.

Sauzet, R. *Contre-Réforme et Réforme catholique en Bas-Languedoc: Le Diocèse de Nîmes au XVIIe siècle.* Paris, 1977.

———. *Les Visites pastorales dans la diocèse de Chartres pendant la première moitié du XVIIe siècle.* Rome, 1975.

Schnapper, Bernard. "La Justice criminelle rendue par le Parlement de Paris sous le règne de François Ier." *Revue Historique de Droit Français et Étranger* 52, no. 2 (1974): 252–84.

Segalen, Martine. *Love and Power in the Peasant Family: Rural France in the Nineteenth Century.* Oxford, 1983.

Sharpe, James A. *Crime in England, 1550–1750.* London, 1984.

———. *Crime in Seventeenth-Century England.* London, 1983.

———. "The History of Crime in Late Medieval and Early Modern England: A Review of the Field." *Social History* 7 (1982): 187–203.

———. "The History of Violence in England: Some Observations." *Past and Present* 108 (August 1985): 206–15.

Slicher van Bath, B. H. *The Agrarian History of Western Europe, A.D. 500–1850.* London, 1963.

Soman, Alfred. "Criminal Jurisprudence in Ancien-Régime France: The Parlement of Paris in the Sixteenth and Seventeenth Centuries." In *Crime and Criminal Justice in Europe and Canada,* edited by L. A. Knafla, 43–76. Waterloo, Ontario, 1979.

———. "Deviance and Criminal Justice in Western Europe, 1300–1800: An Essay in Structure." *Criminal Justice History,* 1 (1980): 3–27.

———. "Deviance and Criminal Justice in Western Europe, 1300–1800: In Search of a Method." Unpublished essay, 1980.

———. "The Parliament of Paris and the Great Witch Hunt." *Sixteenth-Century Journal* 9, no. 2 (1978): 31–35.

———. "Les procès de sorcellerie au Parlement de Paris (1565–1640)." *Annales E.S.C.* 32, no. 4 (May–June 1977): 790–814.

———. "Some Reflections on Torture and Other Punishments as Administered by the Parlement of Paris in the 16th and 17th Centuries." Unpublished essay, 1980.

Spierenburg, Pieter. *The Spectacle of Suffering.* Cambridge, 1984.

Stone, Lawrence. *The Crisis of the Aristocracy.* Oxford, 1965.

———. *The Family, Sex and Marriage in England, 1500–1800.* London, 1977.

———. "Interpersonal Violence in English Society, 1300–1980." *Past and Present* 101 (November 1983): 22–33.

————. "A Rejoinder." *Past and Present* 108 (August 1985): 216–24.

Teall, Elisabeth S. "The Seigneur of Renaissance France: Advocate or Oppressor?" *Journal of Modern History* 37, no. 2 (June 1965):131–50.

Thomson, James K. *Clermont-de-Lodève, 1633–1789.* Cambridge, 1982.

Thompson, E. P. *The Making of the English Working Class.* Toronto, 1968.

Tobias, John J. *Crime and Industrial Society in the Nineteenth Century.* New York, 1967.

Tolstoy, Leo. *Resurrection.* Translated by Vera Trail. New York, 1961.

Tomaselli, Sylvana, and Roy Porter. *Rape.* New York, 1986.

Trénard, L. "Images d'Espagne au temps l'émigration auvergnate." In *Actes du 88e Congrès des Sociétés Savantes,* 731–62. Clermont-Ferrand, 1963.

Traer, James F. *Marriage and the Family in Eighteenth-Century France.* Ithaca, N.Y., 1980.

Trevor-Roper, H. R. "The General Crisis of the Seventeenth Century." In *Crisis in Europe, 1560–1660.* ed. T. Aston, 59–97. New York, 1965.

Trillat, M. "L'Emigration de la Haute Auvergne en Espagne du XVIIIe au XXe siècle." *Revue de la Haute-Auvergne* (1954–55): 257–94.

Vaissière, Pierre de. *Gentilshommes campagnards de l'ancienne France.* Paris, 1925.

Venard, Marc. *Bourgeois et paysan au XVIIe siècle.* Paris, 1958.

Vitrolles, Henri. "La Gabelle en Haute Auvergne." *Revue de la Haute-Auvergne.* (1970–71): 325–38.

Vovelle, Michel. *Piété baroque et déchristianisation en Provence au XVIIIe siècle.* Paris, 1976.

Walter, Gérard. *Histoire des paysans de France.* Paris, 1963.

Weisser, Michael R. *Crime and Punishment in Early Modern Europe.* Hassocks, Sussex, 1979.

Welter, L. *La Réforme ecclésiastique du diocèse de Clermont au XVIIe siècle.* Clermont-Ferrand, 1956.

Welter, R. "Détresse de l'Auvergne du fait des 'gens de guerre' dans la première moitié du XVIIe siècle." *Bulletin Historique et Scientifique de l'Auvergne* (1959): 166–76.

Wheaton, R., and T. Haravan. *Family and Sexuality in French History.* Philadelphia, 1980.

Wills, Antoinette. *Crime and Punishment in Revolutionary Paris.* Westport, Conn., 1981.

Wolin, Sheldon S. "The Economy of Violence." In Niccolò Machiavelli, *The Prince.* Translated by Robert M. Adams (New York, 1977): 185–94.

Woloch, Isser, ed. *The Peasantry in the Old Régime.* Huntington, N.Y., 1977.

Wood, James B. "The Decline of the Nobility in Sixteenth- and Early Seventeenth-Century France: Myth or Reality?" *Journal of Modern History* 48, no. 1 (1976): iii (abstract). Complete article in offprint.

Wrightson, Keith. "Infanticide in European History." *Criminal Justice History* 3 (1982): 1–20.

Yver, Jacques. *Essai de géographie coutumière.* Paris, 1966.

Zehr, Howard. *Crime and the Development of Modern Society.* Totowa, N.J., 1976.

Zysberg, André. "Galères et galériens en France à la fin du XVIIe siècle: Une Image du pouvoir royal à l'age classique." *Criminal Justice History* 1 (1980): 51–115.

————. "La Société des galériens au milieu du 18e siècle." *Annales E.S.C.* 30, no. 1 (January–February 1975): 43–65.

————. *Les Galériens: Vies et destins de 60,000 forçats sur les galères de France.* Paris, 1987.

Index

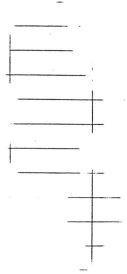